CAPE BRETON RAILWAYS

AN ILLUSTRATED HISTORY

BY HERB MACDONALD

CAPE BRETON RAILWAYS

AN ILLUSTRATED HISTORY

BY HERB MACDONALD

Cape Breton University Press
Sydney, Nova Scotia

Copyright 2012, Herb MacDonald

All rights reserved. No part of this work may be reproduced or used in any form or by any means, electronic or mechanical, including photocopying, recording or any information storage or retrieval system, without the prior written permission of the publisher. Cape Breton University Press recognizes fair use exceptions under Access Copyright. Responsibility for the research and permissions obtained for this publication rests with the author.

Cape Breton University Press recognizes the support of Canada Council for the Arts and of the Province of Nova Scotia, through the Department of Communities, Culture and Heritage. We are pleased to work in partnership with these bodies to develop and promote our cultural resources.

Cover design: Cathy MacLean, Pleasant Bay, NS
    Cover images: Clockwise from top right - Fig. 6.21, p. 125; Sydney Coal Railway 2011, photo by the author; Fig. 2.15, p. 43; Fig. 10.10, p. 197; Fig. 3.8, p. 60.
    Back cover: Fig. 10.17, p. 205; Portrait of the author as a young researcher, courtesy of the author.
Layout: Mike Hunter, Port Hawkesbury and Sydney, NS
First printed in Canada

Library and Archives Canada Cataloguing in Publication

MacDonald, Herb
Cape Breton railways : an illustrated history / Herb MacDonald.

Includes bibliographical references and index.
ISBN 978-1-897009-67-3

1. Railroads--Nova Scotia--Cape Breton Island--History--Pictorial works. 2. Cape Breton Island (N.S.)--History--Pictorial works. I. Title.

HE2809.N6M332 2012   385.09716'9   C2012-902352-3

Cape Breton University Press
P.O. Box 5300
Sydney, NS B1P 6L2

Table of Contents

List of Tables and Maps		7
Introduction		9
Chapter 1	The General Mining Association and Cape Breton's First Railways	14
Chapter 2	Other Early Railways in the Sydney Coal Field	31
Chapter 3	The Intercolonial: Canada's Railway Network Joins Cape Breton	48
Chapter 4	Railways at the Strait of Canso	65
Chapter 5	At the Dawn of the Railways' Golden Age	88
Chapter 6	Moving People	111
Chapter 7	Coal, Steel and Cape Breton's Railways	130
Chapter 8	Other Railway Operations	148
Chapter 9	Working on the Railways	169
Chapter 10	Fading Away: The End of the Railways' Golden Age	191
Chapter 11	Cape Breton's Railway Heritage	210
Notes		222
Bibliography		249
Index		260

Tables and Graphs

Sydney Mines Railways Traffic Estimates, 1830-1860	(Fig. 1.8) **23**
Eastern Extension Railway Rolling Stock, 1884	**54**
The Sydney Coal Field Boom: Urban Populations, 1881-1911	(Table 5.1) **89**
Cape Breton Railway, Revenues and Expenses, 1904-1920	(Table 5.2) **102**
International Company / Cape Breton Company: Passenger Traffic, 1880-1892	(Table 6.1) **113**
Dominion Coal Railway / Sydney & Louisburg: Passenger Traffic, 1894-1920	(Table 6.2) **113**
Inverness & Richmond / Cape Breton Railway: Passenger Traffic, 1905-1919	(Table 6.3) **117**
On the Strait Ferries: CNR Passenger Cars, 1946-1950	(Table 6.4) **122**
Dosco Coal Shipments From Cape Breton, 1946-1957	(Table 7.1) **136**
Intercolonial Railway Coal Purchases, 1892-1910	(Table 7.2) **139**
On the Strait Ferries: CNR Carloads of Coal and Steel, 1946-1950	(Table 7.3) **141**
Disco-Besco-Dosco Rail Production, 1906-1964	**143**
Sysco Rail Production for the Canadian Market, 1970-1987	**145**
On the Strait Ferries: CNR Freight Carloads Other Than Coal and Steel, 1946-1950	(Table 8.1) **150**
Cape Breton Towns: Railway Employment Estimates, 1907	(Table 9.1) **171**
Railway Wage Rates: Scotia, Disco and Canadian Government Railways, April 1921	(Table 9.2) **175**
Changing Railway Employment Trends, CNR, Maritime Region, 1948-1960	(Table 10.1, 10.2) **195**
CB&CNS Carloads Terminating and Originating East of Point Tupper, 1996-2011	(Table 10.3) **207**

Maps and Aerial Photos

Sydney Mines Railways, 1830-1835 (Fig. 1.3) **18**

North Sydney Shipping Wharf and Railways, 1877 (Fig. 1.14) **29**

Cape Breton Mining Railways, 1875 (Fig. 2.13) **41**

Intercolonial Railway, Main Line Reroutings, 1913-1915 (Fig. 5.8) **94**

CNR Railway Yard and Ferry Dock, Point Tupper, 1931 (Fig. 5.13) **99**

Western/Central Cape Breton and the Evolution of the CNR, (Fig. 5.18) **109**

20th Century Coal Railways in the Sydney Coal Field, 1890-1968 (Fig. 5.19) **110**

S&L Railway Yard, Glace Bay, c.1965 (Fig. 9.1) **170**

CNR Railway Yard, Sydney, c.1955 (Fig. 10.2) **191**

Introduction

Once upon a time it was possible to board a train in Sydney or Inverness or St. Peter's and travel to Antigonish or Halifax or far beyond Nova Scotia's borders. But that was once upon a time. For more than twenty years, the only railway passenger service operating in Nova Scotia has been on the Halifax to Montreal route. Fewer and fewer people have ever had first-hand experience of travel by rail or using other services provided by railways. That fact and the rising uncertainty about the survival of Cape Breton's remaining railway freight service make it timely to present a history of the island's railways.

Cape Breton's rail lines are perhaps best known for their substantial roles in the coal and steel industries—and their decline as those industries faded away—but, despite their prominent connections to coal and steel, railways played many other important roles in the life of the island.

For a hundred years, railways carried people to and from Cape Breton as well as between communities on the island. For most of that century, railways carried the mail; before the development of the telephone system, the railway companies provided telegraph service for occasions when the mail was too slow; railways moved freight and express for individuals and businesses; and the railways provided jobs, in large numbers, directly to their own employees and indirectly through companies whose products and services they used.

If asked to recall the island's rail lines, many Cape Bretoners would think first of the Devco Railway, a name that disappeared in 2001 with the closure of the Cape Breton Development Corporation. Those with longer memories or a stronger sense of history might remember the pre-1968 period when the Devco line was the Sydney and Louisburg—the S&L, or the "Slow & Lazy" as some folks called it. Others might think first of the Canadian National Railway that originally linked the island to the rest of Canada when it was built as part of the Intercolonial Railway.

The S&L and the Intercolonial both appeared shortly before 1900 and were central to Cape Breton's railway age. Long before these two, however, as early as the 1830s, the first railways used horse-power rather than locomotives.

The first horse-powered line at Sydney Mines is a contender for recognition as the first railway in Canada, a subject to be examined in chapter 1. The case for that honour requires a definition of "railway" based on a long-run sense of history—but any serious look at railways calls for a long-run view.

For many years, both popular and dictionary definitions have tended to assume that a "railway" or "railroad" uses some kind of locomotive power—steam, diesel or electric. The railways that brought about a worldwide transportation revolution in the 19th century were based on steam-powered engines. People usually overlook the fact that the locomotive-powered railways that first appeared in England in the late 1820s were the products of technological changes that had been under way for a very long time.

It is easy to find references to the Stockton and Darlington line which opened in north England in 1825 that call it the "first" railway, or to George Stephenson, who supervised construction of the S&D and built its first locomotives, as the "inventor" of the railway. The opening of the S&D was a landmark event—but only one of many and far from the first. George Stephenson played an extremely important role in bringing about the railway revolution, but he was not the only significant contributor. The history of the railway in England goes back two hundred years before Stephenson and the opening of the Stockton and Darlington.

Though most of the details of either that earlier history[1] or post-1825 events in England[2] are not relevant to this account of the railways of Cape Breton, a few do warrant brief mention because they set the stage for what began at Sydney Mines.

As would be the case in Cape Breton, the earliest railways in England were closely linked to the coal and iron industries. Until the late 1820s, most of England's railways were found in the northeast, in the coal fields of Northumberland and Durham, where they were built by mine owners to transport coal from the pits to shipping wharves on the coast or on navigable rivers such as the Tyne. Railways had become fairly common in this area during the 1700s and played a vital role in the expansion of mining activity. Though these early lines were operated with horse-power, they moved substantial amounts of coal. As a

Fig. 0.1 A railway approaching the River Tyne c.1820. The drawing illustrates a mine railway typical of the lines that evolved in British coal fields over the previous 200 years. The prominent hand brake on the wagon and the combination of flanged iron wheels running on edge rails were fairly standard in northeast England by 1820. The nature of what supported the track is not clear but the fill between the rails to protect the horses suggests use of stone blocks to carry the rails. The background wharves with railway wagons reflect the very extensive use of railways to transport coal by this time.

Collection of North of England Institute of Mining and Mechanical Engineers, Newcastle upon Tyne, U.K.

passing example, in 1727, almost a century before the opening of the Stockton and Darlington, the Tanfield railway in County Durham was carrying nearly 3,000 t of coal a day on its seven-mile long double-track line.[3]

As new methods and machines appeared in the mines, the same was happening on the horse-powered railways. Coal-hauling capacity improved as better construction standards were introduced. Lines were built as straight as possible and grades were minimized by cutting, filling, tunnelling or bridging. When steep grades could not be avoided, both gravity power and pulley systems controlled by winches came into use. During the 1700s, iron wheels became the norm on coal wagons. Wooden rails were strengthened with iron bars on the top surface to carry the wagons' wheels. Before 1800, solid cast iron rails were introduced and stone blocks were replacing wooden ties to carry the rails.

As changes in railway track and rolling stock appeared, so did the power of steam. Steam engines had been introduced at mines soon after 1700 to run pumps. Later modifications led to engines that could lift cages in vertical shafts or pull loaded wagons out of sloped mine entrances. By 1800, engines were also in use to operate rope or cable systems to power coal wagons on rail lines where the grade was too steep for horses. Soon after 1800, experiments were under way to mount steam engines on wheels.

By the early 1820s, pioneer locomotive builders, most of whom were associated with collieries in northeast England, were trying to harness steam power for "travelling engines" that would run on railways. At the same time,

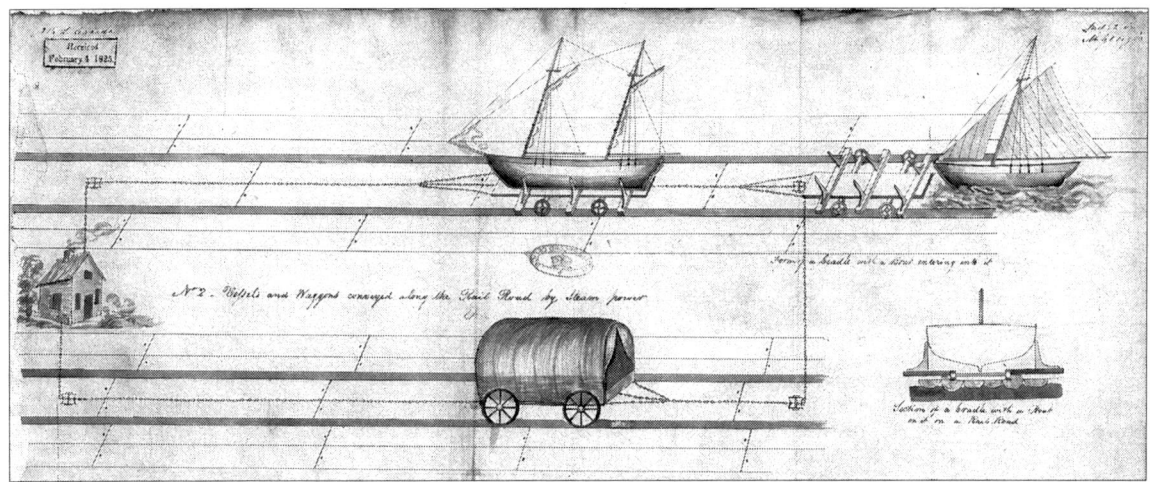

Fig. 0.2 A Canadian sketch of a double track railway powered by a stationary steam engine. The engine would control a set of ropes that would move the wagons, one track for each direction. This was one in a set of drawings sent by James George, a Quebec City merchant, to Lord Bathurst, the Colonial Secretary in London. The date stamp at top left shows receipt at Whitehall on February 4, 1825. These drawings are believed to be the very first Canadian illustrations of any aspect of a railway.[4]

U.K. National Archives, MPG 1/494

Fig. 0.3
The *Steam Elephant*, built c.1815 by John Buddle and William Chapman of Newcastle upon Tyne. This illustration is from an oil painting believed to be from the early 1820s. Buddle was a prominent mining engineer who played important roles in the development of mines and railways in Cape Breton in the 1830s.

Reproduced courtesy of Beamish: The North of England Open Air Museum, County Durham, U.K.

new manufacturing techniques were introduced to make iron rails longer and stronger by shaping them while the iron was still hot and malleable. The new "rolled" rails were strong enough to carry the weight of locomotives. The combination of these two developments made the English railway revolution of the 1820s possible.

In late 1829, only four years after the opening of the Stockton and Darlington in County Durham, the railway age came to Cape Breton. The first lines on the island used horse power for more than two decades. Steam locomotives did not arrive until 1853. The early Cape Breton experience was a direct transfer of early English technology, but what had happened in England over the course of two hundred years occurred in Cape Breton within the span of twenty-five years.

Over the next century and a half, as some areas of Cape Breton evolved from a rural and agricultural society into an urban and industrial one, railways played a central role in supporting the changes that took place. This book looks at those railways in the contexts of what was happening on and beyond the island.

Cape Breton's railways were shaped by factors such physical geography, availability of both capital and customers, and the distribution of population and industries. In response to those factors, railway builders and operators often had to make difficult choices and try to deal with factors they could not control.

A book about those railways faces similar constraints and difficult choices. Reliable source material has often proved to be in short supply. Space is limited. Balances are called for in coverage of different parts of the island over a time frame that spans almost two centuries. Some previously ignored topics such as the early horse-powered railways are examined in considerable detail. Endnotes draw attention to previously unused sources, particularly important references, and instances where details or interpretations have been subjects of disagreement. Other sections of the book have been painted with a very broad brush. To draw the reader closer to the real world of Cape Breton's railways, extensive use is made of photos and original text materials. The first five chapters deal with the appearance of the various sections of Cape Breton's railway network up to the early years of the 20th century. Chapters 6-11 look at the last hundred years through thematic approaches applied to rail lines across the island.

Imagine you're at the railway station platform where your train awaits for a journey through time and space. Listen carefully and you'll hear the locomotive whistle blowing. That will soon be followed by the voice of the conductor alerting everyone that it's departure time. A small portable iron step like the one in the photo is on the platform as a first step up toward your passenger car.

"All aboard!"

Fig. 0.4
Intercolonial Railway passenger car step, c.1900.

Author's photo with permission of Orangedale Railway Museum.

1 – The General Mining Association and Cape Breton's First Railways

The Company

The British-owned General Mining Association (GMA) played a critical role in the development of coal mining in 19th-century Cape Breton. Though the island's mines had been worked as far back as the French era (17th and 18th centuries), it was the GMA that in 1829 first introduced large-scale operations and led the way in establishing the coal industry that emerged over the next hundred years and more. Much has been written elsewhere about the GMA, but it is appropriate to note several points here.

GMA is credited with bringing major changes to Nova Scotia's coalfields; pre-GMA mining activity had been carried out on a very small scale. Previous mine owners had little capital and few employees. Mining methods were primitive. Transport of coal was both difficult and expensive. Output was low and so were financial returns. The GMA brought about change by importing the British mining model.

The company introduced new technology, recruited engineers and managers familiar with modern British practices and brought experienced miners from the U.K. Ownership of the firm was London-based, but on-site management was put in the hands of men with considerable experience and support from consultants who were leaders in their fields in England. These were all based on the GMA's large pool of capital and the firm's willingness to make substantial investments in Nova Scotia.

That pool of capital funded the first railways in both Cape Breton and Pictou County. The GMA's financial resources permitted the company to build railway lines using high standards of design and construction. As a generalization, railway construction in eastern Canada in the 19th century was usually

The Origins of the GMA[1]

When examining what has appeared in print about the GMA, readers are likely to encounter ambiguous, incomplete or conflicting details about the establishment of the firm, its ownership, its stature and the circumstances that brought the company to Nova Scotia.

The firm was first organized in 1825 as the General South American Mining Association (GSAMA). The President was Edward John Littleton, later Baron Hatherton, a prominent long-serving Member of Parliament. Two of the original Directors were of particular interest from a Canadian perspective. Andrew Belcher was the son of the first Chief Justice of Nova Scotia. Charles Poulet Thomson, later Baron Sydenham, became an MP in 1826, held several Cabinet posts in the 1830s and was Governor-General of British North America from 1839 to 1841. In 1829, those three disappeared from the list of Directors, though most of the other original Board members remained with the firm to and beyond 1829. This latter group included: two London bankers, John Wright and Felix Ladbroke; Joseph Marryat, who was Chair of the Lloyd's insurance syndicate; and Edward Blount, a prominent London barrister and also a Member of Parliament.

The company's stated objectives in 1825 were to open mines to bring gold, silver, gemstones and other minerals from South America. Early activity targeted opportunities in Brazil, but quickly expanded to include Mexico and Colombia. The South American focus was behind the presence of two Brazilians, H. I. da Silva and A. I. F. Marreco, on the Board from the outset. It is unclear who had originally led the way in organizing the firm in 1825, but it is perhaps significant that four other original Directors were also partners in the firm of Rundell, Bridge and Rundell. These men would have had a practical interest in gold, silver and gemstones.

From 1804 to 1842, the Rundell partners were the Royal Goldsmiths, craftsmen who provided jewellery plus high-end gold and silver products ranging from silver and gold dinner sets to the coronation regalia of the British Royal Family.[2] The prestige of the Royal Warrant brought the trade of the nobility to Rundell's on Ludgate Hill, a few steps from the west door of St. Paul's Cathedral in London. For the partners, the Warrant was literally a licence to print money. One indicator of the wealth generated is seen in reports in *The Times* of February 21, 26 and 27, 1827, on the will of Philip Rundell, the senior partner in the firm until his retirement in 1823. The estate, "upwards of £1,000,000," was reported as being the "largest sum that ever had been registered" in Doctors' Commons, the probate court of the day.

Firms like Rundell's often extended credit to customers, sometimes to customers whose credit-ratings should have been suspect. In the mid-1820s, debts owed by the Duke of York, a son of

---

GENERAL MINING COMPANY.

CAPITAL £400,000—IN 20,000 SHARES, OF £20 EACH—£7 PAID.

Directors.
EDMOND WALLER RUNDELL, Esq.—*Chairman.*

JOHN BRIDGE, Esq.	FELIX CALVERT LADBROKE, Esq.
THOMAS BIGGE, Esq.	JOSEPH MARRYAT, Esq. M.P.
JOHN GAWLER BRIDGE, Esq.	H. I. DA SILVA, Esq.
EDWARD BLOUNT, Esq.	JOHN PARKINSON, Esq.
Sir F. H. DOYLE, Bart.	GEORGE WARRE, Esq.
A. I. F. MARRECO, Esq.	JOHN WRIGHT, Esq.

Auditors.—FELIX LADBROKE, Jnn. Esq.—E. JERNINGHAM, Esq.—
Secretary.—G. V. DUVAL, Esq.
Bankers.—Messrs. COUTTS and Co.—GLYNN and Co.
Solicitor.—A. HUMPHRYS, Esq.
Mining Engineer.—RICHARD SMITH, Esq.
OFFICE—No. 10, LUDGATE HILL.

Fig. 1.1
Who's who at the GMA in 1830

Quarterly Mining Review, London, vol 1, # 1, 1830: 168.

George III, had become a major concern for the Rundell partners. Their connections with the Palace led to a settlement of the Duke's outstanding accounts in 1826. As a substitute for a cash payment, the partners were granted a sub-lease of the rights to Nova Scotia's minerals which had been granted to the Duke. In contrast to the Rundell partners, most of the Duke's many creditors were still looking for payment when he died in 1827.

It is not known if the Rundell partners transferred the mineral rights to the GSAMA for cash or for more shares in the mining company though the stock option appears to be the better guess. When the GSAMA was restructured in 1829, it was dominated by the four Rundell partners, Edmond Rundell, Thomas Bigge (Rundell's first cousin), John Bridge (a founding partner at the Rundell firm) and John Gawler Bridge, a nephew of John Bridge. Edmond Rundell became Chairman of the renamed General Mining Association and, in April of 1829, about 45 per cent of GMA shares were recorded as held by the Rundell partners, their families or others connected to the Rundell firm. The remaining shares were fairly widely held and were traded on the London stock market. While removal of "South American" from the company name reflected the acquisition of interests in Nova Scotia, the 1829 balance sheet showed that more than 60 per cent of GMA capital was still in South America. It was well into the 1830s before Nova Scotia became the firm's major area of activity.

Other interests and Board memberships of GMA Directors and shareholders point to the scope of the firm's connections in both England and British North America. During the 1830s, names of GMA Directors appear in the lists of shareholders and directors of companies involved in shipping and transportation (the Halifax & Quebec Steamship Company; the Shubenacadie Canal Company), banking (the Bank of British North America; the Bank of Nova Scotia) and colonization and land development ventures (the North American Colonial Association of Ireland; the New Brunswick and Nova Scotia Land Company). Boardroom contacts established links to influential figures in business on our side of the Atlantic (the Bank of Montreal; the British-American Land Company) and the corridors of political influence in London.

Though GMA acquisition of rights to Nova Scotia's coal resources was a combination of accident and coincidence, the company was positioned to tap those resources with extraordinary access to both capital and political clout. The firm's approach to developing the coal fields of Nova Scotia reflected the fact that in its early years it was more than just a company. In its time and place, the GMA was a corporate giant.

focused on cost control and minimization of capital outlay in the short run. The GMA, however, particularly in its early years, took an approach that built quality and longevity into their rail lines in expectation of both short run benefits and long run cost savings.

The initial boom in coal production after the arrival of the GMA at Sydney Mines was duplicated on the south side of Sydney Harbour after 1860. New companies, new mines and new towns appeared in rapid succession. At century's end the coal industry was supplemented by the opening of steel mills at both Sydney and Sydney Mines. From 1829 on, the development of these industries and communities was tied to and supported by the evolution of the railways that appeared first at Sydney Mines.

Cape Breton's First Railway: Sydney Mines, 1829-30

An 1871 book by Richard Brown,[3] the first GMA manager in Cape Breton who spent almost forty years in that position, provides an overview of activity at Sydney Mines once initial problems regarding the company's lease were resolved in 1829. A 200 ft. mine shaft was sunk and steam engines were installed for pumping and winding. A new wharf and a "light temporary railway" were also built though Brown failed to note precisely when or provide any detail about the railway. His omissions and the almost total absence of newspaper coverage of the early years of GMA activity in Cape Breton leave us dependent on company documents that, unfortunately, are in limited supply.[4]

Fig. 1.2
Richard Brown, the first GMA manager in Cape Breton.

Vernon, 16.

A letter, probably from Brown, to the GMA head office in London dated January 15, 1830,[5] indicated that work on the first railway had begun before the end of 1829. The letter reported: "The line of rail-way from the pit to the wharf has been surveyed and leveled, the length of which is 1560 yards." The new wharf was recorded as "built up to the required height, viz 12 feet above high water to the extent of 160 feet, which was as far as could be done that season."

Unknown are when the decision to build the line was made and whether that decision was made in London or in Cape Breton. Also unknown are when this line was completed or when it went into service. It would also be interesting to know if construction began before or after work started on the first GMA railway at Albion Mines (modern-day Stellarton) in Pictou County[6] and to establish which went into service first. These have also proved impossible to resolve though production and sales data suggest that both lines were operational before the end of 1830. The too-close-to-call race between the two sites leaves both as contenders for the honour of having the first railway in Nova Scotia and the rest of British North America.

Few engineering details about the temporary Sydney Mines line have been found. Brown refers to it as a "light" railway, a description that raises questions, particularly about the rails and where they were made.

A tantalizing passage in the letter of January 15, 1830, stated that the "rails &c. it was intended to manufacture at the Albion Mines foundry." Intention is one thing but rail manufacturing is something else. Contemporary press references indicate the first Albion Mines railway was built with iron rail, but there are nagging uncertainties about its origin(s).[7]

For Sydney Mines, there are similar uncertainties. The earliest evidence about rails for Cape Breton appears in letters[8] that confirm arrival on January 9, 1833, of the brig *Mary Anne* from Liverpool with 200 t of "Railway Iron for the Sydney Mines." Brown's letters unfortunately do not include information about the manufacturer, the specifications of the rails or the intended use of this cargo. The timing and size of the shipment, however, suggest it was for the railway built at Bridgeport later that year.

The 1837 Sydney Mines Stock Book,[9] the earliest surviving GMA inventory record from Cape Breton, reported the presence of more than 75 t of "light rails" in the railway's "loose stock." These were recorded as being in 15-foot (4.5 m) lengths and further described as "malleable iron," a term used to refer to rolled rails. The specifications indicate these rails were of British origin. They may have been new stock on hand for future use, but the fact that there was no obvious short-term need for such a large stock suggests they were old rails from the temporary line that had been abandoned by 1835.[10] This assumption, the British origin of the *Mary Anne's* cargo, and specifications recorded for other rail stocks suggest that all the rails laid in Cape Breton by the GMA in the 1830s came from England.

Little has been found about operations on the first Sydney Mines railway, though the 1837 Stock Book's record of old wagons shows the wagon size was ½ Winchester chaldron, a measure of volume that would have translated into load capacity of close to 1500 lbs.[11] More than two years after abandonment of the first line, the inventory showed twenty-two of these still operational plus an additional twenty-nine similar wagon bodies without wheels. There is no basis, however, for speculating about whether the original set of wagons was much in excess of that fifty-one. The 1837 inventory also records an "old incline wheel" located "near the old wharf," suggesting use of a haulage device of some

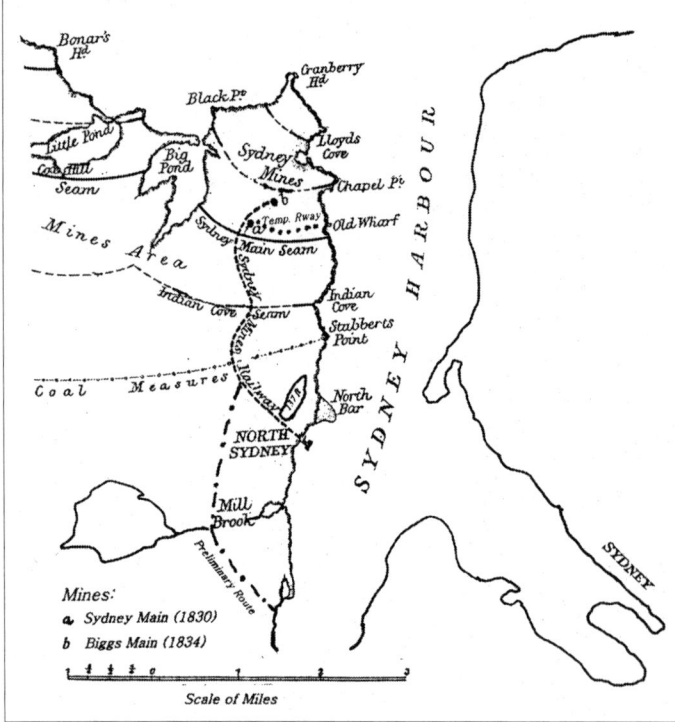

Fig. 1.3 - The Sydney Mines-North Sydney Area in 1835. This map is a simplified and reworked section from a larger map in Brown, 1871.

Fig. 1.4 - John Buddle's suggestion for a wharf frame. This drawing, from a GMA copy of Buddle's 1834 "Railway Report," illustrates how a loading frame would work. The platform was hinged at point "a" and would be in a vertical position when a ship tied up. When the vessel was positioned alongside, the platform would be lowered to the horizontal position shown in the drawing. When loading was finished, the platform would be pulled back to the vertical to permit the ship to depart and another one to tie up. An 1835 British account offered the following description: "A man … unfastens a latch at the bottom of the waggon, which, being made to turn upon hinges like a door, immediately opens and the whole of the coal in the waggon is cleanly poured into the hold. To facilitate this operation the sides of the waggons converge toward the bottom and are lined with smooth iron plates." Nothing has been found to indicate if any of the early wagons in Cape Breton had internal iron plating.

Nova Scotia Archives and Records Management (NSARM), RG 21A, vol 39, # 32: 12.

Fig. 1.5 – This drawing illustrates John Buddle's recommendations for construction of the roadbed for the second Sydney Mines railway. Though the drawing does not have labels to show his intent, Buddle's report included a recommendation that stone blocks, 2 ft x 2 ft x 1 ft, be used to support the rails. Those dimensions are relected in the wording of the tender call.

NSARM, RG 21A, vol 39, # 32: 7.

NORTH SYDNEY

RAILROAD.

TENDERS will be received at this office until the 20th day of MAY from PERSONS disposed to contract for the supply of

STONE BLOCKS OR SLEEPERS,

For the NORTH SYDNEY RAILROAD.

EACH BLOCK to be one foot thick, and to contain four cubic feet; none will be taken of less width than 20 inches. The material to be a strong sandstone, perfectly free from Joints.

SIX THOUSAND Blocks will be required; but TENDERS will be received for lots of Four hundred each or upwards.

TO be delivered at the Mines, Wharf, Plant's Bar, or North Sydney, as may be required, before the 31st day of August next: Security will be required for the performance of Contracts. Further particulars may be obtained at this office, where a specimen of the blocks may be seen

Office of General Mining Association.
Sydney Mines,
April 29, 1834.

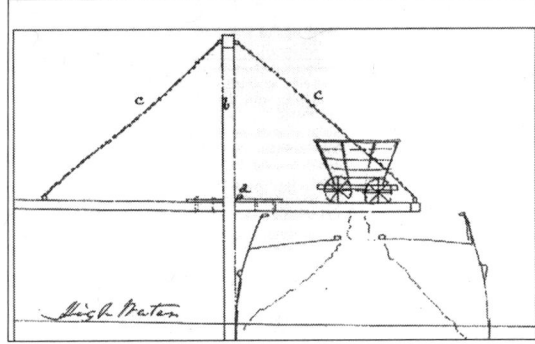

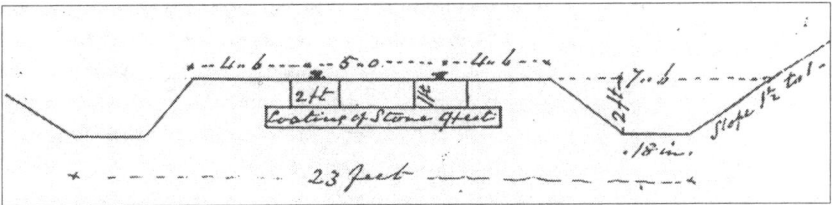

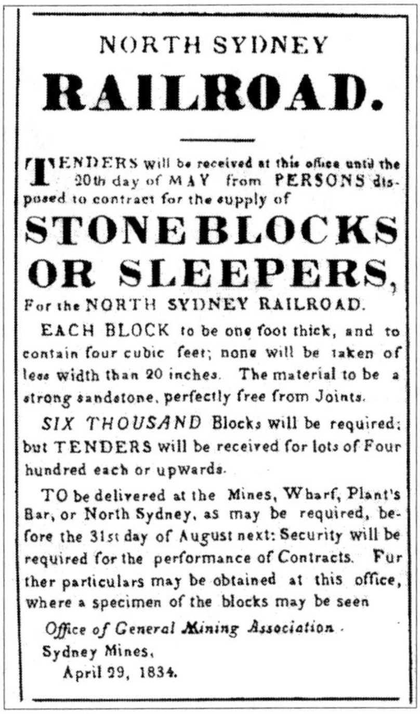

Fig. 1.6 – GMA tender call for stone blocks, 1834. Despite Buddle's recommendation and the tender call, stone blocks were not used, a decision assumed the result of problems of availability and/or cost. "Sleepers" was a British term used for supports for rails, whether made of wood, stone, or (in more recent times) cement. In North America, "sleepers" was gradually replaced by "ties."

The Cape-Bretonian and General Reporter, Sydney, May 24, 1834.

type there—a subject to be dealt with below. The terrain, with a steep slope that dropped about fifty feet down to the shoreline, certainly required one if wagons were brought down to the wharf. There is no basis for drawing any other conclusions about the line's structure or operation though it is possible to calculate estimates of traffic. These will be considered below along with an analysis of traffic on Sydney Mines' second railway.

A Second Railway For Sydney Mines: 1834-35

By 1833, a major expansion at Sydney Mines was being planned. It involved a second mine, a new wharf and a new railway to link the two pits to the new wharf. That summer, J. B. Foord, recently appointed as Secretary to the GMA Board, and Thomas Bigge, a member of the Rundell family, one of the largest GMA shareholders and an important member of the Board, came to Cape Breton.[12] Preliminary decisions about locations for the new wharf and the railway had been made and work had begun on both before the arrival of Foord and Bigge. However, the presence of the visitors from head office seems to indicate concern about some aspect of the new projects. This conclusion is supported by Foord's return to Sydney Mines in January of 1834[13] and the recruitment of two high-profile British consultants, Thomas Telford and John Buddle.[14] Both would be "armchair" consultants; neither crossed the Atlantic to view the site in person.

Telford reviewed plans for location and construction of a breakwater to protect the new wharf from winter storms and ice.[15] Buddle was charged with assessing the plans for operations in the new mine and construction of the new railway.[16] He was provided with an array of maps and documents (that unfortunately have not survived within his papers) and the assistance of Daniel Hoard who went early in 1834 from Sydney Mines to Buddle's home in Wallsend, Northumberland. Two reports, each about twenty pages in length,[17] were prepared and the "Railway Report" provides a starting base of information about the new line.[18]

The initial location chosen by the GMA for the new wharf was four miles further inside the harbour than the original one with a resulting length of about 4.5 miles (72. km) for the railway.[19] While Buddle knew preliminary work had begun on both, he recommended relocating the wharf to just inside the North Bar, a change that would shorten the main line to about 2.7 miles (4.3 km) and reduce both construction and operating costs.

Other key recommendations by Buddle were for the use of locomotives, Newcastle chaldron wagons that would carry about 3 t of coal, relatively heavy weight rail (40 lbs/yard [roughly 20 kg/metre]), stone blocks to support the rails, use of the 4-ft-8-inch gauge (1.42 m) that appears to have been in place on the first railway and use of "loading frames" on the wharf to permit wagons to be dumped directly into ships' holds.[20]

For shipment to Sydney Mines, Buddle ordered a completed Newcastle chaldron wagon, a set of iron work for a second wagon, several chairs (iron plates that supported the rails and attached them to wooden or stone under-supports), and a set of components for a switch, all from Robert Rayne of Busy Cottage Iron Works, Newcastle.[21] These were undoubtedly samples of specifications Buddle wanted to see adopted.

Though Daniel Hoard appears to have met with the GMA Directors in London on his way back to Cape Breton, decisions about the wharf location and railway route were made later by a new player on the scene. Best known for his involvement in ocean shipping, Samuel Cunard had recently become the GMA agent in Halifax and would shortly be a member of the GMA Board. In mid-1834, after visiting Sydney Mines to look at the alternatives, Cunard approved the Buddle-Hoard proposals for the wharf site and the revision of the planned railway route. The new wharf was built at the site that is now the location of the North Sydney wharf for the Newfoundland ferry. Buddle's other proposals were implemented except those for the immediate introduction of locomotives and use of stone blocks to carry the rails (despite the initial GMA tender call for blocks). See figure 1.6.

One interesting detail about the railway as it was built involves the section approaching the wharf where there was a fairly steep slope with a vertical drop of about thirty-five feet (10.6 m). For reason(s) unknown, consideration of that slope on the side of Goat Hill and how to deal with it is conspicuously missing from Buddle's "Railway Report." Despite that, Hoard advised Buddle in a letter in August of 1834 that "we have a self-acting incline plane." Construction of the incline was undoubtedly a result of the decision to defer use of locomotives.

Simply described, a "self-acting incline" (or self-acting engine or balanced incline) was a double-track line on a steep grade with a rope or cable controlled by a large wheel at the top of the slope and rollers to support and guide the rope down each track. One end of the rope would be attached to downward bound loaded wagons at the top of the incline and the other end to empties at the bottom. Gravity power, controlled through the wheel, carried the loads down while the loads simultaneously pulled the empties up the other track. It was a very simple yet highly effective way to deal with grades that were too steep for horse power and low traffic volumes that made a stationary steam engine uneconomical. Use of such a system was obviously more efficient in a setting where the loaded wagons were going downhill though it could also be used to pull loads uphill.

The 1837 Stock Book records the double-tracked section on the incline as 441 yds (403 m) long while Hoard referred to a length of "16 chains" with "a fall of 1 foot in 30." The two are compatible with the terrain and its 35 foot drop (10.6 m). The Stock Book reports the incline was equipped with a wheel valued at £35 and used a 5½ inch (14 cm) rope "200 fathoms" long. This rope length suggests that a total of about 40 yds (36.5 m) of double track was distributed above and below the working section of the incline where the down loads pulled the empties up the slope. Hoard's "16 chains" falls slightly short of the Stock Book references to incline and rope lengths. Perhaps his distance referred only to the part of the incline with a grade and excluded the level sections built at the top and bottom of an incline. This was the first documented self-acting incline in Canada[22] but unfortunately no first-hand accounts of operation have been found.

By 1834, self-acting inclines had been in use in the U.K. for more than seventy-five years and Buddle had included inclines in several railway projects he directed. For example, at Seaham in County Durham, where an artificial harbour and a railway were built under Buddle's supervision for the Marquis of Londonderry in 1828-1831, the Rainton and Seaham Railway included two self-acting engines each more than one-half mile in length.[23]

Despite the absence of reference to the Goat Hill slope in Buddle's "Railway Report," the incline may have been built according to his directions. As noted previously, however, an incline of some type, either a self-acting design or a winch-controlled model, appears to have been used down the slope to the original wharf and construction of the 1834 incline may have been influenced by that earlier model.

The documentation of the Goat Hill incline undermines references that have appeared over the last fifty years[24] suggesting use of "dandy cars" on the slope to the wharf with horses being carried down and pulling the empties back up the slope. "Dandy car" was a widely used name in England for a railway car used to carry horses, usually down grades where loaded wagons either coasted under gravity power or were under the control of some kind of incline.

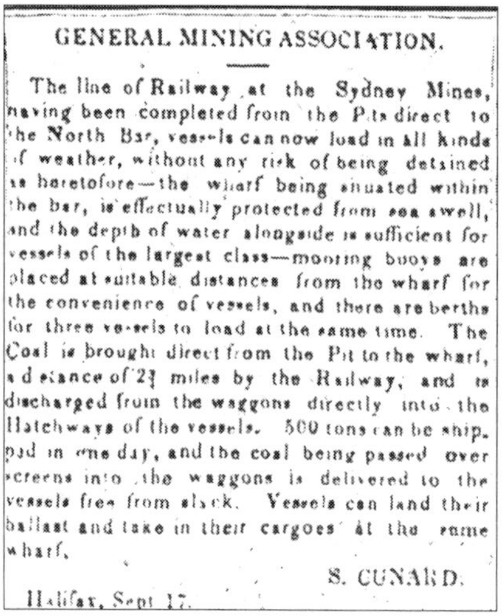
GENERAL MINING ASSOCIATION.

The line of Railway at the Sydney Mines, having been completed from the Pits direct to the North Bar, vessels can now load in all kinds of weather, without any risk of being detained as heretofore—the wharf being situated within the bar, is effectually protected from sea swell, and the depth of water alongside is sufficient for vessels of the largest class—mooring buoys are placed at suitable distances from the wharf for the convenience of vessels, and there are berths for three vessels to load at the same time. The Coal is brought direct from the Pit to the wharf, a distance of 2¾ miles by the Railway, and is discharged from the waggons directly into the Hatchways of the vessels. 500 tons can be shipped in one day, and the coal being passed over screens into the waggons is delivered to the vessels free from slack. Vessels can land their ballast and take in their cargoes at the same wharf.

S. CUNARD.

Halifax, Sept 17.

Fig. 1.7
Samuel Cunard's notice that the new GMA wharf was open for business in 1835.

The Novascotian, Halifax, September 17, 1835.

Despite the relatively recent appearance of references to the use of dandy cars, knowledge of the 1834 incline's existence had not vanished during the 19th century. In a letter written in early 1933,[25] Michael Dwyer, then General Manager of Nova Scotia Steel and Coal, the GMA's successor firm at Sydney Mines, referred briefly though very explicitly to the incline by stating, "the coal was dropped down to the wharf by an endless rope—the full cars going down brought the empties back." The transition between the date of Dwyer's letter and what has appeared in print in recent decades illustrates the problems that emerge as history is written and rewritten without examination of original sources.

While the recent accounts of use of dandy cars on Goat Hill are not literally credible, they may have some other basis in fact. The 1837 and 1838 Stock Books do record the presence of "4 Waggons for carrying horses" and the main line section between the first pit and the top of the incline might have been the location of "dandy" operations. Buddle's report indicated the route leading away from the pits would have had a slight downward grade leading away from the mines toward the top of the incline. With good track and wheels, gravity could have carried the loads to the top of the self-acting engine and the horses, carried down in dandy cars, might have been used only to move empties on the return trip back to the mines. While this suggestion seems possible, it is speculation rather than fact.

Richard Brown's 1871 book stated the new railway opened in 1834 but this seems unlikely. The best evidence for an opening date for both the railway and the wharf appears to be that of Cunard's advertisement that first appeared in Halifax in *The Novascotian* in September of 1835.

An obvious question is if the new railway had any significant effect on activity at Sydney Mines. There was a slow but steady increase in traffic into the early 1840s generated by increases in coal production. GMA employment at Sydney Mines grew from 174 (1832) to 187 (1835), 214 (1836) and slightly above 400 in 1838.[26] Within the 1838 total, for July of that year there is an isolated reference to a railway crew of "20 cart and RailRoadmen" within a surface workforce of nearly 200.[27]

Was any of this increase in activity attributable to the new railway? That is impossible to assess since we have no idea if the earlier railway was ever a bottleneck between pithead and wharf or if the new line had any significant positive impact on the volume of coal the company could ship.

A complementary question from a GMA perspective would have been if the new railway changed the transport cost per unit of coal between pithead and ship's hold. Either an increase in handling capacity without impact on unit costs or a reduction in unit transport costs could have had a positive effect on the GMA Income Statement. Whether the new railway did this and, if so, at a level that exceeded the cost of capital invested should have been of interest to the shareholders. It is impossible, however, to even speculate about this since the surviving records do not contain any data on operating costs for the railway or overall colliery operations.

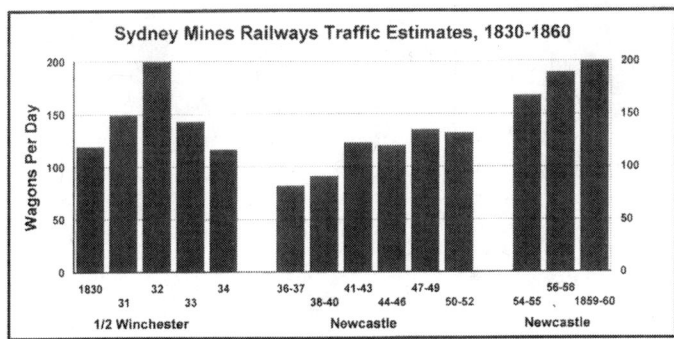

Fig. 1.8
Based on data from *Journals of House of Assembly of Nova Scotia*, 1859, Appendix 22: 389-90 and 1860, Consolidated Appendix: 282; with assumptions of eight-month shipping seasons and six-day work weeks.

Traffic on the Sydney Mines Railways

Since coal was stockpiled at the Sydney Mines pits, sales data provide a basis for estimating railway traffic. As a result of the harbour freezing and the dangers of inshore pack ice, the shipping season was only about eight months long[28] and rail operations were limited to that time frame. Assuming an eight-month season and a six-day work week, it is easy to convert the annual sales data into reasonably reliable estimates of daily traffic volume.

Figure 1.8 plots annual estimates for the first line for 1830-1834 plus estimates for the new railway averaged in multi-year blocks from 1836 through 1852, the year before the adoption of steam locomotives. An assumption in the graph is that the original railway was fully operational throughout 1830 though this is unlikely. The two transition years, 1835 and 1853, are skipped. Stating with 1854 multi-year blocks show estimates for the early years of locomotive operation for comparison. Note that this graph includes two different wagon sizes. The wagons per day on the first line (1830-1834) were one-half Winchester chaldrons carrying about 1500 lb each (680 kg); from 1836 onward, whether handled by horses or locomotives, the wagons were Newcastle chaldrons carrying almost 6000 lb each (2,722 kg).

After 1835, the graph shows a pattern of gradually increasing traffic over the next two decades though there seems no reason to believe that horse-powered operations would have been overly strained by the early 1850s. Even so, the horses were retired and two locomotives, *Sydney* and *Halifax*, went into service late in the summer of 1853.

Other Early Horse-Powered Lines

In addition to the two Sydney Mines lines, the GMA opened two other horse-powered railways in 1833. At Bridgeport, the railway ran about two miles along the beach from the mine to a small wharf. The line at Little Bras d'Or was much shorter, only 431 yds in length (394 m). Neither of these mines was very productive and both were abandoned fairly quickly. Little Bras d'Or was closed in 1837 and the Bridgeport mine in 1842. The mine closures led to abandonment of the railways though it seems certain that rails and other reusable equipment would have been transferred to Sydney Mines.

From the few details available, these railways were likely both quite similar

---

Underground Railways

Following the practice that had become common in England, and the recommendations of John Buddle about colliery operations at Sydney Mines, the early GMA commitment to rail transport was not limited to surface railways. By 1838, the two Sydney Mines pits had 6500 yards of underground track (5,944 m). Eighty per cent was recorded as "metal wagonway," presumably short cast iron rails and probably made in the U.K. The remainder was identified as "malleable iron way." This label indicates these rails were rolled iron, were undoubtedly British-made, probably in lengths of fifteen feet (4.6 m), and perhaps salvaged from the first Sydney Mines surface railway that had been abandoned in 1835. The presence of seventy-seven switches and more than three-and-one-half miles (5.6 km) of track shows these earliest underground rail systems were complex ones. No details about the early underground wagons have been found but it seems likely they were smaller than any used on the surface. Another unknown is whether these earlier pit railways used horses like the surface lines or if the underground carts were moved by miners.

to the first line at Sydney Mines and, given their short operating lives and low traffic levels, they do not require much attention beyond recognition of their existence.

Several points recorded about the Little Bras d'Or railway in the 1838 Sydney Mines Stock Book do deserve to be noted. That line provided the only example of use of wooden rails on a GMA railway anywhere in Nova Scotia. Two hundred yards (183 m) of this line were reported as built with hardwood rails, 8 feet (2.4 m) in length and with a cross-section 5 in x 5 in (127 x 127 mm). The remaining section had rolled iron rails. One detail in the inventory of loose stock at Little Bras d'Or is especially interesting. A small quantity of rolled rails was recorded and noted as being in 15-foot lengths (4.6 m) and weighting 28 lb/yd. This is the only instance before the 1860s where a record combines data on rail length and weight.

Combination of this weight reference with the fact that the low traffic volume on Little Bras d'Or line required relatively low construction standards provides a basis for speculating that the 28 lb/yd weight (ca.14 kg/metre) was likely also used at Bridgeport, may have been the weight used on the first Sydney Mines line, and was likely well below the weight used when the new Sydney Mines line was built in 1834-1835. All this, however, is speculation.

While making guesses about rails, those inclined to venture further out on the speculative limb might find some facts from England interesting. The original rails laid on the landmark Stockton & Darlington in England in 1825 were also 28 lb/yd. Those rails were manufactured by the Bedlington Iron Works, the firm that had introduced the process of rolling rails in England. Michael Longridge, head of the Bedlington Works, had many business con-

> **Cape Breton's First Locomotives**
> *The Cape-Breton News*, Sydney, September 17, 1853: 3
>
> "We had deferred any notice of the introduction of the Steam Engines and Cars, recently put into operation at the works of the General Mining Association, at the Sydney Mines, in the hope that a personal visit to the scene of operation would have enabled us more effectually to report the particulars of the improvement to our readers. But not having up to this time had it in our power to reach the Mines to fulfill this expectation, we now state the fact, and are glad to learn that the Engines or Locomotives 'Sydney' and 'Halifax' are performing their work in the conveyance of coal from the Mines to the Shipping Pier at North Sydney.
>
> "And may we not be permitted to indulge the hope that the same may be the precursor of the establishment of a line of Railway cars, which shall by and by take up the Atlantic Traveller upon his landing in this harbour, or in the adjacent one at Louisburg—which are the nearest ports on the continent of America to the old world—and transport him to the vast and almost boundless territories of the United States, Canada, &tc."

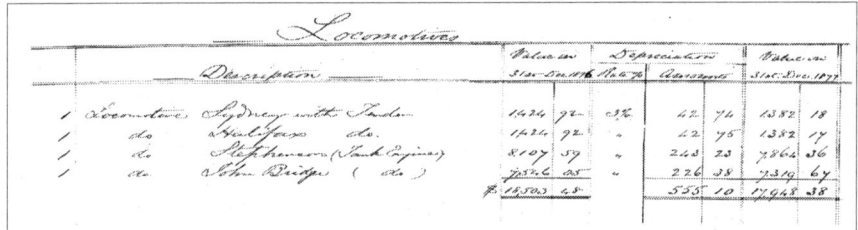

Fig. 1.9
The GMA locomotive roster at Sydney Mines, 31 December 1877.

GMA Papers, B-1-d, Sydney Mines Stock Book, 1877. Beaton Institute, Cape Breton University

nections with John Buddle and credited Buddle for his help in design of the new standards for manufacturing rail.[29] Both Longridge and Buddle had many ties to Timothy Hackworth who, in 1838-1839, built the first three locomotives the GMA brought to Pictou County. The Longridge firm also built *Vulcan*, a locomotive brought to Pictou County by the GMA in 1848. Do these pieces form part of the unfinished GMA jigsaw puzzle or are they all pieces of English puzzles without ties to Nova Scotia? Any answer depends on evidence yet to be found.

The GMA's Iron Horses

Steam engines for pumping and lifting cages were in use in the first Sydney Mines pit by 1830 but the date for the later introduction of steam power on the railway has long been a point of disagreement. Over the past fifty years, dates ranging from the late 1830s to the late 1850s have been offered by various writers. Despite those conflicting and inaccurate assertions, the answer is readily found in Sydney's *Cape-Breton News* and supported by a brief earlier reference in an English newspaper. The first locomotives arrived in the summer of 1853.

Relatively little is known for certain about those first two British-built engines and no photos have been found. One interesting detail, recorded in the GMA Stock Books at the Beaton Institute, is that they were fitted with separate coal tenders, something that sets them apart from most engines used on Cape Breton's 19th-century mining railways. Distances on these lines were short and locomotives did not have to carry much coal or water. Most were tank engines with a small coal compartment built into the frame behind the engineer's cab. The photos below of the GMA's *John Bridge* and *Stephenson* illustrate the basic design of a tank engine.

A number of accounts written over the past century state that *Sydney* and *Halifax* were built by the Neilson Company of Glasgow but a recently discovered newspaper reference from England indicates they came from Newcastle. The April 29, 1853, issue of the Newcastle *Courant* noted that two locomotives, "from the manufactory of Rayne & Burn, called *Sydney* and *Halifax*" had been tested prior to shipment "to a railway originally constructed for horsepower." Rayne's name has appeared previously. The Rayne and Burn name can be seen today on a plate on the locomotive *Albion*, sent to the GMA in Pictou County, NS, in 1854, and now preserved at the Nova Scotia Museum of Industry in Stellarton, NS. As a result of the details from the *Courant* and the *Cape Breton News*, the source of Cape Breton's first locomotives is now also finally established along with the date of their arrival.

A second and perhaps even more significant detail, if it is accurate, appeared in a 1930 newspaper article about Albert Somers of Sydney Mines. Somers was a GMA locomotive engineer who drove *Sydney* and *Halifax* when he was young. One of the mechanical features Somers recalled about those engines was that "The cylinders ... were set up at an angle of 45 degrees."[30] This description sounds like the angled cylinders that can be seen on *Albion* at the museum in Stellarton and suggests that the engines that came to Sydney Mines

Fig. 1.10
Still in Cape Breton: a nameplate from *Stephenson*. This meter long brass plate, almost 150 years old, is one of the most outstanding railway heritage items to have survived in Cape Breton. It is owned by a private collector who kindly permitted the photograph and its reproduction here.

Author's photo

Fig. 1.11
Stephenson at Sydney Mines, showing at least one nameplate in place. The British "bumpers" on the engine and the absence of "knuckle couplers" suggest the photo was taken before the opening of the Intercolonial Railway's connection to the GMA railway at North Sydney in 1891.

Library and Archives Canada (LAC), Andrew Merrilees Collection, 1980-149, Group D, Subseries 1, Box #2000725251.[32]

the year before *Albion*'s arrival may have been quite like *Albion* in design and appearance.[31] Without better evidence, however, this is speculation.

Much more important than arrival date or builder is the question of why the GMA introduced locomotives when they did. Though coal sales and railway traffic levels had been fairly stable over the previous decade, by the early 1850s the company was hoping for a boom in activity. Negotiations had been ongoing toward a trade treaty to give the British North American colonies improved access to the American market. For the GMA, the important goal was the elimination of the American tariff on Nova Scotia coal. No contemporary company correspondence about the potential impact of the treaty has been found although Richard Brown, still the GMA's Cape Breton manager in the 1850s, later wrote that the firm had expected a major increase in sales to the U.S. This optimism appears to have led to the conversion of the Sydney Mines railway to steam power in 1853 as well as to new mines being opened there and at Lingan the next year.

Fig. 1.12
John Bridge operated on the GMA railway at Sydney Mines for about 30 years and appears to have been scrapped c.1900. The 1930 *Halifax Herald* story about Albert Somers referred to earlier stated that Somers had a *John Bridge* nameplate. Is there a descendant of Somers out there with the plate on display or in an attic?

Library and Archives Canada (LAC), Andrew Merrilees Collection, 1980-149, Group D, Subseries 1, Box #2000725251.

Fig. 1.13
The *C. G. Swann* and the men who built the locomotive at Sydney Mines.

Sydney Mines Heritage Museum.

The Reciprocity Treaty was signed in 1854 and did remove the American tariff on Nova Scotia coal, but GMA sales did not increase dramatically until after the outbreak of the American Civil War in 1861. When that happened, most of the additional business went to Lingan rather than Sydney Mines. Upgrading the Sydney Mines railway to steam power was premature, a move that paralleled the large investment the company made in the locomotive-powered Albion Mines Railway in Pictou County in 1838-1840 in anticipation of traffic that did not materialize for more than a decade. *Sydney* and *Halifax* were able to handle the traffic to the North Sydney wharf without difficulty.

In 1866, two more Newcastle-built locomotives, *Fairy* and *Stephenson,* arrived for the GMA. Black, Hawthorn and Co. built *Fairy*, a small tank engine, to transform the horse-powered railway built at Lingan a decade previously, into a locomotive-powered railway. Both before and after the arrival of *Fairy*, the Lingan railway was unusual in one respect. Its track width was 42 inches (106 cm), the only instance where a GMA railway was not "standard gauge" (i.e., 4 feet, 8 ½ inches [1.44 m]). *Fairy*, which appears to have been the first narrow gauge locomotive in Canada, remained in service at Lingan until the

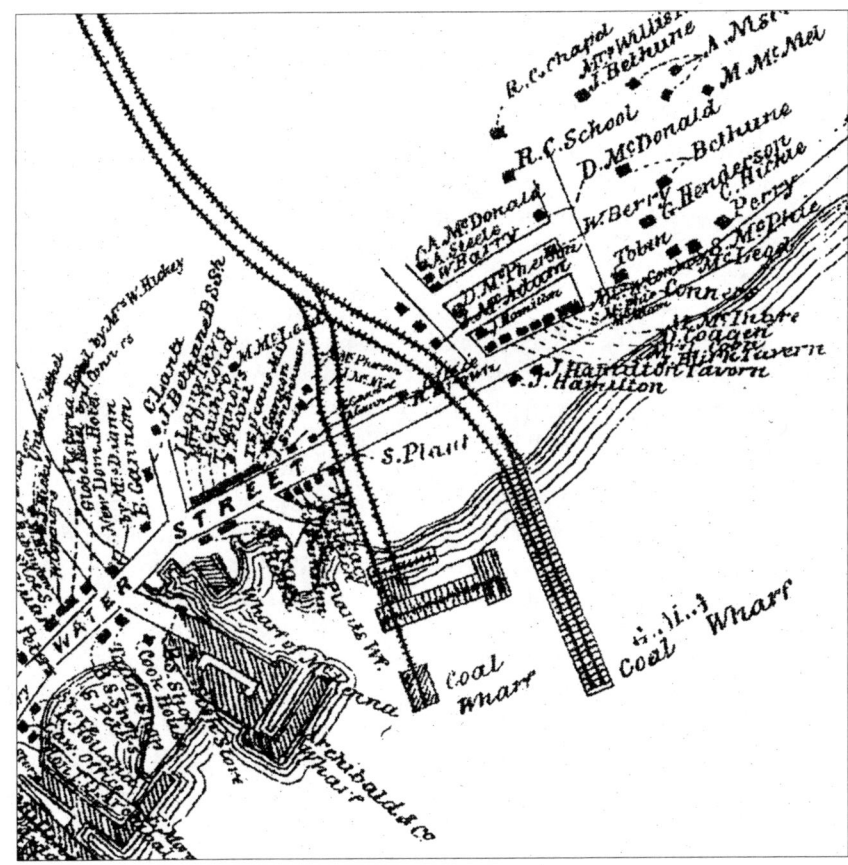

Fig. 1.14
North Sydney in 1877 with the GMA coal piers and their railway lines. Because of the topography, as the railway approached the piers, it must have followed a route very close to that of the modern highway approach to the Newfoundland ferry dock. What is unknown is when this rail line was built to replace the self-acting incline down Goat Hill. Despite the uncertainty, it seems reasonable to speculate this happened upon or soon after the arrival of locomotives in 1853 and that the 1835 wharf was served by the locomotives for about two decades before it was replaced by the piers built in 1876.

Detail from Cape Breton County map, A. F. Church & Sons, Halifax, 1877.

site was abandoned in 1885. The engine was then rebuilt to standard gauge and used at Sydney Mines until it was scrapped after the First World War.

Most writers who claimed that *Sydney* and *Halifax* were built by Neilson, also said that *Stephenson* came to Sydney Mines from the Glasgow firm. Recently found evidence proves this was not the case and also explains the name of the locomotive. The records of Robert Stephenson and Co. of Newcastle show delivery of this engine in May of 1866 to J. H. Burn of Rayne and Burn on behalf of the GMA.[33]

Among later Sydney Mines locomotives were two named after men with GMA connections. The *John Bridge*, built by Fletcher Jennings and Co. of Whitehaven, Lancashire, arrived from England in 1870. It honoured the name of one of the original GSAMA/GMA Directors. The *C. G. Swann*, named after the GMA Board Secretary who retired in 1888, should be the best known GMA engine. It was built at Sydney Mines and is believed to have been the only locomotive built on the island. There is, however, uncertainty about whether this engine was truly built "from scratch" or if it was assembled from parts brought from the U.K. The fact that the engine appears to have been two years in the building suggests the former, but this is a speculative interpretation. Within a few months after completion in June of 1888,[34] the *Swann* went into service on the GMA railway at Victoria Mines, on the south side of Sydney Harbour, where it operated until the mine was sold to H. M. Whitney's Dominion Coal Company in 1893.

During the 1870s and 1880s, other improvements began to appear on the GMA railways. In 1876, a large new wharf complex was opened at North Sydney with a double track rail line approaching the docks. This is illustrated in the North Sydney map published in 1877 (figure 1.14). In the 1880s, the GMA started replacing the older iron rails with steel rails. At 50 lb/yd (roughly 25 kg/metre), these were relatively light weight compared with rails being laid at this time on new main line tracks by railways such as the Intercolonial. Interesting asides to the references in GMA reports on the new steel rails are indications the old rails were to be used on underground lines within the mines. To increase shipping efficiency on the surface railway, larger hopper cars designed to carry 6-ton loads replaced the older 3- and 4-tonne cars that had been in use for decades.

In the late 1850s, the GMA had been forced to give up its monopoly power over Nova Scotia's coal reserves and in 1870 sold its Pictou County mines. Competition emerged from new companies that will be discussed in chapter 2. Consolidation of those new companies on the south side of Sydney Harbour by H. M. Whitney into his new Dominion Coal Company began in the early 1890s. Whitney's attempts to add the GMA properties to his corporate empire were rejected, but in 1900 the GMA's owners accepted an offer from a Pictou County firm, the Nova Scotia Steel Company.[35] The new century began with those new owners preparing to open a steel mill at Sydney Mines and the GMA fading into history.

2 – Other Early Railways in the Sydney Coal Field

After the GMA monopoly on Cape Breton's coal reserves was brought to an end in 1858, new mining companies appeared on the south side of Sydney harbour. In most cases, the mines depended on railways to carry the coal to shipping piers since most of the coal raised was destined for markets outside Cape Breton.

The International Railway

The most successful of the early competitors to the GMA was the International Coal and Railway Company. This New York-based firm was established in 1864, sank pits at Bridgeport and soon built a standard-gauge rail line to a new wharf on Sydney Harbour. The Department of Mines Report for 1869 stated that construction was "being very vigorously carried on" that year and the rail line and the wharf were opened late in 1870.

When making plans for the railway, the International Company attempted to use a model for construction of privately-owned railways which had come into wide use in Canada and would be followed in Cape Breton in later years. The owners tried to obtain financial aid from governments. In 1868, attempts were made to get the new national government in Ottawa to provide a guarantee on a £125,000 loan to fund the railway project. The lobbying effort was widely supported in Cape Breton and on the Nova Scotia mainland.

Charles Tupper, who as Premier led Nova Scotia into Confederation the previous year, was one of Prime Minister John A. Macdonald's key supporters in the new House of Commons. Tupper threw his support behind the company's request. In a letter to Macdonald from London, where he had been sent to try to ensure that Joe Howe did not persuade the British government to undo the Confederation agreement, Tupper tried to convince Macdonald to support the International Company's proposal. He made the case for both the economic benefits to Cape Breton and the potential political benefits in Nova Scotia where anti-confederates held eighteen of the Province's nineteen

International Railway Opens

The Novascotian, Halifax, December 5, 1870.
Special Dispatch ... Sydney, C.B. November 26

"The International Coal and Railway Company celebration, in honour of the opening of the railway, was held today. The Weather was fine. Over two hundred persons left by train for Bridgeport Mines to attend a luncheon. Alfred McKay, Esq, the President of the Company, accompanied the guests. Two barques and two brigs are at the pier loading, all decorated with bunting. Great rejoicings. Capital celebration."

Fig. 2.1
The International Company's shipping pier on Sydney Harbour soon after it went into use. Note the coal cars on top of the pier. In sight are three chutes along the side of the pier plus one on the end. Rail cars were emptied directly into the chutes that carried the coal down into the holds of waiting ships.

Canadian Illustrated News, May 20, 1871: 312.

Fig. 2.2
Henry Day: built in England for the International Company's railway in 1870. The Sydney & Louisburg Museum collection includes photos of the *Alfred MacKay*, the second in the pair of engines built by Black, Hawthorn.

LAC, Andrew Merrilees Collection, 1980-149, Group D, Subseries 1, Box #2000725251.

seats in the Commons. Tupper's letter concluded by saying, "I do hope that the Cabinet will favourably consider an application which I certainly should have sustained had no confederation existed and it had been brought before the local government of Nova Scotia."[1] Despite Tupper's efforts, no guarantee came from Ottawa and the company had to proceed using its own money.

With their new shipping system, International was soon raising as much coal as the GMA on the northside of the harbour. The new firm quickly became one of the province's major mining companies. The railway was just over 12 miles long and built with English-manufactured rail weighing 56 lb per yard (27.8 kg/m).[2] The line was powered by three tank engines imported from England, *Henry Day* and *Alfred MacKay*, both from Black, Hawthorn of Newcastle and *A. C. Morton*, built by the Hunslet Engine Company of Leeds.[3] All were named after International directors or executives. The *Morton* became one of the best known of Cape Breton's English-built engines because of its longevity. That engine wound up on the Dominion Coal Company's Sydney and Louisburg Railway as S&L # 3 and ran until 1942, a working life of more than seventy years.

Before the International Company became part of Whitney's Dominion Coal in 1893, significant changes were appearing on its railway. The introduction of rolled iron rails in England in the 1820s had been a critical improvement in railway track. Steel rails had started to appear in the 1860s and Nova Scotia's first steel rails, 56 lb/yd (27.8 kg/m), were laid between Truro and New Glasgow in 1866-1867 under the direction of Sandford Fleming, the Chief Engineer for construction of the "Pictou Branch." It is possible that the International line was originally built with steel, but no proof of that has been found and the similarity between the weight of its original rails and those on the Pictou Branch may have been a coincidence. By the early 1880s, however, steel rails weighing 60 lb/yd (29.8 kg/m) were being laid on some International Company track.[4]

During the last decades of the 19th century, Canadian and American locomotive builders were replacing their British competitors in the supply of engines to Canadian railways. While the International line was not the first Cape Breton railway to acquire an engine from this side of the Atlantic, shortly before its acquisition by Dominion Coal it purchased an engine called *Sir Donald* from the Rhode Island Locomotive Works of Providence.

The engine was named after Donald Smith, who had added a directorship in the International Company to a wide range of business interests that included a prominent role in the Canadian Pacific Railway. Probably the most famous photo in the history of Canadian railways shows Smith driving the "last spike" in the CPR at Craigellachie, BC, in 1885. Smith was knighted

Fig. 2.3
Sir Donald, locomotive # 4 on the International Company's railway. One of the earliest American-built engines in Cape Breton, this locomotive was named after Sir Donald Smith, a director of the International Company and a leading figure in the construction of the Canadian Pacific Railway.

Sydney Mines Heritage Museum.

in 1886 and so he was "Sir Donald" when the International locomotive was ordered.[5] In 1907, he received a peerage and became Baron Strathcona and Mount Royal. *Sir Donald* was the first of a series of similar locomotives that would be acquired later by Whitney's new firm, Dominion Coal. *Sir Donald*, like the *Morton*, demonstrated the longevity of steam locomotives. It also went to Whitney's railway, was renamed and rebuilt several times, and operated until the end of the age of steam in 1961. Upon Dominion Coal's takeover of the International Company, the original International track was kept in service and became Whitney's main line between Sydney Harbour and Bridgeport.

Glace Bay Mining Company and Caledonia Coal Company

Some early investors in International Coal had interests in other Cape Breton firms. One of these was Gardiner Hubbard of Boston whose name generated the names of Gardiner Mines and the "Gardiner seam" on geological maps. Perhaps best known as the father-in-law of Alexander Graham Bell, Hubbard was involved with both Caledonia Coal and Glace Bay Mining, two firms that opened mines near Glace Bay in the 1860s. Both built short rail lines, documented in government reports as standard gauge, to their shipping wharves. As a result of the Hubbard-Bell connection, it seems that Glace Bay Mining's railway was the first in Canada to use the telephone in its operations.

In 1867, J. H. Converse of Boston, President of both Caledonia Coal and Glace Bay Mining, ordered a small locomotive from Neilson of Glasgow that was the first to operate at Glace Bay[6] and, it appears, the first on the south side of Sydney Harbour. There have been conflicting accounts about which company used the engine though it seems almost certain it went to Glace Bay Mining.[7] While only a guess, it is also possible that the origin of this engine was the basis for the assertions that some of the early GMA locomotives had come from Glasgow. Converse's locomotive acquired the unusual name *Pinkie* which may have been named after Pinkie House near Edinburgh. Glace Bay Mining's railway introduced one other innovation that should be

Fig. 2.4
Horse-powered rail operations at the Caledonia mine in Glace Bay c.1880. Horse-powered rail lines continued in wide use at mines after the arrival of locomotives and it was common to see horses and iron horses working side by side. Principal of Queen's University in Kingston when *Picturesque Canada* appeared, George Monro Grant had an important railroad connection. In 1872, he was recruited from his day job as minister at St. Matthew's Presbyterian Church in Halifax to travel with Sandford Fleming on the transcontinental survey for the Canadian Pacific Railway. The next year, Grant published *Ocean to Ocean*, an account of the survey expedition.

Grant, *Picturesque Canada*, 848.

Fig. 2.5
This photo shows what *Pinkie*, the first locomotive in Glace Bay, probably looked like when new in 1867. The photo shows Neilson & Co's works # 1367, built at the same time and with the same specifications as *Pinkie* which was Neilson's works # 1366.

LAC, Andrew Merrilees Collection, 1980-149, Group D, Subseries 1, Box #2000725251.

Fig. 2.6
Pinkie at work after becoming a Dominion Coal/Sydney & Louisburg locomotive. This photo can be dated to 1895 or later. Another poorer quality copy of this photo shows S&L coal hopper car # 939 to the left of the engine. That car number was one of a shipment of several hundred new hoppers built for the S&L by Rhodes, Curry & Co. of Amherst in 1895. The S&L Museum collection includes several photos from a later date showing *Pinkie* with painted identification as S&L # 1.

LAC, Andrew Merrilees Collection, 1980-149, Group D, Subseries 1, Box #2000725251.

Fig. 2.7
Glace Bay Mining Company's *E.P. Archbold*. Photo date, location, and names of the engine crewmen are all unknown.

LAC, Andrew Merrilees Collection, 1980-149, Group D, Subseries 1, Box #2000725251.

noted. It brought the first American-built engine to Cape Breton. The *E. P. Archbold*,[8] named after a company director, arrived in Glace Bay from the Baldwin Company of Philadelphia in the late 1880s. *Pinkie* and the *Archbold* both survived into the Sydney and Louisburg era and remained in service into the 1920s. In its early days on the S&L, *Pinkie* had the honour of being designated locomotive # 1.

The Glace Bay Mining Company's railway introduced another "first." The Department of Mines Report for 1878 shows that a third rail was added to the line to permit the narrower gauge "coal tubs" used in the pit to be hauled

---

Glasgow and Cape Breton Railway Company (Limited), 1868:
Exerpts From The Company Prospectus

"This company is projected for the purpose of constructing and working a line of railway from Sydney Harbour to Cow Bay, via Bridgeport, in the island of Cape Breton; connecting the great coal district of that part of the province of Nova Scotia with Sydney Harbour, as a Port of Shipment for the Coals raised for exportation.

"The want of such a Railway and Shipping Port is beginning to be greatly felt, and retards very seriously the development of what has already become an important branch of the provincial industry and trade; for with the exception of a small artificial harbour belonging to one of the Coal Mining Companies formed since 1860, and kept open by them at a heavy annual expense, the present mode of shipment at most of the Collieries lying south-east of Sydney Harbour consists in taking the coal in lighters from the shore (the Collieries being situated immediately upon or near the coast) and putting it on board vessels in the open roadstead of the Atlantic....

"The length of the proposed railway is about 25 miles; the country over which it will pass is very level, and it will traverse the Coal area itself. The local Act of Incorporation allows it to be constructed in such portions or sections as the Directors of the Company may determine. Part of the land required for the line is the property of the Government, the rest being owned by a number of private individuals. The former have signified their readiness to grant the necessary right-of-way over their portion, as well as to offer all other facilities to the Company; and the majority of the latter have subscribed engagements in die form to concede a similar privilege and make the proper conveyance as regards their lands upon payment of stipulated sums of a small amount in the aggregate....

"It is shown by preliminary Surveys and Estimates made by a practical Engineer of considerable local experience and familiar with the whole subject matter in its various branches, that the entire line of railway with a gauge of 4 ft. 8½ ins. (that being generally allowed to be the most useful for Coal traffic) can be well and efficiently constructed and completed for an average cost of 10,100 dols., or £2200 per Mile, being 252,500 dols., or £50,500 for the whole distance; that the necessary Wharves, Buildings, &c. would cost about 20,000 dols., or £4,000; and Rolling Stock comprising a sufficient number of Engines and Trucks for the delivery of 2,000 tons of Coals per working day, 77,500 dols., or £15,500; making a total outlay of 350,000 dols., or £70,000. A residue of Capital of 150,000 dols., or £30,000 would thus be available for the purchase of land for the right-of-way, &c....

"Plans of the line of Railway and the position of the Collieries may be seen, and further information obtained, on application to Mr. T. R. Preston, 1 Lime Street Square, London, E.C., or to Mr. W. A Hendry, Halifax, Nova Scotia."

to the wharf by the locomotive. Two possible reasons for this change could have been to eliminate breakage of the coal in the process of transferring it to the original standard gauge wagons and to eliminate the labour costs involved in the transfer process. No documentation has been found to indicate if the standard gauge wagons remained in use after 1878 or how long the shipping method introduced in that year was used. Despite the minimal information available, this event marked the first Cape Breton use of "dual gauge" track, a design that was very rare on railways anywhere in North America.

The Glasgow and Cape Breton Railway

In 1868, a group of British investors had received approval from the Province to open the Reserve Colliery. To move coal from this pit—and others they developed—to their shipping wharf on Sydney Harbour, they built the Glasgow and Cape Breton Railway from Reserve to Sydney in 1871 and soon extended it eastward from Reserve to Schooner Pond near modern-day Donkin. Some elements of the original plan are found in the 1868 prospectus in the James McConnell Library in Sydney.

Despite the original intent to build the Glasgow and Cape Breton as standard gauge, it was constructed as a narrow gauge line with a track width of 36 in (91.44 cm), the only use of this gauge on Cape Breton except for some short sections of line for specialized services within the Sydney steel plant in the mid-20th century.[9] As a caveat to those who read corporate prospectuses, it is interesting to note that a second prospectus[10] issued by the promoters in January of 1871, also found in the James McConnell Library collection, indicated intent to use narrow gauge but without a hint that this marked a significant change in the engineering plans. Neither prospectus made mention of possible use of a second shipping port. In 1874, however, work was started on a branch southward from Reserve to Louisbourg, a port that was normally ice-free even when the Sydney wharf was closed by ice.

In addition to its unusual gauge, the G&CB had three very unusual locomotives. Built by the Avonside Company of Bristol,[11] these were known as "Fairlie Patents" after their designer, Robert Fairlie. The basic design was a mechanical version of the "push-me-pull-you," the two-headed llama of the Dr. Doolittle stories, since the rear of the engine looked the same as the front. As a result, Fairlie Patents were often called "double-enders." A Patent had a central cab, two fireboxes and boilers, two sets of driving wheels and a smokestack at each end. Unlike other British-built engines that operated in Cape Breton, the surviving photos suggest the Patents carried neither specific names nor numbers. It is impossible to tell one engine from another in the few surviving photos. With its three Patents which arrived in 1872[12], the G&CB had 60 per cent of the total Canadian stock of these strange-looking locomotives.[13] The other two, larger than those on the G&CB though also built by Avonside, ran on two Ontario narrow gauge lines, the Toronto and Nipissing and the Toronto, Grey and Bruce.[14]

Fig. 2.8
One of the three Fairlie Patents seen here at the Charlotte Street bridge in Sydney. The narrow gauge line ran from Reserve to a shipping wharf on Sydney Harbour located near the site of Sydney's modern-day City Hall. Despite descriptions in several recently published accounts, this rail line did not go to the International Company's pier.

1893. Photo by Umlah. 77-167-301. Beaton Institute, Cape Breton University.

Fig. 2.9
Frederick Gisborne of the Glasgow & Cape Breton Railway.

Canadian Illustrated News, August 16, 1873: 101.

An obvious question is why a small Cape Breton mining railway opted for the Patent design for its primary source of motive power but neither a documented nor an obvious answer has been found. Few company papers from the G&CB have survived and nothing is offered in the few existing secondary references to the line to account for the choice of Fairlie's design.[15] While they are only speculations, various possibilities warrant consideration if only because they indicate the perils of writing history without good evidence.

Frederick Gisborne, a key organizer of the G&CB and its related mining companies, was also the Nova Scotia government's minerals agent in London when the G&CB was being set up.[16] Given his mandate from the government, he certainly would have been paying close attention to developments in the mining sector including transportation. The possibility of Gisborne meeting Fairlie or seeing early Patents in operation in England or Wales does not seem unreasonable. Equally plausible is the development of contacts between Gisborne and key individuals at the Avonside Company during this period, something that raises the possibility that the Patents were acquired because they were Avonside-built with the Fairlie design being unrelated to the decision. Still another possibility is that the decision was influenced by the substantial flow of publicity in the U.K. about the Patent generated by Fairlie and his supporters at the end of the 1860s rather than by any direct contact between Gisborne and either Fairlie or Avonside. Since there is no evidence of a Gisborne role in the decision, these three possibilities could be restructured with someone else from the G&CB playing the role suggested for Gisborne. Another option is that the choice was made by a broker contracted to obtain locomotives for the G&CB.[17] Still another possibility is that Avonside's involvement was connected to its Bristol location. This was very close to the factory of Fox, Walker and Co. which had provided the first locomotive for the G&CB in 1871, the year before the arrival of the Patents.[18]

While these options are all guesses, they provide an indication of the scope of the possibilities that might have been in play. To go out on a speculative limb, it is possible to suggest that some circumstantial evidence points toward a plausible answer. The 1871 G&CB prospectus identifies James Samuel as Engineer for the company at that time. Samuel was a consulting engineer with extensive experience on railway projects in the U.K. and overseas,[19] who had at least one earlier close link to Robert Fairlie. He was joint holder with Fairlie of an 1869 patent for a "steam carriage."[20] Whether the relationship between the two may have included other interests or activities is unknown, but a Fairlie-Samuel connection might explain why the Patents came to Cape Breton. It must be emphasized, however, that this is an interpretation, a guess, and a good illustration of the uncertainties that abound in the realm of railway history.

Despite uncertainties about the purchase of the Patents, we do have a battery of basic mechanical details about those unusual engines. The technical specifications that have been quoted elsewhere appear to have been based on an 1874 report in the British journal *Engineering*.[21] This account provided details that would appeal to those very interested in locomotive mechanics. The engines were 0-4-4-0Ts[22] with 3-ft-3-in (99 cm) diameter drivers (in wheel sets measuring 5 ft 6 in [1.67 m] between the two axles) and a total engine wheelbase of 21 ft 4 in (6.55 m). The four cylinders were 11 in diameter with a 19-inch stroke (48 cm). The engines had 220 heating tubes, 1.5 in (381 mm) diameter, with a total heating surface of 838 sq ft (78 sq metres). The fireboxes had grate areas of 13.25 sq ft (1.2 sq metres) and added an additional 84 sq ft (7.8 sq metres) of heating surface area. Water and fuel capacities were 1000 gal (4,546 l) and 22 hundredweight (1,118 kg) respectively. These details, the drawing and the photos provide a base for a serious modeller to build a G&CB Patent—or a full-sized replica.[23]

An 1872 letter from E. W. Young, the G&CB resident engineer at that time, showed a high level of satisfaction with the Patents. "The engines ride easily on the rails," wrote Young, "and are comfortable and conveniently arranged for the driver and the stoker. So far as our present experience goes, the engines are a great success. A train of 40 loaded cars[24] can be brought in from the Reserve by one engine."[25]

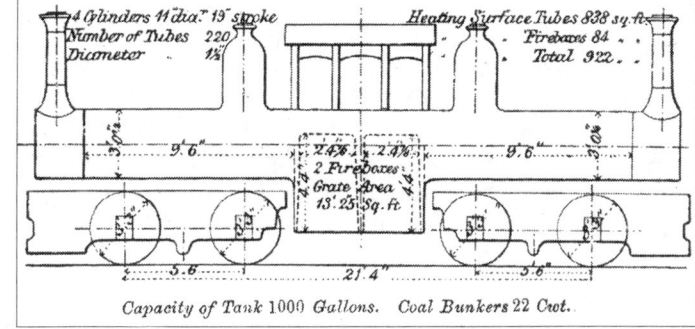

Fig. 2.10 Specifications for the Glasgow & Cape Breton Fairlie Patents: almost everything that would be needed to build one of these engines today.

Engineering, August 21, 1874: 144.

Despite initial confidence about the G&CB and the mines it served, the venture was not successful. A series of financial crises triggered by a long period of boom and bust in the coal industry in the 1870s and 80s led to corporate reorganizations, changes in ownership and several changes in the railway's name. During those years of uncertainty, the branch railway to Louisbourg was built though it is uncertain if work started before or after the first change of company name and the departure of Frederick Gisborne in 1874. Even if work did not start until after he left, Gisborne had obviously been planning

Fig. 2.11 (top) - The bridge that carried the narrow gauge railway over the Mira River on the way to Louisbourg. The *Canadian Illustrated News* described it as an "elegant though exceedingly strong lattice girder iron bridge." A close look reveals the double-ended Fairlie Patent design of the locomotive on the bridge. Along the Mira, the bridge was known as the "Gisborne bridge." The origin of this name raises interesting but unanswered questions since Frederick Gisborne had probably departed the scene before work started on the bridge.

Canadian Illustrated News, June 5, 1875: 356.

Fig. 2.12 (bottom) - The Cape Breton Company shipping wharf at Louisbourg under construction. The photo was probably taken in 1874-75. A.L. Rice had a studio in New Glasgow and was one of the earliest commercial photographers in eastern Nova Scotia. This wharf and the narrow gauge track that ran to it were abandoned when a new standard gauge railway was built to Louisbourg by the Dominion Coal Company in the mid-1890s.

LAC, Sir Sandford Fleming Collection, negative #PA-027636.

to build to Louisbourg. Proof of that will be seen in chapter 4 in discussion of Gisborne's Louisbourg Extension Railway Company that was incorporated in 1872.

Upon Gisborne's departure, D. J. Kennelly became managing director of the firm that had been renamed the Cape Breton Company.[26] Kennelly's background was highly unusual. He had trained in London as a lawyer, served as an administrator in the East India Company and been a senior officer in the Royal Indian Navy.[27] Henry A. Gray, identified as the "engineer in charge" of the line in the Louisbourg wharf photo (figure 2.12), arrived in 1875 from a post on the Intercolonial Railway and stayed with the Cape Breton company until 1878.[28]

While the original narrow gauge line running eastward from Sydney had been a relatively easy engineering project, the branch going south from Reserve to Louisbourg presented challenges to Henry Gray and his men in the form of the Mira River plus numerous stretches of rough country. From that branch, we have one of the most dramatic views of Cape Breton's 19th-century railways. The engraving from the *Canadian Illustrated News* was based on a photo that has survived[29] but the drawing provides a clearer illustration of the site. It and the wharf photo show the construction efforts needed to complete the Louisbourg branch which, according to press reports, was opened in October of 1877.[30] Another illustration of construction on the branch is seen in the photo of Blacket's Trestle in chapter 6.

By 1880, the Cape Breton Company was also on the verge of bankruptcy. A second reorganization took place the next year and the firm was renamed once more, this time as the Sydney and Louisburg Coal and Railway Company.[31] This was not the "Sydney & Louisburg," the standard gauge "S&L," of the 20th century though it was almost certainly the source of the name adopted by that later railway. Then under its third name, the narrow gauge line struggled for another decade with Kennelly continuing as the manager for most of that time. It appears that there were periods when either the mines or the railway ceased operating; an 1894 report on the line indicates the Louisbourg and Schooner Pond sections had gone out of service by 1893. In that year, H. M. Whitney's consolidation of existing companies brought the narrow gauge S&L and its associated mines into the Dominion Coal Company. Most of the narrow gauge track and equipment were quickly abandoned but the name would be recycled by the Whitney group.

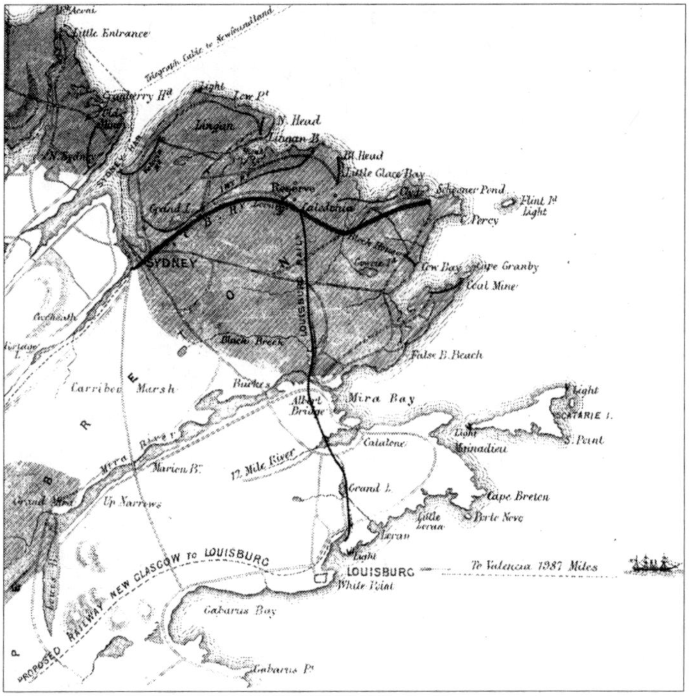

Given the date of the Dominion Coal takeover, references to the Patents being scrapped in 1894 in sources such as Omer Lavallee's *Narrow Gauge Railways in Canada* are reasonable speculations. Despite the scrap date that is usually seen in print, at least one and maybe all of the Patents survived and likely worked for most of another decade.

In 1930, a newspaper account told of Dominion Coal's modification of the narrow gauge branch from Reserve to Dominion: "To continue using the narrow gauge engines, a third rail was laid on this branch, and the strange spectacle of a narrow gauge engine hauling a train of standard gauge cars was a regular thing for years."[32] The account went on to comment about the curious structure of the switches in use and the challenges faced by brakemen setting switches for trains with narrow gauge locomotives hauling standard gauge cars. This undermines the conventional version of the end of all narrow gauge operations and also provides a second Cape Breton example of the use of dual gauge.

At least two Patents appear to have survived to run on the dual gauge branch until they were scrapped toward the end of 1902. A railway industry journal published early in 1903 stated that "the old double-end locomotives … have recently been taken apart at the Reserve, and will be disposed of as old junk. The machinists who took them apart say it was the hardest job they ever tackled, as the engines were very strongly built and the parts mostly forge-made."[33]

Fig. 2.13
The Cape Breton Company's narrow gauge railway route in 1875. Note the inclusion of a "proposed railway" to run westward from Louisburg to New Glasgow on the mainland. The evolution and significance of that project will appear in chapter 4.

Cape Breton Company Limited, Notice to Ship Owners and Coal Agents, London, March, 1875.

Dominion Coal Company coal bunker at Reserve. Figure 2.14 illustrates several aspects of the complexity of the early years of the S&L as well as the potential problems in interpreting photographic evidence. The photo could not have been taken before 1895. As with the second photo of Pinkie above (figure 2.6), that earliest possible date is based on the numbers visible on the S&L hopper cars that came from Rhodes, Curry and Co. in 1895. Despite frequent references in usually reliable sources that say the Fairlie Patents were scrapped in 1894, there is a narrow gauge Patent in  the foreground. An added interesting detail is that neither the track on which the Patent sits nor the other tracks visible has a third rail to permit the dual gauge operations described in the 1930 newspaper account. Such would have been useful since the Rhodes, Curry hoppers inside the bunker were standard gauge. The locomotive in the background has not been identified. In theory, it might have been the first G&CB locomotive that arrived in 1871 but there are no known photos of that engine to use for comparison and the limited evidence regarding the roster of the narrow gauge line seems to suggest that engine had been scrapped before 1895. The second engine is more likely one of the standard gauge Black, Hawthorn engines that had come to the International Company in 1870. This suggestion is based on the absence of alternatives plus some physical similarities. Compare the background engine with the *Henry Day* at the beginning of this chapter (figure 2.2). However, another aspect of the photo raises a relevant question. The three lines of track outside the bunker appear to have the same gauge. The presence of the Patent on the track in the foreground indicates that track's gauge was the 42 inches of the G&CB. If either or both of the interior tracks had been standard gauge, 33 per cent wider, that great a difference should be apparent. The track on which the S&L hoppers sit inside the bunker was standard gauge, four feet, eight and one half inches, but the rails are not visible to assist in assessing the photo's content. In 1897, B. T. A. Bell had the good sense to not offer any details about the photo other than to identify the location as Reserve.

Bell, 1897.

Dominion Coal Company and the New S&L

At the beginning of the 1890s, a group of financiers headed by H. M. Whitney of Boston brought forward a plan to consolidate all coal mining in Cape Breton under a single corporation. Various factors were in play including the interest of some of Whitney's Boston associates in a secure supply of coal for their gas manufacturing and related companies in the Boston area. Canadian participants included Donald Smith, previously on the International Company Board, and W. C. Van Horne, another name prominent in the history of the Canadian Pacific Railway.[34] Given the railway focus of this book, it should be noted that the investors with CPR connections appear to have been interested in the potential profits from the company rather than the development of ties to railway companies like the Canadian Pacific.

Mixing Berry-picking and Narrow Gauge Railroading

The Halifax Herald, Halifax: March 1, 1941: 17.

Stories about how trains were so slow that train crews were able to go berry-picking while on the job are common in Cape Breton and elsewhere in the Maritimes. These stories were perhaps true on occasion but they were more likely to have been a gentle way of poking fun at the slow speeds of trains. Non-railroaders were usually not aware that those slow speeds were often dictated by rules, whether written or unwritten, to enforce safe train operation on poor track.

"R. A. (Bob) Macaulay, retired CNR (Canadian National Railways) Fuel Inspector was born in Port Morien, March 2, 1871. In his younger days, like the majority of the boys in the mining district, he went to work in the pit with his father. Bob then went railroading on … the old narrow gauge between Sydney and Reserve and later to Louisburg. In a radio address over CJCB in Sydney, he discussed the days of the narrow gauge railroads and coal mining in Cape Breton.

"In one instance he told about these old locomotives. There were some fairly steep grades on this line between Sydney and Reserve and by the time the locomotive reached the top of the first one, the engineer had to stop in order that the fireman could get up steam enough to reach the top of the next one. This took considerable time so the conductor and the brakeman would wander off in the woods picking the berries that would be in season. When the locomotive was ready to go the conductor and the brakeman would have strayed away a considerable distance so the engineer would have to blow the whistle to attract their attention to the fact that the train was ready to go."

Fig. 2.15 - Another illustration from the beginning of the Dominion Coal Company era. The locomotive, new in 1893, was named *H. M. Whitney* to honour the new boss. It was identical to the International's *Sir Donald* and came from the same builder, the Rhode Island Locomotive Works. This engine, later renamed as # 31, ran on the S&L for almost 70 years until the end of the age of steam in 1961. The passenger cars in the photo still carry the International name, probably an indication the photo was taken soon after the new Whitney firm was established. Passenger operations will be discussed in chapter 6.

Sydney & Louisburg Railway Museum, #SL-X90-4-118.

Behind the scenes, the Nova Scotia government was interested in seeing the coal industry strengthened and output increased to boost the flow of royalty payments to the Province. Critical roles were played by Benjamin Pearson, a Halifax lawyer and businessman who had strong backroom connections to the Liberal party and Premier Fielding. After initial negotiations broke down, Pearson appears to have negotiated the 1892 deal that satisfied both the Whitney syndicate and the government. Within a few years, Dominion Coal owned virtually all the collieries on the south side of Sydney Harbour. While Whitney's name dominated the Sydney area over the next decade, Pearson's importance drew little attention even though he was on the Board of the new coal company and would be a key player in the establishment of the Dominion Iron and Steel Company a few years later. Pearson's name will appear again in conjunction with other railway projects.[35]

The rise of Dominion Coal led to consolidation of the railways that had been built by the companies bought by Whitney and his associates. Hiram Donkin, a native of Wallace, Nova Scotia, had been a senior engineer involved in survey work and construction of the new Intercolonial railway, recently opened between the Strait of Canso and Sydney. He was hired by the Whitney group to direct the reorganization of Dominion Coal's railways.[36] Sections from Donkin's 1894 account below provide a contemporary summary of the formation of the "new" S&L. The Sydney and Louisburg name, borrowed from the final version of the name of the narrow gauge line, quickly came into use to refer to Dominion Coal's railways. For example, both the full name and the abbreviated "S&L" can be seen on photos of railway cars before 1900. This common use was much more important than the legal detail that the name had no official status until the 1910 incorporation of the railway as a separate firm, the Sydney and Louisburg Railway Company.[37] Donkin probably made the decisions about retaining the International Company's standard gauge railway, retaining some pieces of the narrow gauge line in the short run, and construct-

Fig. 2.16
Rail activity at Reserve colliery c.1900. The drawing is a good illustration of the focus of the new S&L on moving coal.

Vernon, 199.

The Railway System of the Dominion Coal Company

Hiram Donkin, C.E.

"The railway system acquired by the Dominion Coal Company Limited, at the time they came into possession of their coal property in Cape Breton, consisted of the International, a standard gauge railway 12 miles in length, with a branch to Old Bridgeport mines ½ mile in length, and a branch 1½ miles in length connecting with the Canadian Government railway at Sydney; a standard gauge railway from New Victoria mines to shipping pier, Sydney Harbour, in length 5 miles; a standard gauge railway 1 mile in length, from Caledonia mines to shipping pier Glace Bay; a standard gauge railway ½ mile in length, from Glace Bay mines to its shipping pier; the Sydney & Louisbourg railway (so called), a narrow gauge extending from the harbour of Sydney to the harbour of Louisbourg, in length 34 miles, with a branch to Schooner Pond 10 miles additional; and a narrow gauge railway 1¼ miles in length between Gowrie Mines and the shipping Pier, Cow Bay.

"The aggregate length of these railways, not including length of sidings and yard accommodation, amounts to 64½ miles. Of these railways, the International carried the outputs of that name, the Old Bridgeport and Gardiner mines and was also carrying freight and passenger traffic. The Sydney and Louisbourg railway carried the outputs of the Reserve and Emery mines to the Shipping Pier, Sydney Harbour, a distance of 12 miles, but was not in use for traffic from Reserve mines in the direction of Louisbourg or Schooner Pond. The Victoria, Glace Bay, Caledonia, and Gowrie Railways carried the output of their respective collieries.

"In addition to the railways enumerated and in view of the increased facilities for transportation which would be required to meet an enormously increased output of coal, the Dominion Coal Co. Ltd. decided to build a standard gauge railway from Sydney to the winter port of Louisbourg, and which should connect with the collieries in operation.

"To this end survey parties were organized and took the field in the spring of 1893. The question of modifying the gradients and curvature of the existing Sydney and Louisbourg Railway (so called), substituting structures intended to carry a heavier class of rolling stock, and adopting a standard gauge was first taken up and after due consideration (in which the remoteness of the so-called Sydney and Louisbourg railway from the collieries in operation in the Glace Bay and Cow Bay basins formed the most important factor) was abandoned in favour of extending the railway between Sydney and Bridgeport, hitherto known as the International Railway, on to Louisbourg....

"The railway now under construction between Sydney and Louisbourg differs in some respects from railways intended for general traffic, inasmuch as, for the present at least, its heavy traffic will be in one direction only, therefore, in adjusting the grades, advantage has been taken of this peculiarity in order to reduce the cost of construction and to economize distance.

"The total length of the line from Sydney to Louisbourg when completed will be 37 miles in length. The maximum gradient opposed to the traffic will not exceed 42½ feet to the mile on tangents, and is equated for curve resistance. The sharpest curve on the main line has a radius of 1,443 feet, and even this curve has been sparingly used. The width of the road-bed in cuttings is 22 feet, on embankments 16 feet; there will have to be moved in the formation of it about 600,000 cubic yards of material, of which a large percentage is rock. For the passage of steams and proper drainage of the road-bed there will be required about 7,000 cubic yards masonry of a class not surpassed by any other on this continent. The important structures on the line, taken in their order from Bridgeport to Louisbourg, are as follows; Little Glace Bay Brook, Big Glace Bay Brook and Black Brook, steel trestles 150 feet in length each, and in heights from 25 to 30 feet; Mira River bridge, three spans of steel and iron of 100 feet each, of which one is a serving span; outlet of Catalone Lake, a span of 50 feet and a steel trestle (between the crossing of Catalone Lake and the Summit), 360 feet in length and having an average height of 50 feet.

"There will be over 3,000 cubic yards of ballast per mile, the rails are of steel, weighing 80 lbs per lineal yard, and these will be supported on cedar ties placed two feet centres.

"The joint fastenings are of the latest, heaviest, and most approved type, and steel "Servis" tie plates will be used throughout the whole length of the line. With the class of locomotive engines now in use hauling coal for the Dominion Coal Company Ltd., the average train load of coal need not be below 600 tons to Louisbourg, but the permanent way and structures are designed and intended for a heavier class of engine, so that train loads can be materially increased if desired. The design proposed [for the] shipping pier at Louisbourg harbour will be 600 feet in length and 90 feet in width, will have 26 feet of water at inner and 30 feet at outer end at low water, will be built of hard pine resting upon creosoted piles and will be approached by a trestle 450 feet in length.

"In addition to the roads now in use and under construction, the writer has received instructions to extend the Victoria Mines Railway a distance of 1 mile, and also make surveys for and to report upon the best location for a railway to serve the Low Pont coal fields.

"Whilst the railway from Sydney to Louisbourg is essentially a railway for the cheap transportation of coal, and has been located solely with that object in view, it will not be without interest to the travelling public...."

From *The Canadian Mining Review*, vol. XIII, no. 8, August, 1894: 154.

ing a new standard gauge track from Bridgeport through Glace Bay and along the coastal route to Louisbourg. Regular service on the new line to Louisbourg began in June of 1895. See page 110 for a S&L system map.

As noted by Donkin upon the creation of the new S&L in 1894, and illustrated by the 1903 sketch of activity at Reserve (figure 2.16), transport of coal to shipping wharves, to the steel plant complex that appeared in Sydney at the turn of the century, and later, to area power plants, was always the focus for the S&L. Despite that focus, the S&L also offered regular passenger, freight, express and mail service. These areas of activity will be examined in later chapters.

Other 19th-Century Mining Railways

Several other railways warrant mention if only to recognize their existence. Little firm information is available about them and what is to be found, either in print or online, is often contradictory.

The Gowrie Company began mining at Cow Bay, near Port Morien, in the early 1860s. The firm was owned by the Archibald family of Sydney Mines and named after the family home there (a name adopted from Scotland). A number of pits were sunk between the 1860s and 1880s. The Mines Report for 1873 noted that a "light locomotive" was placed on the railway. The wording suggests that a horse-powered line had been operating previously though this is uncertain. Some details appear in the first issue of the annual "Railway Statistics" compiled and published by the federal government in 1876.[38] One locomotive is recorded along with 80 coal wagons on the line at the end of 1875. The tables for later years indicate the arrival of a second locomotive in 1879. Both were tank engines built by the Hunslet Engine Works of Leeds. No photos have been found though it appears that the 1873 engine was originally intended for the Prince Edward Island Railway and of a design similar to the six sent to PEI the previous year.[39] The Railway Statistics tables show the Gowrie line, slightly over a mile in length, was built to the same narrow gauge, 42 in (106 cm), used by the GMA at Lingan and by the PEI Railway in its early years. The Gowrie site was bought by Whitney's Dominion Coal Company in 1894 and both the mine and the railway were closed.

Another railway existed at a mine at New Campbellton overlooking Great Bras d'Or channel, a short distance from the north end of the modern-day Seal Island highway bridge. This mine was originally opened in 1862 but output was low and the mining activity was irregular. An 1865 report to the owner, Charles J. Campbell of Baddeck, indicates the presence of a horse-powered railway built with "strap rails" which were wooden rails topped with iron bars. Another report done in 1874 states that the line had been rebuilt with iron rails, "chiefly 35 lbs to the yard," with a gauge of 42 in (106 cm), the same as used at Lingan and Gowrie. The 1874 document also indicated that "a locomotive is about to be supplied."[40] The Mines Report for the same year noted purchase of a locomotive and the "Railway Statistics" from Ottawa at the end of 1875 records the engine, 45 coal cars, the 42 in gauge, and a track length of 2.5 miles (4 km). A drawing of the area appeared in the *Canadian Illustrated News* of July 1, 1876, but this seems to have been New Campbellton's moment of greatest fame.

A promotion brochure on the New Campbellton mine that appeared in 1880 included a report done that year by the Inspector of Mines, Edwin Gilpin. That report confirmed the presence of a locomotive. However, Gilpin stated that, "up to the present date, the depression of trade has rendered its [the engine's] use unnecessary."[41] The mine was reopened in the 1890s but soon closed again and this time the site was abandoned permanently. It is unknown if the locomotive was ever used. Also unknown are the sources of the engine, the rolling stock, or the rails or what became of the railway's equipment. Of all the island's railways, this is one of the two about which the least information has been found, at least to date, and it calls out for future research. A second strong contender for such research activity will appear in chapter 4.

3 – The Intercolonial:
Canada's Railway Network Joins Cape Breton

Railway Dreams and Mainland Beginnings

Even before the General Mining Association had brought the first locomotives to Cape Breton, both the island and the Nova Scotia mainland had dreams of railways, railways that would do much more than just move coal. In the public mind, railways had quickly evolved into the idea of "common carriers" for passengers, freight, express or mail in exchange for payment from the passengers or shippers. After 1830, railways such as the Liverpool and Manchester in England and the Baltimore and Ohio in the United States quickly became famous and served as examples of this new form of transportation.

British North America's first common carrier line, the Champlain and St. Lawrence, opened in 1836 to connect the south shore of the river opposite Montreal with the headwaters of Lake Champlain. Other proposals for railways were gaining the attention of governments, investors, and the general public in many countries. In the mid-1840s, one idea that became prominent on both sides of the Atlantic was that of a railway to connect Quebec City or Montreal with an Atlantic coastal post, Halifax being the most frequently proposed eastern terminus.[1] One of the active promoters of the "Halifax & Quebec," as the project was generally named, was John Wright from the General Mining Association's board of directors.

In addition to proposals for an east-west railway linking the British North American colonies, there was also interest, on both sides of the border, in establishing rail links between the colonies and the northern United States. From the American side, John A. Poor[2] of Portland, Maine, played a leading role in promoting a railway from Portland to Montreal that might draw Montreal's trade to his home town. On our side of the border, a key supporter of Poor was Alexander Galt,[3] an important railway promoter who was also active in politics and, twenty years later, played a major role in events leading to Confederation in 1867.

Companies were established on both sides of the border in 1845 and construction was soon under way, northward from Portland and southward from Montreal. The St. Lawrence and Atlantic opened for business in 1853. That same year it was leased—and later purchased—by the Grand Trunk Railway that Galt helped to develop. By 1856, the Grand Trunk's routes stretched from Levis, opposite Quebec City, through Montreal and Toronto as far west as Sarnia on the American border at Lake Huron as well as from Montreal south to Portland.[4]

In 1850, with the railway from Maine to Montreal well under way, Poor hosted a meeting in Portland to promote a rail connection from Maine into New Brunswick and on to Nova Scotia. Out of the "Portland Convention," with the support of both American railway promoters and representatives of the colonial governments, the European and North American Railway Company was incorporated in Maine in 1850. The goal was a railway from Bangor, Maine, to Nova Scotia. South from Bangor, another American line would lead to a connection at Portland with the St. Lawrence and Atlantic, which was nearly ready to open through to Montreal.

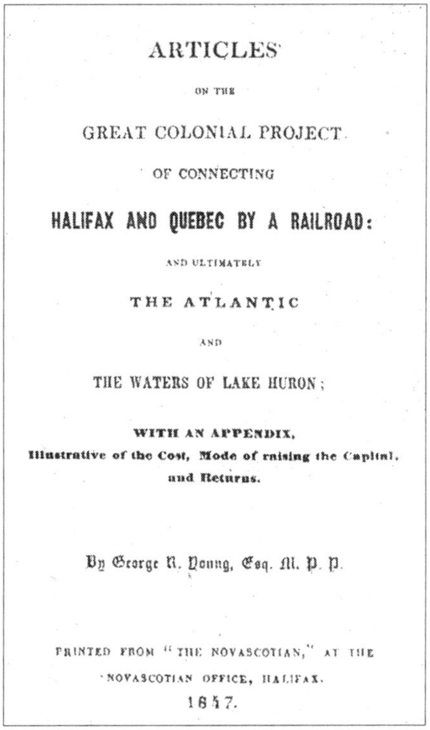
ARTICLES

ON THE

GREAT COLONIAL PROJECT

OF CONNECTING

HALIFAX AND QUEBEC BY A RAILROAD:

AND ULTIMATELY

THE ATLANTIC

AND

THE WATERS OF LAKE HURON;

WITH AN APPENDIX,
Illustrative of the Cost, Mode of raising the Capital, and Returns.

By George R. Young, Esq. M. P. P.

PRINTED FROM "THE NOVASCOTIAN," AT THE NOVASCOTIAN OFFICE, HALIFAX.
1847.

Fig. 3.1
Promoting the Halifax and Quebec project. George Renny Young, a Nova Scotian lawyer, journalist and politician, was very active in the project from 1845 until his death in 1853. In 1847, in his role as MLA, Young also joined a campaign that led, ten years later, to the end of the GMA monopoly on mining in Nova Scotia. In 1849, as a member of the Uniacke-Howe government, he was one of the commissioners who directed construction of an electric telegraph between Halifax and New Brunswick.

For Cape Bretoners, the critical phrase in the European and North American prospectus was the reference to a Nova Scotia destination.[5] The only specific option identified was Halifax, but the document included the qualification, "or whatever eastern port is adopted." A survey report issued soon after the prospectus included a map showing Halifax as the eastern destination, but a possible alternate route was shown running eastward from Truro.[6] On Cape Breton, it went along the south coast to Louisbourg. These documents appeared to leave the door open for Cape Bretoners and the response was quick. A public meeting was called in Sydney:

> for the purpose of taking into consideration the best means of developing the great natural resources of the island; and more particularly to point out the capabilities and advantages of the Harbour of Sydney, as one of the termini of the projected "European and North American Railway" across the provinces of Nova Scotia and New Brunswick.[7]

The meeting led to the result that often comes out of public meetings—the appointment of a committee.

The committee included Judge Dowd, the three Island members of the Legislature, Richard Brown of the General Mining Association and a number of other local businessmen. Subsequent issues of the *Cape-Breton News* provided details from the meeting and reports on discussions in the Legislature about the railway project. The committee's report went into circulation in May of 1851, but it was all for naught.[8]

The Sydney Railway Meeting, 1851

Cape-Breton News, Sydney, March 1, 1851.

"A public meeting was held at the Court-House in Sydney on Thursday February 27th, 1851, at which a very large number of the inhabitants of the County was present. The Deputy Sheriff in the absence of the High Sheriff read the requisition and notice. On motion of Mr. Justice Dowd, seconded by R Brown Esquire, Charles E Leonard was chosen Chairman. On motion of T. D. Archibald, Esquire, D. N. MacQueen, Esquire was chosen Secretary. The Chairman briefly stated the objects of the meeting. Mr. Justice Dowd addressed the meeting and moved the following resolution, which was seconded by P. H. Clarke, Esquire.

"Whereas public attention has for some time past been engaged in considering the speediest and most practicable line of communication by steam between Europe and America, in connection with a Railway across the Provinces of Nova Scotia and New Brunswick; and whereas it is the opinion of this meeting, that a large amount of valuable information in connection with the advantages and capabilities of Cape Breton bearing on this important subject, which has not yet been brought before the public in Great Britain or this Country can be readily obtained. And this meeting, being also of opinion that the general resources of the Island,—not limited to its valuable Mines, Minerals, Fisheries, and Agriculture, but extended to many other sources of internal improvement,—might be made available for useful purposes, in promoting Colonization, Emigration, and Manufactures, if more generally known.

"Resolved therefore, that a Committee be appointed to prepare a report embracing these several subjects, more particularly with reference to connecting this Island by steam navigation with the Mother Country, and by Railway with the United States and neighboring Colonies, and to put the same in general circulation."

Funding for such a project was one major challenge. In the absence of private local capital or the ability of the colonial governments to undertake their shares of construction costs, the Imperial government in London had been involved for some years in discussions with the colonies about how to fund the Halifax and Quebec project. The Portland idea offered an alternative and the Nova Scotia and New Brunswick governments decided to try to sell it in London.

Though Joseph Howe had not been a member of the Nova Scotia delegation at Portland, he was sent to persuade the British government to provide a guarantee on loans raised by the Province to finance Nova Scotia's section of the line.[9] After months in the British capital and optimistic that his proposal would be approved, Howe came back to Halifax to await the decision. In a famous speech soon after his return, he suggested to his audience that:

in five years we shall make the journey hence to Quebec and Montreal, and home through Portland and St. John, by rail; and I believe that many in this room will live to hear the whistle of the steam engine in the passes of the Rocky Mountains, and to make the journey from Halifax to the Pacific in five or six days.[10]

Howe's long-run prediction was correct but the news from London was a great disappointment. The British government rejected the Portland project.[11]

London did offer a financial guarantee for some version of the Halifax and Quebec project, but only when the colonies reached agreements in a form acceptable to London about sharing costs and about a route that would be militarily secure, in other words, located far away from the American border.[12] That decision shaped the development of railways in New Brunswick and Nova Scotia until after Confederation. With the demise of the European and North American project and little prospect for agreement on an "all-British" railway route to the St. Lawrence valley, Cape Breton's hope for a rail connection to the rest of Nova Scotia and beyond would remain but a dream for decades.

Howe, a key member of the provincial government, shifted his focus back to Nova Scotia and his earlier ideas about rail lines going out from Halifax.[13] The quick result was the Nova Scotia Railway (NSR), built and operated by the Province. The line's two branches, from Halifax to Windsor and Truro, were both operational before the end of the 1850s[14] and the Truro branch was extended to Pictou County in 1867.

The Confederation agreement of 1867 promised construction of the Intercolonial Railway of Canada (IRC) by the Canadian government to link Nova Scotia and New Brunswick to Quebec and Ontario. The Halifax-Truro section of the NSR would be transferred to the Intercolonial, an arrangement that assured that the new railway would have its eastern terminus at Halifax. The NSR section east of Truro, the "Pictou Branch," was also transferred to the IRC but initial attempts to interest Ottawa in extending it toward or into Cape Breton fell on deaf ears.

While the new national government had assumed responsibility for a "main line" to the Maritimes, this did not carry over to the construction of branch lines, a view opposed by the provincial government in Halifax. The prospects for building from the eastern end of the Pictou Branch to the Strait of Canso and beyond into Cape Breton remained a basis for disputes between Halifax and Ottawa for nearly two decades.

An interesting observation appeared in the 1868 letter from Charles Tupper to Sir John A. Macdonald, referred to in the previous chapter, about International Coal's quest for government aid to build their company railway. While referring to the International request, Tupper noted in passing: "It is quite possible that the day may come when the Railway from Pictou or rather New Glasgow may be extended to the harbour of Sydney as the most easternmost point of the Dominion of Canada."[15] Had the letter become public, most people would have assumed that, between the lines, Tupper was telling Cape Bretoners that they should not hold their breaths.

> **The British North America Act, 1867, Section 145**
> Inasmuch as the Provinces of Canada, Nova Scotia, and New Brunswick have joined in a Declaration that the Construction of the Intercolonial Railway is essential to the Consolidation of the Union of British North America, and to the Assent thereto of Nova Scotia and New Brunswick, and have consequently agreed that Provision should be made for its immediate Construction by the Government of Canada; Therefore, in order to give effect to that Agreement, it shall be the Duty of the Government and Parliament of Canada to provide for the Commencement, within Six Months after the Union, of a Railway connecting the River St. Lawrence with the City of Halifax in Nova Scotia, and for the Construction thereof without Intermission, and the Completion thereof with all practicable Speed.

In 1872, as completion of work on the Intercolonial line between Halifax and the St. Lawrence was in sight, Nova Scotia Premier William Annand revived the idea of extending the Pictou Branch and the Legislature passed an *Act* offering land grants and subsidies to any firm that would build from Pictou County to the Strait. Several years later, Ottawa agreed to grant the Pictou Branch to anyone who would construct the line, though this was made contingent on successful completion of the railway project and provision of an operating ferry at the Strait.

Numerous early proposals were made to construct the "Eastern Extension" to either the Strait or beyond to either Sydney or Louisbourg. One propsal worthy of note, though it was withdrawn, came from a partnership of E. R. Burpee, a New Brunswick railway contractor, and Collingwood Schreiber, who had been an assistant to Sandford Fleming during construction of the Pictou Branch in the mid-1860s.[16] Like Fleming, Schreiber quickly went on to bigger things and in 1879 became the Chief Engineer of Canadian Government Railways. In that and other senior positions that he would hold in Ottawa for more than twenty-five years, Schreiber played an important role in resolving Cape Breton's long-standing quest for a railway connection to the mainland.[17]

Another series of proposals came from the groups involved in the Glasgow and Cape Breton railway and its successor, the Cape Breton Company Railway. In 1872, Frederick Gisborne and others incorporated the Louisburg Extension Railway Company to build a line from New Glasgow to Louisbourg.[18] The *Act* included authorization for possible construction of a railway tunnel under the Strait of Canso. This proposal and its 1875 sequel will be examined in chapter 4 in the background to the construction of a railway from the Strait to St. Peter's.

The absence of results generated increasing discontent in eastern Nova Scotia and it circulated throughout the province and beyond. An 1876 newspaper story from Saint John, New Brunswick, captured the mood in its first sentence, "The Cape Breton people feel sore on the railway question."[19]

In 1877, a proposal was accepted from a group headed by two Montrealers, Hugh Allan and Harry Abbott, who both had powerful business and political connections. Allan had become an important shareholder in coal companies in Pictou County though this had been a small venture for one of the richest men in Canada.[20] He had been a key member of a group working toward the contract to build the Canadian Pacific Railway. Part of that work involved Allan and his associates making very large contributions to John A. Macdonald's

Conservative Party in the 1872 election campaign. Allan's name was central to the Pacific Scandal that arose soon after the election with the revelation of a telegram from Sir John A. calling on Allan for last minute campaign funds. The scandal brought down Macdonald's government in 1873 and contributed to a Liberal win in the national election in January of 1874. The information revealed in the Pacific Scandal was a prime example of "railway politics" at work in Canada.

The Conservative connections of Allan's partner were equally strong. Harry Abbott was a brother of John Abbott who would assume the Conservative leadership and the Prime Minister's office upon Macdonald's death in 1891. While Abbot and Allan's Conservative friends were on the opposition benches in both Ottawa and Halifax, they won support from the Nova Scotia government. Premier Hill wanted to see work on the railway under way, even if the contract was to go a pair of prominent Tories.

Despite financial and legal difficulties, and more than a few instances of shady dealing on the part of Allan and Abbott,[21] the Eastern Extension railway got built. The line opened as far east as Antigonish in September of 1879 and reached Mulgrave on the Strait of Canso at the end of 1880.[22] Even as track was being laid, the project, which had become known as the "Halifax & Cape Breton (H&CB)" (the name of the Allan-Abbott company), was complicated by disputes between Halifax and Ottawa and between both governments and the H&CB. The contract soon turned into a nightmare for the Province which had funded a major part of the cost of construction.[23] The national government unilaterally changed some of the terms regarding the turnover of the Pictou Branch which the Province had committed to turning over to the H&CB. The alternative available to the Province, a result of an 1880 agreement with Allan and Abbott, was for the Province to purchase their new railway.

In 1882, a new Liberal government came to power in Halifax. Premier William Thomas Pipes and his cabinet were desperate to get the Province out of the railway business. A settlement was reached with Allan and Abbott to sell their interests to the Nova Scotia government. After extended negotiations,

Fig. 3.2
Destination Cape Breton – or at least in that direction. This is the only known photo that shows a Halifax & Cape Breton train. The photo had no details attached to indicate where, when or by whom it was taken. Logical guesswork points to New Glasgow, the western end of the H&CB, and to A.L. Rice whose photo studio in New Glasgow later became the Waldren Studio. Rice's name appeared in the previous chapter as the source of the photo of the Cape Breton Company wharf at Louisburg.

Dalhousie University Archives, Waldren Studios Collection, PC 2 #297.17

53   THE INTERCOLONIAL

> ### Railway Partners: The H&CB and the Nova Scotia Government
>
> The testy relationship that had developed between the government and the H&CB is apparent in the following exchange of telegrams on November 4, 1882. The story of the ongoing legal battle between the government and the company was sufficiently newsworthy to make the *New York Times* on the day of the exchange of these telegrams.
>
> "To Captain T. D. Milburne, Vice-President, Halifax & C.B. Ry. And Coal Co.
>
> "Sir: The Government demand possession of the line of railway of the Halifax and Cape Breton Railway and Coal Company with all its appurtenances. They require a categorical answer, Yes or No. If you decline answering definitely, the Government will consider it a refusal. Of course they will comply with the terms of the contract.
>
> "I have the honor, &c, Albert Gayton, Commissioner of Public Works and Mines of Nova Scotia."
>
> ========
>
> "To The Honourable Albert Gayton, Commissioner of Public Works &c
>
> "Sir: I have the honor to inform you that I decline to give possession of this line of railway to the Government except upon the terms and conditions and within the time mentioned in the contract with the Government.
>
> "I have the honor, &c, T. D. Milburne, Vice-President, H. and C.B. Railway."
>
> *Journals of the House of Assembly of Nova Scotia*, 1883, Appendix 12, Railway Papers, 8.

> ### Eastern Extension Rolling Stock, November 1, 1884.
>
> 9 locomotives
> 6 first-class passenger cars
> 4 second-class passenger cars
> 6 baggage and smoking cars
> 30 box cars
> 70 flat cars
> 150 hopper/coal cars
> 2 conductor's vans
> 1 snowplow
>
> Parliament of Canada, *Sessional Papers*, 1885, vol. 7, Sessional Paper # 11, Appendix 4; Canadian Government Railways Report, 1883-1884: 19.

in 1884 the Province then transferred the new railway to Ottawa along with all provincial claims to the Pictou Branch.[24]

Other details about the Eastern Extension demonstrate equipment and operating standards that would be used or exceeded when construction eventually reached Cape Breton.[25] The rails were 56 lb/yd steel (27.8 kg/m), this having become the norm for main line track. New turntables for turning engines were built at Antigonish and Mulgrave. Engine sheds and towers for both water and coal for the locomotives were in place at New Glasgow, Antigonish and Mulgrave. The coal towers indicated that the days of wood-burning locomotives were coming to an end. Additional water towers were located about every 16 kms (10 miles) along the line. All but one of the water towers had steam-powered pumping systems. Semaphore signals were installed to direct locomotive engineers at the yards at New Glasgow, Antigonish and Mulgrave.

The rolling stock was equipped with an early system of air brakes, controlled by steam from the locomotive. Also used were Miller couplers, a design patented in the United States in the mid-1860s that had been quickly adopted across North American railways. A step toward the Janney "knuckle coupler" system that became the North American standard, Miller couplers provided stronger connections between rail cars in motion, could close their connection automatically, and made the work of railway brakemen much safer. The source of the locomotives is significant. All the engines were made by the Kingston Works of Kingston, Ontario.[26] Canadian-built engines were starting to take the place of British and American imports.

With the complete Truro-Mulgrave line in the hands of the federal government, Cape Bretoners' lobbying efforts were redirected toward Ottawa and results were eventually achieved. In 1886, ten years after railway passenger and freight service had been opened all the way between Halifax and Montreal and beyond, Macdonald's Conservatives, now back in power, made a commitment to extend the Intercolonial to Sydney.[27] While the decision may have been made primarily on the merit of the idea, politics certainly played a role. An election was looming in 1887 and the Conservatives knew that the railway issue was important on Cape Breton.

Fig. 3.3 - A modern knuckle coupler. Before the first versions of this type of coupler appeared toward the end of the 19th century, a number of different manual coupling methods had been in use. All had been dangerous and led to many injuries to the brakemen whose duties also included coupling and uncoupling cars.

Author's photo.

The Intercolonial on Cape Breton

Participants in a public meeting in Sydney in April of 1886 (see below) would surely have been pleased by events over the next two months. In June, an *Act* was passed in Ottawa "to authorize the construction of a railway from the Strait of Canso to Louisburg or Sydney, as a public work."[28] The key role leading to action by the government appears to have been the lobbying effort within the ranks of Conservative Members of Parliament by H. F. McDougall, MP for Cape Breton County.

With a mainland terminus in place at Mulgrave, it was obvious that the Cape Breton section of the Intercolonial would begin on the opposite shore and the site selected was at Point Tupper.[29] Surveys offered alternate routes on each side of the Bras d'Or.[30] One of the surveyors, and subsequently a supervising engineer for construction of part of the line, was Hiram Donkin whose name appeared in chapter 2 in his later roles with the Dominion Coal Company.

A Message to Sir John A

"Moved by J. A. Gillis, Esq., Barrister; seconded by County Councillor M. Neil.

"Whereas it has been recognized by both Legislatures of the country that Cape Breton is entitled to a railway through the Island;

"And whereas universal and deep-seated discontent exists throughout the whole length and breadth of the Island owing to the apparent negligence and continued indifference manifested by the different governments in awarding Cape Breton her just and long desired rights;

"And whereas it is expedient to press vigourously and at once our claims in such behalf upon both governments;

"Therefore resolved that our representatives are hereby called upon, as the express wish of this meeting, to end all party and political feeling in making our claims for immediate railway construction throughout the Island, and thus secure to ninety thousand people a small instalment of those rights so long, so unreasonably, and so unjustly withheld.

"Carried unanimously.

"This is a true copy of the first resolution passed at public patriotic meeting held in Sydney, CB, on Saturday, Ap 3/86, at 11 a.m., David McKeen, Esq., County Warden, in the Chair.

"Signed, E. A. MacKeen, Secretary."

LAC, Sir John A Macdonald papers, MG 26-A, vol. 143: 58657.

Schreiber report (opposite) Parliament of Canada, *Sessional Papers*, 1889, vol. 9, Sessional Paper # 10, Appendix 5; Annual report upon the Oxford and New Glasgow and the Cape Breton divisions of the Government railways now under construction, 14-15.

Consideration of the options involved intense local and partisan interests in addition to the engineering considerations. The Intercolonial had become more than just a railway. It was also a channel used by the federal government to deliver political patronage and rewards to constituencies as well as to individuals and companies and everyone was aware of that fact.

The subject of the railway route was prominent in campaigns for Cape Breton seats in the federal election in February of 1887, which was won by Macdonald's Conservatives. Voters in Inverness elected a Conservative MP. The constituency of Richmond abandoned the Tories and elected a Liberal. Voting against Sir John A. certainly did not help Richmond's chances of having the railway built along the south coast though it appears that the decision had been made before the election but not made public. Had the election results been reversed in the two constituencies, it is possible that the railway's route might have been different as well. That suggestion, however, is speculation.

The route announced was to run northward from Point Tupper, along the north side of the Bras d'Or to Iona, across Barra Strait to Grand Narrows and then on to Sydney with a short branch line to North Sydney. The route was the subject of a long and spirited debate in the House of Commons on June 6, 1887, four months after the Macdonald government had been returned to office. E. P. Flynn, the member for Richmond, did his best to present the case for a route that would go south of the Bras d'Or—and through his constituency. The

Building Toward Sydney, 1887-1888

"Messrs. Sims and Slater commenced work on their contract for the construction of the section between the Grand Narrows and North Sydney and Sydney in the winter of 1886 and prosecuted the work during the following year until December, 1887, having been favored with a most propitious season for carrying on works of railway construction, it having been almost unprecedently dry.

"The clearing of the right of way was done and considerable progress had been made with the grading, but very little masonry had been built and the quarries were in a most unsatisfactory condition, the daily output of stone therefrom being very trifling, and the organization, if organization it could be termed, for carrying on this class of work was very defective. In fact at the time they were relieved of the management of the contract, the works were dragging along very slowly, the workmen and mercantile community having apparently lost confidence in them. So unsatisfactory was the state of affairs that it became necessary for the Government to take the work out of the contractors' hands and finish it to the best possible advantage....

"In the month of June last the Government assumed control of the work and at once arranged for vigorous prosecution by jobbing out the grading, cribbing, &c., in small contracts and organizing efficiently for carrying on the mason work by day's labour. Several scows for carrying stone from the quarries to the sites of the structures were built, steam tugs chartered to tow them, additional teams employed to haul the stone, the force very largely increased in the quarries, and about eight gangs of builders and a large number of stone cutters were employed at the site of the structures, as well as a force preparing the foundations.

"The station buildings were let to a responsible contractor and the work generally is making good progress. The masonry, of which there will be about 16,000 cubic yards, will, I have no doubt, be finished this year. The crib wharfing will also be completed this season, but the grading and the station buildings will probably not be fully completed until next spring. A number of steel bridge superstructures have been erected and the balance should be in place before next spring.

"About 2,000 tons of rails are to be delivered at the Grand narrows this season, and it is proposed to deliver an equal quantity at Sydney in the early spring, so that the laying of the track may be proceeded with from both ends at the same time until the entire line is covered. While this work is in progress, the ballasting of the road will be carried on.

"The work on this section is being conducted under the careful supervision of Mr. Hiram Donkin, an engineer favourably known in the profession for his ability, energy, close application to his work, his uprightness of character, and for his frugal management of work in his charge, who, with the faithful aid of his staff, will, I am satisfied, carry the work through with economy and despatch, in an efficient manner, so as to have this division ready for traffic by September next.

"The present proposition is to cross the Grand Narrows by a steam train ferry, and to this end preparations are being made, but it may be worth considering whether or not a steel bridge resting on iron cylinders filled with concrete would not be preferable. The length of such a structure would be 1,600 feet....

"I have the honor to be, Sir, Your obedient servant,
"Collingwood Schreiber
"Chief Engineer and General Manager, Canadian Government Railways
"17 September 1888"

lengthy transcript indicates the extent to which both geographic and partisan loyalties split over the possible spoils from the railway project.

The total route was 98 miles (158 km long)— 42.5 (68) from Point Tupper to Iona, 52.5 (84.5) from Grand Narrows to Sydney, plus 3 (5) on the branch into North Sydney. Some work on the eastern end had started before the election and the subsequent official announcement of the selected route. By mid-1887, the project was well under way. Schreiber's report from September of 1888, printed opposite, provides a sense of the scope of the work and the sort of difficulties that might be encountered on such a job.

From the time of the decision for the railway to cross Barra Strait, there had been controversy about the plan to use a ferry. This was one of the more contentious topics in the long debate about the route in the House of Commons in June of 1887. Some time between Schreiber's report of September 1888 and February 1889, the original plan for a ferry was abandoned in favour of bridging the crossing. That decision has been credited by some to a personal involvement by Sir John A. following a visit to Grand Narrows in 1888 though no documentary evidence has been found to support that claim.[31]

The Grand Narrows bridge was the most challenging engineering project on the Intercolonial line through Cape Breton. It was built by two Montreal firms. Responsibility for the main body of the bridge was given to Job Abbott's Dominion Bridge Company. Abbott was an American by birth and no relation to Harry Abbott of the H&CB. Dominion Bridge had completed major projects across the country including the Canadian Pacific's Lachine Bridge over the St. Lawrence at Montreal. The contract for the vital underwater foundations went to Reid and Isbester, who were also building the western section of the line between Point Tupper and Iona.[32] Following his activity in Cape Breton, Robert Reid became the key figure in the development of the railway across Newfoundland and the North Sydney-Port aux Basques ferry link between the Intercolonial and the Newfoundland Railway.

As Schreiber's letter to Sir John A. (see below) suggested might happen, the bridge was opened by the Governor-General. In mid-October of 1890, a five-car special train carried Lord Stanley, probably best known as the donor of hockey's Stanley Cup, from the Strait to Sydney.[33] The opening of the bridge also served as an "official opening" for the entire line though regular traffic had to wait a bit longer. The section east of the bridge started carrying scheduled trains in November and the western end of the line, between Iona and Point Tupper, opened for regular business at the beginning of 1891. Despite the technicality that the route included a railway ferry at the Strait of Canso, Canada had joined Cape Breton by rail. See page 109 for an IRC route map.

During its early years, the Intercolonial was much criticized, partly because of the extent to which it was used by governments for patronage purposes, and partly because of problems with employee performance. In his history of the Canadian National Railways, G. R. Stevens used the title, "Case History of a Horrible Example," for his chapter on the early days of the IRC. Sobriety, or rather lack of it, was one particular problem with employees, so much so that in 1885, an edict from the Minister of Railways decreed that "any officer

Fig. 3.4 (left)
The tender call for the Grand Narrows bridge. The advertisement was widely circulated in newspapers across Canada in early 1889.

Fig. 3.5 (below)
Grand Narrows bridge
LAC, negative #PA-021553.

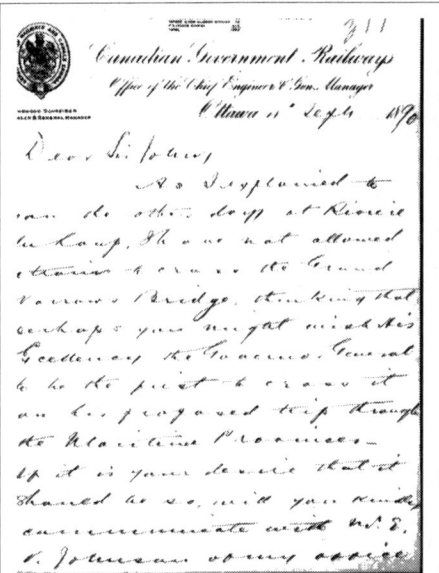
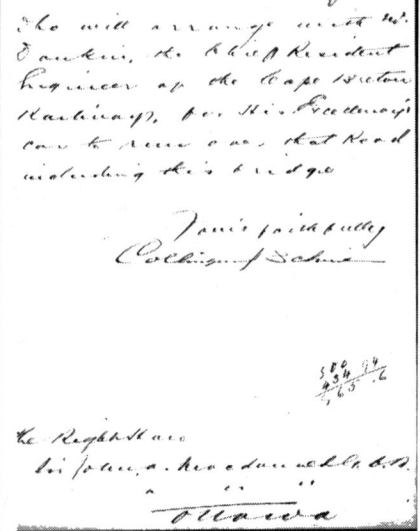

Fig. 3.6 - Who should open the bridge? The railway boss, Collingwood Schreiber, consults the political boss, Sir John A. Macdonald.

LAC, Sir John A. Macdonald Papers, MG 26-A, vol 137: 56814-15.

Fig. 3.7 - A working HO scale model of the swing section of the Grand Narrows bridge.

Author's photo by courtesy of Orangedale Railway Museum.

Fig. 3.8 - This Beaton Institute photo is believed to show the first train to cross the Grand Narrows bridge. The people posing on the flat car closest to the photographer were probably local residents invited to make the crossing. The train, however, was obviously a construction train. Note the workmen with timber on the second flat car as well as the

loading (or unloading) of timber taking place on the car beyond the locomotive. Schrieber's reference in his letter to Macdonald stated that he had not permitted a train to cross the bridge. That statement obviously referred to any scheduled train providing public service but excluded work trains as seen in this photo.

Photographer unknown. 77-847-981. Beaton Institute, Cape Breton University.

Fig. 3.9 - On first discovery, this photo appeared to be a very early Intercolonial locomotive, perhaps one of the first IRC engines on Cape Breton. When the photo was acquired in 1977, a note was attached reading: "Hoag Engine, fast starter – ran between Georges River and Port Hawkesbury." But the note and research on the photo raised some problems. On further research the conclusion is that, despite the note on the photo, this locomotive was never on Cape Breton and that the photo was taken on the mainland no later than 1875.[34]

Photographer unknown. 77-618-752. Beaton Institute, Cape Breton University.

or employee known to be intoxicated, whether on duty or not, will at once be dismissed from the service."35 Despite the orders from Ottawa, it appears that the problem did not disappear at once. IRC reports show that employee discipline was a long-standing concern of David Pottinger, the Pictou native who served as General Manager of the IRC from 1879 to 1913.

Pottinger and his immediate boss, Collingwood Schreiber, who was in charge of the Intercolonial plus all other federal government railways, waged a long struggle to free the railway from political interference regarding construction, operations and employment. Two early Cape Breton examples illustrate the problems they had with the politicians and the fact that the political involvement often went to the highest level—the Prime Minister's desk.

In May of 1891, Schrieber wrote to Sir John A. about conflicting pressures coming from Hugh Cameron, Member of Parliament for Inverness County and John Archibald McDonald, MP for Victoria.36 Each wanted to see the station being considered for a location near the Estmere bridge to be built on "his side" of the county line. It is uncertain who made the final decision but it was an ingenious one that treated the MPs equally. The station was not built. The second example deserves reproduction of the original letter to Sir John A. from Rev. Isaac Murray, DD, of North Sydney. Murray's objective was a job

Fig. 3.10 How do you get your son a job on the Intercolonial?

LAC, Sir John A. Macdonald Papers, MG 26-A, vol 286: 131208-09.

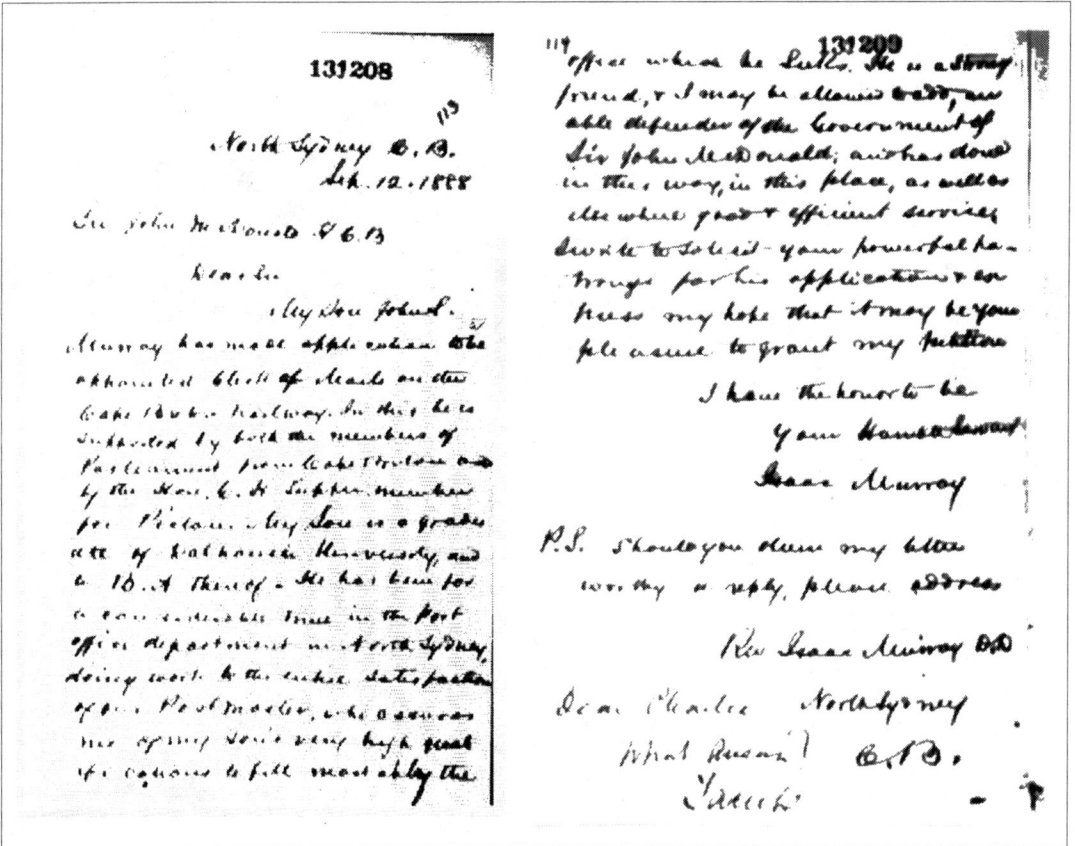

for his son as a railway mail clerk. At the bottom of page 2 of the letter, note in Macdonald's hand the query, "Dear Charlie What reason? JAMD."

"Charlie" was Charles Hibbert Tupper, son of Sir Charles Tupper and Minister of Fisheries in Macdonald's cabinet. In the absence of his father, in London in a second tour of duty as Canadian High Commissioner, the younger Tupper had an important voice in dispensing party patronage in Nova Scotia. Tupper's reply, dated September 17, stated he did not know the Murrays, but that he had "told MacDougall and MacKeen I would join in any recommendation they might make in favour of Mr John S. Murray for a railway mailclerkship."[37] MacKeen and McDougall were presumably David MacKeen and Hugh Francis McDougall, the two Conservative MPs for the riding of Cape Breton. No attempt has been made to determine whether or not John Murray got the job. With the involvement of two MPs, a cabinet Minister, and Sir John A, it is quite likely that he did.

Though the Estmere station was not built, many others were, in centres large and small along the route. Some, like Grand Narrows, were regular stops for passenger and freight service. Other smaller communities like Christmas

Fig. 3.11 - Grand Narrows station. The building was one of several standard Intercolonial designs. Identical stations were built ca. 1890 at a number of locations including North Sydney Junction, West Bay Road and Orangedale. The Orangedale station has been preserved as a museum and is a vital part of Cape Breton's railway heritage.

North Sydney Museum.

Fig. 3.12 - While the date of this photo is uncertain, the design and vertical clapboard finish suggest the Christmas Island station was built when or soon after the Intercolonial opened through to Sydney in 1891. The door on the left would have led into a small waiting room for passengers and the agent's office. The open door on the right led into a shed for freight and express. The sloping ramp, seen in the photo running from the shed porch down to the station platform, could be repositioned to reach upward and into an open door of an express or freight car.

Reproduced by permission of Hughena MacKinnon, Christmas Island.

Fig. 3.13 - The cover of an Intercolonial timetable in effect when the Cape Breton line was officially opened in October of 1890. For a sample timetable for the Cape Breton section of the route in later years, see Fig. 6.17.

1893: People are Clamouring for Railroads

By J. M. Gow

"It is true that we now have in Cape Breton a railway through the centre of the island, from the Strait of Canso to the harbour of Sydney. And this railway is a great convenience. You can now travel from Sydney to the Strait in three or four hours. Formerly the journey in winter time sometimes occupied as many days. The snow banks used to be somewhat obtrusive, and impeded the liberty of the subject. The locomotive now bowls merrily along where the disgusted horse used to be winking with his ears—the only visible part of his anatomy—out of the snow-drifts. This taste of railway has only whetted the appetite of the people for more. They say now they need a railway along both the south and north shores—the former within reach of Arichat and the settlements along the south shore as far as Louisburg and Main a Dieu; the latter to Port Hood, Mabou, Margaree to Baddeck, and thence down the north shore to the neighbourhood of Cape Smoke. It is said the system of railways in Cape Breton would then be complete. There is quite a population along these districts, and no doubt the presence of a railway would stimulate intercourse and benefit all these settlements which are now comparatively isolated. The very fact that people are clamouring for railroads, and feeling the want of them, indicates that use would be made of them were they constructed."

Gow, *Cape Breton Illustrated*, 408.

Island received irregular service for both freight and passengers depending on the size of the community. At these small "flag stations," some passenger trains would stop on signal or to let passengers off while "express trains" would not stop at all. Schedules were, of course, set down and passenger train schedules were widely circulated. "Running on time" was one of the prime duties for all train crews.

Despite the many complaints about the IRC in its early years, its construction finally provided the railway connection that Cape Betoners had been demanding for forty years. The opening of the line, however, did not end the Island's quest for railways. If anything, it brought a reaction reminiscent of a famous line from Charles Dickens's *Oliver Twist*. After finishing his serving of workhouse gruel, Oliver said, "Please, sir, I want some more." J. M. Gow's assessment, two years after the opening of IRC service to Sydney, was that Cape Bretoners wanted more.

One challenge that remained to be dealt with by the IRC was the Strait of Canso. When construction activity had started, a ferry inherited from the Halifax and Cape Breton Company was used. It was still in place when IRC trains began to run through to Sydney. Freight had to be unloaded and passengers had to leave their trains at Point Tupper or Mulgrave. The ferry provided the connection to a waiting train on the other side. This, of course, added to the cost and transit time involved. In 1891 the IRC started moving railway cars across the Strait on a barge attached to a tug or the ferry. Other changes would follow to permit the railway to deal with the Strait, the last of which was the opening of a rail line on the Canso Causeway in 1955.

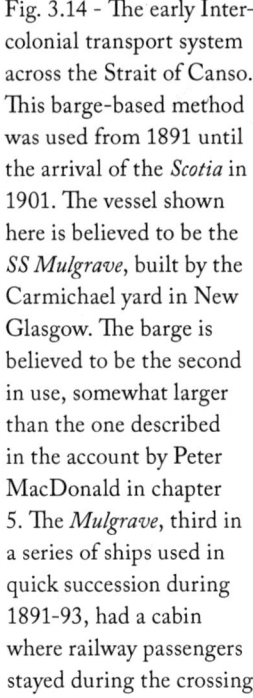

Fig. 3.14 - The early Intercolonial transport system across the Strait of Canso. This barge-based method was used from 1891 until the arrival of the *Scotia* in 1901. The vessel shown here is believed to be the *SS Mulgrave*, built by the Carmichael yard in New Glasgow. The barge is believed to be the second in use, somewhat larger than the one described in the account by Peter MacDonald in chapter 5. The *Mulgrave*, third in a series of ships used in quick succession during 1891-93, had a cabin where railway passengers stayed during the crossing.

Vernon, 331.

4 – Railways at the Strait of Canso

Soon after the Intercolonial was extended into Cape Breton, two independent railways were built near the Strait of Canso. Both quickly established connections with the IRC. In 1901, the Inverness and Richmond (I&R) opened to link coal mines in Inverness County to a new wharf at Port Hastings and to the IRC near Point Tupper. Two years later, the Cape Breton Railway (CBR) introduced service from Point Tupper to St. Peter's. Since the CBR had its origins in the quest for a railway to link the mainland to the eastern side of Cape Breton in the 1870s and 1880s, it is appropriate to turn to it first. The origins and the twists and turns of its story warrant examination in some detail.

The Quest for a South Coast Line

As the 1870s campaign developed for a railway from Pictou County to Sydney or Louisbourg, the south coast was a strong contender for the Cape Breton section of the route. A coastal route could offer three potential advantages. It would be shorter than a route north of any part of the Bras d'Or lakes. It would eliminate the need for a ferry or a bridge to cross one of the Bras d'Or channels. And a southern route would also be able to connect to the line from Sydney and Reserve to Louisbourg which was under construction by 1874.

Frederick Gisborne and the Glasgow and Cape Breton group had started planning a south coast route even before work began on their branch to Louisbourg. In 1872, they obtained incorporation of the Louisburg Extension Railway Company[1] to build from Louisbourg to New Glasgow with either a rail tunnel under the Strait of Canso or a ferry to serve the railway. A separate 1872 statute spelled out the assistance the Province would provide to the company. The Province offered up to 60,700 ha (150,000 acres) of crown land and a cash subsidy of 50 per cent of the royalties on coal from all the mines on Cape Breton Island for a period of forty years. These were both conditional upon completion of the railway within five years.[2] Soon after the *Acts* were passed, however, the parent Glasgow and Cape Breton firm was in financial trouble and unable to do anything about the project.

When the G&CB was restructured into the Cape Breton Company, the idea of an extension was revived. By mid-1874, D. J. Kennelly, the General Manager of the new firm, began discussions with Premier William Annand about the concept. Agreements were reached and statutes passed to reincorporate the Extension Company and revise the terms for provincial aid to the Cape Breton section of the project.[3] A cash subsidy of $3,100 per km ($5,000 per mile) replaced the 1872 *Act*'s offer regarding coal royalties. Ongoing payments of the subsidy were authorized as work progressed, an arrangement that would improve the company's cash flow. The land grant was to be doubled and mineral rights to be included for 50 per cent of the land granted.

Kennelly was unable to get everything he sought in the negotiations leading to the two *Acts*, however. The Province turned down his request to have the Pictou Branch turned over "in gift for the construction of the Railroad from New Glasgow to Louisburg." The five-year time limit set in the 1872 *Act* was also reduced to three years. A potential problem created by the 1875 *Act* was a requirement for the line to be built to standard gauge. The G&CB/Cape Breton Company railway, to which the extension line would connect, was narrow gauge and would have to be rebuilt if it was to be used as the new line's link from Louisbourg to Sydney.

It appears that Annand was confident that Kennelly's firm could meet the railway needs of the eastern mainland and provide the desired cross-island line. The degree of the Premier's interest is indicated by an 1874 invitation by Annand to Kennelly for the two to travel to Ottawa, presumably to seek support from the federal government.[4] No evidence has been found of the trip actually taking place, though the company did approach Ottawa about financial aid. The company's goal was reflected in the inclusion of the "proposed railway" on the Cape Breton Company's 1875 map reproduced in figure 2.13.

Like the G&CB before it, the Cape Breton Company was in a losing battle for financial survival in the midst of the economic depression of the 1870s. No start was made on the extension railway and the project lost its legal status when its three-year time limit ran out in 1878. In mid-1879, in a quest for cash to avoid bankruptcy, the Cape Breton Company was trying, without success, to sell its existing railway to the Province.[5]

In 1877, the contract for a railway from Pictou County to the Strait of Canso was given to Allan and Abbott. After 1877, proposals for a railway along Cape Breton's south coast would be focused on that specific route unencumbered by any requirements for construction on the mainland. Hindsight shows that another change also took place. With the demise of Kennelly's project, all subsequent railway proposals for cross-island lines by either route came from the mainland. None had connections with railways already existing on Cape Breton Island and few had any participation by Cape Breton residents.

Despite the absence of local proposals to build, lobbying efforts directed toward the provincial and federal governments continued. Until 1887, these were directed toward getting the first cross-island railway built along the south coast. That was changed by the 1887 decision to build the Intercolonial north of the Bras d'Or as far as the channel between Iona and Grand Narrows. With that decision, any south coast line would have to compete with the IRC.

Pre-1887 opposition to a northern route option is seen in documents that made their way to the attention of the provincial government. From a "large and influential Public Meeting" at St. Peter's in 1876 came pleas to have the cross-island railway avoid "isolated" places like West Bay and Whycocomagh on the north side of the lake and build through St Peter's, "the most favourable point on the Bras d'Or Lake for the temporary terminus of the railway in view of its ultimate extension to Louisburg."[6] An 1880 petition from St. Peter's was a bit more subtle. It just called for construction of a railway that could be eventually continued "toward Louisburg." That destination implied a south coast route through St. Peter's though the petition's resolutions avoided an explicit request for the line to go through the community.[7]

The focus on Louisbourg rather than Sydney as the eastern destination made sense in a Richmond County context. A Louisbourg line would be much more likely to follow the south coast. For a line to Sydney, on the other hand, a stronger case could be made for a northern route. Support for the south coast option was not limited to Richmond County. It also came from advocates in the Sydney area like Marshall Bourinot.

As Quickly As Possible … To Louisburg

Marshall Bourinot,
Exerpts from a letter to the editor, *Cape Breton Advocate*, Sydney, February 2, 1878

Marshall Bourinot was a son of John George Bourinot, one of the organizers of the 1851 railway meeting in Sydney described in chapter 2. In 1859, Marshall Bourinot obtained a licence to open the Blockhouse mine near Port Morien, the first pit opened following the end of the GMA monopoly. In later years he was involved in other mining projects in Cape Breton and Richmond counties.

"We must have a railway as quickly as possible to connect Cape Breton with the great system of railways on this continent, and do let us adopt and insist on having what we really can secure—certainly branches will follow, as a natural consequence, to other parts of the country as soon as we have the main trunk railway completed. Too long has Nova Scotia got all the benefit, so let us now get what we really can, if our representatives are all faithful and sincere to the interests of Cape Breton. Let us watch and see that they act energetically and do not play into the hands of those who not only always get the lion's share, but the whole….

"I am firmly convinced that any Government of the Dominion will look most favourably upon the direct route to the harbour of Louisburg, and this perhaps is the only chance of getting assistance from them. All capitalists and persons well acquainted and alive to the desirability of building to the closest point to Europe desire that the most direct route be followed.

"With all my heart I hope that one of the lines will be built, and construction going on at both ends simultaneously. I earnestly advocate the direct line from Hawkesbury to Louisburg because I think in this way we will succeed in our wishes and branch lines will follow…."

Twenty Years of South Coast Projects

The two decades of railway proposals that appeared and vanished left many unanswered questions about where projects had come from or why they did not proceed.[8] The cycle of proposals also made a strong impression on the people of Richmond County. In October 1901, soon after a first-sod ceremony at St. Peter's that actually led to some track being laid, the Sydney *Daily Record* captured the essence of the local mood. "People had become so accustomed to companies appearing annually to the scene, doing some preliminary surveying and a lot of talk, that scepticism had become very deep."[9] That scepticism had undoubtedly been shaped by the area's experience with the St. Peter's canal. Though it ran only a very short distance from the Bras d'Or to the Atlantic, it took more than forty years to build. The first serious survey work had been done in 1825 but the canal was not opened until 1869. It was probably no surprise, therefore, when a never-ending cycle of schemes failed to produce a railway.

In 1878, Edmund Plunkett, who had made overtures to the Province about a tender for the Eastern Extension a few years previously, incorporated a company called the Cape Breton Railway, Coal and Iron Company authorized to build a line "by way of St. Peter's." No construction work was ever done though newspaper accounts show Plunkett still trying to raise capital as late as January of 1882. His associates have not been identified but the company's name raises the question of whether Plunkett had connections to any coal companies operating in Cape Breton at that time.

With an imposing name, the Great American and European Short Line appeared in the Nova Scotia statutes in 1882. The firm was established by a group of New Yorkers including A. L. Blackman who had just participated in starting construction of the first railway in Newfoundland. By 1882, the small Newfoundland Railway Company was in trouble and the "Great American" idea was, in part, an attempt to save the Newfoundland project. In Nova Scotia, the new firm got rights to build railways from a point "at or near Cape North" to the Strait of Canso and along Northumberland Strait from New Glasgow to Oxford. It was also authorized to acquire running rights on existing rail lines running through eastern Canada and into the United States. The objective was establishment of the railway component of a fast rail-sea route from England to New York. The scheme was ambitious and the company actually got as far as starting work on the section near Oxford before it collapsed. Cape Bretoners may well have wondered if anyone connected with the project knew anything about the geography of the Cape Breton highlands and the engineering challenges to be faced in the construction of a railway southward from Cape North.

The Gisborne-Kennelly "Extension" name came back into circulation in 1884 with the Cape Breton Railway Extension Company, though there is no evidence of involvement that year by Kennelly or any other participants in the 1872 or 1875 companies. The 1884 firm was created by a number of Americans, mostly from Ohio, with several Ontario associates. The Ontario group included James J. White of Ottawa, the Canadian agent and editor for the *American Railroad Journal*. This firm was reincorporated in 1886 and again in 1890 with some continuity from the 1884 group. Nothing has been found, however, to explain the interest of men from Ohio and Kansas in Cape Breton. White might have been brought in because of his potential capacity to provide publicity. Two new names in 1890, Robert Mitchell and Murdock Chisholm, raise questions about who they were since the 1890 *Act* did not provide information about where the principals lived. The real source of the question is the fact that Mitchell and Chisholm reappeared in another project a few years later in a context that suggests they may have been Cape Bretoners.

In 1886, the Cape Breton Rail and Annex Steamboat Company offered a new approach. It proposed construction of rail lines from the Strait to St. Peter's and from East Bay to Sydney. Between St. Peter's and East Bay, a ferry run of approximately 35 miles (56 km) would take the place of a railway. The promoters included a New York broker, the Mayor of Halifax and A. C. Ross of North Sydney. This was probably Alexander C. Ross who had real estate holdings in North Sydney and was involved over the next twenty years in a number of other proposed railways on Cape Breton. Ross was also publisher of the *Daily Record*, the Sydney paper that supported the Liberal party, and a future Liberal Member of Parliament for Cape Breton North-Victoria. His name raises questions about other possible participants of the Liberal persuasion not named in the 1886 *Act*, a speculation based in part on the fact that in 1882 the party had acquired a grip on political power in Nova Scotia that would last until 1925. As will be seen below, well-connected Liberals were as likely to become involved with railway projects as well-connected Conservatives like previously named Hugh Allan and Harry Abbott.

The Cape Breton Railway Extension Company appears to have been taken over by a New York syndicate by 1891. From that date through 1895, there is surviving correspondence showing the efforts of Col. Henry Alton, (who in 1895 held 1680 of the company's 2230 shares) to arrange financing from the United States and England and get support from the Province. Kennelly reappeared in the 1895 list of shareholders. He held twenty shares as did Henry Paint, a prominent businessman from Port Hawkesbury and the Conservative MP for Richmond County in the 1880s. Despite the position of the Liberal party in Nova Scotia, Conservative connections were still useful in Ottawa though that would cease with the election of a Liberal government led by Wilfrid Laurier in 1896.

Alton's activity also included the 1893 incorporation of the Lennox Island Bridge and Railway Company to build a branch railway from Arichat on Isle Madame to connect with the Extension Company's proposed line along the south coast. This project showed that Alton recognized the need to provide at least the appearance of local participation. The *Lennox Island Act*'s list of promoters included five Arichat men, Edmund Flynn, Remi Benoit, George Shaw, Abraham Le Blanc and Isodore LeBlanc. Over the next decade, Isodore LeBlanc would be a prominent name in Richmond County railway projects.

While the Alton group was at work, an Ontario-based group appeared on the scene under the name of the Canso and Louisburg Railway Company. They received a federal charter in 1892 to build "by way of St. Peter's" to Louisbourg and Sydney. In the list of founders, D. J. Kennelly was the only local name. Four years later, in 1896 the Canso and Louisburg reincorporated in Nova

Scotia with new names added, including Isodore LeBlanc and Chisholm and Mitchell from the 1890 Extension Railway group. By 1899, a report in the *Railway and Shipping World* suggests that the Extension Company and the Canso and Louisburg had formed some kind of relationship. One possibility is that the two firms merged under the name of the newer company. Alton remained on the scene and in 1899 was identified as Vice President and General Manager of the Canso and Louisburg Company.[10]

Though its efforts came to naught, one other detail about the Canso and Louisburg group should be noted. Its list of 1896 incorporators also included B. F. Pearson—a name that automatically raises questions. Benjamin Pearson of Halifax had very influential links to the provincial Liberal government, had played several critical roles in bringing H. M. Whitney and his associates to Cape Breton; and he was a member of the board of Dominion Coal. His presence in the Canso and Louisburg group suggests that others from the Whitney group might have been in the background. As with the possibility raised regarding Alexander Ross, however, this is speculation. Pearson had many business interests separate from those involving his associates in Dominion Coal.[11]

Regardless of possible political and corporate connections or the fact that the Canso and Louisburg appears to have still had legal standing as a result of an 1898 extension of its original time limit, that firm was pushed aside by another group of would-be railway builders.

A Project Under Way

A new syndicate recycled the oft-used name, "Cape Breton Railway Extension Company," and obtained incorporation from the Province in March of 1899.[12] The *Act* authorized building a railway "providing a shorter and more direct route between Canso and Louisburg than at present exists." It is assumed that "Canso" was intended to mean some point on the Cape Breton side of the Strait of Canso at or near the Point Tupper ferry dock used by the Intercolonial. Despite the fact that the company was authorized to establish a "bridge, tunnel or ferry over, at or under the Straits of Canso," no reference has been seen to any consideration of activity on the mainland side of the Strait.

Nine promoters were named in the *Act*, five Americans and four Nova Scotians. Three of the Americans identified were from New Jersey with one each from New York City and Philadelphia. Only one has been identified in connection with previous Cape Breton railway projects and all vanished from the stage so quickly that their names do not warrant recognition beyond a footnote.[13] They were all conspicuously missing from the only official list of company shareholders found, a list that dates from July of 1901.[14]

The Nova Scotia group included three Cape Bretoners: Isodore LeBlanc and Duncan Finlayson of Arichat, plus Simon Joyce of D'Escousse. From the mainland came John Ouseley, a lawyer from Windsor, Hants County. It seems certain these men were recruited for their political connections. Finlayson and Joyce were the two sitting Liberal members of the Assembly for Richmond.

LeBlanc had been a Liberal Richmond MLA and in 1899 was a member of the Legislative Council. Ouseley had become the Clerk of the Assembly after the Liberals took power in 1882.

At that time, the Assembly *Debates and Proceedings,* the record of activity in the House, did not attempt to capture the full flow of debate. Its reports for March of 1899 do not indicate that any concerns were raised about possible conflicts of interest. The record does show that Simon Joyce moved both first and second readings of the Bill to incorporate the company.[15] Not even the *Halifax Herald*, at that time the loudest voice of the Conservative party, noted the Bill's passage through the Assembly; the railway project was overshadowed by a much bigger issue being debated, the proposals by H. M. Whitney and his Dominion Coal associates to establish a steel plant in Sydney.

The first Canadian source to present some important context for the new railway company appears to have been the Toronto *Mail and Empire*. On October 11, 1899, more than six months after the company's incorporation, that paper reprinted an article about the railway project from the previous day's New York *Daily Tribune*. The *Tribune* piece may have been the first time the project appeared in the New York press, but it would not be the last. "It is understood," said the New York original and the Toronto reprint, "that the interests behind the enterprise are the Vanderbilts, Dr. W. Seward Webb being mentioned as its principal promoter." The Vanderbilts were one of the richest families in the United States. Webb's wife was a Vanderbilt and both his brother and father-in-law were vice presidents of the Vanderbilt-controlled New York Central Railroad, one of the largest and most profitable American rail lines. The story about a Vanderbilt connection made it to the front pages of Nova Scotia newspapers very quickly.

The Liberal-leaning Halifax *Morning Chronicle* reported the story and also noted arrival in Nova Scotia of senior representatives from the new railway company including Robert Campbell, the President, and Edmund Guerin of Montreal, the company counsel. In the Conservative *Herald,* the story appeared under a header, "Vanderbilt Line in Cape Breton." The papers associated the appearance of Vanderbilt wealth behind the project with certainty that a railway would actually be built this time. This assumption became a recurring story in the Nova Scotia press.[16]

Fig. 4.1
Dr. William Seward Webb, c.1901

Harrison, vol. 1, 365.

The story of this venture is one of the most complicated and intriguing in the history of Cape Breton's railways. Like the railway itself, the story was incomplete from the outset and remains incomplete to the present day. Most of what is known comes from surviving newspaper accounts though they provide only a limited record of the events and the cast of characters involved. Those accounts included facts, speculations and outright fantasies. At the time, it must have been difficult on occasion to separate one category from another. Even with the wisdom of hindsight, those difficulties are still present.

While preparations for activity in Cape Breton were getting under way, a *New York Times* article on August 21, 1900,[17] revealed the proposed scope of the railway project. The story's header optimistically reported, "The Cape Breton Railway Now An Assured Fact." The lengthy report illustrates a number of the strands of the story that would develop over the next two years. In addition to the line from the Strait to Louisbourg, the *Times* said there would be a branch to Sydney and a bridge built across the Strait of Canso. On a much wider scale, the story reported that "ultimately this road will, it is said, make a link in the contemplated Atlantic-Pacific Railway" with other lines to be built or purchased. In addition, the *Times* noted that, "From the terminals at Louisburg it is intended to run fast steamships to Liverpool." Most readers of this story and the versions of it that worked their way into the Canadian press did not pay much attention to qualifying words or phrases like "intended" or "it is said."

By the summer of 1901, things started to happen. In June, Campbell and other New Yorkers were back in Halifax and Cape Breton.[18] Press coverage reported that Seward Webb would soon take over as CBR President and Campbell would step down to the position of Vice President. Surveys for the route were underway under the direction of the recently appointed Chief Engineer, Reuben W. Leonard, whose prior experience had included positions on the Intercolonial and the Canadian Pacific. Notice of his appointment was included in a letter from Webb to Premier George Murray.[19]

Fig. 4.2 - *Nova Scotia Royal Gazette*, Halifax, June 12, 1901: 250

> Cape Breton Railway Extension Company (Limited).
> NOTICE.
> A SPECIAL meeting of the shareholders of the Cape Breton Railway Extension Company (Limited) will be held at the office of the company, No. 214 New York Life Building, at Montreal, P. Q., on the 17th of July, A. D. 1901, at 10.30 o'clock in the morning, to consider a proposition to issue five per cent. gold bonds to the amount of $2,400,000, to be secured by a first mortgage, and to consider such further business as may properly come before said meeting.
> ROBERT J. CAMPBELL,
> President.
> JOHN M. GUERIN,
> Secretary.
> Montreal, 8th June, 1901.   june12—5i

Also in June, news from New York announced establishment of a new investment firm, the Dominion Securities Company, with Webb as President. Described by the *New York Times* as established "to develop Nova Scotia," its directors included John Jacob Astor, from another prominent New York family, and S. R. Callaway, the President of the New York Central.[20] Dominion Securities would wind up holding most of the Cape Breton Railway Company's common shares as well as the bonds that were issued following a meeting in July.

Soon after the notice about the bond issue, the *Royal Gazette* announced the railway company's legal name had been changed by Order-in-Council. "Extension" disappeared and the line became the "Cape Breton Railway" (CBR).[21] Later in August, Reuben Leonard's wife wielded a pick in a "first sod" ceremony at St. Peter's.[22] The south coast railway was finally under way.

In October, just after Premier Murray's Liberals took 36 of the 38 Assembly seats in a stunning election victory, Seward Webb, now installed as CBR President, came to Cape Breton. His visit received almost as much attention as the local papers would have given to a Royal tour.[23] With work on the railway under way, expectations of its impact ran higher and higher.

Relatively little has been found about construction though it appears to have been very labour-intensive. In early 1902, the *Railway and Shipping World*, the prime source of news about the railway industry in North America, reported more than 1500 men at work grading the 40 km (25 miles) of roadbed west of St. Peter's. At the same time, the first rails were being laid eastward from Point Tupper. Some contractors were local, for example Archibald and Sutherland from Port Hastings and J. Mackey of Grand Anse. Others came from as far away as Sault Ste. Marie, Ontario.[24] Due to a shortage of local labour, many workers were recruited "from away," from points both east and west. In January 1902, ads were placed in St. John's, Newfoundland, looking for 500 men for the project.[25]

By the autumn of 1902, the roadbed was approaching completion as far as St. Peter's, and rails had been laid on most of that distance. Ballasting was ongoing where track had been laid and station buildings at Point Tupper and St. Peter's were being built. A major bridge was under construction at River Inhabitants with its steel to come from the Dominion Bridge Company of Montreal, the firm that had done much of the structural work on the Intercolonial's big bridge at Grand Narrows.[26] Chief Engineer Leonard was still directing construction, but by this time he was reporting to a new boss in New York, Myron Evans.

Evans had come to Cape Breton on inspection trips at least twice, during the summer of 1902 and again in November.[27] The earliest reference located to identify him as the new CBR President dates from December of 1902,[28] but he probably assumed the position some months before as a result of important developments in New York. In the immediate flow of the CBR story, however, New York is less important than St. Peter's, and the New York events will be

---

September 7, 1903: A Big Day in St. Peter's

Sydney Record, September 12, 1903: 3

"The Cape Breton Railway was formally opened Monday, the first through train running over it from Point Tupper to St. Peter's that morning. Large numbers were on board. The run to St. Peter's was made in slow time so as to give the excursionists an opportunity of seeing the road and points of interest on the way. The Train arrived at St. Peter's at 10 o'clock where the citizens of the town had prepared a reception in honour of the occasion. Addresses were made by several of the leading citizens and the event of the first arrival of regular passenger trains in that town was duly celebrated. The town was also gaily decorated with flags and bunting. Jay Downer, chief engineer and general manager of the road had charge of the train. The road is now opened for passenger and traffic service. It is 32 miles [51 km] long and was completed a few days ago."

The Sydney *Post* covered the story a few days later, on September 18 and 21, though with several points that differed from the content in the *Record*. The *Post* correctly identified the senior CBR man as Downey, not Downer, though what was likely a typographical error in the *Record* is of little consequence. More interesting is the beginning of the *Post* story on 21 September. It observed that the reception upon the arrival of the train "was somewhat marred in consequence of the absence of Chief Engineer Jay Downey." Again, it doesn't matter much if Downey was present that day or not. However, the discrepancy between the two papers regarding the presence or absence of the new Chief Engineer is a useful reminder that, on even very basic "facts," details found "in print" may prove unreliable.[29]

dealt with in due course. Two years plus a month after the first sod was turned, the line from Point Tupper to St. Peter's opened for business. In the context of things that had happened in New York, that was perhaps a miracle.

The Stock Market Bubble[30]

While the CBR was being built toward St. Peter's, reports had indicated that work would continue to Louisbourg and perhaps beyond. In addition to the confidence about finances created by the Vanderbilt connection, a front page story in the Sydney *Daily Post* on June 26, 1901, reported CBR President Robert Campbell saying that "they has concluded satisfactory arrangement with both the local and federal governments last fall regarding the matter of subsidies." In February of 1902, the *Railway and Shipping World* noted that "plans for the extension ... to Louisburg, about 80 miles (129 km), will be completed in March, and construction will be gone on with immediately thereafter." That report noted that surveys were also being carried out for a branch line to Arichat on Isle Madame. Even more significant in that story was news of a CBR purchase of a large block of land in Louisbourg "for terminals." Such a purchase was presumably related to the story that had first appeared in the *New York Times* of August 21, 1900, about an "intended" line of fast steamships between Louisbourg and England. In April of 1902, *Railway and Shipping World* reported that survey work had been completed for the line between Louisbourg and Sydney and started for a branch from Sydney to North Sydney.[31]

Other stories had been appearing with even more exciting projections. On October 7, 1901, when Seward Webb was in Cape Breton, the *Daily Record* learned, "in the course of a conversation with one of Dr. Webb's party," that "hotels will dot the shores and mountains bordering on the lakes, and every modern effort will be made to attract tourists to Cape Breton." This was big news and appeared where it belonged, on the front page. The same day, the *Daily Post*, had an even bigger scoop, on the front page of course, under the header that read "Colossal Scheme" with a subhead, "Vanderbilts to Rival the Great C. P. Railway: To Build a Transcontinental Railway From Sydney To The Pacific Coast." The fine print in the *Post* noted that Webb was "not prepared to say" things to confirm the headlines just yet but the paper appeared confident in its understanding of what was planned. The impression created by stories like these was that a railway along the south coast was only a very small part of what was to come to Cape Breton.

More than a few people in St. Peter's, Louisbourg and beyond likely suspected that all this was a bit too good to be true—and that was the case.

During 1901 and early 1902, there had been a comparable flow of reports in the New York press and beyond about Webb, Dominion Securities, where he was President, Arthur L. Meyer, Dominion's Vice President, Robert Campbell, the original CBR President, and other companies that they owned, controlled or were interested in.[32] The news was always positive and much of it had to do with railways in Canada. There were stories about acquisition of control of the South Shore Railway which operated from St. Lambert, opposite

Montreal, to Sorel, Quebec along with plans for its extension to Levis, opposite Quebec City; plans for a new railway bridge across the St. Lawrence to Montreal; moves to acquire control of the Canada Atlantic Railway which ran from Lake Huron through Ottawa to Montreal; and plans for construction of a Montreal subway system that would include a tunnel under the St. Lawrence.[33] Great things were going to happen, and the prices of shares in the various companies rose accordingly. Dominion Securities shares, which first traded at just over $60 in mid-August of 1901, were quoted at $113 on March 25, 1902.

The bubble burst a month later. On May 2, 1902, the headline for a *New York Times* story read, "Webb Syndicate Stocks Break Heavily: Vast Paper Profits Converted Into Vast Losses." The next day's paper stated that a warrant was out for Arthur Meyer's arrest. Three "investment" firms were suspended by the New York Stock Exchange. Dominion Securities shares, the most readily available benchmark of Webb-Meyer stock prices, collapsed from their March high of well over $100 to below $30. By mid-June, they were down to $10½.

Post-crash press coverage does not provide enough to draw many firm conclusions about the market bubble. It is clear, however, that it was more than just a case of excessive speculation. Rising share prices had been created, at least in part, by stock "washing," artificial trading that when reported looked like real market activity.[34] The usual goal of this kind of market manipulation is captured by the cynical label given to it—"pump and dump." As share prices are inflated, those doing the inflating start unloading their shares to others. It seems, however, that some people had at least one other goal. Substantial loans were obtained from a large number of banks with the inflated shares in Webb-Meyer syndicate companies deposited as security.[35] The story got to Nova Scotia quickly and on May 8 the headline on a front page story in the *Halifax Herald* began with the essential question, "Who Got All The Money...." Unfortunately, nothing has been found to suggest who was really behind the market manipulation or to answer the *Herald's* question. It is also unclear what caused the bubble to collapse when it did.[36]

Webb tried to distance himself from Arthur Meyer, Dominion Securities and the related companies though many of his explanations seemed to play fast and loose with what appeared to be the facts. Regarding the CBR, he was quoted as saying, "I have never had one dollar invested in the Cape Breton Railway Company either in its stocks or bonds,"[37] despite the fact that his name had appeared at the head of the list of shareholders at the Montreal meeting in July of 1901 that approved the bond issue. It must be noted, however, that his statement might have been literally true if he had received shares without making any payment. It was not unusual at the time for company organizers to acquire shares without making any contribution of capital to a company. The crash did not affect Webb's ongoing search for deals. Less than a month after the crash, he was back in Canada in his private railway car for discussions with William Mackenzie and Donald Mann, builders of the recently-opened Inverness and Richmond Railway, about possible joint ventures.[38]

Despite the arrest warrant, no indication has been found that Arthur Meyer was charged let alone convicted of any wrongdoing. He appears to have been involved soon afterward with a stockholders committee established to reorganize Dominion Securities. When a new board was established for that firm in August of 1902, Meyer became one of the directors and was the only one carried over from the original board.[39]

The Dominion stockholders committee was likely the body that named Myron Evans as CBR President to replace Seward Webb. Several members of the new Dominion board accompanied Evans to inspect work on the CBR and meet with Premier Murray in November-December of 1902. Their presence suggests that Dominion still held most of the CBR shares and bonds as reported at the end of May, 1902.[40] That could have reflected an ongoing serious interest in the Cape Breton Railway. It might have been because the securities probably had no market value.[41]

The Political Scandal that Might Have Been

The list of names of those who incorporated the Cape Breton Railway Extension Company in 1899 included four active Nova Scotia Liberals: two sitting members of the Assembly, a member of the Legislative Council, and the Clerk of the Assembly. From this group, Isodore LeBlanc and Simon Joyce appear in the 1901 list of CBR shareholders, the only such list found. LeBlanc, Joyce, plus Duncan Finlayson also appear in the list of those who, along with Arthur Meyer of New York, incorporated the North American Coal and Development Company in Nova Scotia in March of 1902. No Cape Breton Liberals were directly connected to Webb's Dominion Securities Company but on the Dominion board was Thomas Robertson, formerly a Liberal Member of Parliament for Shelburne, Nova Scotia, and at this time, an MLA and Speaker of the Nova Scotia House of Assembly. Edmund Guerin, who appears to have accompanied all the CBR delegations to visit the Premier's office in Halifax, was a sitting Liberal MLA in Quebec and a partner of J. A. C. Madore, Liberal MP for the Quebec riding of Hochelaga. The CBR was, in its time and place, a small-scale illustration of railway politics in practice. But where was the scandal? The connections between the CBR and the Liberal party, then in power in both Halifax and Ottawa, did not demonstrate anything new or different in the mixing of corporate and partisan interests.

But things could have become very interesting in the 1901 Nova Scotia election that the Liberals won so handily. All that required was a Nova Scotian equivalent of George Norris, the confidential secretary of John Abbott who had copied the documents that triggered the Pacific Scandal—after the copies had been sold to the Liberals who piously denounced corruption from their seats on the opposition benches in Ottawa.[42] Had an entrepreneurial secretary in Premier Murray's office played the same role, the provincial Conservatives might have generated a "Cape Breton Scandal" and brought down the Murray government with just one interesting quote from a letter in the Premier's files.

When writing to Murray in 1899 on behalf of the Cape Breton Railway Extension Company, Edmund Guerin had included the following: "It is thoroughly understood with all our New York friends that this road will give its influence and support to the Liberal party and I will take my cue from you for whatever may be required to be done."[43]

No evidence has been found to indicate if Murray or the provincial Liberal party cashed this blank cheque.

The Stump of Line

When the Webb-Meyer shares crashed, there was considerable local concern about the possible effect on the CBR. Work did continue, though rumours about the railway's future circulated. Just after the crash, Mackenzie and Mann were in Halifax about their ongoing consolidation of lines in western Nova Scotia into what became the Halifax and Southwestern Railway. Sydney's *Daily Record* suggested that "the Cape Breton Extension may fall into their hands,"[44] a logical speculation given their ownership of the Inverness railway. In December of 1902, when reporting on the visit of Myron Evans and others from New York, the *Record* suggested that the line would be completed only as far as St. Peter's and then put up for sale. That story went on to identify the Canadian Pacific as the expected buyer.[45]

Despite qualified reports during 1903 from the new CBR management of their intention to continue the line to Louisbourg, no track was laid east of St. Peter's. After the first section of the line was opened, there were hints that construction would proceed but nothing came of them. Governments in Halifax and Ottawa offered additional inducements to the CBR or others who might take the bait but no offers came forward. Gradually it came to be accepted that the south coast railway was not going to be built.[46] St. Peter's would remain the eastern end of what was later described as a "stump of line."[47] Stump or not, at least that section of the CBR was open for business. William Calder provided a sense of what it meant to the people of Richmond County. See page 109 for a map of the route to St. Peter's.

Fig. 4.3
Cape Breton Railway # 3 and crew at Point Tupper, 1911: F. T. McGlasher, Engineer, (left) and J. R. Morrison, Fireman (right).

Port Hastings Museum and Archives.

The Cape Breton Railway's Impact on Richmond County

J. William Calder

"The Cape Breton Railway had its work spelled out. It had to make money, and that without delay! It certainly could not depend on the few town folks who were thrilled at the novelty of taking joy rides to Pt. Tupper and back, or those passengers who were travelling away on legitimate business. It had to carry freight, lots of it, and express, for that was and still is the monied backbone of railways. It had to have revenue to pay for the tons of coal the locomotive gobbled and money for the wages, so that the men who kept the roadbed and the tracks in good condition and the operating crew were rightly paid cash each month and there were the two bosses and the "boy" in the station at the end of the line.

"It was not too long after the first run that the C.B.R. was awarded the contract to carry the mails. His Majesty's Government said: "We will pay you so many cents per bag per trip;" and the C.B.R. said: 'Thank you', and went to work. All this was a fine bit of business for the C.B.R. But all this was far from sufficient to sustain the system.

"General merchants of the village, along the line and to the east began to move in goods and material by the carload. Hardly an evening passed but the little engine pulled one or two cars of flour and feed or a hopper of Sydney or Inverness coal. And cars of pressed hay moved in the winter or spring if the crop the summer before was inadequate. Merchants ordered perishables by express. These were smartly handled so that fresh fruit arrived in good order and in the fall a carload or more of barrels of apples from the Valley arrived. The train brought certain luxuries which were hard to come by including anthracite, commonly called hard coal, from the coal fields of the United States. All this was gradually eating into the livelihood of the coastal schoonermen.

"Some merchants contracted with the Dominion Coal Company to supply pit props for the mines in the Sydneys and with local farmers to supply the timber. The pit props were loaded in box cars placed along the line and merchants advanced cash to reputable workers. This was a boon to the farmer in the non-productive winter....

"D.Y. Stewart incorporated his fishing interests under the name of Stewart Fish Company, dealers in fresh and cured fish. Before long, box cars were spotted on the Stewart spur [a short branch or siding connecting to a main line railway], some incoming loaded with coarse salt, others empty, ready to take on outward shipments.

"The local management of the C.B.R. were delighted and optimistic; the keys of the Empire typewriter clicked cheerfully as George E. Johnson, general manager, two-fingered a letter to New York:

> "We are happy to inform you that an industry with great potential is now operating here. It will mean an addition of considerable revenue to us. Inward and outward carload shipments will be increasing."

Excerpted and edited from Calder, 57-59. Reprinted by permission of Formac Publishing Cmpany Limited.

The Inverness & Richmond

By the time construction was about to begin on the CBR, the western side of Cape Breton Island saw another railway built. As on the south coast, there had been decades of dreams and schemes for railways that would run northward into Inverness County.

The county had a small population and little industry to provide an economic base for a railway. Unlike the south coast, a route through Inverness was not an option for a main line to the larger coal mining district in the eastern part of the island or the harbours at Sydney or Louisbourg. But Inverness County did have one thing to attract a railway: coal. Attempts were made to develop mines at Port Hood, Mabou and Broad Cove (renamed and incorporated as the town of Inverness in 1904) starting in the mid-1860s but with little success. The prospects for mines in Inverness County were limited by a serious shipping problem. The shoreline of the Gulf of St. Lawrence did not have harbours appropriate for shipping coal. As a result, proposals to develop the coal industry and a railway were tied together from the outset. The prospects for coal traffic were supplemented by the potential for development of gypsum deposits located at Chéticamp, on the coast to the north of the coal district. Development of the mineral resources or a railway were hampered, however, by the fact that the required investment capital could not be raised locally and the external capital coming to Cape Breton was being drawn toward the mines developing around Sydney and Glace Bay.

What happened or did not happen in Inverness County over the period 1876-1899 was very like the Richmond County experience except for the railway-mining linkage. That pattern was established with the first railway survey carried out in 1876.[48] Over a 26-year period, 1874 to 1899 inclusive, more than sixty provincial and federal statutes were passed dealing with railways and mines in Inverness County. There were forty-six acts passed involving companies with a name beginning with "Inverness." The promoters included the usual suspects: American financiers; local politicians and active partisans (including a future Premier), usually though not always grouped together by party affiliation; a few local entrepreneurs; and, after work had started on the Intercolonial, an occasional contractor or engineer from the mainland or central Canada who had come to Cape Breton in conjunction with the IRC project.

It appears that there were at least five distinct projects, most of which lasted for some years and saw membership in the group of promoters change over time. After the previous detailed examination of twenty years of proposals for the south coast line, there would be little of value gained by attempting to dissect the various projects for Inverness County, save for two that do warrant some mention for several reasons.

In 1888, William Penn Hussey, a Boston coal merchant, arrived on the scene. Hussey's enterprise, eventually incorporated as the Broad Cove Coal Company, sank a mine shaft, built a shipping wharf, and opened a short narrow gauge railway between the mine and the wharf. Hussey's firm had to struggle to keep the channel to the wharf open, but over the decade of the 1890s, the mine produced some coal for export. The scope of Hussey's activity is something of a mystery. Annual Reports from the Department of Mines offer little detail and secondary sources have conflicting information about the output of the Broad Cove Company. It seems certain, however, that activity by the Broad Cove Company did not even begin to match the coal boom on the eastern side of the island.[49] It is also unknown why Hussey abandoned Inverness in 1899.[50] It appears likely, however, that Hussey's experience provided the stimulus for construction of a railway southward to deal with the shipping problems in the vicinity of Broad Cove.

A second venture worth noting was the Boston and Nova Scotia Coal Company. It was unusual, at the most superficial level, because its name did not start with "Inverness." The firm, established in 1893 to develop mines at Broad Cove,[51] also acquired the rights granted several years before to the Inverness and Victoria Railway Company.[52] That railway idea was one of the few that did not suggest a route following the coast northward from Point Tupper, the ferry terminus of the Intercolonial Railway. The Inverness and Victoria was authorized to build a line that would branch off the Intercolonial some 66-80 km (40-50 miles) inland and proceed northward. The statute's wording "via Whycocomah to Broad Cove coal mines, Margaree and Baddeck, with a branch to Chéticamp and other points as may be desirable" leaves considerable uncertainty about the intended route—assuming that a decision had actually been made by the promoters. The original Inverness and Victoria group seems to have been entirely Cape Breton-based except for Hiram Donkin, then working on the island as a senior civil engineer for the Intercolonial. The successor firm, the Boston and Nova Scotia, was also controlled in Nova Scotia though with only a minority stake from Cape Breton. The largest shareholder, with 30 per cent of the stock, was William J. Fraser of Halifax. Another Fraser from Pictou had 10 per cent. Cape Breton shareholders were Alexander Ross of North Sydney, a name that has appeared several times previously, with 20 per cent and John McKeen, Warden of Inverness County, with 10 per cent. The additional 30 per cent interest was held in Boston and Providence, RI.

In its November 1898 issue, *Railway and Shipping World* carried a note about the Inverness and Richmond Railway Company (I&R) that had been incorporated more than a decade before.[53] The company was now controlled by two Torontonians, R. H. Bowes and P. Ryan, who were identified as trying to attract American capital. Survey work had been done along with some preliminary grading of a 24-km (15-mile) section running north from Port Hawkesbury. Approval had been gained for subsidies to the extent of $7,400 per mile (per 1.6 km) from Ottawa, Halifax and the municipal government. This was a typical report about a venture that might or might not lead anywhere. Four months later, however, in March of 1899, the journal had a follow-up report stating that Bowes and Ryan had "given an option ... to Mackenzie, Mann & Co, & it is expected that firm will take it over & build the line."[54] The arrival of William Mackenzie and Donald Mann on the scene marked the transition from decades of dreams to two years of action. By June of 1901, I&R trains were running from the junction with the IRC near Point Tupper to Broad Cove. See page 109 for a map of the route to Inverness.

The partnership of William Mackenzie and Donald Mann was one of the extraordinary stories in the history of Canadian railroads. Over the period 1896-1917, they built nearly 13,000 km (8,000 miles) of track and equipped it with all the supporting infrastructure and systems needed for operating lines—an average of a mile a day, every day, for more than twenty years. Their long-term achievements and problems, particularly in a Cape Breton context, will appear in the next chapter. In 1899, the two were just beginning to gain prominence at a national level.

Natives of Ontario, Mackenzie and Mann had started careers as railway contractors for the Canadian Pacific in western Canada in the early 1880s. Their first joint venture grew out of separate contracts for the CPR on the "short line" from Montreal via Maine to Saint John, New Brunswick in 1888. By the mid-1890s, out of several railway projects in Manitoba, a partnership developed and the contracting firm of Mackenzie, Mann and Company was established.

Since most of their activity up to 1899, separately or together, had been in western Canada, an obvious important question is: what brought Mackenzie and Mann to Cape Breton? There are several possible explanations though no one can be offered with any certainty.

Perhaps they were approached as potential contractors. Mackenzie was operating from a Toronto base at this time, was involved in the development of the Toronto street railway company, and could have been known to Bowes and Ryan who were from Toronto. It seems more likely, however, that the overture came from Mackenzie and Mann in pursuit of business regardless of the location of a possible contract. The geographic scope of their activities shows that the partners were constantly on the hunt for opportunities at this time.

The I&R project was probably particularly interesting to Mackenzie and Mann because of its connection to potential development of the coal resources of Inverness County. In his account of the rise of the "meteors in the sky," as he called the partners, George Stevens described Mann as "coal obsessed."[55] Over the years, many of the partnership's railway projects had connections to coal, iron and gypsum mining ventures across the country. Mann, said Stevens, "never ceased to be a prospector at heart."

Other personal influences and connections might also have been at work. The CPR project in Maine in 1888 had been under the direction of James Ross who subsequently partnered with Mackenzie and Mann on other CPR contracts in the west. The Toronto street railway, in which Mackenzie was an investor, was headed by Ross. In the late 1890s, Ross had developed a link to Cape Breton; he had joined the board of Whitney's Dominion Coal Company and became a director of the related steel company when it was set up in 1899.

Throughout 1899, *Railway and Shipping World* recorded the developments.[56] On the financial side, arrangements were quickly made to float a bond issue and the terms of government subsidies were finalized. The Province agreed to increase its normal subsidy of $3,200 per mile to $4,000 a mile (per 1.6 km). While arrangements were being finalized, Mann wrote Premier George Murray seeking subsidy payments "as every ten mile section is completed" rather than upon final completion of the line. As an alternative, he asked if the project and

Fig. 4.4

In 1902, the legal name of the I&R was changed to the Inverness Railway and Coal Company. The bond illustrated here was issued just after the name change. Though it had no legal status after 1902, the traditional "I&R" name lasted longer than the bonds which went into default before their 1922 maturity date.

Inverness Miners' Museum.

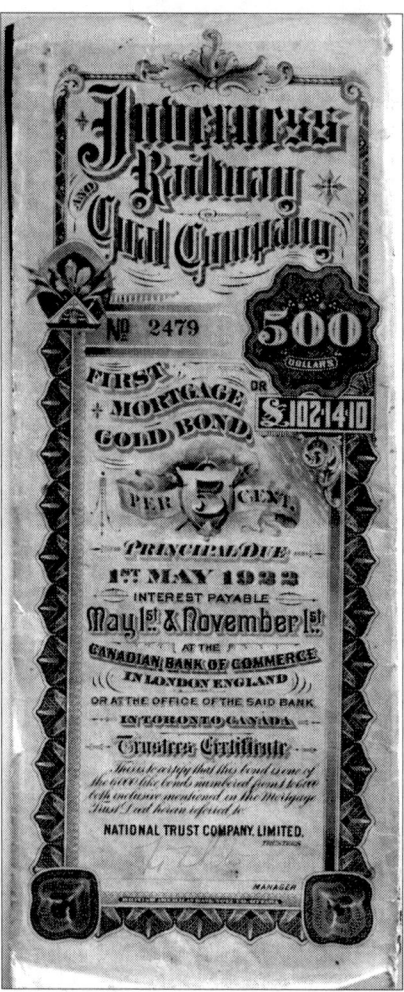

its subsidy could be split in two with payment for the first section to be made before the second section was started. This, Mann noted, would "greatly assist us in financing the scheme."[57] The partners' financial model was to maximize both the amount of government subsidization and the speed with which the funds came in. Regardless of that approach, the partners did have access to other capital as needed and construction proceeded rapidly. Before the end of the summer, more than a thousand men were at work on the section between Port Hastings and Port Hood. That section opened for traffic at the end of September 1900.

On the I&R, as on many of the partners' other undertakings, the financial model had a counterpart on the construction side. The basic strategy was to try to curtail costs in the short term. Deficiencies in railway construction could be made up later, to be funded by the flow of revenue after a line became operational. In Nova Scotia, the Provincial Engineer had to confirm that construction standards had been met before the Province's subsidy payments could be made. Correspondence within the Provincial Engineer's office and to Premier Murray indicate that corners were cut when the I&R was built. When the railway became operational through to Broad Cove in June of 1901, speed limits were imposed until necessary construction improvements were carried out.[58] Late in 1901, a short extension was completed to connect the new line to the Intercolonial near the IRC's Point Tupper ferry dock.

With the link made to the Intercolonial, the core part of the railway project was completed, but there was unfinished business. Before construction had been started, the plan had been to locate a new shipping wharf at Caribou Cove, now Port Malcolm, Richmond County, a short distance southeast of Point Tupper, perhaps influenced by an offer of a subsidy by Richmond County. That proposed wharf site had not been mentioned in the contract signed in May of 1899[59] and the wharf was built at Port Hastings, adjacent to the I&R main line and a short distance north of the point where it met the Intercolonial. The location was very near to the point where the Canso Causeway comes ashore at Port Hastings. It is uncertain about when construction began or exactly when the wharf opened. Despite that uncertainty, the output of more than 20,000 t of coal at Broad Cove in 1902 suggests the wharf must have been at least partly operational before the end of that year.

Development of the coal deposits at Broad Cove had been built into the contract governing the subsidies from the Province. While capital was going

---

Lines Of Steel Are Now Joined

Halifax Herald, December 13, 1901: 1

"The first through car to Broad Cove went out over the Inverness & Richmond Railway today, this being Mackenzie and Mann's private car *Atikokan*. It was shunted from Point Tupper to Point Tupper Junction, where the car was attached to a special engine of the Inverness and Richmond Railway and run to Broad Cove. On board the car were Messrs. Mackenzie and Mann; Mr. Sinclair, the general manager of the road; Charles Fergie, Westville; Mr. Wallace, a Toronto capitalist; and Mr. Bristol, solicitor for the company. Heretofore the cars going over this road were transferred from Mulgrave to Hastings. Now they will be ferried across to Point Tupper. Completion of the link between Hastings and Tupper gives the through train service from Sydney to Broad Cove. The ferry service between Hastings and Mulgrave will be discontinued. The object of the present visit of Messrs. Mackenzie and Mann is to examine the progress of the work at Broad Cove. Mr. Mackenzie feels confident that with the introduction of improved methods of mining and shipping facilities which they propose introducing they will be prepared for an output of a quarter of a million tons by the close of next season."

Fig. 4.5 - I&R coal pier at Port Hastings. Note the five hopper cars on top of the pier and the chutes that carried coal down into the holds of ships. The facility had storage capacity for 4500 t of coal on site.

LAC, negative # PA-125172.

into railway track, investment was simultaneously going into two new mines and refitting a third. One opened each year over the period 1901-1903. In 1902, coal output was more than 20,000 t; in 1903, it rose to 120,000 and in 1904 was almost 150,000 tons. Broad Cove was incorporated as a town in 1904, taking the name Inverness, and had all the signs of a boom. The workforce in the mines was nearly 500. Central Avenue, the new town's main street had twenty-seven bars and saloons to cater to all those thirsty miners.[60]

In 1902, the railway company and the Inverness-Richmond Collieries and Railway Company were merged into a single firm, the Inverness Railway and Coal Company. That restructuring may have had as much to do with clarification of ownership as anything else. Presumably in payment for funds owed them by the original shareholders of the I&R, Mackenzie and Mann acquired enough stock to have effective control of the new company.[61] Strictly speaking, after that reorganization the railway should be referred to as the IR&CC. Despite that technical detail, the traditional short form, the I&R, remained in popular use as long as the railway survived as an independent company and so it will remain the I&R in this book.

Another aside fits in here. In 1901, Mackenzie and Mann had responded to offers of provincial subsidies to complete a major section of railway between Halifax and Yarmouth and take over a small operating section of the line that was in trouble. The result was the partners' Halifax and Southwestern that ran down Nova Scotia's south shore with several branches crossing the province to the Bay of Fundy side.

There remained one piece of unfinished business, the northward extension of the line from Broad Cove to Chéticamp. As a result of the focus on Broad Cove, there were local concerns that the railway would not continue northward, concerns that reached the Premier's desk.[62] The concerns were valid; the line was never built, by Mackenzie and Mann or by anyone else. To put this into proper context, however, it is important to note that neither Mackenzie and Mann nor the government had been on public record as saying the I&R line would go to Chéticamp. The 1899 contract did not include anything about construction north of Broad Cove and effectively excluded construction to Chéticamp through a restriction of the subsidy to a maximum distance of 109 kms (68 miles). The line built to Broad Cove was 100 km (62.4 miles) long. An extension to Chéticamp would have required about another 56 km (35 miles) of track and either a separate financial deal or a willingness by Mackenzie and Mann to build without a subsidy. Neither of these was forthcoming.

Other Railways That Never Were

The original popular expectation that the I&R would go as far north as Chéticamp and the plans of the CBR to build eastward from St. Peter's marked just two of the uncompleted railways in western Cape Breton.

Mention has already been made of the Inverness and Victoria (I&V) and its proposal for an inland route to Broad Cove and either a coastal route or an inland route further north to Chéticamp. This 1887 proposal may have been the basis for another project that appeared a decade later.

Soon after 1900, references appear to the plans for the Broad Cove, Baddeck and North Sydney (BCB&NS). The reported objective was a railway that would bring Prince Edward Island agricultural produce through port(s) such as Inverness or Margaree Harbour and onward through Baddeck to the Sydney area.[63] That route would have included a bridge over the Bras d'Or Channel at Seal Island, an engineering undertaking comparable to the IRC bridge at Grand Narrows. No evidence has been found of a company formally established under the BCB&NS name. It seems likely that this was the firm incorporated as the Cape Breton Northern in 1902[64] for a route similar to the one associated with the BCB&NS. Hiram Donkin, whose name had appeared in the I&V statute, was one of the incorporators of the Cape Breton Northern along with others including James Burchell, at that time the owner of the small mine at New Campbellton. Nothing came of any of these projects.

Another railway company established in 1902 was the Mabou and Gulf (M&G)[65] by American owners who had acquired the Mabou coal mine the previous year. The company was to build a railway from the mine to Mabou Harbour and from there southward to Whycocomagh and beyond to connect with the Intercolonial at Orangedale. This would have been a shortened version of the western part of the route proposed by the CBN. The Mabou and Gulf was different in one critical respect. Some preliminary work was done[66] and rails were laid on the first section from the mine to a wharf at Mabou.[67] The line had a few coal cars plus a locomotive, but by 1910 it had faded away, perhaps as a result of protracted negotiations with the I&R about how the two railways could cross, perhaps as a result of a lack of success in the mining operations. The Department of Mines Reports for 1908 and 1909 indicate the company ceased to operate in August of 1908.[68] The mine was apparently taken over by the provincial government for some five months but abandoned in January 1909 when the mine flooded. It is unclear whether the flooding caused the Province to walk away from the mine or if the flooding took place as a result of abandonment by the Province.

There were a number of other projected railways that did not get their trains to run. For example, in almost every year between 1904 and 1916, statutes were passed by the Nova Scotia legislature dealing with the Margaree Coal and Railway Company which was authorized to build rail lines from Inverness to Chéticamp as well as on an inland route to connect to the IRC at or near Orangedale. Nothing has been found that any construction work was ever done on a rail line. One other project that deserves mention was an infrastructure venture rather than a railway.

In 1902, the Strait of Canso Bridge Company was incorporated federally to build a railway and general traffic toll bridge across the Strait.[69] Four provisional directors were named, three of whom have appeared previously. Those three were: Robert Reid of Isbester and Reid and the Reid Newfoundland Company; Hiram Donkin, who had recently left Dominion Coal for a senior position at Nova Scotia Steel and Coal at Sydney Mines; and Alexander Ross of

Fig. 4.6
Mabou & Gulf # 4. Accounts of this locomotive suggest it originally ran on the Lehigh Valley Railroad in Pennsylvania and passed through several owners before coming to Cape Breton. The assigned number raises an obvious question: what about numbers 1, 2 and 3? Given the modest and short-lived scope of M&G operations, it seems doubtful that the line had more than one locomotive. Perhaps the # 4 had been allocated by a previous owner. Information attached to the photo in the museum at Port Hastings suggests # 4 survived in "a roundhouse at N. E. Mabou until 1942" despite assertions by several railway historians that the engine was scrapped c.1910. Equally intriguing is wording on the photo's information sheet suggesting in three places that more than one M&G locomotive was in that "roundhouse." Perhaps some reader can shed light on these Mabou mysteries.

Port Hastings Museum and Archives, # P83-103.

North Sydney. The fourth was Graham Fraser, Vice President of Scotia Steel.[70] These names suggested a serious project with immediate connections to two of the three largest enterprises in Cape Breton and Newfoundland and indirectly to financial and banking interests in Halifax through Scotia's President, John F. Stairs.[71]

The concept drew extensive press coverage, locally, in central Canada and in New York. The earliest newspaper story found appeared in the New York *Daily Tribune* in March of 1902 shortly before the *Act* of incorporation was passed. The timing and the New York publicity base raise suspicions that the project was connected to activity of the Webb-Meyer syndicate and that the provisional directors had been recruited as window-dressing. That is only a suspicion, however, and there is evidence to the contrary. The bridge project did not vanish when the bubble of the Webb-Meyer companies burst in May of 1902.[72]

Survey work was done and the bridge design prepared. In May of 1904, with the statutory deadline for commencement of work about to expire, the company's *Act* was amended to extend the required start date to 1906 and make 1910 as the required completion date.[73] At the same time, the Montreal *Gazette*

To Bridge Strait of Canso: Proposed Structure To Cost $4,500,000

Daily Tribune, New York, March 4, 1902: 5
Halifax, N.S. March 3 (Special) –

"Civil Engineer Hiram Donkin, formerly resident manager of the Dominion Coal Company at Glace Bay, has prepared several plans for the projected railway bridge over the Strait of Canso. Soundings that have been made reveal the fact that the strait has a solid rock bottom and that, in spite of the great depth and the strong current, there are no difficulties in the way which modern engineering skill cannot overcome. The bridge will probably be erected from Cape Porcupine to near McMillan's Point, Post Hastings.

"The plan most likely to be adopted provides for a cantilever bridge of 1,800 feet, with two piers in eighty feet of water, with approaches of 1070 and 300 feet of trestle work on either side. The bridge is to carry two lines of railway tracks, with wide carriage roads on either side. The bottom girder of the bridge will be 150 feet above high water mark. The bridge will cost about $4,500,000 and will probably be built by the Dominion Bridge Company of Montreal. It is believed in Cape Breton that the promoters will succeed in floating the necessary capital and that construction work will start at an early date."

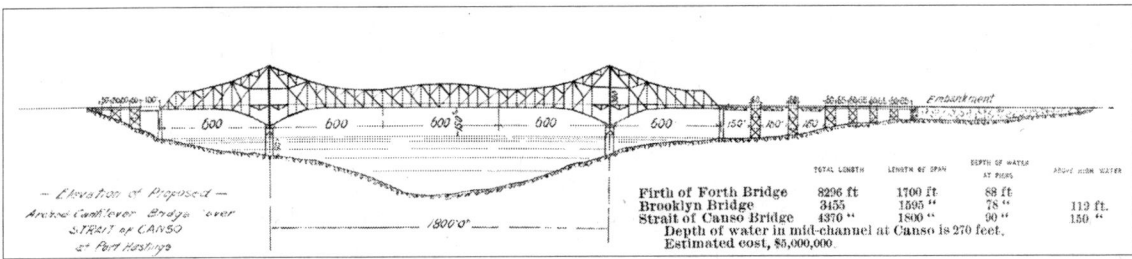

Fig. 4.7 (below)
Vernon, 330

ran a story on the continuing efforts of Alexander Ross to promote the idea but nothing came of the project.[74]

It is unknown just how serious the original promoters were about the proposed bridge though the *Gazette* interview with Alexander Ross noted an obvious link to Scotia Steel's new steel mill at Sydney Mines. Ross stated that all the steel for the crossing would be made in Cape Breton. Had the bridge been built, the primary user would certainly have the Intercolonial Railway. The Annual Reports of both the General Manager and the Chief Engineer of the IRC over the period 1902-1907 made no mention of the project. Perhaps IRC management was of the opinion that the bridge would never be built, that it was simply too large and costly a venture for its time and place.

5 – At the Dawn of the Railways' Golden Age

The first decade of the 20th century saw important changes in the Cape Breton economy, particularly in the urban centres on the eastern side of the island. For the island's railways, the period marked the beginning of more than five decades during which they were, for most people and businesses, the heart of the transportation system.

Around Sydney Harbour, the steel industry developed to complement the continued growth of coal mining. On the south side of the harbour, the Whitney group established the mills of the Dominion Iron & Steel Company (Disco) which opened in 1901. On the north side, Nova Scotia Steel and Coal (Scotia), the successor to the GMA, matched Whitney's entry into the steel business and opened a competing steel mill at Sydney Mines in 1904.

At the time of the appearance of these new firms, there were shuffles in positions of power among some whose names have appeared previously. Whitney sold his controlling interests in both Disco and Dominion Coal and departed from the companies and Cape Breton. James Ross, who has been named in conjunction with Mackenzie and Mann, became the key figure at Dominion Coal. At Scotia Steel, Graham Fraser, one of the founders, had difficulties with his fellow directors, left the company and in 1904 was hired as Director of Operations at Disco. Hiram Donkin, who had spent a period at Scotia Steel and then returned to Dominion Coal, left Domco in 1907 to become Deputy Minister of Mines and Public Works in the provincial government though this new job did not end his interest in Cape Breton's railways.

The development of new mines and the steel plants led to a population boom in the communities around Sydney Harbour. Some of this was the result of immigration, from as near as Newfoundland[1] or as far away as eastern Europe. Another contributor to population change was the continued migration from rural areas to urban centres, away from an economy based on some combination of farming, lumbering and fishing, to one of working for wages in the mines and steel mills, and of course for the railways. The population boom also brought a growing number of potential customers for the various services being provided by railways.

Table 5.1 - The Sydney Coal Field Boom: Populations 1881-1911				
	1881	1891	1901	1911
Sydney Mines	2340	2442	3191	7470
North Sydney	1520	2513	4646	5418
Sydney	1480	2427	9000	17723
Glace Bay		2459	6945	16562
Total	5340	9841	23782	47173
Canada Year Book, 1913, Ottawa, King's Printer, Populations Table 6: 58-59.				

The Railway Network in 1914

On the north side of Sydney Harbour, the Scotia railway's lines moved ever-increasing volumes of coal from the company's pits to the North Sydney shipping wharves which had been rebuilt under Hiram Donkin's direction in 1901-1902 and the new steel mill at Sydney Mines. New hopper cars that carried 16 t of coal replaced the old 8-t cars. The track was relaid with heavier rails weighing 80 lb/yd (40 kg/m) to upgrade the 50lb/yd (24.8 kg/m) rails that had been in place for several decades. Soon after 1891, connections had been made with the Intercolonial branch line to North Sydney. In 1906, the IRC branch was extended to Sydney Mines providing Scotia with capacity for another junction. Other connections would be made between the two when the IRC expanded further into the district where the Scotia line operated.

Fig. 5.1 - A postcard of Nova Scotia Steel & Coal's Princess Mine in Sydney Mines c.1905. Opened in 1867 by the GMA, the Princess mine was the largest colliery on the north side of Sydney harbour for decades. It was the site of the highest death toll in a single mining accident on the northside when 16 miners were killed and 50 injured on a runaway rake in 1938. A rake was a set of small rail cars that carried miners in and out of the pit.

Sydney Mines Heritage Museum.

Fig. 5.2 - Nova Scotia Steel & Coal's new shipping docks at North Sydney ca. 1905.

Cape Breton Miners' Museum, Glace Bay #6A1-62.

Fig. 5.3 - Sydney Mines Intercolonial Station built c.1906.

Sydney Mines Heritage Museum.

As part of the series of reorganizations of the Sydney-based companies that had begun with the establishment of Disco, the Sydney and Louisburg Railway was turned into a separate corporation in 1910. All shares, however, remained in the hands of the parent company which in 1910 was renamed the Dominion Steel Corporation. No S&L shares were available for public purchase. With its line south and east from Sydney, the S&L linked collieries to shipping wharves, the Sydney steel plant and communities along the shore

Fig 5.4 - The second Intercolonial Railway station in Sydney; built ca. 1905.

Photo restored by Terry Power, Sydney, NS. Reproduced by permission of Mr. Power.

Fig. 5.5 - A Sydney & Louisburg passenger train at the Sydney station. Loco #23 was built in 1900 by the Schenectady Locomotive Works of Schenectady, New York. The engine ran on the S&L for over half a century and was scrapped in 1953. The bell from #23 was recently donated to the S&L Museum in Louisbourg after an extended retirement in the care of a S&L family.

Sydney Mines Heritage Museum.

to Louisbourg. The S&L also maintained the connection to the Intercolonial main line at Sydney, originally established by the International Company Railway in 1891.

By 1914, twenty years after its birth, the S&L had almost doubled its rolling stock. The number of locomotives went from nineteen (1895) to thirty-one (1914) and the inventory of coal cars expanded from 923 to 1550. Coal traffic increased dramatically, from fewer than one million t in 1895 to more than four million t in 1914. There was an equally large increase in the number of "passengers" carried during the same period, though the number of passenger cars on the line changed only slightly, increasing from six to eight.[2] Most of the passengers being carried by rail were miners going to and from the pits who did not pay fares on the trains and who did not get passenger-class cars to ride in.

Fig. 5.6 - S&L hopper # 610, built by Rhodes, Curry & Co. This car, one of a large 1895 order, was presumably photographed at the builder's plant in Amherst before transfer to Cape Breton. The Sydney & Louisburg name on the car illustrates official use of the name long before the S&L was set up as a separate company in 1910.

Sydney & Louisburg Railway Museum, #SL-96-1095.

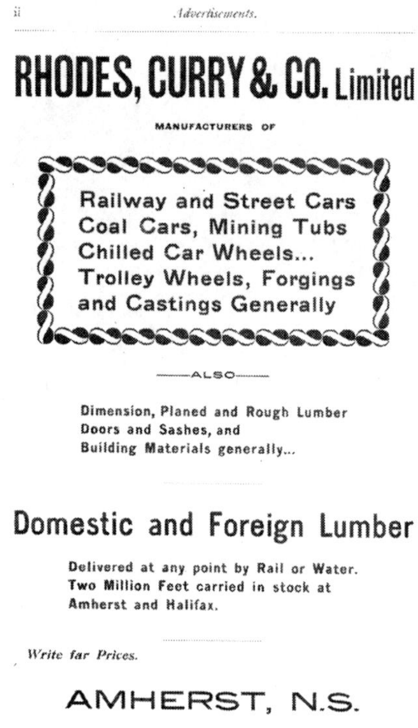

Fig. 5.7 - The ad provides a sense of this company's activity in 1900. Started as a lumber and milling firm in 1877, it became a major builder of railway rolling stock about 1890 and maintained that position for over two decades. At its peak, the Amherst plant was the town's largest employer with a workforce that ranged between 1000 and 1500. In 1909, in a deal arranged by Max Aitken of Royal Securities, the company was merged with two Montreal firms under the name Canada Car & Foundry. Nathaniel Curry moved to Montreal as president of the new company. By the early 1920s, the Amherst plant was closed and all production relocated to Montreal—an all too familiar story in the economic history of the Maritimes.[3]

Bell, 1900.

The Intercolonial and the Battle of the Sydneys

When the IRC line was under construction, a number of local rivalries had appeared. One of the strongest of these was between North Sydney and Sydney. Both had contended for the status, the potential jobs and the possibility of

---

Train Service on Cape Breton Division

House of Commons Debates, June 21, 1900: 7972-73

"Sir Charles Tupper (Cape Breton). Mr. Speaker, before the Orders of the Day are called, I want to draw the attention of the Hon. Minister of Railways and Canals (Mr. Blair) to a matter of some importance. I have received the following telegram from the Board of Trade of Sydney:

"At a large meeting of the Sydney Board of Trade held this afternoon, the following resolution was unanimously passed:

"Resolved, that this meeting of the Sydney Board of Trade has witnessed with exceeding regret the departure made by the management of the Intercolonial Railway from their published time-table, in running the fast express into and out from North Sydney twice a day. That this diversion from the main line to a branch delays the arrival of the train by schedule time thirty minutes, and from past experience, it can be concluded that the delay will largely exceed that limit, that this delay is particularly annoying, as it prevents the possibility of delivering any mails that come in by that train on the night of its arrival; that it is contrary to the spirit and object of the system of fast travel, and is a source of annoyance to each and every traveller whose destination is Sydney; that the large volume of passenger traffic at present is to Sydney, and the slight inconvenience of changing cars at North Sydney is trivial in comparison with the unnecessary and annoying delay caused by running the whole train down to the North Sydney station, and very frequently down to the North Sydney wharf; that the time-table, as arranged, settled and published by the Department of Railways, was acceptable to this board as a compromise, in view of the fact that the early express was still allowed to continue the old system of running on the North Sydney branch on the up and down trips, but the unexplained change compelling both trains to run into North Sydney is an act of injustice and injury to the town of Sydney which this board regards as utterly unjustifiable; further resolved, that the representatives of this county in the Dominion parliament and local legislature be asked at once to demand of the Department of Railways its adherence to the printed time-table, and that copies of this resolution be sent to the representatives of the county, to the Minister of railways and to the Minister of Finance."

"(Sgd.) D. A. Hearn, Secretary, Sydney Board of Trade"

During the lengthy debate, the closest Tupper got to a response for the Sydney Board of Trade from Andrew Blair (Minister of Railways in Laurier's Liberal government) was the following:

"The Minister of Railways and Canals (Mr. Blair ... I am in communication with the department at the present time, and am in hope that we will be able to arrive at the solution moderately agreeable to both parties. If not, we will have to determine the question according to what we conceive to be the interests of the different localities, the interests of the railway, and the interests of the public service, and make our decision accordingly, even though neither of the parties might be content with it."

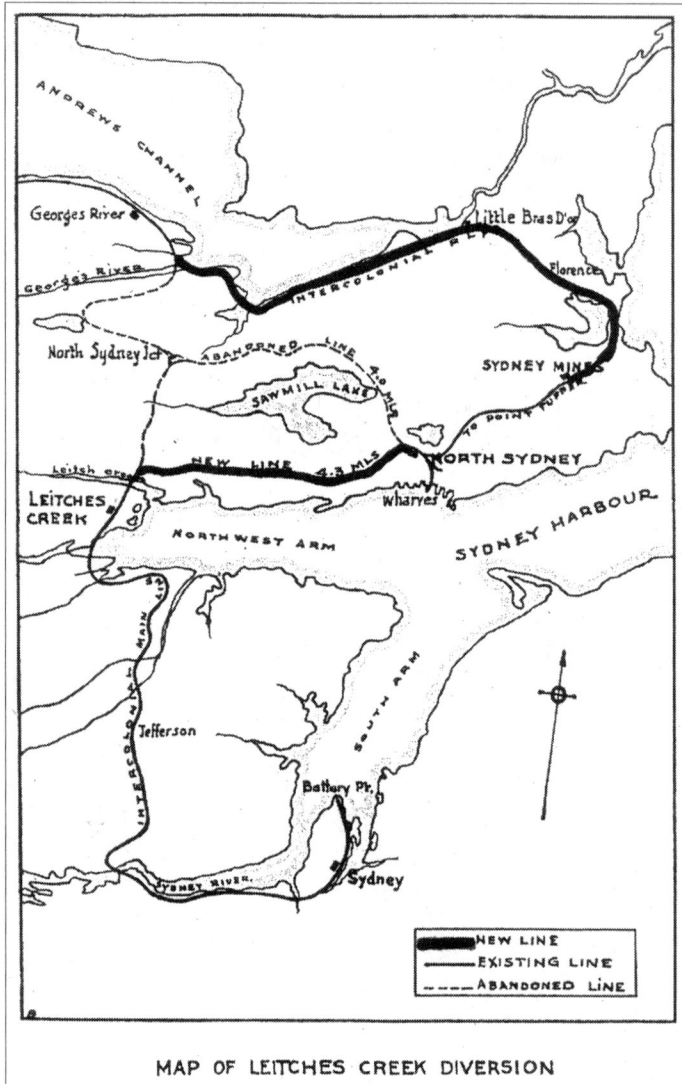

MAP OF LEITCHES CREEK DIVERSION

Fig. 5.8
Parliament of Canada, *Sessional Papers*, 1916, vol 15, Sessional Paper # 20, Department of Railways and Canals, Annual Report, 1914-15, part X.

better service associated with being the eastern terminus. The prospect of being located on a branch line had little appeal to either community. Sydney won the honour when the line opened in 1891, but the controversy over scheduling and discontent in North Sydney about that town's branch line status continued for years.[4] The rivalry became a partisan issue and on more than one occasion was carried to Ottawa and the railway's political masters. For example, in June 1900, the House of Commons was the scene of an extended and vigorous discussion of the conflicting claims of the two towns that took up nine pages of the parliamentary record.[5] The debate was triggered by a telegram from the Sydney Board of Trade, which Sir Charles Tupper, then Leader of the Opposition and MP for Cape Breton, presented to the House.

The conflict between the two towns over schedules, plus the demands from Nova Scotia Steel and Coal for improved rail connections were resolved, to the extent they could be, by the realignment of the IRC main line on the north side of Sydney Harbour. This involved new track bringing the line through Little Bras d'Or and Florence to Sydney Mines from the north in 1913. Here, connection was made with the North Sydney branch that had reached Sydney Mines in 1906. This older section was retained and linked at North Sydney to a few miles of new track to Leitches Creek in 1915.[6] Here, the new section rejoined the 1891 route to carry trains the rest of the way into Sydney. Completion of this rerouting ended the branch line location of the large northside towns and also brought IRC service to Florence and Little Bras d'Or, both of which had become important mining communities.

The IRC and Shipping Connections

The importance of the opening of the Intercolonial to Cape Breton was increased by the construction of a rail line across Newfoundland, a development that led to a new transport role for North Sydney. The narrow gauge

Fig. 5.9
The Intercolonial North Sydney Junction station was built c.1890 at the junction where the branch line went into the town. The photo shows the building being moved, probably in 1915. A new station, much like the one in Sydney Mines shown previously, was built in North Sydney ca. 1914.

North Sydney Museum.

Fig. 5.10
The Intercolonial station at Little Bras d'Or, built at the time of the rerouting of the IRC main line through that community in 1913.

Orangedale Railway Museum.

Fig. 5.11
SS Bruce, the first Reid Newfoundland Company ferry for the North Sydney – Port aux Basques run.

North Sydney Museum.

Newfoundland railway reached the island's west coast at Port aux Basques in 1898. The railway company then established a ferry service to North Sydney, where passengers and freight could transfer to IRC trains. By the time the Newfoundland railway was fully operational and the ferry running, both were controlled by Robert Reid whose construction firm had built both piers of the Grand Narrows Bridge and the IRC line between that bridge and Point Tupper.[7] The Newfoundland experience, where the contractor acquired ownership of the railway, was similar to what had happened on the Inverness and Richmond which had wound up under the control of the contractors, Mackenzie and Mann.

The first ship on the North Sydney to Port aux Basques run was the fabled *SS Bruce*.[8] The vessel's schedule, with departures three days a week in each direction, was tied to arrivals of the connecting trains. Departures from Newfoundland awaited the express from St. John's. Departures from North Sydney were governed by arrival of the Cape Breton-bound express that had connected in Truro with the express from Montreal. The *Bruce* linked the two islands until 1911 when it was wrecked near Louisbourg. For more than sixty years, the ferries to and from Newfoundland handled passengers and freight without taking railway cars across Cabot Strait. The narrow gauge Newfoundland cars could not run on the track on the Cape Breton side just as standard gauge cars could not be used in Newfoundland. As a result, passengers and freight had to transfer from train to ferry to train to cross the Strait and move onward into Newfoundland. Transshipment of Newfoundland freight became an important part of the North Sydney economy and probably generated more jobs than would have existed had rail cars been carried on the boats, something that did not happen until 1968.

While the Intercolonial's link with the Newfoundland ferry was the railway's most important shipping connection, there were others, most of which had short lives falling sometime during the period between 1891 and 1914-1918. As a snapshot example, an IRC schedule from January of 1907 showed that steamship connections would be made at Mulgrave with three vessels, *SS John L. Cann* sailing two days a week for Guysborough and three days a week for Canso; *SS F. M. L. Paint* sailing daily except Sunday for Port Hawkesbury and Port Hastings and *SS Percy Cann* sailing daily except Sunday for Arichat and Petit de Grat. When inland navigation opened, that is after the Bras d'Or was free of ice, trains 19 eastbound and 20 westbound would connect at Iona, with *SS Blue Hill* sailing daily except Sunday to Baddeck. No reference was made to vessels out of North Sydney or Sydney heading north to or beyond Ingonish.

In the years just before and after 1900, the Sydney and Louisburg also made steamer connections. These were with the Mira River Company's steamboat at Mira. The morning train from Sydney and the early evening train from Louisbourg each connected with the steamer for travellers taking the boat to upriver destinations.[9]

Early Days at the Point Tupper Ferry Dock

Peter MacDonald, Big Beach, Cape Breton County

"The first improvement was the use of a small scow capable of carrying two cars, which was loaded and unloaded on an apron on the north side of the wharf. Improvements, in time, did come; an enlarged scow with capacity for eight cars, four on each track. The facilities for handling this scow were placed on the southern side of the wharf, and a breakwater erected which formed a dock, into which the scow was placed for unloading in the winter. The dock often filled with drift ice and had to be cleaned out with poles in order to get the scow into the apron. A boat would bring the scow over in the morning, leaving it in the dock, and take passengers off the Sydney train to Mulgrave, and then go back for the scow, which had in the meantime been unloaded and reloaded.

"On one occasion in January a terrific snowstorm started. The passenger train was due to leave for Sydney at seven o'clock and was heavily loaded with passengers with some distinguished gentlemen among them. The train started but never got out of the yard. The train was backed into the station and did not leave for the next seventy-two hours. There were no hotels at Point Tupper, and passengers used to have their supper at the Grand Narrows hotel. The people of Point Tupper were not prepared to feed them. In twenty-four hours, all available foodstuffs were exhausted. The wild storm still raged and it was impossible for any person to venture over to Port Hawkesbury to procure food. The trackmaster was Simon Fraser and all available men were employed to assist the trackmen in trying to get the track cleared, and it was not until the third day that an engine came through."

From "History of Cape Breton Railroad," Beaton Institute, Reports: Transportation, # 82-98-1568, pp. 3-4. Date uncertain but believed written c.1948. An article by Peter MacDonald, "How the Railway Came to Cape Breton," appeared in the Sydney *Post-Record* of 23 April 1948.

Reprinted with permission of the Beaton Institute, Cape Breton University.

At the Strait of Canso

In the first years of IRC service across the Strait of Canso, the company used a barge system to transport cars, a photo of which appeared at the end of chapter 3. This system presented problems, especially in winter. Peter MacDonald's account indicates that a winter voyage on the Strait might be somewhat less fun than a tropical cruise.

To solve at least some of the problems, a new vessel, *Scotia*, was put into service to carry a larger number of rail cars as well as passengers across the Strait. Built at Newcastle-upon-Tyne, U.K., *Scotia* had a harrowing Atlantic crossing in the summer of 1901.[10] The arrival of the vessel was complicated by the fact that the new Mulgrave dock was not ready to handle traffic on and off the ferry. As a result of the wharf problems and a period in drydock in Halifax, *Scotia* did not go into regular service until April of 1902. From that date onward, however, the vessel worked the Strait crossing, decade in and decade out. With three rail tracks running the length of the deck, *Scotia* carried nine

Fig. 5.11a (above) - The first *Scotia* at work soon after it went into service.

Vernon, 326.

Fig. 5.12 (below) - The Point Tupper yard, probably post-1903 and definitely no later than 1912. The station in the background was destroyed in a fire in July of 1912. The two-coach passenger train by the platform was probably a CBR train for St. Peter's.

Point Tupper Heritage Association.

passenger cars or eighteen freight cars. There was no cabin capacity for passengers so they stayed in the rail cars during the crossing that normally took about half an hour. In 1915, in response to growing traffic volumes, a sister ship arrived and was named *Scotia II*.

The new ferry came from the same Newcastle shipyard that built the first *Scotia*, Armstrong, Whitworth and Co. The new *Scotia* was a bit larger than the first one and had a slightly greater railcar capacity. Both ships remained in use until the opening of the Canso Causeway and the ferry-based jobs were a mainstay of the Strait communities during that time.

As traffic on the Intercolonial increased, Mulgrave and Point Tupper grew into towns where life revolved around the railway and its ferries. In addition to the ferry crews, many other railway jobs appeared in the communities. Normally, locomotives were not carried across the Strait and both train crews and roundhouse employees were based in the two towns.

Main line traffic on the Intercolonial was supplemented by activity on the two independent lines at the Strait, the Inverness and Richmond running north to Inverness and the Cape Breton Railway running south and east to St. Peter's. By 1914, however, both were in financial trouble.

Railway Restructuring at a National Level and in Cape Breton

The financial problems faced by the independent lines at the Strait were far from unique. Railway construction had been in a boom period across Canada for two decades prior to the outbreak of war in 1914. Like all booms, it came to an end.

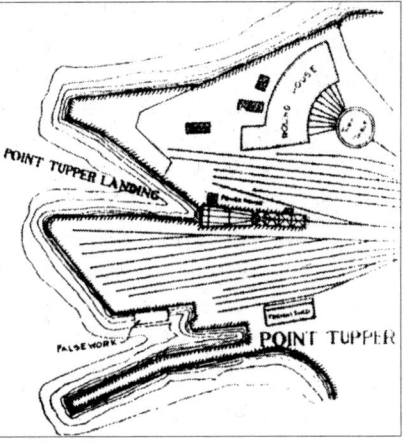

Fig. 5.13 - Though dating from 1931 and illustrating reorganization of the Point Tupper yard the previous year, this map illustrates the scope of the rail and ferry facilities at Point Tupper from the 1890s until the opening of the Canso Causeway in 1955.

Contract Record and Engineering Review, June 17, 1931.

Fig. 5.14 - An Inverness & Richmond passenger train at Inverness in the days before the passenger car was relegated to the end of a freight train. The photo was probably taken in the decade before 1914. I&R #s 4 and 5 were built for the new Inverness line by the Canadian Locomotive Company of Kingston, Ontario, in 1903. Both engines were scrapped in 1924 when the then-bankrupt line was leased by the newly-formed Canadian National Railway.

Reproduced by permission of Janice Ferguson, Inverness.

Mackenzie and Mann, the contractors who had gained control of the Inverness and Richmond in Cape Breton, had become involved in an infinitely more ambitious project. Between their arrival in Cape Breton in 1899 and 1914, they had created Canada's second almost-transcontinental railway, the Canadian Northern (CNoR), which stretched from Montreal to Vancouver.[11] Statistics from a 1919 federal report on the growth of the CNoR recorded an amazing period of growth. In 1899, Mackenzie and Mann companies were operating 407 km of track (253 miles). This expanded to 3109 km (1932 miles) in 1904, 7820 km (4859 miles) in 1909, and 11914 km in 1914 (7403 miles). Most of this was owned outright by the CNoR. A small proportion was found in other small companies like the Inverness and Richmond that were controlled by Mackenzie and Mann.[12] In almost all cases, the only external interests held in the lines were through ownership of bonds. There were, however, a lot of bonds outstanding on which interest had to be paid regularly.

During the same period, the Grand Trunk Railway, with financial backing from the federal government, extended its Quebec City-to-Winnipeg line eastward to Moncton, New Brunswick and west to Prince Rupert, British Columbia.

Despite the big increases in rail traffic produced by the war, the financial implications of a period of overbuilding caught up with these new railways. Starting in 1915, a series of administrative and operational changes came out of the financial wreckage that appeared along the tracks of the Canadian Northern and the Grand Trunk.[13]

The first of these mergers gathered together the Intercolonial, the Prince Edward Island Railway, which had been owned and operated by the federal government as a separate entity reporting to the same administration as the Intercolonial, plus the eastern section of the Grand Trunk system which had been called the National Transcontinental Railway. This group of lines was consolidated into the Canadian Government Railways. That name had been in use at an administrative level in Ottawa for decades. Recall the 1890 letter from Collingwood Schreiber, "General Manager of Canadian Government Railways," to Sir John A. Macdonald about the opening of the Grand Narrows bridge reproduced in chapter 3. In 1915, the CGR name was taken out of the administrative headquarters to appear in the public eye on timetables, tickets, railway stations, rolling stock, etc. The Intercolonial ceased to exist under its original name. Its motto, "The People's Railway," and its moose logo, or "herald" as logos were called in the world of railways, were replaced with signage proclaiming the new "Canadian Government Railways."

The next two mergers brought the Canadian Northern and the Grand Trunk Pacific, the western section of the Grand Trunk, into the government fold. Legal and financial work preceded the appearance of the new face of the consolidation in public, but by 1923 the process was completed with yet another name change. The CGR became the Canadian National Railways—the CNR. The restructuring of the big Canadian railways that operated over vast distances was duplicated on a small scale in Cape Breton.

From the time it was opened in 1901 until 1918, the railway to Inverness showed an operating profit. The accounts for the mines were less consistent, but losses recorded in the colliery accounts for some years were offset by profits in other years. This, however, was not the full financial picture. The bad news was in the non-operating accounts. The key components there were the annual interest payments, most of which went to the holders of the outstanding bonds. The limited detailed financial information available[14] shows that in an average year over the period 1907-1914, more than $60,000 in interest was payable every six months. Over those years, the company never earned enough to cover all the interest payable. The only conclusion that can be drawn is that additional funds were advanced during those years from some outside source, presumably from Mackenzie and Mann's other ventures.

When the first interest payments for 1915 came due on May 1, the cash crunch arrived. There were no funds available from the company's internal cash flow. Mackenzie and Mann had been unable to raise additional money from their other companies or their personal funds and their credit had been exhausted. The interest payments were not made and the company went into receivership. The losses had averaged nearly $100,000 per year and the cumulative loss on the books at the end of 1914 stood at over $1.1 million. The amount may not sound particularly large but when inflation is considered, it would be comparable to at least $20 million today

Both the railway and the mines continued to operate but they came under the direction of the Eastern Trust Company acting as receiver on behalf of the creditors. In 1924, Canadian National leased the rail line for $25,000 a year and outright purchase of the railway to Inverness was completed by the CNR in 1929 for $375,000. The money went to Eastern Trust for distribution to bondholders. The sale included the railway's rolling stock, seven locomotives and more than 150 cars, almost all of which were scrapped. The railway's core holdings of property were part of the deal but the Port Hastings coal wharf and the mines were excluded.

Fig. 5.15 - Inverness & Richmond bond interest coupons that were not honoured after the company was unable to make the interest payments due in May of 1915. The bondholder was left holding worthless promises to pay at future dates.

Inverness Miners' Museum.

William Calder's account of the impact of the Cape Breton Railway in chapter 4 began on a realistic note, "The Cape Breton Railway had its work spelled out. It had to make money."

Despite the initial optimism, that railway never made money either; though had it been built through to Louisbourg, the financial results would probably have been worse and sooner. Realistically, the results should not have surprised anyone. There was a very thin population to generate passenger traffic, few users of freight service, and, with only a few short-lived exceptions, the rail line did not stimulate the appearance of new industries. At the time of the

Webb-Meyer crash in 1902, the *New York Herald* had captured the essence of the problem that emerged. "Standing by itself," the *Herald* had said, "the road would seem to possess but little earning capacity."[15]

From the outset, expenses exceeded revenues. That pattern remained in place without any particular reason for anyone to expect a change and, before the end of its first decade, there were worries about what would happen to the CRB. There were other lines in the Maritimes in trouble and the federal government recognized that some of them might go bankrupt. In early 1909, a number of Intercolonial managers included St. Peter's in a series of stops to prepare a report on branch lines "that it is proposed should be taken over and made part of the Intercolonial Railway system."[16]

No takeovers took place as a result of the report, perhaps a result of the political change that took place in Ottawa in 1911. The new Conservative government under Robert Borden was less inclined than Laurier's administration to use public money to support railways, whether privately owned like the CBR and the I&R or publicly owned like the Intercolonial. That shift in policy had implications for the IRC that will appear in chapter 8.

By 1914, the CBR, like the I&R, was heading down the track toward bankruptcy. In comparison with the consolidated results for the rail and mining operations of the I&R Company, the annual operating losses on the CBR had been relatively small, never exceeding $20,000 a year. The fundamental problem, however, was in the pattern—the railway was never able to break even let alone make a profit. Over the period from 1914 to 1920, losses did decline as a percentage of revenue but they continued to increase in dollar totals. This more than offset the fact that between 1906 and 1920 passenger traffic had doubled and freight traffic had increased almost three-fold.[17] The following table records the level of operating expenses for each dollar of revenue and clearly illustrates the pattern that spelled the end of the CBR.

The New York owners were unable or unwilling to continue to cover the losses that, in dollar terms, had reached a cumulative total of $150,000 by 1919.[18] In 1920, the St. Peter's "stump of line," as George Stevens had described it, was sold to the federal government for $100,000. Upon purchase by Ottawa, it was added to the Canadian Government Railways system. In 1923, the CGR St. Peter's branch became part of the Canadian National system. William Calder provided an account of the day in 1920 when the CBR ceased to exist as an independent company.

Table 5.2 - Cape Breton Railway: Operating Expenses per Dollar of Operating Revenue, 1904-20									
	1904	1906	1908	1910	1912	1914	1916	1918	1920
$ Expenses	2.06	1.92	2.14	2.31	2.11	2.10	1.45	1.83	1.65

Sources: Provincial Engineer's Reports for 1904-1920 inclusive, *JHANS*, 1905 -1921, Appendix 7 or 7B in each volume. A 17-year table that records only every second year might distort a statistical trend, but that is not the case here. The average figure for the eight omitted years was $1.92 and the closest to a statistical error was $1.28 in 1919.

One Day in St. Peter's

J. William Calder

"Early in 1920 rumours trickled through the village; trickled, dried up and then started again. It is not known whether J. W. Doyle [the local CBR manager] was cognizant of what was actually afoot, or whether negotiations were being carried out solely with the New York syndicate. It is a fact that on the first day of July 1920 when the 'forlorn' little Cape Breton train clanged its bell and pulled away from the station in St. Peter's at 8:15 that morning, all the crew, all the sectionmen and the manager and the 'boy' were aware this was the last day for the Cape Breton Railway Company Ltd.; the orphan—'a bastard born' was to be adopted....

"It was just minutes past noon and most folks were at their dinner tables, when the special arrived. It was the same little engine with its two coaches that had left on schedule that morning, but coupled to the rear was the executive car from headquarters of the Atlantic Region of the Government System....

"J. W. Doyle was about to leave the office and go on board to welcome the officials, when a young man descended from the executive car and walked smartly to the office and entered. Mr. Doyle was about to offer his hand when he was interrupted. The young man smiled, introduced himself as secretary to Mr. Brown, superintendent of the Atlantic Region and said: 'Mr Brown sends his compliments. He wishes to inform you that some of his staff will be ready shortly to take inventory; and at that time it would please him to have you come aboard.'

"An offer was apparently made to Doyle to stay on as station agent at St. Peter's but he turned it down and moved to Halifax. The 'boy,' William Calder's brother Jamie, became the new agent, a post he would hold for 47 years."

Excerpted from Calder, 73–74. Reprinted by permission of Formac.

Railway Accidents and Wrecks

For a host of reasons, during the early days of railways, wrecks were common. Poor quality of track construction and maintenance were certainly factors. Lack of adequate employee training and supervision was another. Poor procedures for train control and the lack of signalling systems often led to collisions. While sweeping statements are risky, the risk of death or injury to either passengers or employees did decline at a fairly steady rate over the years and decades leading into the 20th century.[19] Despite that trend, however, risks did not disappear. This was particularly true for the men who ran the trains and especially for the brakemen. These men were often required to move back and forth on the train, often over the tops of moving cars, to handle brakes. They also looked after coupling and uncoupling cars and positioning track switches as cars were dropped or picked up.

To provide some examples, 1914 has been selected to provide examples without any attempt to establish if it was a good, bad, or average year as far as injuries and deaths were concerned. Accident data for the Intercolonial on Cape Breton records fourteen incidents.[20] One passenger was injured when he jumped from a moving train in Sydney. Ten employee injuries were reported.

The Dangers of the Steel Plant Railway

Lew Allan Davis

The following is excerpted from an interview with Lew Allan Davis who went to work at the Disco steel mill in 1909 at age 22. He began as a labourer and soon became a brakeman on the railway in the plant, a job he held until he retired in 1959. Davis had strong memories of the dangers of working on the railway. His observations are preceded by LED while interviewer questions are introduced by RC: Ron Caplan, the publisher of *Cape Breton's Magazine* and the interviewer.

LED: Those were all steam engines, burning coal. Things were so ancient. They used to have a lot of accidents.

RC: You hurt your hand....

LED: Caught between two cars. Cars were coupled up, you know, with link and pin. You had to put the link in and drop the pin, and sometimes you'd get caught—pinched. It was common. That was the original equipment over the old country. I lost 3 months for that hand. I got 5 dollars a week.

RC: From the company?

LED: No, from our benefit society—and if we hadn't a union, I'd have had nothing. But, oh, I've seen accidents there, terrible bad accidents. I know one fellow, he wasn't working on the railroad, but he was walking, crossing the track in the plant—and we were just after having lunch, and there were two engines there in that department. And this engine backed down and the man got out of the way. But he didn't see the next one coming—and it knocked him down—cut him right in two. But, oh, I've seen men there would be killed and never had a mark on them. Hit by the train but the way they fell, you wouldn't see any injuries. Or perhaps stumbled and fell. I knew a man there, when the train backed in, this brakeman wasn't there. So the conductor investigated, walked up the track a piece—there he was on the ground, dead.

RC: What happened?

LED: Goodness knows. In the early years there were a lot of accidents.... There was a man driving an engine. He had three heavy loads on it. And he was coming up this hill, and a train of coal coming down ran into him. Same track. The driver was killed.... The fireman, he was lucky, he jumped out....

RC: And wasn't there even a train, a shunter, known as the mankiller?

LED: Yes, # 125. And she had a screechy whistle. You heard it and it would go through you. And this engine had killed quite a few. I don't know why. It just happened that way. There was no reason for it, in a way. Nothing wrong with the engine. And nothing wrong with the man that was driving it. But that's the way. It had run people over. Man would be working on a track and this engine would come by and hit him.

RC: Considering the noise, aren't you surprised that people would get hit by trains?

LED: Yes, but that happens yet.[21]

Excerpted from "Lew Allan Davis & the Railroad," *Cape Breton's Magazine*, # 27, 1980: 10-12.

Four of those involved brakemen with all happening when cars were being coupled or uncoupled. Three injuries involved "others," people on tracks or trains who should not have been there. On Cape Breton, the IRC did not record any fatalities though the news from the mainland was not as positive. Thirty-five deaths were recorded between Halifax and Chaudiere near Quebec City; three passengers, twelve employees and twenty "others."

On the independent lines, sixteen incidents were reported, all but one on the S&L.[21] One passenger was injured as were twelve employees. As on the Intercolonial, injuries to brakemen were frequent and they were often received when cars were being coupled. Crushed or lost fingers were very often a brakeman's fate. Three reports involved "others," one injury and two fatalities. Both deaths were reported as "run over while trespassing," a description used to account for most of the twenty "others" killed on the Intercolonial's mainland track that year.

As improvements in railway technology and procedures increased, some of the risks faced by employees decreased. The Intercolonial usually led the way in introducing changes, primarily because it had more financial resources to do so than smaller lines in Cape Breton or elsewhere in the Maritimes. For example, air breaks, controlled by steam from the engines, had started to appear on the IRC in 1883. Reference has been made previously to the beginning of changes in coupler systems, developments which eventually made the work of brakemen much safer. Signalling systems appeared and improved and, again, the Intercolonial led the way in the region. Semaphore signals, manually controlled by station masters who received orders by telegraph or, twenty years later, by telephone, marked the first step. During the First World War, the IRC began to install electric "block signals" that communicated with each other and introduced telegraph-based dispatch systems issuing centralized orders to direct train movements.[22] These last two developments appeared on the busiest sections of the IRC line in 1914 though they were not introduced in Cape Breton until some years after the end of the war.

Sometimes factors from outside the railway contributed to accidents. One of the best known S&L photos shows a locomotive nose down in the waters of Mira Gut. The photo does not tell the whole story of either the location or the circumstances. The bridge had a "swing" section that could be rotated to permit vessels to pass through the narrow mouth of the Mira River. If the swing section was positioned for vessel traffic, the track on the adjacent section closest to Louisbourg led directly to air and then water, neither of which would carry a train in motion. There were no signals to provide warnings to train crews. The limited view of the bridge available to the engineer of an approaching train gave only minimal time to stop a train if that was necessary. These dangers were regarded as more theoretical than real since few of the vessels using the Gut passage needed to have the bridge rotated.

On the afternoon of April 14, 1903, however, the dangers became real. The bridge was opened to permit passage of the steamer *Alameda*. Before the steamer came through, another steamer appeared on the scene. S&L loco #62 was heading for Glace Bay from Louisbourg with a long train of empty coal cars. When he saw the position of the bridge, the only braking capacity avail-

Fig. 5.16
The Mira bridge wreck on the Sydney & Louisburg, 1903.

Sydney & Louisburg Railway Museum.

able to the engineer, James Parsons, was to throw the throttle into reverse and apply sand to the wheels. The engine was slowing down as it entered the first span of the bridge but the attempt to bring the train to a complete stop did not succeed. Fireman Charles Dickson was able to leap from the engine cab and grasp a bridge girder. Parsons went to the bottom of the Gut with the locomotive and was killed. The photo was taken during the final stage of retrieval of the engine. In hindsight, the wreck had another sombre element in addition to the death of Parsons. Harry Cann, one of the brakemen on Parsons's train, was killed some years later in a railway accident at Morien Junction.[23]

Fig. 5.17
The Glendyer wreck on the Inverness & Richmond, 1912.

Reproduced by permission of Janice Ferguson, Inverness.

Another well-documented wreck from this era occurred at Glendyer on the Inverness and Richmond line. For readers inclined to search for newspaper accounts, the date was July 11, 1912. The morning train left Inverness with half a dozen hoppers of coal, one box car, the baggage-mail car plus the coach. On a down grade about 24 km (15 miles) south of Inverness, engine # 79 left the rails and pulled the freight cars with it. The loco rolled down the slope visible in the photo. The engineer, William Campbell was killed. The fireman, Stephen Gillis, was badly scalded by steam, but did recover. Following a funeral in Inverness, a special I&R train carried Campbell's body to Port Hastings for burial. When the engine was repaired and put back into service, it was given a new number, something that often happened with locomotives involved in accidents leading to the death of enginemen.[24]

More Railways that Never Were

Chapter 4 introduced some railway projects at the Strait of Canso that did not get beyond the planning stage. Such dreams were not limited to the western side of the island. An early uncompleted project in the Sydney area was the Sydney and East Bay line. The first of several companies using this name was set up in 1873 under the leadership of Frederick Gisborne who had played a major role in establishing the narrow gauge Glasgow and Cape Breton. Other firms planning to build on this route would be incorporated in 1899, 1904 and 1911. The 1911 company also obtained rights to build eastward from Sydney to New Waterford to offer competition to the S&L.[25] No record has been found of any work actually being done on any of the versions of the Sydney and East Bay project.

In 1911, a Sydney group established a company with a very intriguing name, the Sydney, New Waterford and East Bay Monorail Company.[26] The idea of mononrail lines, using only a single rail, had been around from the very early 1800s[27] but without much practical success. The 1911 *Act* empowered the company to build two routes out of Sydney, one to New Waterford and a second to East Bay. The *Act*'s fine print included a very important word, "or," within the phrase "a line of railway or monorail." As a result, it is possible that the "monorail" in the company name was strictly for promotional reasons. It would, however, be interesting to discover the intentions of the Sydney promoters. Nothing has been found to suggest anything was ever done by this company regarding any of the activities authorized by the *Act* which had also included telephone and telegraph services, mining and operation of shipping wharves.

One other mining railway should be mentioned here even though it got a bit beyond the promotional stage. The Cape Breton Coal, Iron and Railway Company was established in 1895 to develop a coal property south of Glace Bay though no work was done for a decade.[28] In 1905 the firm was reorganized by a predominantly English group headed by Horace Mayhew, a retired army Colonel. Ambitious plans were prepared to develop a mine, build a railway and establish a new town for 10,000 people. Mayhew named the site Broughton after his estate in England. William Harris, a noted architect, was hired to prepare the town plan and design some key buildings. A mine was opened and a railway branch was built to connect the site with the S&L's main line.

Much effort went into planning the town but only about sixty buildings, including two hotels designed by Harris, were built. The venture soon proved a failure. The S&L refused to carry Broughton coal to a shipping wharf and the company did not have funds to construct its own railway and pier. In addition, there were legal problems with Dominion Coal over ownership of a critical piece of property. In early 1906, negotiations with Premier Murray for financial aid from the Province to help fund construction of a new railway failed to produce results. By the middle of that year, the Broughton dream was dead. Over the next decade, several attempts were made to revive the scheme and a $2 million bond issue was floated in 1912. The attempts did not succeed and the Mayhew mine closed for the last time in 1915. The stillborn site was used for a short period in 1916 as the headquarters for the 185th Battalion, Cape Breton Highlanders. When the Battalion went overseas, however, the Broughton site was abandoned.

In hindsight, the Broughton experience was interesting in two respects. At a theoretical level, Broughton was a unique Cape Breton example of serious town planning to prepare for development of new community—even though the community did not come to fruition as planned. In the real world, the fate of Broughton was a clear demonstration of the power that could be exercised by any company that dominated the coal and steel industries, at that particular moment the dominant firm being the Dominion Coal Company.

Two Maps for the 20th Century

The two maps that follow illustrate the core routes of Cape Breton's railways as they emerged between 1890 and 1914.

The map on page 109 captures the lines that were consolidated into the Canadian National Railway system and were operated by the CNR into the 1970s when the abandonment of routes began. Note that the main line from the Strait of Canso to Sydney as shown reflects the route changes made in the vicinity of North Sydney and Sydney Mines over the years 1906-1915. This route is as recorded in a 1954 timetable for passenger trains in Figure 6.17 and as operated in the post-CNR years by the Cape Breton and Central Nova Scotia Railway.

The map on page 110 captures the core routes of the 20th century railways in eastern Cape Breton operated by coal companies that evolved into the Dominion Steel and Coal Company (Dosco). The map records a number of the branches of the Sydney and Louisburg, but there were numerous smaller branches that are not shown. The process of abandoning branches started as soon as Dosco was taken over by the Cape Breton Development Corporation (Devco) and the map does not reflect the post-1968 Devco Railway.

Western / Central Cape Breton and the Evolution of the Canadian National Railway

Fig. 5.18

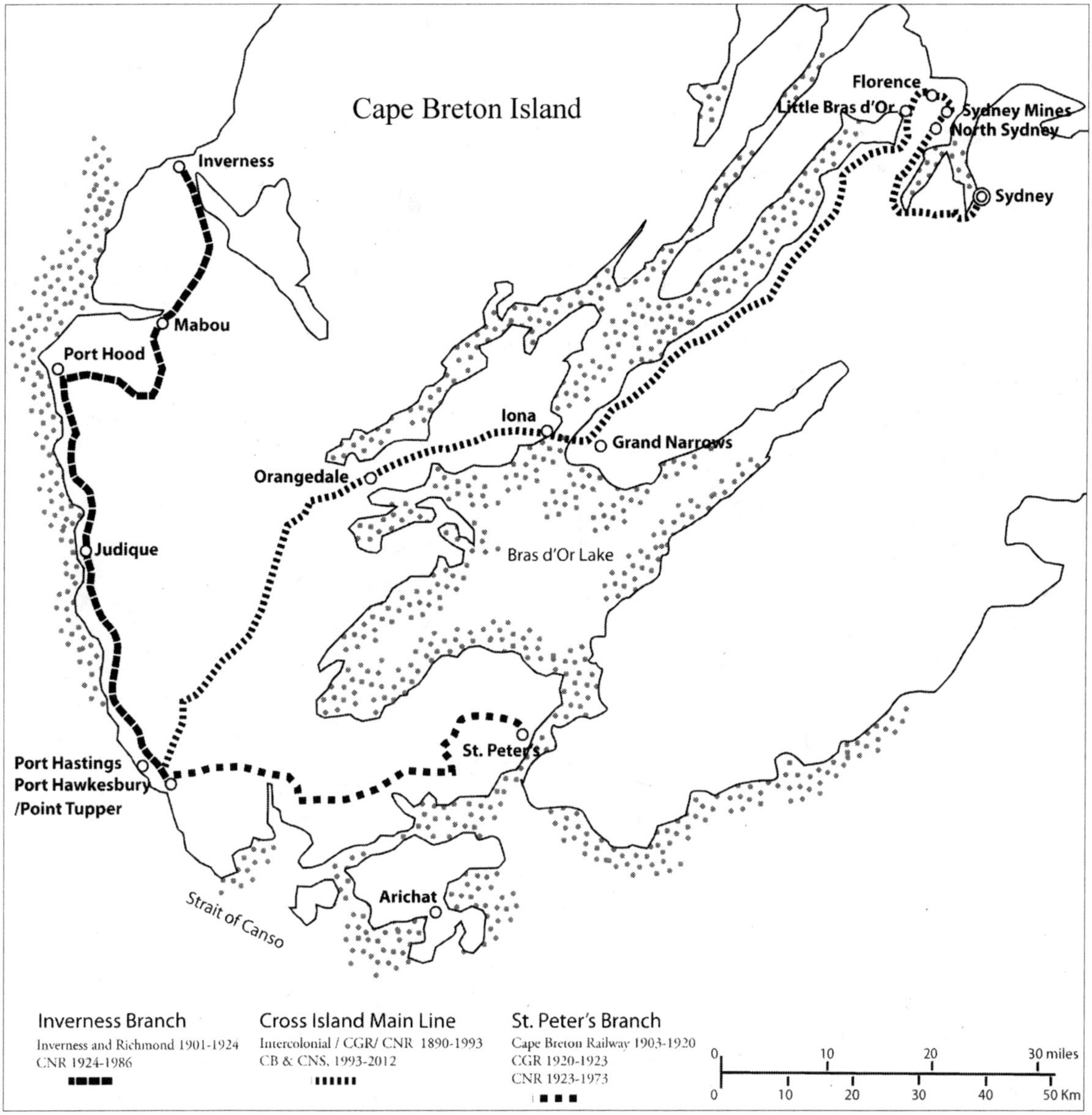

Twentieth-century Coal Railways in the Sydney Coal Field, 1890-1968

Fig. 5.19

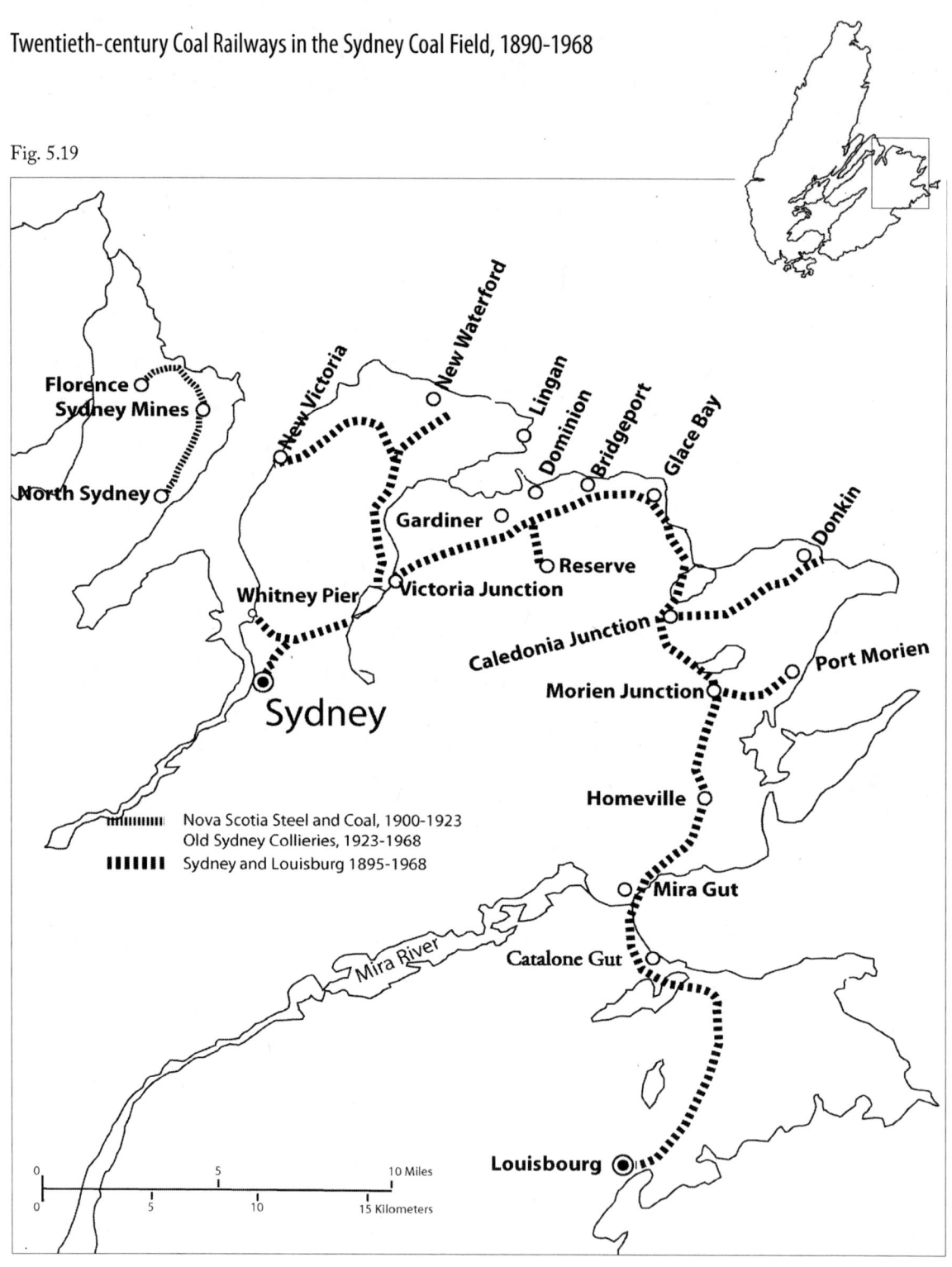

HERB MACDONALD 110

6 – Moving People

The S&L and its Predecessors

It appears that the International Company Railway, running between Sydney and Bridgeport on the outskirts of Glace Bay, was the first of Cape Breton's mining company lines to also carry passengers. The first annual report of the Provincial Engineer, found in the House of Assembly *Journals* for 1880, shows that the International line carried more than 1,200 passengers during its eight months of operation in 1879. The rapid growth in numbers over the next few years suggests that 1879 marked the introduction of service. That is speculation, however, and there may be evidence still to be found to show International passenger operations before 1879. It is also an assumption that the absence of a report on passengers on the narrow gauge Cape Breton Company Railway in 1879 indicates that the Sydney-Reserve-Schooner Pond-Louisbourg line did not start carrying passengers until the next year.

The table below indicates how quickly the passenger business grew for both railways starting in 1879-1880. Despite the trend shown by the data, there are numerous unanswered questions about these early passenger operations. Perhaps the most important involves the definition of a passenger. The primary role of these railways was to support the mines and it is likely that most of the "passengers" were miners and other company employees being carried to and from places of work and probably without charge. There are reports on passenger revenue but no way to determine how many of the people reported as riding the trains were "revenue passengers" as opposed to "deadheads," as free riders are often called in the world of transportation.

Fig. 6.1
Conductor Malcolm MacDonald of the S&L, at Glace Bay c.1950

Sydney & Louisburg Railway Museum, #SL-04-271.

Fig. 6.2 - Blacket's trestle, on the Cape Breton Company's Louisbourg branch. The source of the name is unknown. J. R. Blackett was cashier of Dominion Coal twenty years later. Perhaps he had been involved with the narrow gauge line but that is only a guess. The inclusion of Gray's name suggests the photo was taken during or soon after construction of the branch since Gray appears to have departed in 1878.

LAC, Sir Sandford Fleming Collection, negative #PA-027634.

No information has been found about train schedules or the equipment used to carry passengers in these early days. It is likely that, in the beginning at least, cars for passengers on both the International and G&CB lines were attached to coal trains.[1] This had been the model for Nova Scotia's first railway passenger service introduced on the GMA's Albion Railway in Pictou County in 1840.[2] It is also possible that Cape Breton's earliest "passenger cars" were little more than box cars refitted with windows and bench seating. The photo (figure 6.2) of a narrow gauge Fairlie Patent locomotive with several coal cars also shows a car with windows that may have started life as a freight car. It may have been put into service to carry construction workers building the Louisbourg branch. It may, however, also reflect the first cars used for general passenger service on both the G&CB and the International railway at the beginning of the 1880s.

Despite the absence of photographic or descriptive evidence, however, it seems safe to assume that the narrow gauge line had at least one respectable coach in service in the summer of 1880. Perhaps it was the car seen on Blacket's trestle. In August of that year, the Governor General, the Marquis of Lorne, paid a short visit to Cape Breton. He arrived at Louisbourg by ship and travelled to Sydney by rail for a reception and luncheon at the home of Senator Bourinot. We might wonder if Bourinot told Lorne about his involvement in organizing the Sydney railway meeting in 1851. After a short tour around Sydney, Lorne returned to Louisbourg, again travelling by train.[3] A photograph of the Governor General's train is one of those "missing" pictures that could add a great deal to our appreciation of the early days of Cape Breton's railways.

By the end of its life as a separate line in 1893, the International line was running at least some trains dedicated to passenger service with conventional passenger coaches, though it is uncertain when service reached this level. Figure 2.15 of the passenger train with the locomotive *H. M. Whitney* and two International cars shows those coaches were car numbers, # 2 and # 3. That suggests that International had at least one other coach that would have carried # 1.

Table 6.1 - International and Cape Breton Company Railways: Passenger Traffic, 1880-92

Year	International			Cape Breton		
	Passengers	# Months Operating	Monthly Average	Passengers	# Months Operating	Monthly Average
1880	3279	8	410	447	7	64
1882	9901	9	1100	4398	11	400
1884	8980	11	816	8620	12	718
1886	8029	10	803	4012	10	401
1888	6871	8	859	5884	10	588
1890	9556	10	956	6270	10	627
1892	17606	12	1467	4930	10	493

Annual Reports of the Provincial Engineer of Nova Scotia, *Journals of the House of Assembly*, 1881-93, Appendix 7 or 7B.

Variability in both the number of months of operations in a year, and in the later years in the number of reported passengers was a reflection of the health of the coal industry. Following the Dominion Coal takeover of these lines, passenger trains ran year-round, but the volatility in the number of passengers continued. Despite that, the growth in traffic shown in table 6.2 reflects the increase in activity in the mines, the establishment of the steel plant in Sydney in 1902 and the population growth on the south side of Sydney Harbour. As with the data in the first table, it is unknown how many of the Dominion Coal or S&L passengers were company employees. It seems likely that only a relatively low percentage of the "passengers" shown were fare-paying travelers.

The numbers for the S&L during the First World War mark the highest levels of recorded passenger traffic on this line. The totals during 1914-1920 would never be seen again though it is likely this reflected use of more accurate definitions of passengers in later years. Post-1920 traffic for all classes of passengers was certainly also affected by Cape Breton's slide into the two decades of depression that gripped the economy of the Maritimes until after the outbreak of the Second World War in 1939.

Table 6.2 - Dominion Coal Railway / S&L Passenger Traffic, 1894-1920

Years Ending	Passengers	Monthly Average
1894	37391	3116
1897	66233	5519
1900	71348	5946
1903	69570	5798
1906	49491	4125
1909	50542	4211
1912	120,135	10011
1913	142,052	11838
1914	176,166	14680
1916	160,294	13358
1918	160,395	13366
1920	172,833	14402

Annual Reports of the Provincial Engineer of Nova Scotia, *Journals of the House of Assembly*, 1895-1921, Appendix 7 or 7B.

The schedules for passenger service on the S&L appear to have changed relatively little over the years. There were morning trains daily except Sunday to Glace Bay from both Louisbourg and Whitney Pier. The train from Whitney Pier stopped at the main Sydney station en route. Return trips left Glace Bay in the afternoon or the early evening. In the early years, as indicated in the 1903 timetable below, these trains were "express"—dedicated to passenger service. During periods of economic depression, they were turned into "mixed

Fig. 6.3a and b (above) - The 1903 timetable shows all S&L passenger trains. The 1935 table does not include either the daily service on the Victoria branch to New Waterford or the Saturday service on the Port Morien and Number Six branches.

1903 timetable from *Daily Post*, Sydney, September 9, 1903: 8; 1935 timetable from Sydney & Louisburg Railway Museum collection.

Fig. 6.4a (above) - The S&L station at Glace Bay, c.1960

Sydney & Louisburg Railway Museum.

Fig. 6.4b (right) - This photo, probably c. 1950, provides another perspective on the S&L yard in Glace Bay as seen from upstairs in the station. Note the two cream cans on the platform.

LAC, Andrew Merrilees Collection, 1980-149, Group D, Subseries 1, Box #2000725251.

trains" that had passenger cars attached to freight or coal trains. The section from the 1935 timetable illustrates such a period.

Soon after 1903, service began between New Waterford and Victoria Junction to connect with the train running from Whitney Pier and Sydney to Glace Bay. The Victoria Junction connection accommodated travellers going from Sydney to New Waterford or from New Waterford to Glace Bay. In 1935, as in the last years of passenger service in the 1950s, these were mixed trains. Through most of the S&L's operating life, there was also Saturday service between Glace Bay and both Port Morien and "Number Six," modern-day Donkin. Trains running on Saturdays, when there was likely to be more paying passengers, were more likely to haul only passenger cars. This is reflected by the designation of the "express" status of the Port Morien and Number Six trains in the 1935 timetable.

Most of the S&L's passenger car roster was acquired before the end of the First World War. Six new coaches were built by Rhodes Curry and Co. of Amherst in the years before and after 1900. A second-hand coach arrived in 1911 followed by another two, also second-hand, in 1918. The only other addition was a car brought from Dosco's Cumberland Railway and Coal Company at Springhill in 1940.[4] A single "combination car" handled baggage

Fig. 6.7 - S&L # 22 with crew; photo probably taken c.1920. The engine was scrapped in 1925. The high smokestack in the background at left suggests a location near the S&L roundhouse at Glace Bay.

Sydney & Louisburg Railway Museum, #SL-96-1367.

Fig. 6.5 - A busy day at the S&L station at Mira Gut. The date is uncertain but the automobiles suggest mid-1920s. The crowd and length of the train suggest some special event may have been drawing passengers to Sydney though that interpretation is only a guess.

Sydney & Louisburg Railway Museum.

Fig. 6.6 - A non-so-busy S&L passenger train, probably in the 1950s. Passenger car # 4, built by Rhodes Curry of Amherst, has been preserved at the Canadian Railroad Historical Association museum at St. Constant, PQ.

Sydney & Louisburg Railway Museum, #SL-X93-558.

Fig. 6.8 (above left) A family excursion on the S&L in 1960, three years before the end of all passenger service on the line.

Sydney & Louisburg Railway Museum, #SL-00-461.

Fig. 6.9 (above right) The ticket cabinet at the Louisburg station.

Sydney & Louisburg Railway Museum.

Fig. 6.10 (right and p. 117)

S&L workers' coach # 116, new at Eastern Car Company at Trenton. This was the first in a set of ten "hobo" cars delivered to the S&L in 1923.

Dalhousie University Archives, Waldren Studios Collection, PC 2 / 298.2 and 298.4.

and express. It had started life as a box car that was rebuilt at the Glace Bay shops in 1928. Most of these cars survived until the S&L abandoned passenger service in 1963. Two of the coaches have survived, one at the S&L museum at Louisbourg and the other at the Canadian Railroad Historical Association Museum, Exporail, at St. Constant near Montreal.

In addition to the scheduled passenger trains, others known as "hobos" or "man trains" took miners to and from their shifts in the pits. These were several steps down on the comfort scale and originally used old box cars fitted with windows and wooden bench seating. In 1923, ten new "workers' coaches" were ordered from the Eastern Car Company in Trenton for use on the hobo trains though they did not offer much in the way of improved comfort. These cars, nos. 116-125, continued in use until the early 1950s. The hobo trains usually had right of way priority over all others, an indication of the importance attached to getting the miners to work on time. Not all of these trains were timed to shift-changes in the pits, however, and some could be used by people other than miners going to or from work. For many years, for example, a Saturday

night return run was made from Louisbourg to Glace Bay.[5]

Two interesting and unanswered questions about the hobo trains are why and exactly when they acquired the "hobo" name. The name appears to have emerged during the 1920s and was certainly a transfer of the term "hobo" that was given to "travellers" who often took free (and illegal) rides on trains. It is unknown if the hobo trains were given their name by those who travelled in them, by S&L employees, or by someone from outside the mining-railway community.

At the Strait of Canso

Fig. 6.10b - Interior of a "hobo" car.

The independent lines at the Strait provided year-round passenger service from the opening of their services to Inverness and St. Peter's. As in the Sydney area, growth in passenger traffic was rapid. The table below outlines the traffic volume at the Strait in the early years. For the period included, the I&R was part of the local coal company. As a result, it is likely that I&R numbers, like those in the two previous tables, are inflated by deadheads travelling to and from work at the mines at Inverness. In the case of the St. Peter's line, however, there is no doubt that most passengers recorded were paying customers.

Table 6.3 - Inverness and Richmond and Cape Breton Railway: Passenger Traffic, 1905-1919					
Year	I&R			CBR	
	Passengers	Monthly Average		Passengers	Monthly Average
1905	27479	2040		6850	571
1910	35196	2933		7332	611
1914	39703	3309		9415	785
1915	36129	3011		7901	659
1916	36232	3019		9443	786
1917	34076	2840		10394	866
1918	37527	3127		13230	1110
1919	39340	3278		14756	1230
Annual Reports of the Provincial Engineer of Nova Scotia, *Journals of the House of Assembly*, 1906-20, Appendix 7.					

Schedules on the Strait lines were quite similar from the beginning of

Fig. 6.11 (above) - The *Judique Flyer* at Inverness, ca. 1950.

Reproduced by permission of Buddy MacMaster, Judique

Fig. 6.12 (right) - Waiting for the *Flyer* at Judique, ca. 1910.

From the Windows on the Past Collection, the Storyteller's Gallery, Judique.

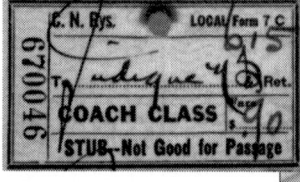

Fig. 6.13 - A stub, the passenger's receipt, for a CNR ticket to Judique ca. 1950.

Fig. 6.14 - Waiting for the *Flyer* at Port Hood. Built in the late 1920s, this was the second Port Hood station.

Both courtesy Chestico Museum & Historical Society, Port Hood.

independent operations through to the end of the CNR years. The Inverness railway saw one train a day in each direction with an early morning departure from Inverness reaching Port Hastings and Port Hawkesbury by mid-morning with a return trip arriving in Inverness around 7:00 pm. On the St. Peter's branch, there was a morning departure from St. Peter's and a return run arriving in St. Peter's in the early evening. As on the S&L, the composition of the trains to Inverness and St. Peter's changed over time. As a generalization, however, mixed trains were the norm on both lines, especially after 1920. The photo above of the *Judique Flyer*, as the Inverness train was commonly called, is probably a fairly typical view of what was offered to passengers on these two lines.

The 1919 I&R timetable called for the train from Inverness to Point Tupper to cover the 62 miles (100 km/h) in three hours and thirty-five minutes—a breathtaking speed of slightly more than 15 mph per hour (24 km/h). By the 1950s, thirty-five years later, improved service had cut twenty minutes off the running time. The St. Peter's branch offered an even more relaxed trip to passengers. In the 1950s, the afternoon train from Point Tupper to St. Peter's was scheduled to complete the 29 miles (47 km/h) in two hours and thirty-five minutes, a leisurely pace of 12 mph (19 km/h).

The Intercolonial and its Successors

The Stations of the Inverness and Richmond

By Allister MacBean

MacBean grew up in Inverness where his father served as station agent for the I&R and then the CNR over the period from 1902 to 1946.

"The stations were small, and the one building contained a waiting room, office and freight and baggage room. Inverness, Port Hood, Port Hastings, and Port Hawkesbury had in addition a freight storage shed. The stations were all alike except Mabou and Port Hood; these two were alike and slightly larger, and had two waiting rooms. All were heated by stoves, and in my day only the one at Inverness had electric lights. A telegraph line ran from Point Tupper to Inverness, with telegraph keys in the open stations (those with agents on regular duty), the general office, and the train despatcher's residence in Inverness. A telephone line also ran from Port Hastings to Inverness, and in addition to the open stations, was installed in several flag stations (stations without agents), Black River, Glendyer, Glencoe, and Creignish.

"By 1917 a larger office and waiting room were built on to the original station in Inverness, and the partitions in the original building were removed and it was used as a baggage room and express room. Part of this is still standing although it has been remodelled. All other station buildings have been removed....

"Including Inverness but excluding Point Tupper there were fourteen stations along the line. Seven of these were open or booking stations, and of the remaining, four had caretakers who showed up at train time, and the others were just a shed with a stove and were overseen by the sectionmen. Strathlorne, Mabou, Port Hood, Judique, and Port Hawkesbury were each staffed by one man, an agent-operator. At Port Hastings the agent also acted as coal sales agent; he was in change of the coal shipping piers, and would oversee the shipping of all cargoes. There was also a telegraph operator and at times a clerk. All Point Tupper station personnel were Intercolonial and later Canadian National employees."

Excerpted from MacBean, p.52-54. Reprinted by permission of Robert D. Tennant Jr.

> **General Specifications, Second Class or Smoking and Baggage Cars, Halifax and Cape Breton Railway and Coal Company, 1878**
>
> "Forty-five feet body, over platforms fifty-one feet. Miller platforms and couplers. Monitor or Deck roof with sash lights and ventilators. Frame of white oak, outside sheeting of narrow clear pine matched. Upper panel or Frieze boards of white wood. Enclosed passage way on one side of baggage compartment. Baggage compartment fitted with stove and lamp. Passenger compartment fitted with slatted reversible seats. Patent cast-iron ends. Hat-racks, stove, saloon, water-cooler, lamps, window shades, painted inside, oak-grained, with white or tinted roof. Full passenger car trucks with equalizing bars and elliptic springs. Smith's Vacuum brake, and all fittings complete including Royalty."
>
> *Journals of the House of Assembly of Nova Scotia*, 1879, Appendix 7, "Eastern Extension Railway," 46.

Fig. 6.15 - An Intercolonial express c.1910

Cape Breton Miners' Museum, Glace Bay, #6B1-A23.

Fig. 6.16 (p. 121, top) CNR express at North Sydney, c.1930

North Sydney Museum.

Serious attention to passenger service came to Cape Breton with the Intercolonial Railway in 1890. By then, the IRC was a mature line that had a mandate to move people and freight across eastern Canada. It had an obvious advantage in the form of the financial resources that came from the federal government's purse, that is from the taxpayers. The attention the Intercolonial paid to passenger service had been matched on the pre-IRC branch that had reached Mulgrave in 1880. At the time of its acquisition by the federal government for transfer to the IRC in 1884, the short-lived Halifax and Cape Breton Railway from New Glasgow to Mulgrave had sixteen cars for various classes of passenger service. To put this into some context, recall that the S&L operated a total of twenty-two passenger cars over the period 1899-1963. Only one photo has been found of the passenger cars used on the H&CB and none from the IRC's early days on Cape Breton. The 1878 H&CB car specifications, provided to the Nova Scotia government by Harry Abbott, and the photo of the H&CB train, figure 3.2, provide some sense of what passengers experienced when IRC service began on Cape Breton Island.

Data on passenger numbers in Cape Breton on the main line Intercolonial-CNR trains between Sydney and Halifax have not been found. Despite this, timetables tell many things about the service. One train a day ran in each direction between Sydney and Halifax from 1891 to 1900. This was expanded to two trains a day, with morning and evening departures between 1900 and the middle years of the Second World War. From 1900 to 1915, one of the two trains would make a diversion into North Sydney for transfers of Newfoundland ferry passengers. This limited service ended in 1915 with the relocation of the track and all passenger trains through Little Bras d'Or and Florence to Sydney Mines and North Sydney. Before the end of the Second World War, a second evening train was added to the schedule in each direction and the "three a day" model stayed in place until the 1960s. Unlike

Cape Breton's "local" passenger trains on the S&L and the lines at the Strait from their early years, the IRC-CNR "expresses" looked like main line passenger trains in the rest of the country. More than a dozen cars was the norm for the expresses, this included cars for baggage, mail and express, plus refrigerator cars.

Until the 1950s, morning departures had coach seating plus a "parlour car" for those willing to pay a premium for extra comfort. These cars included a small restaurant section offering full meals in contrast to what was available from the "newsie," the seller of sandwiches, snacks and newspapers to coach passengers. It appears that the Sydney-Halifax expresses never included full "dining car" service as found on trains like the *Ocean Limited* between Halifax and Montreal.[6] The evening trains did offer Pullman or "sleeping cars" in addition to coaches. One evening train in each direction also transferred at least one sleeper to and from the *Ocean* in Truro. Someone leaving Sydney in the evening could board a "sleeper" that would be added to the *Ocean* in Truro the next morning and arrive in Montreal twenty-four hours later. Sleeping car service remained in place until 1967 when the night expresses were replaced by the diesel-electric trains called "Railiners" that had been introduced on the daytime runs ten years earlier.

Though it is a poor substitute for data on the number of passengers moving on the IRC/CGR/CNR trains, there is some information about traffic

Fig. 6.17 - The CNR timetable for service to and from Cape Breton as at mid-1954.

Canadian National Railways, Timetable #D-190, April 25, 1954.

121   MOVING PEOPLE

in the late 1940s in the form of statistics on passenger cars being handled by the ferries at the Strait of Canso. It would be a leap of either faith or folly to try to estimate the number of people implied by the statistics. It does seem likely that the "passenger car" data excludes cars that carried mail, baggage and express. A second reasonable assumption is that the typical or average passenger car in use at this time would have carried about fifty people. However, there is no basis for making even estimates of the numbers of full and empty seats. As a result, attempted conversions of the data to passenger numbers would be wild guesses at best.

Table 6.4 - On the Strait Ferries: CNR Passenger Cars, 1946-1950				
	From Cape Breton	To Cape Breton	Total	Total Per Day
1946	7435	7497	14,943	41
1947	6970	6966	13,936	38
1948	7502	7509	15,011	41
1949	7824	7844	15,668	43
1950	7760	7769	15,529	43

Data source: Pierre Camu, "The Strait of Canso and Cape Breton Island," Geographical Bulletin, Canada Department of Mines and Technical Surveys, # 3, 1953, Table II: 56. The data were provided by the CNR.

Running-time over the 290 miles between Sydney and Halifax did not change much between 1900 and the late 1950s. In either direction, the trip took about twelve hours at an average speed of about 25 mph (40 km/hr). That speed was often blamed on the limitations of steam locomotives though this was not the explanation. In the 1950s, the engines that hauled the Sydney expresses at such a leisurely pace were capable of pulling the same loads at more than three

Fig. 6.18 - CN Railiner units after the transfer of CN passenger service to VIA Rail. This photo shows VIA train # 605 at North Sydney, September 1989.

Photo by Bill Linley, Port Lorne, NS. Reproduced by permission of Bill Linley and the Orangedale Railway Museum.

times the speed on the Sydney-Halifax route. All they needed was good track and license to exceed speed limits. Slow speeds on Cape Breton's main line were the result of two factors, the more significant of which was that the quality of the track that was never up to the standard of many other heavy traffic routes. Safety considerations imposed reduced speeds. A second factor was the frequency of station stops. For a significant part of their "running time," the expresses were preparing to stop, standing still or starting to build up speed after a stop.

The opening of the Canso Causeway in 1955 did not have a significant effect on rail travel time though technological change would shortly bring a marked improvement. The first "Railiners" went into service on daytime passenger trains shortly after the opening of the causeway. They reduced the Sydney-Halifax time to seven hours though with smaller passenger loads. Not recognized at the time, the gradual introduction of these trains marked the beginning of the demise of main line passenger service in Cape Breton.

Fig. 6.19 - The ticket window at the CNR station at Orangedale.

Author's photo with permission of Orangedale Railway Museum.

Travellers and Their Train Trips

Two of the images earlier in this chapter illustrated passenger tickets. Buying a ticket was of course the first step in a passenger's trip, whether the destination was only a short distance away or on the other side of the continent. In a few larger stations like Sydney, there were agents with specialized responsibility for the sale of passenger tickets. In most stations, however, agents handled tickets, freight, express and all the other tasks that might come through the station door or down the track. Orangedale in central Cape Breton was one such station. The museum now based at the station demonstrates several aspects of the passenger's initial relationship with a railway.

Fig. 6.20 - A CNR agent's pin from the 1930s.

Author's photo.

The ticket window, as it is now seen, was a counter where tickets were purchased. The notice displayed beside the window reminded passengers boarding trains at a station where tickets were sold that they were expected to buy their tickets before boarding. Those who boarded at very small stations where tickets were not sold could pay their fares on the train.

On the agent's side of the counter, there would be a cabinet of tickets, like the one at the Louisburg station seen earlier in the chapter. For short distances or frequent destinations, railways prepared small pre-printed tickets like those in the Louisburg ticket cabinet. For long trips involving changes of trains or travel on more than one railway, tickets were much more elaborate with multiple sections completed by the agent to meet the traveller's needs. The receipt stub from the ticket to Judique illustrates a section from this ticket format. Several photos in chapter 9 will illustrate the uniforms worn by train crews on passenger trains. As seen in the photos of

Martin Boston at the Orangedale museum in chapters 10 and 11, some agents also wore uniforms though this was not a consistent pattern. It was usually a reflection of the size and status of the station. In smaller stations, the agent's "uniform" was often limited to a small badge or pin.

Unlike the situation in many parts of Canada, railways did not play a very active role in the development of a tourist industry in Cape Breton that might benefit the island or attract railway passengers. On the Nova Scotia mainland before 1900, the Dominion Atlantic Railway had labelled itself "The Land of Evangeline Route" and used the story of Evangeline and the 1755 expulsion of the Acadians to market the Annapolis Valley, the railway and its hotels and steamships to a growing tourism market in New England. The Evangeline campaign was highly successful and kept in place until into the 1970s.[7] Before 1900, the Canadian Pacific Railway had started to tout the scenery of the Rockies and build CPR hotels which tourists could reach on CPR trains.[8] The same strategy was used after 1923 by Canadian National in competition with the CPR. Both national railway lines developed chains of hotels in major Canadian cities and also entered the steamship business. Best known to most Nova Scotians was Canadian National's "Lady Boat" fleet which sailed out of Halifax to the West Indies.[9]

The Intercolonial did make some attempts to promote tourism but most advertising campaigns focused on what the Maritimes offered to hunters and fishermen. Brochures and booklets published by the railway carried titles like "Moose in the Micmac Country" and "Forest, Stream and Seashore." Occasionally, the marketing pitch was specifically directed to attractions such as the beaches of the Maritimes, but these efforts were the exception rather than the rule. The CGR brochure featuring the Bras d'Or Lake district is one of the few examples found of tourism promotion that highlighted Cape Breton. Even though the island did not get much attention in railway advertising, Cape Breton destinations were included in special fare offers designed to attract summer travellers. For the summer season in 1910, for example, a special "round trip summer excursion fare" was offered, valid from the beginning of June to the end of October, from Montreal to Sydney for $33.00.[10]

In addition to regularly scheduled passenger service, until the 1950s it was not unusual for Canadian railways to run passenger trains for special occasions or to provide either a complete train or a locomotive for what might be described as a chartered train. Many such trains were seen in Cape Breton, especially in the period before the Second World War. Some specials served local needs or events. Allister MacBean's book on the I&R records "Dominion Day" picnic specials from Port Hawkesbury to Inverness. The Intercolonial ran specials out of Sydney for picnics in locations such as Iona.[11] The cover of Campbell and Johnston's book *Tracks Across the Landscape* features a photo of the special train to Louisbourg on June 17, 1895 for ceremonies to dedicate a monument commemorating the 1745 capture of the fortress by Pepperell's forces from Boston. That special also marked the opening of the new Louisbourg line. In future years, the S&L ran company specials for miners' picnics at Mira and provided service clubs and church organizations with specials for social and religious oc-

Fig. 6.21 (below left) - This illustration loses some of its impact in black and white. The original was the colour back cover of an elaborate IRC book promoting the railway's options for prospective tourists.

Intercolonial Railway, *An Intercolonial Outing: Along the Shores of the Lower St. Lawrence and the Provinces by the Sea*, n.d., [1893?].

Fig. 6.22 (below right) - Detail from the cover of a CGR promotion piece on Cape Breton, ca. 1919. The brochure had eight pages, many photos and a full colour map as a centerpiece.

Nova Scotia Archives and Records Management, #F / 108 / G54 / #6.

casions.[12] When the First World War ended, specials brought people to Sydney from surrounding towns for the victory parade and celebrations.

One of the most interesting types of passenger specials in Eastern Canada was the harvest excursion. In contrast to local specials, these trains ran most of the way across the country. Over four decades, from 1890 until the 1930s, the railways offered cheap fares on old cars to attract farm labourers from the Maritimes to Western Canada to work on the grain harvest. When the crops were in, harvester trains brought the workers home again. A. A. MacKenzie, for many years a member of the History Department at St. Francis Xavier University in Antigonish, offered an insightful look at these excursion trains and the Cape Bretoners who travelled on them.

At the beginning of this chapter attention was given to the numbers of miners who travelled as "non-revenue passengers" on the Sydney and Louisburg and the Inverness and Richmond. Across North America, trains were

---

Cape Bretoners on the Harvest Excursions
A. A. (Tony) MacKenzie, St. Francis Xavier University

"Organized in 1890 by government and railroad co-operation, harvest excursions existed to bring seasonal labourers to harvest the western crop of grain. Labour was scarce in the West. Easterners could buy excursion tickets to Winnipeg and points west of there at less than one half of the regular fare, returning home at slightly higher rates.... After a few years the excursions came to be invested with an aura of glamour and excitement.

"Born of this myth was the conviction that, of all the pugnacious, drunken and violent elements on the harvest trains, Cape Bretoners were by far the worst. In 1922 a North Sydney youth was dismayed to learn that men from his native island had been 'branded as wild men, savages, roughnecks since 1892.' Men from the different Cape Breton mining towns often fought among themselves till they reached the mainland. Then they 'stuck together like glue' and fought all 'foreigners.' In drunken glee they threw stove lids through coach windows, and 'put the rocks' to lineside buildings and section crews. In North Bay, where a train was forced to stop because of a hot box (an overheated wheel) in 1922, the Cape Bretoners ran amok, wrecking a pool parlour and assaulting people on the street. 'I played traffic cop for a while,' said a Sydney Mines youth, who appears to have entered thoroughly into the spirit of the thing; 'nobody got arrested ... what could the police do with 800 harvesters?'

"Lineside merchants, it must be said, invited trouble when they doubled or quadrupled the price of food and tobacco in anticipation of the harvesters' arrival. Hardly any trains carried dining or lunch cars (they charged very high prices anyway) and harvesters' supplies were often gone after three or four days on the train. Many harvesters carried little money. Often they borrowed from friends or relatives, peddled fish, or pawned a watch to raise the fare. Many of the Cape Bretoners were striking or laid-off miners and steelworkers, resentful of their treatment at the hands of Montreal and Toronto-controlled corporations. They believed in forceful action, individually or en masse, to avenge real or imagined wrongs. Cooped up on the rocking jolting train from five to seven days (Cape Bretoners were on the train longer than anyone else), pugnaciously proud of their island and their way of life, they pushed back—hard—if anyone tried to push them around.

"Leaving economics aside, the excursions were pre-eminently successful in creating a myth, a legend—the legend of the wild Cape Bretoners raising hell across the country, then buckling down to work like slaves in the furnace heat of the prairie. The excursions provided endless grist for the storytellers at firesides and in taverns. Only a few scattered magazine articles,[13] fewer scholarly works, and a stray thesis here and there have attempted to record and analyze their significance. The harvest excursions deserved better."

Excerpted from MacKenzie, "Cape Breton and the Western Harvest Excursions, 1890-1928," 71-74 and 83. Footnotes from the original have been omitted and one footnote, [13] added for this reprinting.

patronized by another variety of ticketless passengers, those who travelled without any form or approval or acceptance by the railway companies. Collectively known as hobos, these were travellers, almost always men without money to pay the fare but on the move, either looking for work or avoiding it. In the years before the option of hitchhiking on the highways, an illegal ride on a freight train was a possibility for a hobo willing to accept the risks involved. Riding the freights was particularly common during the two decades of widespread depression between 1919 and 1939.

Hoboing Days

Interview With Peter Willy Murphy, New Waterford

"Before she'd pull out, you'd go like hell down the track ahead of the train and you'd pick a good spot so you could land it. Your best bet was on the outside of a bend. You'd get on the outside of the bend because the engine would be gone down here and the back of the train would be there, so the couplings would be all at their best width—be all wide on the outside. Where on the inside of the bend the engineer could look back and see you—fellow on the caboose could look down and see you—you had no chance to run at the train. Then you'd get good at it. You'd make a jump or a leap for the rungs either on the box car or baggage, I never rode rods. I've seen fellows do it but I can't do it, I never picked up the courage to do it.

"For hoboing you wear high gloves, very high gloves, strong gloves. For jumping and scuffing in the ashes, see. See, you'd jump, you wouldn't always land on your feet. Maybe you'd go like that, that far for cripe's sake, and you'd be skinned, practically to there. You see, the firemen on the tenders weren't bad, the engineers on it, but you had to watch out for the conductor, the train police, and the trainmen.

"I got kicked off one time in Orangedale, On an early morning train, I saw the shadow coming behind me, and I was peeping out the baggage and Lord, before I knew it, I got the boot right in the tail bone, boy, and Whoosh! He kicked me good and hard so I wouldn't fall under the wheels. And Lord, I went out into space. Well, I laid there for pretty near half a day dazed, I couldn't move—paralyzed me."

Excerpt from interview by Elizabeth Beaton; *Cape Breton's Magazine*, # 15, 1976: inside front cover.

Railways in the Streets in Eastern Cape Breton, 1902-1947

Toward the end of the 19th century, there was a boom across North America in the construction of a different type of railway. A by-product of the appearance of cheap electricity in cities and large towns, electric-powered "street railways" or "tramcars" marked an important step toward the end of the age of the horse and buggy. The first street railways appeared in major metropolitan centres like New York, Boston and Toronto. In the late 1880s, H. M. Whitney, who later would lead the organization of the Dominion Coal Company, was heavily involved in street railways in the Boston area.[14] Over the next decade, the new technology spread rapidly and street railways appeared in smaller cities and large towns. In Nova Scotia, the first companies were established in Yarmouth in 1892 and Halifax in 1895.[15] Just after the turn of the century, street railways appeared in Cape Breton. The Cape Breton lines were typical of the technology. The cars ran on lightweight railway tracks set in the streets and drew electric power from overhead cable systems.

To be financially viable, street railways required a significant population concentration in a relatively small area. The coal and steel communities in eastern Cape Breton provided such a population density. The first line opened in 1902 was the Sydney and Glace Bay Railway, a subsidiary of the Cape Breton Electric Company (CBE) which provided electric power in the area. The line was 34 km (21 miles) in length from Sydney through Reserve to Glace Bay with a return loop north and east of Glace Bay back to Reserve. A map of the line looked like a figure "6" tilted 90 degrees to the left. Much of the line running east from Sydney was built along the roadbed that had carried the Glasgow and Cape Breton Railway and its narrow gauge successors. In exchange for property belonging to the Dominion Coal Company, CBE gave the coal company a 50 per cent interest in the street railway. At the opening, when nine cars were operating, running time from Sydney to Glace Bay was 40 minutes. Using the 1903 schedule as an example, cars ran hourly from 6.00 a.m. to 11:00 p.m. from Sydney and 7:00 a.m. to midnight from Glace Bay. An additional morning express car from Glace Bay was scheduled to connect with the Intercolonial express that left Sydney at 7:30 a.m.[16]

In 1903, CBE opened a second line, 10 km (6 miles) in length from North Sydney to Sydney Mines. The North Sydney and Sydney terminals were both near wharves and to connect the two branches, CBE operated a ferry service with departures every two hours. In 1911, the separate companies were consolidated into the CBE firm with Dominion Coal receiving CBE shares in exchange for its holding in the Sydney and Glace Bay line.

The street railway system in its various forms was owned by an American company, Stone and Webster, which operated electric utilities and street railways across North America. No reference has been found to any connections between Whitney's railway interests in Boston and the Stone and Webster firm, so it may be a coincidence that the CBE street railways appeared at a time when Whitney still had a role, though a reduced one, in the Sydney economy.[17] While Whitney was still on the boards of both the coal and steel companies, by this time control of both firms had shifted to a Montreal-based group led by James Ross.[18]

The real question about Whitney and the Sydney area street railways is why he did not take the lead in introducing a system in the 1890s when Dominion Coal was emerging as the dominant force in the local economy. That question seems all the more pertinent since Whitney and David MacKeen, then the resident manager of Dominion Coal, were both involved in 1895 with Benjamin Pearson, another Dominion Coal board member, in the establishment of a company that consolidated the street railway and the supply of electricity in Halifax.

CBE operated the street railways as a side venture until the entire company went bankrupt in 1931 in the wake of the depression that had so ravaged Cape Breton. The new owners of the power-production side of the firm wanted to abandon the streetcar system, but the Sydney-Glace Bay service was rescued by the employees who put together a company called Cape Breton Tramways. The goal was to keep the cars running and protect jobs until another buyer could be found. Projected as a short-run venture, the employee-owned company operated the lines for sixteen years.[19] One of the results of the revival of the economy during the war years was the increase in the ownership of automobiles and the appearance of competition from buses. A sharp decline in streetcar traffic in 1945-1946 was interpreted as a sign of changes to come. The company was sold to a local bus company in early 1947 and streetcar operations ended in May of that year. Cape Breton Tramways is a fascinating example of a successful employee response to absentee owners preparing to abandon a company, a situation that has appeared all too frequently in Cape Breton's history.

Fig. 6.23 - Sydney and Glace Bay tramcars at the junction at Reserve.

[ca.1906]. Photographer unknown. 77-1181-1315, Beaton Institute, Cape Breton University.

7 – Coal, Steel and Cape Breton's Railways

The importance of coal and steel to Cape Breton's economy in the 20th century, and the relationships between those industries and the railways, call for consideration of the linkages at work. It should be noted, however, that a review of such complex subjects over the span of many decades and in wider contexts, all within a few pages, is an exercise akin to visiting a large coal mine or steel plant for an hour or two: such a visit would generate some general impressions, but many things would not be seen or understood. And many of the things seen might not be understood in the contexts of the mine or plant setting, the industry or the community or region. It must also be noted that what follows has been shaped by the resources available. A recurring challenge has been unavailability of documents or detailed sources that could permit a thorough understanding of some of the linkages that existed.

Two key trends emerged well before 1900 that would shape the economy of eastern Cape Breton for most of the 20th century.[1] The American market for Cape Breton coal had vanished in the 1860s after the non-renewal of the Reciprocity Treaty and the end of the American Civil War. There was the hope that H. M. Whitney's consolidation of most of eastern Cape Breton's mines in 1893 would lead to a revival of sales to the United States, but that did not happen. Coal output did increase dramatically after 1893 but most of the rising output went in two other directions. One was to markets along the St. Lawrence River, particularly to Montreal. The second was to a local market that appeared when Cape Breton's steel industry was established just after the turn of the century. That market was complemented by household and industrial purchases of coal. Those, however, did not appear to account for a major proportion of coal sales until the 1970s when coal sales to power plants became more important as output from the mines declined.

A second important trend arrived with Whitney—that of corporate consolidation. The mines and the steel plants would be the subject of ongoing attempts by groups of financiers, most of whom were from outside the province, to bring all the companies under their control. Decades of complex evolution took place with profound implications for the people of Cape Breton

Fig. 7.1 - This drawing shows the Scotia company steel mill at Sydney Mines. It is uncertain if the drawing was done while the mill was under construction or after its 1904 completion. Regardless of the drawing's date, the three-car passenger train in the foreground must be attributed to artistic license. The Scotia railway did not run passenger service. The Intercolonial's main line did not come that close to the steel plant and IRC passenger trains would have been much longer than the three-car train in the drawing.

Sydney Mines Heritage Museum

Fig. 7.2 - The *Harvey Graham* was built for the Scotia company in 1908 by Andrew Barclay & Sons of Kilmarnock, Scotland, and used at the Sydney Mines steel mill. The crane was named after one of the Pictou County founders of the company that evolved into the Scotia firm.

LAC, Andrew Merrilees Collection, negative PA-208780.

and the island's railways. This evolution began with three anchor companies: the two Whitney firms, Dominion Coal (Domco) and Dominion Iron and Steel (Disco) established in the 1890s, and Nova Scotia Steel and Coal (Scotia), which had purchased the General Mining Association's Cape Breton properties in 1900.

Shortly after 1900, Whitney's role was taken over by James Ross[2] of Montreal who, with his associates, gained control of both Domco and Disco. The steel company soon passed into the hands of a group of investors from Toronto headed by James Henry Plummer along with William Van Horne (of CPR fame) of Montreal. After a prolonged struggle,[3] the Ross group at Domco was bought out and the two companies were merged into the Dominion Steel Company. The Sydney and Louisburg Railway became a separate company as part of this 1910 reorganization, though ownership of the railway was entirely in the hands of the new parent steel company. Dominion Coal became another division of the parent firm.

On the north side of Sydney Harbour, control of Scotia passed into hands of Halifax financiers. That transition had started when John F. Stairs of Halifax became President in 1901 in conjunction with the financing of Scotia's new steel mill at Sydney Mines. The shift in control from Pictou County to Halifax was taken one stage further[4] during the First World War when control of Scotia was acquired by American investors.[5]

In 1921, a comprehensive consolidation of coal and steel took place. Dominion Steel and Scotia merged to create the British Empire Steel Corporation (Besco) headed by another Montreal financier, Roy Wolvin, whose financial base was Canada Steamship Lines plus other shipping and shipbuilding firms.[6] This merger brought the Scotia railway under the same ownership as the S&L. The northside companies including the railway were operated under the name Old Sydney Collieries (OSC) while the S&L kept its name and remained a separate company owned by Besco.

The history of the coal and steel communities of eastern Cape Breton, especially for the period between 1900 and the 1930s, has been well documented. Studies have tended to focus on the legacy of concentrated corporate power—the decades of stormy relations between miners and steelworkers and the companies they worked for. Closely related were the struggles between competing miners' unions and the political results of the general pattern of support given to the companies by governments in both Halifax and Ottawa.[7]

Two reflections of that period from the Besco years capture the time, place and conditions. From a narrative poem originally published in Glace Bay in 1926, a short excerpt indicates the workers' disdain for Roy Wolvin, the Besco President. Lawren Harris' drawing, "Glace Bay," appeared in 1925 in the midst of one of the longest and most bitter of the miners' strikes.

Roy the Wolf
by Dawn Fraser

"Now, of all the bosses that e'er were cursed,
Roy the Wolf was called the worst,
He was the leading parasite
That fed on the workers day and night;
Greedy, growling wolf for more,
He stole the bread from the workers' door,
Grew fat on starving children's cries
And filled the papers with foolish lies—
That his company couldn't afford to pay—
Yet he got three hundred dollars a day
For doing nothing but looking wise,
Starving kids and telling lies;
Thus he promoted the capitalist game
'Til babies were taught to curse his name,
And Roy the Wolf and his thieving band
Spread distress throughout the land."

The except from "The Case of Jim McLachlan," is from a reprint of Dawn Fraser's *Echoes From Labor's Wars*, Wreck Cove, Breton Books, 1992. The Harris drawing, originally published in *Canadian Forum*, vol. 5, no. 58, July, 1925: 303, is reproduced courtesy of the Lawren Stewart Harris Estate.

The title of the narrative poem, from which the portrait of Roy Wolvin is taken, points to J. B. McLachlan, a labour leader who was a towering figure in Cape Breton in his day. David Frank's book, *J. B. McLachlan: A Biography*, is too important to bury in a footnote. It is, in this author's opinion, the most important book on any aspect of the history of Cape Breton in the 20th century and a must-read.

An extended financial crisis led to the 1928 reorganization of Besco into the Dominion Steel and Coal Company (Dosco), a name that continued until 1968. Under Dosco, the S&L and OSC names were retained for the railways.[8]

From Cape Breton and Nova Scotia perspectives, the last in this series of the struggles for control of the coal and steel companies also merits brief mention. After 1928, control of Dosco remained in Montreal and Toronto. Over much of the post-1928 period, the key directors had close connections to the Royal Bank of Canada and Wood Gundy and Co., a leading investment dealer. In 1957, in the wake of the death of Lionel "Laddie" Forsyth, the first and only Maritime-born Dosco President, overtures to take over the company came from A. V. Roe (Avro), an emerging Toronto-based aircraft manufacturer controlled by the Hawker Siddeley group in England. Some sources suggest that the impetus for the takeover came from within the Dosco board. One Nova Scotia director, Roy Joudrey of Hansport, NS, strongly opposed the takeover and led a prolonged struggle that captured newspaper headlines for months during the summer and autumn of 1957.[9]

In the end, however, the takeover went ahead and Dosco came under the control of the company that was about to launch the *Avro Arrow*, a sophisticated new supersonic jet fighter aircraft. In early 1959, the *Arrow* program was killed by a government decision made in Ottawa. Nearly 15,000 employees at factories in and around Toronto were fired[10] and the *Arrow*s that had been completed were cut up. The fates of the *Arrow* project and the Avro employees were indicators of what was to come for Dosco.

During the Second World War years and after, Dosco had been the largest private sector employer in Nova Scotia and one of the largest companies in Canada. Nova Scotia operations included virtually all coal mines on both Cape Breton and the mainland, the Sydney steel plant, other large firms such as the Eastern Car Co. in Trenton, Pictou County, and the Halifax shipyards. From 1940 into the mid-1950s, the Dosco workforce in the province averaged around 15,000.

But what of the railway connections? Having reached the 1950s with this summary of the coal and steel industries, it is time to go back in time to consider the railways.

From the beginning of the 20th century, railway freight traffic on Cape Breton had been dominated by the movement of coal and steel. In terms of weight or volume, most coal was handled by the S&L and Scotia/OSC railways. Until the Second World War, most shipments were short hauls from the mines to the shipping wharves or the steel plants, sometimes with interim stops at wash plants such as the one near Port Morien captured in a photo from the 1890s. The "steel plants" became a single destination in 1921 when the Scotia mill at Sydney Mines was closed as part of the Besco consolida-

Dominion Coal Co.   Coal Washing Plant near Port Morien, Cape Breton.

Fig. 7.4 (above top) - Dominion Coal's wash plant near Port Morien, ca. 1897. At facilities like this, coal was washed and screened to remove rock content before it was taken to shipping piers or, in later years, to the steel plant.

Bell, 15.

Fig. 7.5 (above bottom) - Dominion Coal's shipping wharf at Louisbourg built when the standard gauge S&L was completed to Louisbourg in 1895. It replaced the earlier wharf on the opposite side of Louisbourg harbour, built to handle coal shipments on the narrow gauge railway branch from Reserve. This photo was probably taken soon before the wharf was abandoned in 1962.

Sydney and Louisburg Railway Museum, # SL-00-935.

tion. Most coal that left Cape Breton went by sea, from the main shipping wharf in the Whitney Pier district of Sydney which had been the site of the original International Company wharf illustrated in chapter 2. The wharves at North Sydney and Louisbourg remained important coal shipping ports, but Glace Bay's role as a coal port came to an end soon after the Whitney consolidation of the companies in 1893.

The rolling stock rosters of the S&L and Scotia/OSC lines always reflected their focus on coal traffic. In the 1950s, when coal production was at its post-1920 peak, the S&L had more than 1,000 coal cars in service, mostly "hoppers" like # 4203 (figure 7.8), and was handling in the range of four million t per year.

After the Besco merger, S&L and OSC trains obtained "running rights" on CNR track to transport coal between the north and south sides of Sydney harbour. It became common to see cars belonging to one of the lines on the other's track. Actual operation of coal company trains over the CNR between North Sydney and Sydney appears to have been carried out by CNR crews—perhaps to ensure that train operations were in the hands of crews completely familiar with the rules on Canadian National track.

Coal traffic reflected the "boom and bust" cycles of the mines generating the traffic. When things were busy, they were very busy. But in slack times, such as during the extended downturn in the Cape Breton economy between the two world wars, both railways were hard pressed to cover the costs of maintaining their infrastructure.

The traffic volatility and resulting pressures applied equally to the Intercolonial and its successors. During the years of both wars, the main line

Fig. 7.6 (top) - The S&L doing its job – c.1950. The presence of the single box car in the photo is probably statistically appropriate. The S&L had relatively little use for box cars and had few of them. For example, during the period 1940-41, the railway ordered 350 new 50-ton coal hoppers and 15 box cars.

Sydney and Louisburg Railway Museum, #SL-96-1118(1).

Fig. 7.7 (right) - Old Sydney Colleries # 25 at work at Sydney Mines, June 23, 1952. This photo was originally published in the Canadian Railroad Historical Association journal, *Canadian Rail*, # 525, July-August, 2008. See chapter 11 for a 2011 photo of #25 in retirement at the CRHA museum at St. Constant, Quebec.

Photo by Ronald Ritchie, Hudson, Quebec; reprinted by permission of Mr. Ritchie.

Fig. 7.8 - # 4203 was one of an order of 100 cars (#s 4200-4299) built by the Eastern Car Company in Trenton in 1951. These 60-t cars were the last hoppers acquired by the S&L.

Sydney and Louisburg Railway Museum, #SL-96-1098.

Fig. 7.9 - # 1000 was one of an order of 60-t hopper cars built by Eastern Car in 1946 for Old Sydney Collieries.

Dalhousie University Archives, Waldren Studios Collection, PC 2 / 350.24.

between Sydney and the mainland was frequently being used to capacity. The Strait of Canso rail ferries were often in continuous service for days or weeks at a stretch. This situation was sometimes intensified by special circumstances. For example, in 1942, when the regular flow of water-borne coal shipments to St. Lawrence River ports was curtailed by the successes of German U-boats in the Gulf of St. Lawrence,[11] the CNR experienced a surge in long-haul coal traffic from Cape Breton's mines to destinations in Quebec.

The 1950s was a second period with a significant boom in coal shipments to Quebec by rail. The following table provides an overview of the railway's role in handling Cape Breton coal during twelve years close to the end of the era when "coal was king." The trend appearing in the years after 1951 was influenced by several events within Dosco operations on the mainland. Starting in 1951, coal from Cape Breton mines accounted for increasingly larger shares of total Dosco coal sales. In Pictou County, the Allan shaft, the most important mine in Stellarton, was lost to fire in 1951 and the MacGregor mine, where nineteen men had died in 1952, was abandoned in 1957. The table also reflects the loss of Springhill's No. 4 mine with thirty-nine lives in 1956. Those events would shortly be followed by the second Springhill disaster, the 1958 "bump" in No. 2 mine that killed seventy-four men and ended mining in the Cumberland County town.

Table 7.1 - Dominion Coal Company Shipments From Cape Breton, 1946-1957						
Two-year Period	By Rail to Maritime Destinations (000 t)	By Rail to Quebec Destinations (000 t)	Total Rail Shipments (000 t)	Total Shipments By Sea (000 t)	Total All Shipments (000 t)	Percent of Total Shipped By Rail
1946-47	1326.0	136.2	1462.2	2095.2	3537.4	41.3
1948-49	1559.7	535.3	2095.0	4342.5	6437.5	32.5
1950-51	1524.4	719.2	2243.6	3708.8	5952.4	37.7
1952-53	1286.1	471.3	1757.4	3540.8	5298.2	33.2
1954-55	960.8	788.7	1749.5	4293.6	6043.1	28.9
1956-57	1271.2	1383.1	2654.3	3426.6	7080.9	37.5
Data source: Dominion Coal Company, "Submission to the Royal Commission on Coal," 1960, Appendices 16 and 19.						

From a rail-based perspective, the table illustrates something of particular interest: the increasing level of long-haul traffic into Quebec. The final two-year period shown is the first when rail shipments to destinations beyond the Maritime provinces exceeded shipments within the Maritimes. The tonnage for that period, the two years immediately after the opening of the Canso Causeway, converts to about 180 cars of coal a day (assuming an average carload of 40 t), seven days a week, moving westward across the causeway.

There were a number of factors at work that do not appear in this table, all of which were mentioned in the Dominion Coal submission to the Rand Royal Commission. Cape Breton coal was becoming more expensive to mine as mines went ever deeper and, in many cases, farther out under the ocean floor. For decades, it had been recognized that Cape Breton mines required modernization and mechanization. Improvements came slowly lagging developments in the mines of large American coal producers. When investments were made in Cape Breton's mines, they were generally too small and too late.[12]

Beginning with John A. Macdonald's "National Policy," import duties were charged on American coal coming into Canada. They did not, however, prevent imported American coal from dominating the Ontario market by the 1890s and challenging Nova Scotia producers for the Quebec market by the 1920s.[13]

Starting in the 1920s, federal shipping subsidies and railway freight rate reductions were introduced to offset some of the costs of shipping coal with a primary goal being to increase sales of Nova Scotia coal in central Canada. These subsidies certainly assisted the industry. As an illustration, over the period 1928-1944, approximately 25 per cent of Nova Scotia's coal output was shipped under some form of transport subsidy.[14] The subsidies were also consistent sources of political controversy. They were traditionally seen in Nova Scotia as inadequate gestures that did not meet the needs of the industry. In central Canada, they were often regarded as inappropriate government interventions in the marketplace or a wasteful handout to an uncompetitive region.

By the 1950s, the most important development was the onset of decline in the overall market for coal. Both industries and households in central and eastern Canada were converting from coal to oil which, in the short run, appeared to offer lower energy costs and security of supply.

One of the most relevant examples of that trend appeared on Canadian railways in the 1950s. For close to a century, those railways had themselves been an important market for coal. The Dominion Coal submission to the Royal Commission noted that the total purchase of coal by all Canadian railways had decreased from 12.4 million t in 1948 to only 1.4 million t in 1958. "This market," the company recognized, "is continually decreasing and holds little hope for the future."[15] Within a few months of Dominion's presenta-

Fig. 7.10 - S&L # 210 at # 26 Colliery in Glace Bay in the 1960s, soon after the S&L abandoned its steam locomotives. The engine, built in 1950 by Alco, the American Locomotive Company, was one of a set of four similar engines acquired second-hand from the Wisconsin Central Railway in 1961. It ran on the S&L and then the Devco Railway until it was scrapped in 1982.

Photo by Robert Durning, Dartmouth, NS; reprinted by permission of Mr. Durning.

tion to the Rand Commission, the S&L joined the trend and acquired its first diesel engine. A bit more than a year later, the coal company's main railway abandoned coal-fired locomotives and the S&L became an all-diesel railway. The photo at # 26 Colliery in the early 1960s is a perfect illustration of the transitions taking place, initially on the railways and soon to be followed in the production side of the coal industry.

In 1966, Dosco announced it would abandon its remaining Cape Breton mines.[16] The next year, they were taken over by the federal government's Cape Breton Development Corporation (Devco). The Devco mandate was to operate some mines, but phase out all coal production by 1981. Within that period Devco was to promote development of new industries to provide employment prospects for the future.[17] Devco represented a new, more direct approach to the subsidization which, through tariff and freight rate policies, had been supposed to support the coal industry for decades. The end of Devco coal production did not come until long after the original target date of 1981. Some mines struggled on for another two decades supported by what was left of the S&L which had been renamed the Devco Railway. In 2001, the federal government announced that Devco was to be wound up. The last mine was shut and disposal of other assets began. Most of the surviving pieces of the Devco Railway were abandoned at this time.

The Railway Market for Cape Breton Coal

The importance of railways as customers for Cape Breton's coal producers merits examination to the extent that it can be done. The S&L and Scotia/OSC lines, owned by companies that also operated the mines, used local coal. But with never more than fifty locomotives in service at any one time and only relatively short routes in service, they never generated an important demand for output from the mines.

The Intercolonial and later the CGR and CNR, with their large numbers of locomotives, used huge amounts of Nova Scotia coal but most, it appears, came from the mines in Pictou and Cumberland counties. Statistical evidence about the railway marketplace for coal is hard to come by, though it does exist for two brief periods.

Nova Scotia Department of Mines Annual Reports include data for the years 1892-1911 that provide a detailed picture of what was happening during the two decades after the Intercolonial reached Sydney. To put a sample of that data into some context, in mid-1910 the IRC had 435 locomotives in service between Sydney and Montreal. No comparable data on railway purchases of coal have been found for the period after 1911, but fragmentary information suggests the pattern in place by that time continued until the 1940s, long after the IRC had become part of the Canadian National system.

Table 7.2 - Intercolonial Railway Coal Purchases, 1892-1910				
Fiscal Year	IRC Purchases in Nova Scotia Including Cape Breton (1,000 t)	IRC Purchases in Cape Breton (1,000 t)	Cape Breton Purchases as Percent of Total IRC Purchases	IRC Purchases in Cape Breton as Percent of Cape Breton's Total Coal Output
1891-92	179	5.6	3.2	0.5
1895-96	196	20.7	10.5	1.6
1899-00	271	36.2	13.3	1.7
1904-05	384	83.4	21.7	2.5
1909-10	488	164.8	33.7	3.7

Data Source: Nova Scotia Department of Mines Annual Reports, Appendix 6 in *Journals of the House of Assembly*, Halifax, 1893-1911.

While the table does show a large increase in IRC coal purchases from Cape Breton mines over the two decades, the rate of growth in purchases was only slightly greater than the rate of growth in the total output of Cape Breton's mines. The single most significant figure in the table is the percentage of the island's coal going to the IRC in 1910: 3.7 per cent. That year's results marked the highest percentage of Cape Breton coal sales to the IRC over the period for which data are available. As a customer, the Intercolonial was of relatively little consequence.

At the producer level, there were exceptions to that generalization. The latter part of the table records the period just after the Inverness & Richmond line had opened. That event had stimulated a major increase in mining activity at Port Hood and Inverness.

Output from the mines in Inverness County was relatively small in comparison with the coal raised in Cape Breton County. For most of the 1905-1911 period, the Inverness and Port Hood mines were producing between 300,000 and 400,000 t a year, only about one-tenth of the output from the Sydney coal field. For the Inverness County mines, however, the Intercolonial was a much more important customer. During those years, the IRC was buying close to 20 per cent of the coal raised at Port Hood and Inverness.

The Inverness County boom was one that did not last. The Port Hood mine flooded in 1911. Though it reopened for a short period just after the First World War, output was low compared to the pre-war period. At Inverness, production peaked in 1911 and a long period of decline began. By the mid-1920s, Inverness output was less than one-third of that being raised in the years 1907-1914.[18]

For part of this period, 1907-1911, the Department of Mines statistics provide an additional data subset of interest. For those five years, shipments to the Intercolonial were recorded in two categories, deliveries by rail and deliveries by sea. Most of the sea-borne shipments went up the St. Lawrence River, to IRC coal depots at locations such as Lévis, to meet the railway's needs on the western end of its line. For the brief period reported this way, about 75 per cent of all Cape Breton shipments to the IRC went by ship rather than by rail despite the fact that the railway was the buyer. It was significantly cheaper to

Fig. 7.11 - Bankhead at the Inverness mine, ca. 1905-1910.

Postcard. Photographer unknown. 79-1163-4143. Beaton Institute, Cape Breton University.

move high weight, low value products like coal by ship than to haul it by rail and most of the coal shipped from Cape Breton to Quebec went by sea.

The pattern shown in the table and its projection into future years had implications for the workforce in Cape Breton's mines as well as for Cape Breton's railway employees. Without the competition from mainland mines in Cumberland and Pictou Counties, demand from the region's big railway could have led to much higher employment levels in Cape Breton's mines and on the island's railways.

From 1921 onward, the consolidated coal companies, Besco and then Dosco, had a different perspective on the source of coal purchased by the CNR. These firms also owned the mines at Springhill in Cumberland County as well as Acadia Coal, the major producer in Pictou County, so the relative absence of sales of Cape Breton coal to the railway was of less concern to the companies.

A second set of data is available to tell something about the importance of the CNR as a customer for Cape Breton's mines in the years just after the Second World War. The original source, a study of rail ferry traffic at the Strait of Canso, provided detailed data on numbers of rail cars crossing the Strait in each direction with counts by type of car and/or the products being moved. Westbound shipments of coal and steel make a logical combination to present together.

Fig. 7.12 - The rail approach to the Port Hastings coal pier, ca. 1914. A photo showing the main body of this pier appeared in figure 4.5.

Port Hastings Museum and Archives, # AAQF00aa008i.

Table 7.3 - Westbound on the Strait Ferries: Railcars of Coal and Steel, 1946-1950									
	Coal To CNR	Coal Other	Coal Total	Steel Rails	Steel Other	Steel Scrap	Steel Total	Coal & Steel Total	Average Per Day
1946	6543	19,721	26,264	1158	3414	65	4637	30,901	85
1947	2197	9324	11,521	821	5550	63	6434	17,955	49
1948	6413	17,372	23,785	1487	5499	76	7062	30,847	85
1949	4249	17,227	21,476	1709	6495	44	8248	29,724	81
1950	7416	21,458	28,874	2343	6834	117	9294	38,168	105
Data source: Camu, Table II, 56. Camu indicated the data were provided by the CNR.									

As an indication of what was moving on the railway ferries and westward from Mulgrave, the numbers are both interesting and valuable. For example, coal purchased by the CNR was accounting for more than 20 per cent of the coal moving by rail during this period. But the ferry-based numbers provide only about one-third of the total picture. What is missing from this table is information about coal deliveries to the CNR and to other customers by sea, about two-thirds of the coal sales at the time. The first table in this chapter does provide details on sea-borne traffic, most of which went to Quebec or Newfoundland, though it is not broken down with any information about customers. As a result, it is impossible to draw any firm conclusions about the relative importance of CNR purchases of Cape Breton coal at this time to compare with the data from the previous table outlining Intercolonial purchases. Despite that, it is easy to conclude that railway purchases were significantly more important than during the years before the First World War. Based on two conservative assumptions, that none of the water-borne coal went to the CNR and that the average hopper then in service carried 40 t, the rail-based shipments to Canadian National would have accounted for more than 8 per cent of Cape Breton's coal sales during the period—a considerable increase over the 3.7 per cent peak recorded in 1910.

The 1946-50 data also provide a valuable indication of the relative importance of outbound coal and steel traffic that was being handled by the railway. Ignoring 1947, where the ratio is skewed as a result of an extended miners' strike, coal shipments accounted for about three times as many carloads as steel. Within the steel classifications, we can also see the relative importance of rails, most of which were going to the CNR. Over the period covered, rails were accounting for about 25 per cent of all steel shipments. Again, the table excludes details on steel products that left Sydney by ship. No alternate data source has been found and, as a result, no sense of the wider picture can be offered.

The Railways and the Cape Breton Steel Industry

In the early years of the 20th century, the railway marketplace was much more important to Cape Breton's steel industry than it was to the coal mines. From mid-1905, shortly after the Disco plant opened at Sydney, one of its main products was rails. The decision to enter the rail market was certainly influenced by the strong demand for rails at the time. A boom in railway construction, especially in central and western Canada provided the key market for the plant's rail mill. But that boom did not last. After the end of the First World War, the Canadian rail market became a highly cyclical one. Demand for rails was based on maintaining or upgrading existing rail lines rather than building new ones. That activity was in turn more sensitive to the general health of the economy.

Trends in sales were driven primarily by these market conditions despite research and efforts to improve the quality of the product coming out of the Sydney rail mill. In the early 1930s, experiments by Cam Mackie led to adoption of the "Mackie Retarded Rail Cooling Process" at the Sydney rail mill. This involved a slower cooling process for red-hot rails that would significantly reduce the risk of cracking after the rails went into service. The process was widely adopted across North America and, by 1940, most rail manufacturing in Canada and the United States was using the Mackie method.[19]

There was a long-term downward trend in demand for rails in eastern Canada where Sydney's output was most competitive. At the same time, the central and western Canadian markets came to be dominated by Algoma Steel in Sault Ste. Marie, Ontario. In addition to the changing market conditions and the increasing impact of shipping costs, another factor that affected the Sydney plant's output of rails, and other steel products was a long-term decline in efficiency and productivity. Equipment and processes became increasingly outdated, factors that drove up production costs, cut into profits or increased losses, in turn further diminishing Dosco's capacity or inclination to modernize.

Fig. 7.13 - Dominion Iron & Steel Co coke ovens complex, Sydney: a drawing from 1901-02 when the Disco plant was under construction.

Vernon, 205.

Dosco lost out on government aid to modernize steel plants during and immediately after the Second World War.[20] At the same time and into the 1950s, the company expanded its capacity to produce finished steel products in Quebec. Except for production of rails, the Sydney plant was left to focus on the output of semi-finished steel ingots, blooms and billets, the market for which was more uncertain and competitive.[21]

During a short period in the late 1950s and early 1960s, rail production once again exceeded the level of the boom years just before the First World War, but this also failed to last. The following graph illustrates the volatility in average annual production by periods during the first six decades of operation of the rail mill. Within those nearly sixty years, highlights include annual outputs of more than 180,000 t in 1912 and 1913, a collapse to 17,000 t in 1920, the prolonged impact of the depression in the 1930s when average annual output remained less than 40,000 t for eight years and the recovery during the period 1957-1964.

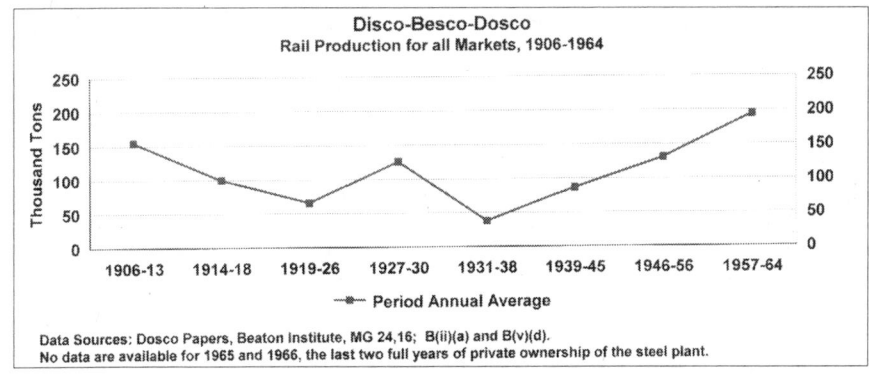

Fig. 7.14 - CN flatcars with rails at Sydney Steel Plant, 10 May 1994.

Ratel Photography. 95-292-26383, Beaton Institute, Cape Breton University.

Fig. 7.15 - Increases in coal and steel traffic on the CNR during WWII led to longer and heavier freight trains, especially those heading to the mainland. One response by the railway was use of larger and stronger locomotives on the CN line through eastern Nova Scotia and Cape Breton. # 6021, photographed at Sydney during the war years, illustrates the last generation of CNR steam engines that handled freight and passenger traffic on the island. The locomotive, built at Kingston, Ontario in 1924, was scrapped in 1959.

Photo by Harry Hynes, Glace Bay; from the author's collection.

The years after the end of the Second World War saw mounting concern, political debate and a stream of studies about the future of Cape Breton's steel industry, a direct parallel to worries about the future of the coal mines. In 1967, a year after they announced their intent to abandon the mines, Hawker-Siddeley, the last of Dosco's private owners, abandoned the steel plant. As had happened with the mines, the plant was taken over by government. The Sydney Steel Corporation (Sysco), owned by the Province, was set up to operate the complex.

Soon after the establishment of Sysco, sales of Sydney rails to Canadian buyers began to trend downward again. Exports started to account for a rising percentage of sales of rails, but generally failed to offset what was happening domestically. The shrinking Canadian market after Sydney's last 200,000 t year in 1970 is illustrated in the second graph, based on surviving Sysco data. At the same time, Sysco's markets for semi-finished steel were also in decline.[22]

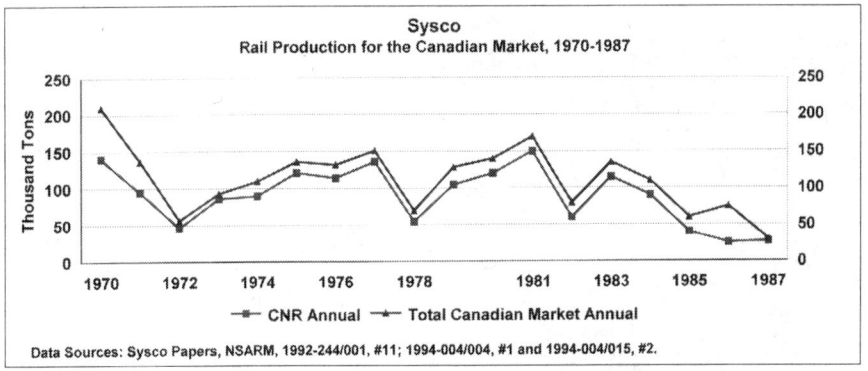

The two graphs tell only one part of the story of the rail business. For example, for either a private or public company, long-term profits and losses will ultimately be a more important measure than the physical output levels that the two graphs illustrate. And it must also be remembered that the rail business was only one part of the wider story of the decline of Sydney's steel industry.

Fragmentary evidence suggests that from the late 1970s rail production was an increasingly important part of the plant's total output. Data for the period 1978-1979 through 1983-1984 show rail output rising from one-third of total plant tonnage to 90 per cent in 1983-1984. During that period, total annual output of all steel products declined from half-a-million t to less than 150,000 t.[23]

Despite their limitations, the two graphs show Sydney Steel's long-term experience in the market for rails, an experience that was an increasingly important factor leading to the decision by the Province to close the steel plant in 2001.[24]

In a wider and more recent perspective, Sydney's experience with steel has not been unique. Canada's other primary steel producers have fallen on hard times over the past fifteen years. In the years from before the Second World

War through the 1990s, Canada had three primary steel companies larger than Dosco/Sysco, those being Algoma in Sault Ste. Marie, the Steel Company of Canada (Stelco) and Dominion Foundaries and Steel (Dofasco), both in Hamilton. Stelco went bankrupt and is now controlled by United States Steel of Pittsburgh. Algoma experienced several bankruptcies and is now a subsidiary of the Essar Group with headquarters in Mumbai, India. Dofasco is the only one of the three that remained profitable and it was bought by ArcelorMittal based in Luxembourg. All three firms are still operating but at much lower levels of output and employment than was the case twenty or fifty years ago.

Sydney Steel and the Railway Rolling Stock Marketplace

Fig. 7.16 - Rails cooling in the Sydney rail mill.

Sydney Steel Museum Society.

The volatility in the rail business emerged in another important market served by the Sydney steel plant, although indirectly. The Eastern Car Company of Trenton, on the Nova Scotia mainland, was a major manufacturer of railway freight cars set up as a subsidiary of Nova Scotia Steel and Coal in 1912. After the 1921 merger, the Trenton works became a part of Besco and retained a corporate connection to the Sydney steel plant until 1967. Over its operating lifetime, which lasted for forty years after the departure of Dosco, the Trenton plant produced more than 100,000 rail cars. For much of that time, most output went to Canadian railways. Throughout its history as a Dosco subsidiary, Eastern Car built virtually all the rolling stock acquired by the S&L and the OSC lines. The two hopper cars seen in the photos earlier in the chapter were examples of sets of Trenton-built cars that went into service in Cape Breton. While it was a Dosco subsidiary, Eastern Car's advertising material was often illustrated with photos of cars built for the Cape Breton rail lines.

During its later years, as Canadian demand sagged, the plant's new owners, first the Lavelin Group and then Greenbrier Industries, attempted the same strategy as the Sydney steel plant and pursued export as well as North American markets.[25] The export markets proved even more volatile than the domestic market for railway rolling stock and Greenbrier closed the plant in 2007.[26]

From 1912 until 2001, extensive use was made of Cape Breton steel for Eastern Car's rail cars and their wheel and axle sets. A complementary positive economic impact of the relationship between Sydney and Trenton came from the role of the railway in transporting the raw materials from Sydney. There is no basis for making estimates about what percentage of the steel recorded in the table showing Strait of Canso ferry traffic was destined for Trenton. Having said that, the numbers were probably statistically significant and likely remained so into the 1980s.

The fates of the coal and steel industries in Cape Breton are recent examples of the process of deindustrialization that has stalked the Maritimes since the 1920s. The impacts of shifting trade patterns and economic globalization have given central Canada some experience with this process. In that location, however, there has usually been one difference. A crisis in a setting such as the Ontario automobile and auto parts industries is likely to be seen as a national problem and receive an appropriate level of national attention from the federal government. When the same process has affected the Maritime economy, the results have tended to be seen as regional problems which, by national definition, are of much less consequence. In a recent book dealing with the economic experience of the Maritimes within the Canadian federation, Donald Savoie of l'Université de Moncton captured the essence of this approach to economic policy in a chapter title: "The Problem: Big Dogs Eat First."[27]

The decline and eventual fall of Cape Breton's coal and steel industries have of course had a major impact on the railway between Cape Breton Island and the mainland. The subject and the question of whether or not the line will survive will be addressed in chapter 10.

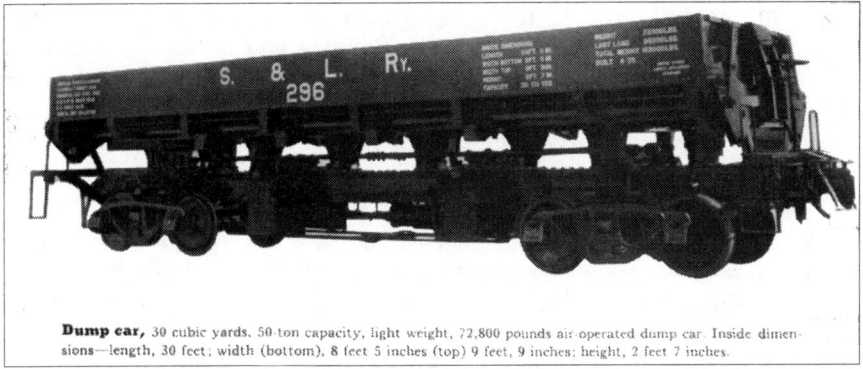

Fig. 7.17 - This side-tipping dump car is one in an order of seventeen (#s 294-310) built by the Eastern Car Company for the S&L over the period 1935-40. The photo comes from a large binder, prepared c.1950 for Eastern Car's sales agents, with many illustrations of the company's output over several decades for the S&L as well as for other railways.

Whitney Pier Historical Society Museum.

8 – Other Railway Operations

"Mixed trains" that combined passenger and freight services were mentioned several times in previous chapters. This chapter is a print version of a mixed train: a range of topics about railways and their services in Cape Breton that merit some mention.

Freight and Express Services

William Calder's account of the post-1903 impact of the railway on Richmond County reprinted in chapter 4 shows how the opening of the railway offered new advantages to local businesses in one Cape Breton community. The most important of these was the railway's capacity to handle freight. In communities on or near rail lines, retail merchants came to rely on the trains to bring in goods from wholesalers and suppliers. Woodlot and sawmill owners were able to start sending out logs, lumber and more specialized products like pit props for the mines. Farmers were able to bring in grain and fertilizer by the carload and deliver products like milk and cream to urban dairies. Shipments like milk and cream that required speedy or special handling could be shipped in "express" cars that were attached to passenger trains. The cost of express shipments, by item or by weight, was much greater than shipment by freight, especially for small individual items or consignments, but quick transit was provided in exchange for the higher cost. In Cape Breton, most of the express services were provided by the Intercolonial and its successors and available in communities on or close to the IRC/CGR/CNR lines.

Detailed information on the scope and volume of shipments by businesses exists in archival records. Unfortunately almost all the records are in the collection of IRC/CGR/CNR documents at the National Archives in Ottawa. Small samples can be found, however, in local collections such as that of the Orangedale Railway Museum.[1] As random examples, express and freight waybills from the late 1960s record outbound shipments from Orangedale such as 328 cases of oysters to a wholesaler in Montreal, a boxcar load of 727 bales of

Christmas trees bound for Chicago (in a Santa Fe boxcar being routed back to the United States) and a heavy piece of construction equipment identified as a "Northwest shovel" sent to Nova Scotia Tractors and Equipment in Halifax on a CNR flatcar.

For decades after the railways appeared, their capacity to deliver goods was often equally important to individuals as recipients and as consumers. In the 1880s, a Toronto retailer named Timothy Eaton started to expand his customer base through his "mail order" catalogue. Delivery of goods by rail became a common practice for Eaton's and other firms that adopted mail order marketing. The delivery model ended the dependence of buyers on local merchants, their inventories or their ability to handle special orders, and marked the first step toward the series of changes in retailing that led to shopping centers, big box stores and online shopping sites.

In 1920, Eaton's established a large regional distribution centre in Moncton, New Brunswick; over the next four decades, this company dominated the mail order trade into Cape Breton and other parts of the Maritimes.[2] Until the 1960s, shipments from Eaton's formed an important part of the freight and express traffic coming into many of the island's railway stations.

No data have been found to form the basis for a big-picture analysis of freight moving to and from Cape Breton but Pierre Camu's study of rail ferry operations at the Strait of Canso in the years just after the Second World War offers one statistical snapshot. The following table excludes the coal and steel traffic that was summarized in the previous chapter. Unfortunately the data quoted below do not provide details about the nature of the goods

Fig. 8.1 (top) - Handling express at the CNR station at Point Tupper ca. 1950. Quick loading and unloading of express, baggage and mail had to be carried out while passengers were getting off and on the train.

Port Hastings Museum and Archives, photo #AAQF00aa0002.

Fig. 8.2 (bottom) Handling freight at North Sydney ca. 1950. The scene shows part of the interior of the CNR freight shed and ramps leading into the cargo holds of a Newfoundland-bound ferry.

Abbass Studios Ltd. Collection. 87-418-16948. Beaton Institute, Cape Breton University.

being moved. A second limitation from a Cape Breton perspective is that the data include shipments for and from Newfoundland via the ferry connection out of North Sydney.

Despite those problems, the numbers do show one very important thing—the great gap between inbound and outbound freightcar loads crossing the Strait of Canso. The data, which exclude empty cars, clearly indicate that two of every three cars bringing freight to Cape Breton or to the Newfoundland ferry went back to the mainland empty. This fact speaks to the extent of the imbalance of trade in products other than coal and steel between the combined Cape Breton and Newfoundland economies and the rest of Canada. While no comparable data has been found for the years reported or other time periods, it seems almost certain that a record of rail traffic on the western and northern borders of New Brunswick would have shown a similar imbalance between the Maritime region and central Canada.

Table 8.1 - On the Strait Ferries: Freightcar Loads Other than Coal and Steel, 1946-1950				
	From Cape Breton	To Cape Breton	Total	Total Per Day
1946	6927	21,294	28,221	77
1947	6910	21,854	28,764	79
1948	8373	22,200	30,573	84
1949	7337	23,061	30,398	83
1950	7150	22,299	29,449	81
Data source: Camu, Table II: 56. Camu indicated that the data were provided by the CNR.				

The Intercolonial and the Maritimes

In 1876, the Intercolonial was completed to open the rail link from Nova Scotia and New Brunswick to Quebec with connections to Ontario and beyond. In 1879, the year after being returned to office after a five year period on the opposition bench, Sir John A. Macdonald's government introduced the "National Policy," a package of tariffs designed to protect many types of Canadian businesses from foreign competition. In the short term, the combined effects of these two developments stimulated the growth of industry in Nova Scotia communities on the IRC route between Halifax and central Canada.[3] Truro and Amherst[4] on the main line plus New Glasgow,[5] on the "Pictou branch" that had opened in 1867, were the prime locations along the railway for new processing and manufacturing industries that could reach extended markets through the Intercolonial. These towns were established centres before their railways opened and had local business communities, workforces and sources of capital, some of the critical ingredients for economic growth that could respond to the opportunities offered by the extension of the IRC's reach.

The Iona Gypsum Company and the Railway

Michael MacKenzie

"About two box cars or hopper cars of coal were brought in to the mill weekly from the Sydney area mines. The coal was used to keep a good head of steam in the various mills and especially to maintain a good fire under the two kettles to drive off the moisture in the gypsum. Thus a fireman and a stationary engineer were employed on each shift. Many men were employed in the warehouse bagging or filling the barrels, transferring the finished product either to the boats or waiting box cars. A 'donkey' engine [a small improvised/locally-built engine] then hauled one (or at most two) car(s) on the two mile spur to the Iona CNR siding. This operation required a driver and fireman.

"The two-mile spur line was by no means a bed of roses. Leaving the mill proper, from the level beach, they had a steep grade to climb. It was such a problem that the donkey engine often had to make several runs at the hill before they could make it with their heavy load of plaster. On their return trip, they brought back two empty cars.

"Their second problem, more troublesome and expensive, was that after every heavy wind and high seas from the east, or even the south east, the railway tracks would be covered with sand and gravel in about four extensive places. As a result, this two-mile company spur line had to employ a small gang of men to keep it clear and operational. It appeared that without the beach problems one man could have maintained the line. Ninety per cent of the two miles was on the salt-water beach at about the high water mark.

"This railway spur was a necessity, yet a costly operation. Highway trucks were not common in the area when the mill was functioning. (Alex MacKenzie purchased the first truck in nearby Benacadie in 1929.) The author and several students rode a push car over the line in the spring of 1932, probably the last to use the line. About a month later the gravel piled up on the tracks calling a halt forever to the use of these tracks. Some years later the rails were removed for scrap steel at the Sydney steel plant."

Excerpted from Michael MacKenzie, *Tracks Across the Maritimes*, 48-50. Reprinted by permission of Breton Books, Wreck Cove, Cape Breton.

During its early years, the IRC offered a means for Maritime firms to reach additional local markets plus the markets of central Canada. It did so with freight rates designed to stimulate the development of industries in the region.[6] IRC rates were somewhat lower than those on railways running west of Montreal. In addition, there was a preferential rate system with westbound rates that were lower than those for comparable shipments coming into the Maritime region. There is little doubt that the IRC and its rate structure provided an initial boost to the Maritime economy though that boost was geographically limited and it did not last.

For a number of reasons, Cape Breton was one of the areas within the region where the impact of the IRC and its rate system was much less significant. The time gap between 1876 and the opening of the Intercolonial's Cape Breton branch in 1891 was one factor. Cape Breton was also faced with other disadvantages that inhibited the development of new industries. The population was relatively small and predominantly rural. In the towns, most of which were concentrated on the eastern side of the island, the focus was coal mining and in Sydney and Sydney Mines after 1900, the steel industry. Despite the disadvantages, examples can be found over the decades following 1891 of industries that appeared as a direct result of the arrival of the railway.

One example of this was the Iona Gypsum Company at Grass Cove, near Iona in central Cape Breton. The company opened a mill that processed gypsum from a nearby quarry and produced processed ready-to-use plaster mix. The service offered by the Intercolonial permitted this firm to bring in coal and ship its finished product from a location where no other cost-effective transportation option was available. During its short life, 1916-1931, Iona Gypsum sold its plaster across eastern Canada. At its peak, the firm employed as many as 100 men and was an economic giant in its immediate area.

The appearance of firms like Iona Gypsum was somewhat exceptional on Cape Breton and it, like many earlier firms that had depended on the Intercolonial, had a relatively short life. By the time the IRC was made a part of the Canadian Government Railway system during the First World War, many changes were under way to affect it, the Maritime region and the country.

The more rapid population growth of central Canada after 1890 was accompanied by economic growth, especially in the Montreal-Windsor corridor which became the emerging business heartland of the country. The post-1876 boom in the Maritimes came to an end and the region became more and more an economic hinterland, a market for firms in central Canada. As its population declined in relation to the rest of the country, the region's political influence declined as well. Along with these developments, the Intercolonial, and after 1915 the CGR, also underwent important changes.

Fig. 8.3 - The *Canadian Illustrated News* noted the opening of through IRC service from Halifax to Lévis, Quebec in 1876 with this drawing that took the journal's entire front page – 10 x 14 in. Maritimers expected the railway's primary role would be to carry their products into central Canada. The drawing proved to a more accurate prediction of the IRC's longer-term impact – opening the Maritime market to goods from Quebec and Ontario.

Canadian Illustrated News, Montreal, September 30, 1876: 1.

The Politics of Freight Rates

The economic histories of Cape Breton and the Maritime region are subjects far too big and complex to receive more than the observations that have been made to this point.[7] Equally big and complex is the topic of freight rates in the context of the economic and political history of the Maritimes, but it is a subject that cannot be ignored.

While it had no immediate effect on the Maritimes, a benchmark event came in 1903 with the Laurier government's establishment of the Board of Railway Commissioners, a federal agency that would, among other things, have power to regulate railway freight rates.[8] Though IRC rates were initially excluded from the authority of the Board, in 1912 the recently elected Conservative government headed by Robert Borden began what one historian called "the attack on the Intercolonial's rate structure."[9] The attack was not completed until 1918, after the consolidation of the IRC, the Grand Trunk Railway and the Canadian Northern into the CGR. In the context of that consolidation, the Intercolonial headquarters at Moncton was transferred to Toronto and the IRC freight rate structure was dismantled.

Over the period 1918-1920, Maritime freight rates increased dramatically more than those in central Canada to "equalize" shipping costs.[10] The preferential rates for westbound traffic were eliminated removing the aid to Maritime producers shipping into central Canadian markets. The capacity for individual shippers to negotiate special rates with the railway for their products or for particular destinations was also eliminated. The broad rationale was to remove what was regarded as regional favouritism with special subsidies delivered through the railway freight rate system.

In the economic recession that followed the First World War, the Maritime region was especially hard hit—chapter 7 provided a glimpse of the problems in Cape Breton's coal industry. In manufacturing and other sectors, many businesses closed and unemployment soared. In the absence of alternatives, people in the region adopted the "going down the road" solution. Estimates indicate that a hundred thousand Maritimers left the region in the 1920s. Numerous factors were involved but the changes to the freight rate system were widely seen as playing a critical role. As a result, freight rate policy quickly became an important political issue, contributed to wide and rapid swings in popular support for political parties and generated previously unseen moves toward regional co-operation to try to influence federal government policy.

In the federal election of 1921, Mackenzie King's Liberals were the beneficiaries of rising regional discontent with the Conservative government despite Borden's departure from the Conservative leadership the year before. King and the Liberals won twenty-five of the thirty-one Commons seats in the Maritimes. Despite that block of Liberal MPs and strong lobbying efforts, King's government failed to make any strong moves to address regional concerns. Prior to the 1925 election, the Conservatives led by Arthur Meighen offered support to the developing Maritimes Rights movement. Though it has often been presented as an essentially partisan venture controlled by the Conservative party, the movement went beyond that.[11] Voters responded and the

Fig. 8.4 - "Room For More": The flags flying on Donald McRitchie's "Maritime Rights" train indicate some of the key regional grievances of the period. In addition to freight and express rates, another railway-related issue was the routing of goods from central Canada and grain from the west through CNR-owned harbour facilities at Portland, Maine. These wharves and the Portland to Montreal line had become part of the Grand Trunk Railway before Confederation. Portland Harbour was well established as a winter port for Montreal before the Intercolonial opened service through to the Maritimes in 1876. When the Grand Trunk became part of the government-owned CNR during World War I, shipping interests in the ports of Halifax and Saint John became very vocal about the continued use of Portland's harbour. The cartoon originally appeared in the *Halifax Herald*, February 13, 1924: 3.

Donald M. McRitchie fonds, 1900.007-RIT/113; Acadia University Archives; reproduced by permission.

Fig. 8.5 - In addition to previously-mentioned railway issues in the Maritimes in the 1920s, there were perceptions that the railways were not doing enough to support existing regional businesses or help new ones get started. These criticisms were closely related to the "Maritime Rights" cause. Because of its dominant role in Nova Scotia, the CNR was a particular target for this charge which is humourously captured in this cartoon. The drawing was identified as "contributed" but it appears to be in the style of Donald McRitchie, the resident cartoonist at the *Herald*.

From the *Halifax Herald*, May 28, 1928.

Conservatives won twenty-three of the twenty-nine regional seats in Ottawa (including eleven of the fourteen Nova Scotia seats) to support a short-lived Meighen government. In Nova Scotia, it could be suggested that one of the strongest forces behind the Conservative campaign was Donald McRitchie, the cartoonist at the *Halifax Herald*, the major voice of the party in Nova Scotia.[12] The federal results had been preceded by a provincial election in Nova Scotia earlier in the year. In that contest, the provincial Liberals, who had held power for over forty years, were swept from office, in no small measure because of their unqualified support to Besco during the long and bitter miners' strike in Cape Breton.[13]

The Maritime Rights movement was closely tied to local and provincial Boards of Trade and local "clubs" they organized. These organizations recruited support from the three provincial governments, all of which were Conservative by 1925, as well as from the press, farmers' organizations, major firms and organized labour. There were gaps in the level of active support for the movement, some geographical and some reflecting particular sectors. Cape Breton and its major industries constituted one of those gaps.

Cape Breton's relative inattention to the movement was a result of several things. The issue of railway freight rates was somewhat less significant to the coal and steel industries, at least in the short term, because most of their outbound shipments were going by water rather than by rail. At a more basic level, from the time of the Besco consolidation in 1921, the company and the unions were locked in an intense ongoing struggle. In the context of that struggle, the Maritime Rights issues were generally viewed as mainland and partisan subjects that had little relevance to Cape Bretoners' immediate priorities. The Sydney *Daily Post* did address the issues on occasion though that may have been at least in part a reflection of the paper's pro-Conservative loyalty at the time. Despite its partisan interest, however, the *Post* recognized that issues such as freight rates and tariff policy had implications for the local coal and steel industries, their employees and their communities.[14]

In 1926, after Mackenzie King regained office in Ottawa, he resorted to the great Canadian strategy for dealing with an important problem. A Royal Commission was appointed to investigate transportation topics, trade and ports policies and issues related to federal land and cash grants to the Provinces. The study was headed by Sir Andrew Rae Duncan who had just led a provincial Royal Commission investigating the problems in the Cape Breton coal industry. Like most comparable documents, the Commission's report[15] was filled with compromises.

On freight rates, the subject of immediate concern here, the Commission concluded that the Maritime economy had been adversely and unfairly affected by the post-war changes to rates and the procedures for rate-setting. The key recommendation was for a 20 per cent reduction in existing rates east of Lévis, Québec. This was adopted by King's government and implemented through the *Maritime Freight Rates Act* (*MFRA*) of 1927.

That *Act* provided the rate reduction recommended by Duncan and restored a part of the preferential rate system. The rate reductions made did not apply to eastbound traffic that originated west of Levis. For the longer term, the *Act* restored a means for subsidies to be provided through regional freight rates that were separated to a degree from those in effect in central and western Canada. Though the advantages restored in 1927 would be under constant pressure and gradual deterioration,[16] they provided many decades of benefits to the regional economy. Those benefits applied to the Nova Scotia coal industry and the mines in Cape Breton as well as the steel industries in Pictou County and Sydney.[17]

The presence of a separate federal *Act*, the establishment of the body that became the Maritimes Transportation Commission (MTC) to advise the Provinces, and the precedent for use of a Royal Commission established a model that would last until almost the end of the century. Royal Commissions on transportation came and went in response to perceived problems or political needs.[18] The MTC became a vital source of research and advice for the provincial governments and a regular participant in the ongoing freight rates debates.[19] Railway subsidies under *MFRA* and other rail, trucking and marine subsidies under the *Atlantic Region Freight Assistance Act* continued until they were eliminated by the Chrétien government in 1995.

While the regional freight rates issue has vanished from the political radar, at least for the short run, it has not disappeared as a subject for discussion and debate to historians, economists and others who attempt to assess the role of railway policy in the development and subsequent relative decline of the Maritime region. References have previously been noted to several important studies by two historians, Ernest Forbes and Ken Cruikshank. Other accounts by those authors and two other scholars also warrant mention. An ongoing Forbes-Cruikshank debate focused on three key questions from the Intercolonial era. Did the IRC or its political masters intend the railway to play an active role in regional economic development? Was the railway really important enough to have an influencial impact on regional economic growth and/or decline? Why was the IRC and its freight rate system dismantled at the end of the First World War?[20] Two other important works come from economists. Kris Inwood has tackled the subject in a specifically regional context while Howard Darling looked at the topic within a book on freight rate issues across Canada.[21] The issues involved are of more than just historical or academic importance. They have major implications for understanding the problems that have beset the region for a century and for decisions that will play a role in shaping the future of Cape Breton and the rest of the region.

Lest Maritimers think that they have a unique heritage in the form of their long-lasting regional freight rates issue, that is not the case. Western Canada's experience with the "Crowsnest Pass Freight Rates" has been similar in many ways. The "Crow Rates" grew out of an 1897 agreement between the Canadian government and the CPR and provided reduced rates on western grain going to ports on the Great Lakes. While they offered one form of immediate benefit to farmers, the rates were also seen as inhibiting non-agricultural economic growth in the west. As in the Maritimes, the Crow Rates were a hot topic in the Prairie Provinces for business interests and politicians for almost a century and have long been an important subject for analysis by economists and historians in Western Canada. The Crow Rates were abolished in 1995 at the same time as the system of regional freight rates in eastern Canada.

Mail, Telegrams and Financial Services

As elsewhere, the arrival of railways on Cape Breton led quickly to rail transport of mail for both short hauls and long distance deliveries. The Intercolonial had been carrying mail long before its extension to Cape Breton was completed in 1891. As noted by Calder's account in chapter 4, the Cape Breton Railway received a mail contract soon after it began service to St. Peter's in 1903. Post Office records show no evidence of the International Railway or the G&CB or its narrow gauge successors carrying mail, but the S&L was added to the Post Office list of railway mail carriers in 1906.

In addition to regular mail which moved by rail until the 1960s, the Intercolonial also ran mail specials from North Sydney to Montreal from 1891 to about 1914. These carried large shipments of mail from England destined for central Canada that were unloaded at North Sydney from ocean liners en route to Halifax or American ports. Speed was of the essence and the IRC mail specials were given right of way over all other trains.

For urgent communications, before the availability of widespread and reliable telephone systems, larger railway companies like the IRC delivered news, both good and bad, by telegram. The Intercolonial's own telephone system was, in theory, just for railway use but for decades it would also be used by station agents in response to medical emergencies, fires or other urgent local needs. The IRC went into competition with the Post Office and banks by selling money orders that made it easy to transfer funds over long distances. Another form of railway company support for freight and express traffic was provision of "Collect On Delivery"

Fig. 8.6 - A CNR mail and express car, probably photographed in the 1950s. Some mail "cars" were like the one shown here, a separate section in a car that had another section for express. Others, more likely to be seen on longer runs such as between Halifax and Montreal, occupied entire cars and were complete travelling post offices where mail would be sorted en route.

Abbass Studios Ltd. Collection. 87-417-16947, Beaton Institute, Cape Breton University.

Fig. 8.7 - Mail from Britain being unloaded at North Sydney in July, 1905 for an Intercolonial mail special to Montreal. The running time for regular passenger service at this time was about thirty-six hours (with twenty-five minutes for a change of trains in Truro). The mail specials apparently did the run in about ten hours less.

LAC, Post Office Department collection, negative #PA-061883.

(COD) service. A customer could order goods COD and make payment at the railway station when they arrived. The railway would then transmit the payment to the supplier.

Mail and express shipments were frequently valuable and called for appropriate caution by railway employees who were responsible for them. On occasion, procedures were not as carefully followed as they should have been, a potential problem illustrated by a story from St. Peter's found in the next chapter. Despite the possible attraction of what the railways carried, the 19th-century western American tradition of train robberies did not carry over the Canadian border. There were exceptions to that, of course, and Cape Breton was the location for what may have been the only train robbery that took place in Nova Scotia. On Friday, April 18, 1958, virtually all provincial newspapers carried the story as the lead item on the front page. The morning headline on the Halifax *Chronicle Herald* was "Police Set Dragnet For Railway Bandit."

The robbery took place on the CNR's overnight express bound for Sydney. Soon after departure from Port Hawkesbury in the early hours of Thurday, April 17, the two clerks in the mail car were held up by a masked man armed with a shotgun. The clerks were tied up and deposited in the car's washroom and the mail car's contents ransacked. The robbery was not discovered until the train reached Little Bras d'Or when a mail driver boarded the car to find out why his mailbag was not being unloaded. From mailbags found at Orangedale, it was concluded that the bandit had left the train there.

The excitement about the story did not last long. The Saturday papers reported the arrest of a former railway mail clerk and recovery of money orders, a large inventory of postage stamps, cash, jewellery and other items that had been taken from the mail car.[22] The newspapers also reported rumours that perhaps the bandit's real target was a large shipment of cash for a Dosco payroll though the company denied that its payroll funds were moved in cash by rail.

Fig. 8.8 - Bob Chambers, the *Chronicle Herald*'s resident cartoonist for many years, captured the essential elements of the 1958 train robbery story in this drawing that appeared on the paper's front page.

The *Chronicle Herald*, April 18, 1958: 1.

The Railways and the Military

During the years of the two world wars, railway operations were frequently adjusted to meet military priorities. Regular passenger trains were often complemented by troop train specials that carried thousands of Canadians to training camps and military postings within the country as well as to ports to embark for Britain or other overseas destinations. Military equipment, goods destined for Britain and materials deemed essential to the war efforts were given priority over other freight and express traffic.

This pattern appeared before the beginning of the First World War. On July 31, 1914, as war between Britain and Germany became imminent, "great crowds" gathered at the Intercolonial station in Sydney to welcome a detachment of soldiers from Halifax sent to guard the cable station at North Sydney and the wireless station at Glace Bay.[23] Over the next few days, before and after the formal declaration of war on August 5, the Intercolonial brought more troops from Halifax and a Prince Edward Island artillery unit that had travelled by ship to Port Hawkesbury.[24] In addition to carrying military personnel posted to Cape Breton, the railway's link to the Newfoundland ferry played an important role, especially during the Second World War, for transport of personnel travelling via the Newfoundland Railway to or from the island's wartime naval and air bases.[25]

Special local military needs in Cape Breton were also met by the railway during both conflicts. As an example, in 1944-1945 the CNR carried new heavy guns and support equipment to upgrade the coastal defence battery at Chapel Point at Sydney Mines. A series of seven-car shipments included 28-t barrels of new artillery pieces, the most modern heavy guns put in place in Canada during the war.

Fig. 8.9 - The IRC troop train special with the 36th Field Battery at Sydney in 1915.

Old Sydney Society.

Before the end of the first month of war in 1914, the Sydney station was the scene of another type of military event. An Intercolonial special carried the men, field guns and horses of the 17th Field Battery from Sydney to Camp Valcartier in Quebec for additional training prior to active service in Europe. The departure of the 17th was a highly emotional and patriotic event that established the model for many others over the years 1915-1918 and 1939-1945. In the autumn of 1915, a second artillery unit, the 36th Field Battery, left Sydney on another IRC special. The 1915 departure of the 36th is the only such event during either of the world wars from which a photo has been found.

Sydney Harbour did not play a major role during either war as a point for loading cargo or military personnel bound for England. That activity was concentrated at Halifax for a number of reasons. Halifax had the most extensive system of docks found on the east coast for cargo and passenger ships. The port was also the location of the most important Canadian naval base. In early 1917, in response to the rising number of ships being sunk by German submarines, virtually all merchant ships bound to and from Britain started moving in groups known as convoys. They were accompanied by warships to offer protection from German U-boats. Halifax's large sheltered inner harbour offered a location where large numbers of ships could anchor, before and after taking on cargo or troops, as convoys were formed in preparation for sailing. While the convoy shipping strategy appeared only after the mid-way point during the First World War, it was introduced at the beginning of war in 1939 and remained in effect throughout the Second World War.

Sydney's port was used primarily for the formation of convoys of previously loaded ships though there were occasions when both supplies and troops bound for Britain were brought by rail from points west of Cape Breton to meet ships in Sydney. Cape Breton coal topped up fuel stocks to ready ships for the long and dangerous crossings.

In 1917-1918, Sydney became the marshalling harbour for all slow convoys for Britain, a role that would be repeated during the first years of the Second World War. To support the "SC" convoys, as those sailing from Sydney were coded starting in 1940, Sydney became a base for naval escort vessels that sailed with the convoys to provide protection with varying degrees of success. The risks at this phase of the war are illustrated by the fate of SC-7, a 35-ship convoy that sailed from Sydney for Liverpool in October of 1940. For most of the crossing SC-7 had only one escort, *HMS Scarborough,* a Hastings-class sloop from the Royal Navy. Over the span of several days and nights, SC-7 was attacked by a "wolf pack" of seven U-boats and twenty of the thirty-five merchant ships were sunk.

During the years of the Second World War, the CNR line between Sydney and the Strait of Canso and beyond was frequently being used to capacity and the Strait rail ferries were often in continuous service for days or weeks at a stretch. This situation was sometimes intensified by special circumstances. During 1942, a German submarine offensive extended the war from Atlantic coastal waters near Cape Breton into the Gulf of St Lawrence. Between May and October that year, nineteen freighters and two Canadian warships were sunk in the Gulf or close to it.[26] Convoy shipping was introduced in the Gulf in September, and ships carrying Cape Breton coal to the St. Lawrence had to travel in those convoys. As a result, the CNR experienced a surge in long-haul coal traffic from Cape Breton's mines to destinations in Quebec.

The war was brought closer to home to Cape Bretoners in the autumn of 1942. The iron ore for the Sydney steel plant was coming from Bell Island in Conception Bay, Newfoundland. In September and again in November, Bell Island's anchorage was attacked by U-boats. Four ore-carriers were sunk, one owned by Dosco and the others under charter to carry ore to Sydney. Seventy merchant seamen were lost between the two attacks.[27]

The most traumatic event of either war with a specific railway connection occurred between the attacks at Bell Island. The Newfoundland Railway ferry *SS Caribou*, sailing on the run between North Sydney and Port aux Basques, Newfoundland since the mid-1920s, was torpedoed and sunk by the U-69 in October of 1942. Of the 251 passengers and crew aboard, fewer than half survived.[28]

Fig. 8.10 - A 1928 Newfoundland postage stamp showing the *SS Caribou*.

Extensive use was made of the CNR and its predecessors for another military-related purpose. During periods of labour unrest in Cape Breton's mines or steel plants, it was not unusual for soldiers, militia or "special police" to be brought from Halifax or further afield. In theory, this was to protect company property and prevent violence under the terms of the federal *Militia Act*. In reality, it was also to use the threat of armed force to intimidate striking workers. The role of the CNR in bringing in these "armies of occupation" did not endear the railway to the strikers, their families or their supporters. While numerous accounts can be found in the Sydney press about the arrival of these special trains, those from August 1922, June and July 1923 and June 1925 are particularly vivid.

The Sydney *Daily Post* of July 9, 1923, reported the arrival of a sixteen-car special with soldiers to bolster the force that had arrived previously. The force included "mixed drafts of cavalry, artillery and infantry from Ontario and western Canada." Another train was reported to be en route. The next day's *Post* recorded its arrival from Manitoba with 250 men from Lord Strathcona's Horse and Princess Patricia's Light Infantry. This special, the *Post* said, had come from Winnipeg in four days. The arrival of this particular set of reinforcements was undoubtedly related to the fact that J. B. McLachlan and Dan Livingstone, the key leaders of the miners' union, were in jail in Halifax charged with seditious libel, unlawfully publishing false tales "whereby injury or mischief was likely to be occasioned to a public interest."[29]

Fig. 8.11 - Part of a CNR military special, believed to have been taken at Glace Bay during the 1920s.

Cape Breton Miners' Museum, Glace Bay, #9B1-221.

Circus Trains

The roles of the railways in wartime or in Cape Breton's stormy years of labour unrest are not especially cheerful subjects. In contrast, the railways also brought other special trains that brought enjoyment to Cape Bretoners. From the opening of the Intercolonial until about 1950, Sydney and the larger surrounding towns in eastern Cape Breton were often included in the routes of railway circuses. The outbreak of the First World War was accompanied by the presence of a circus in eastern Cape Breton. Operating out of a twenty-car circus special, Robinson's Famous Show arrived in Sydney on August 3, 1914, and gave shows there that day. On the 4th, they moved to North Sydney for an evening show that began just after the British ultimatum for the Germans to withdraw from Belgium expired. By the time the show was over, Britain and Canada were committed to war with Germany.

Except for locomotives chartered from local railways, circus companies had their own complete sets of rail cars. Passenger cars carried performers and work crews and served as the circus hotel during stopovers. Customized stock cars filled the same roles for performing and work animals. Flat cars carried wagons that were loaded with tents, poles and other equipment. When a new show site was reached, the wagons could be rolled off the flat cars while carrying their loads. Once unloaded, they would be moved from the rail yard to the site of the day's show, a process that was usually turned into a publicity-generating parade. Use of its own train permitted a circus to finish an evening show, reload the rail cars, travel overnight to the next town and set up in the morning for afternoon and evening shows at the new location. Larger circuses often used enough rail cars, perhaps thirty or forty, to warrant having several "sections" (i.e., separate trains).

Most shows would play in several Cape Breton towns. One of the first large shows to come to Cape Breton was the Great Pan-American Show that played both North Sydney and Sydney in July 1903. In June 1920, Howe's Great London Circus visited three towns, New Waterford, Glace Bay and Sydney Mines. In 1938, Robbins Bros. Circus gave afternoon and evening shows in Charlottetown, PEI, on Saturday, June 11. The two sections then travelled the 400 miles with at least two ferry runs to reach Sydney by Monday morning. An account of the Robbins tour notes that this run, including a stop in Stellarton to feed and water the animals, "was made in record time ... with the excellent service given by the C. N. Railroad." The circus played in Sydney on Monday and Tuesday and moved to North Sydney for a Wednesday night show. By the early hours of Thursday morning, the Robbins trains were en route to Point Tupper, the ferry dock and the next day's show back on the mainland.[30]

In August 1949, Daily Brothers circus narrowly avoided a serious accident en route to Cape Breton. The first section of the two-section train went through an open switch west of Truro and ran into some gondola cars loaded with sand on a siding. Fortunately the train was moving at slow speed and there was little damage. Following performances in Truro the show continued eastward with the two trains requiring three ferry runs to cross the Strait of Canso. On August 11, there were two shows in Glace Bay followed by a two-day stand in Sydney on the 12th and 13th. Following the last Sydney show, Daily Bros. headed back to the mainland and their next stop in Halifax.[31] Though other circuses came to the island after 1949, Daily Bros. appears to have run the last circus trains to Cape Breton.

The Night Jesse James Almost Held Up the Passenger Train

Pat Meagher

Pat Meagher, a native of Mulgrave, had a long career with the CNR. He was Station Agent at Point Tupper when the Canso causeway opened in 1955 and retired in 1973 from the position of Ticket Agent in Sydney. His story about his cousin Bernie indicates that "circus-type" events might be local and spontaneous. Meagher did not attach a date to the following story though it seems likely that it took place before the 1958 mailcar robbery. Cousin Bernie's prank would not have been amusing in the years soon after the real holdup.

"My cousin Bernie Meagher was one of those people who got his kicks out of pranks. He worked on the Canadian National out of Mulgrave but when work was scarce exercised his seniority and worked in the Point Tupper roundhouse. He came to work across the strait from Mulgrave to Point Tupper on his own boat....

"One night while I was busy selling train tickets for No. 8, the passenger train was soon due, I heard a commotion on the platform. Looking out the big window, I saw Bernie astride an old black horse.... He had a black handkerchief over his face and was waving a toy pistol over his head.

"Of all things, he was shouting, 'I'm Jesse James and I'm going to hold up the passenger train'.

"The driver of the shunter, Alex MacKinnon, saw Bernie going to the railway station and knowing his intentions decided to get in on the act. After climbing aboard the shunter, he came up the passing track with the engine at full throttle, his whistle blowing and his head out the cab window.

"He was yelling, 'Wyatt Earp to the rescue'!

"When the docile old horse saw that big black devil coming at him with headlight gleaming, whistle blowing, and steam puffing, he bolted and flung Bernie into the air, after which Bernie made a three-point landing on his rump, back and head. Regaining his feet, Bernie gingerly flexed his muscles, and began turning his head and neck to the left and right. To nobody's surprise except his own, he had become victim of his own joke.

"One of the passengers going out on the train that night was Senator MacLellan from Port Hastings, bound for Ottawa. I heard the senator, who never caught the practical joke at first, tell the story again and again reveling in its sheer excitement. He never saw anything to compare to the night when Alex MacKinnon and Bernie Meagher played the roles of a legendary lawman and outlaw."

From Meagher, *Scotia People*, 41-42.

Industrial Railways

An "industrial railway" is by definition a line that operates solely within or to support some commercial or industrial venture. Such a railway is different from a "common carrier" line because it does not provide any kind of service outside its business setting. Industrial lines do not provide public passenger or freight service or carry out any of the other activities associated with railways like the Intercolonial and the CNR. Over the course of the 20th century, Cape Breton had a number of industrial railways appear, operate for a time and vanish.

One of the longest lasting industrial lines was the one operating within the Sydney steel plant. While a part of the corporate structure that owned the Sydney and Louisburg, the rail operations within the plant were separate from the S&L and never identified as a distinct entity. The steel plant line at Sydney had an equivalent at Sydney Mines, the railway that served the mines in that area and the Sydney Mines steel plant while it operated. The GMA/Scotia railway, known after 1921 as the Old Sydney Collieries line, was Cape Breton's biggest industrial line based on the amount of traffic it handled for its owners. There have been numerous references in previous chapters to OSC along with the S&L because of their similar roles in handling coal traffic. The two did differ, however, because OSC was an exclusively industrial railway while the S&L was a common carrier line that also provided public passenger and freight services.

Most of Cape Breton's other industrial railways were associated with mines or quarries, many of those being at gypsum quarries. For several decades, Ché-

Fig. 8.12 - One of the most interesting photographs from the Scotia Steel & Coal Co. railway is this image (ca. 1920) of the hospital car that was available for emergencies at the company mines in the Sydney Mines area. The car was in service until about 1922.

Kelly Photo. 80-774-4954. Beaton Institute, Cape Breton University.

ticamp was one of the island's major gypsum producers. When the Inverness and Richmond failed to extend its line north of Inverness, Chéticamp and adjacent communities were left with their hopes for a rail connection to the south unfulfilled. Despite that, an industrial railway soon appeared to handle moving gypsum from the quarry to the dock for the Great Northern Mining Company. Established in 1907, the company changed its name to the Great Northern Mining and Railway Company in 1910[32] and acquired authority to build its railway. The 3.5 mile (5.6 km) railway, opened in 1911, was a modest undertaking but it met the needs of the company to transfer the processed gypsum from the company's mill to dockside. The company output in its early years apparently went to Quebec and Montreal. While it operated, the line was the most northerly railway on the island though relatively little detail is available about it. The provincial Department of Mines report for the year it opened indicated it was standard gauge and had a single locomotive. Several years after opening, the company was reported to employ sixty-five men, twelve of whom were on the railway.[33] The company underwent a series of reorganizations and changes of name over the years until mining activity ended in 1939.[34] The original Great Northern Company was unusual in one respect: it was not a "come-from-away" firm but one locally organized under the leadership of Father Pierre Fiset, the parish priest in Chéticamp.[35]

Another short industrial railway to carry gypsum operated at St. Anne's in Victoria County. The Victoria Gypsum Mining and Manufacturing Company was established by W. H. McCurdy of Baddeck who had previously operated small mines closer to Baddeck. The Victoria company was incorporated in 1890 with Alexander Graham Bell identified in the *Act* as one of the other founders.[36] Unlike the Great Northern firm, the Victoria company did not process its gypsum. In the decade before the First World War, crude gypsum was being shipped to Pennsylvania. The two quarries, which apparently employed more than 100 men in their early years, were linked to a shipping wharf by a 4-mile (6-km) narrow gauge railway with two locomotives in service.[37] The company appears to have ceased operations in the early 1920s.

A second company operated in Victoria County at Ottawa Brook, west of Iona. The Newark Plaster Company, opened in 1907, was based in New York. It appears to have been a much smaller operation than the Victoria company though it also exported unprocessed gypsum by ship to the American market. The provincial Department of Mines report for 1912 reported the quarry to wharf railway was only one mile (1.6 km) in length, was narrow gauge, and was powered by "locomotives"—plural. Like the Victoria company, it also appears to have ceased operations in the 1920s.

In more recent days, gypsum production at various points around the Bras d'Or increased considerably. It reached a scale where small railways could not provide efficient transport to shipping docks. In the 1990s, a subsidiary of U.S. Gypsum was exporting more than a million t a year using an endless conveyor system to carry the stone from quarry to dockside. Another large company, Georgia-Pacific, moved comparable volumes by rail from a quarry at Big Brook to Port Hawkesbury though the trains moved on the CNR line. The company had its own locomotive at the shipping terminal.

Fig. 8.13 - This 50-t diesel, built by General Electric in 1956, was donated to the Orangedale Station museum in 2000 by the Georgia Pacific company after the firm ended railway shipment of gypsum to its terminal at Port Hawkesbury. This small diesel is the only "preserved" railway engine on display in Cape Breton.

Author's photo with permission of Orangedale Railway Museum.

A different kind of small industrial railway found in Cape Breton was the marine railway. The all-inclusive definition of such a line would be that it was one designed to carry boats. That role implied that at least one end of the rail line went to at least the edge of water and perhaps down into water, whether a harbour, river or lake. Boats could be floated or hauled into place on a rail car designed for the purpose. The concept is illustrated in a drawing (figure 0.2) in the introduction of this book. See the top section of the 1824 drawing by James George of Quebec City where a boat is being loaded onto the rail car at water's edge.

Marine railways could serve two basic purposes other than serving as substitutes for locks within a canal. One option was as an *alternative* to a canal. Carrying boats overland between two bodies of water might make sense under certain conditions—though marine railways of this category were uncommon and frequently unsuccessful. The closest that Maritimers came to seeing this type of railway in operation was in the 1880s when Henry Ketchum's Chignecto Marine Transport Railway Company began construction of a marine railway to connect the Bay of Fundy with Northumberland Strait. The ambitious project ran out of both financial and political support in 1891 though Ketchum attempted to keep it alive till he died in 1896.[38]

The marine railways that operated in Cape Breton and elsewhere in the Maritimes were much smaller and more specialized. These were lines at shipyards or drydocks for use in launching newly built vessels or taking ships out of the water for maintenance or repair work. While somewhat similar methods using wooden slipways had been common at shipyards for many centuries, the new term "marine railway" came into use in the mid-19th century and appeared in several locations in Cape Breton in the 1860s.

The Archibald family, mentioned previously in conjunction with the Gowrie Coal Company, established the North Sydney Marine Railway Company in 1865. Ships weighing up to 2,000 t could be handled at this site. The year before, the Strait of Canso Marine Railway was opened at Point Tupper. This firm operated under several names until the 1960s. The North Sydney Marine Railway still operates under a successor company.[39]

Ghosts Along the Track

A final topic that should not be overlooked is that of the stories of the supernatural related to railway lines. Stories of this type are deeply rooted in Cape Breton's oral culture and reflect traditions that came with the early settlers from Scotland and Ireland, though other traditions may have been at work along this particular track. Ghost stories connected to railways were common throughout eastern North America in the 19th century and appeared in locations without any strong Celtic connections.

In the 1920s, Mary Fraser collected stories of the supernatural across Nova Scotia.[40] Among the stories she found involving railways, some were about forerunners, sightings that were premonitions of things to come. While forerunners were often predictions of death, they were sometimes benign and several of Fraser's railway forerunners were merely predictions of where railways would be built at a later date. One of those came from Mabou and told of visions of a train at a point where the Inverness and Richmond line would run in the future. A similar story came from a farm outside Point Tupper when the first surveyors were examining possible routes for the Intercolonial. "The old farmer came out to them," recorded Fraser, "and told them that they were wasting their time there, for the trains would pass at the rear of the house, for he had seen them there. The next year, a new survey was made, and sure enough to-day the trains pass behind the old farmer's house." From Barrachois, on the St. Andrews Channel leading to the Bras d'Or, came a more traditional forerunner—an omen on death on the Intercolonial.

The Phantom Train at Barrachois

By Mary Fraser

Some years ago, people who lived on a certain hill at Barrachois, Cape Breton, used to watch a phantom train glide noiselessly around the headland of the Bras d'Or, and come to a stop at a gate leading to one of the houses. One who saw it herself told me how at seven o'clock every evening for a whole month, every family on the hill would go out of doors to see it. Every coach was lighted, but no people could be seen. At the hour of its approach, some people sometimes went down to the track to get a better look at it, but were disappointed at its not coming at all, although the watchers on the hill saw it as usual. At the end of the month, a man was killed by the train just at the gate to which the phantom train used to come. Nobody saw it afterwards.

From Fraser, *Folklore of Nova Scotia*, 45-46.

Jay Underwood, a railway historian from Elmsdale, Nova Scotia, has published a book about the supernatural stories specifically connected to the province's railways.[41] In the absence of details from Fraser about the date of the sightings of the Barrachois phantom train, Underwood speculated that the story may be tied to the death of Alexander McDonald in 1901. McDonald, the deputy warden of the county, died of injuries suffered when he was struck by an Intercolonial snowplow train at Boisdale, a short distance from Barrachois.

Though the "ghost story" genre is rooted in the years before or around the turn of the 20th century, more recent versions can also be found. Michael MacKenzie of Christmas Island has published an account of several "forerunners" associated with the death of Rod MacKenzie, a CNR section foreman, run down and killed by a freight train near Christmas Island in 1936.[42] During the 1940s and later, there was a tradition of a spirit of some kind in the S&L roundhouse at Glace Bay. The spectre was seen by many employees over the years, but was not regarded as a threat. One account of the roundhouse ghost has been provided by Leo Evans, a long-time S&L employee. Evans remembered his first day on the job when he was told by the foreman. "Oh, by the way, ignore the ghost. He won't bother you."[43]

9 – Working on the Railways: Railways As Employers

At their peaks, railways were important sources of jobs in a number of Cape Breton communities. The work done by railway employees changed over time in response to changes in technology but there was always a wide range of jobs. There were the crews responsible for construction of track, bridges, turntables, stations and other infrastructure. Local crews called section gangs looked after short sections of track in use. At larger stations, station agents were supported by freight and express handlers, sold passenger tickets, looked after baggage, express and freight shipments and handled the cash. In earlier years they were also responsible for operating signals or passing on train orders to engineers on trains coming through their stations. Central administration offices had the upper layers of supervisors and managers plus specialized staff such as auditors who did annual detailed reviews of the records in each station.

Administrative centres were often locations for "roundhouses" where locomotives were stored. These facilities were railway equivalents of bus garages. A roundhouse complex like the S&L site at Glace Bay had crews of machinists and other skilled workers providing maintenance and repair services for locomotives, freight and passenger cars and other equipment. Last, but far from least, were the train operating crews. These included brakemen, train conductors, locomotive firemen and engineers, the "drivers" who ran the locomotives.

Most Intercolonial/CNR employees were based in Sydney, North Sydney or the ferry towns at the Strait of Canso where there were roundhouses at both Mulgrave and Point Tupper. As a result of the location of the S&L roundhouse and shop facilities in Glace Bay, that town and its adjacent communities appear to have been home for most S&L employees.

The independent lines at the Strait, the I&R and the CBR were small by comparison but within their local areas they were also important sources of jobs in their early years. Inverness and Richmond employees were concentrated at Inverness, the line's northern terminal, though that pattern changed after the line became a part of the CNR when Point Tupper became the base for many Inverness branch employees. Available data on railway employment is fragmentary but what is available indicates the importance of railway jobs in

Fig. 9.1 - This aerial photo c.a1 965 is centered on the S&L yard at Glace Bay. The steam locomotives have disappeared from the roundhouse but the rest of the site is still a hub for railway activity. Note the roundhouse's interior turntable which rotated to permit locomotives to move in and out of the stalls. To the right of the roundhouse (in this photo) were the machine shops for maintenance and repair of locomotives, rail cars and other equipment. Across the tracks (and near the upper right hand edge of the photo) were the passenger station and freight shed positioned between the railway and Union Street. Several of the Glace Bay photos in chapter 6 can be looked at as detailed components of this aerial shot.

Collection of Carole MacDonald, Halifax.

these communities. The following table's estimates for 1907 provide a snapshot of the relative importance of railway employment in Cape Breton from 1900 to the 1960s.

Railway Employment: A Sample Year—1907

The table below offers estimates of railway employment in 1907 in five key railway towns. To provide perspective, estimates have also been made for labour force totals based on the town populations from the 1901 census. The railway employment estimates are then shown as percentages of the towns' labour forces. The estimates are a bit simplistic but they provide a rough indication of the importance of the railways as generators of jobs and incomes.

Table 9.1 - Railway Employment Estimates for 1907				
Town	Estimated Total # Railway Employees	1901 Town Population	Estimated 1901 Town Male Labour Force	Estimate of Railway Employment as percentage of Town Male Labour Force
Inverness	48	2000 (est)	400	12%
Sydney Mines	52	3198	640	8%
North Sydney	56	4646	929	6%
Glace Bay	158	6945	1389	11%
Louisbourg	34	1046	209	16%
Totals	348	17834	3567	10%

Data Sources: Railway employees: based on *McAlpine's Nova Scotia Directory, 1907-1908*, Halifax: McAlpine, 1908; 1901 Town Populations from 1901 census data in *Canada Yearbook*, 1907 and 1914; 1901 Labour Force Estimates are extrapolated from 1901 census data using the percentage of national male "wage earners" "at regular work" as percentage of total national population in *Canada Yearbook*, 1907.

As a generalization, it can be suggested that at least some of these jobs were perhaps even more significant than the data in the table indicate. Railway employees, especially on the Intercolonial and later the CNR where often-volatile coal traffic was not the focus of activity, were less subject to temporary or extended layoffs triggered by downward cycles in the coal industry. In addition to greater long-run job security than most workers in other industries, they tended to have higher and more stable incomes. Wage levels, benefits and working conditions on the IRC and CNR were the result of the early appearance of strong unions on the government railway system.

Railway Employee Unions

John A. Macdonald's government passed a *Trade Union Act* in 1872 that legalized trade unions in work areas under federal jurisdiction. Under the protection of this Act, the railway unions which had appeared in the United States expanded into Canada and recruited members from the ranks of railway employees in this country. Most of these were "craft unions" whose members came from specific trades or employee groups, a pattern that has survived in the union movement on railways to the present. In its early days, the union movement on the railways was led by employees in the "running trades," the men who ran the trains. The Brotherhood of Locomotive Engineers, the Brotherhood of Locomotive Firemen and Enginemen, the Order of Railway Conductors and the Brotherhood of Railroad Trainmen—often referred to as the "Big 4"—led the way in the quest for recognition by railway companies, something that was not automatically provided by the 1872 *Act*. As collective bargaining rights were achieved, the unions negotiated contracts and sought improvements in wages, hours and working conditions and the introduction of other benefits such as

Fig. 9.2 - Cover of a beneficiary certificate from a B.R.T. union insurance policy c.1914.

Port Hastings Museum and Archives, RG 6, 14.

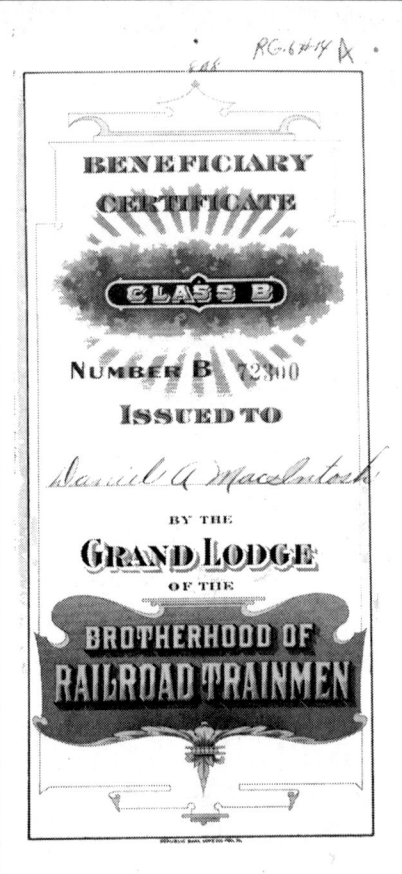

pensions and insurance programs. Seniority rights protected employees with work experience; in the event of lay-offs, those most recently hired would be the first to lose their jobs.[1]

One other benefit that employees and family members enjoyed was that of free travel. The extent of the travel permitted was based on years of service. Employees with a significant number of years could travel virtually without limit on distance though a "pass" normally applied only to coach class. Sleeping car or dining car services had to be paid for. Railways usually recognized each other's passes or would issue reciprocal passes. This meant, for example, that a CNR or S&L employee from Cape Breton with enough years of service would be able to get passes for travel throughout the United States as well as across Canada.

Once in a while, employee perseverance might be called for. Dan MacKinnon, an S&L brakeman and later a conductor, recalled a story about a trip to Boston in 1937 for which he hadn't been able to get a pass from the Boston and Maine. On the way down, he paid the B&M fare for the last section of the southbound trip, that from Portland into Boston. While in Boston, he went to the B&M pass bureau to request a pass for his return. When his request was being considered, the B&M staff member checked on the status of the S&L and observed, "it's only a small, little railroad." MacKinnon responded, "Yes, it is … but it's just as wide as the Boston & Maine."[2] MacKinnon's account of the story did not indicate if he got a B&M pass or not.[3]

Despite early recognition from some lines such as the Great Western and the Grand Trunk, union attempts to gain collective bargaining rights were initially opposed by most of the privately-owned railways. By 1890, however, when the Intercolonial reached Cape Breton, the "Big 4" and other unions had come to represent large numbers of railway workers across the country. On the Intercolonial, General Manager David Pottinger had initially opposed union

Fig. 9.3 - As holder of a pass valid over the entire CNR system, W. A. McLean must have had a considerable amount of seniority.

Port Hastings Museum and Archives.

John the Grit and the Open Bridge

by Michael MacKenzie

"A few years after the opening of the CNR (the old ICR [sic]) mainline between Grand Narrows and Sydney in 1890, 'John the Grit,' as he was called, was one of the two bridge tenderers. He was employed for about two years, but became dissatisfied with conditions of employment, especially his wages, which were relatively low, even for those years.

"Having concluded that he was underpaid, John MacKinnon or 'John the Grit' was not a fellow to beat around the bush. He requested an increase in his salary forthwith. The wheels of justice were not going to grind slowly for him—he devised an apparently quick and simple solution to the whole problem, he thought, yet one which might remove the problem from him instead of solving it. To put his plan into execution he proceeded to open the drawbridge on the seven-span Grand Narrows bridge across the Bras d'Or lakes where he worked, or at least to open it sufficiently that he could jump across the abutment yet prevent the trains from using it. John then hied himself up to his boarding house at Dan Joe MacNeil's, about half-a-mile away.

"John the Grit assumed that the inconvenience to the freight trains and the passenger train would compel the Intercolonial Railway (ICR), the predecessor of the CNR, to grant him his 'reasonable' request for higher wages. But the ICR did not view it that way. Two freight trains heading east were held up west of Iona. The ICR agent at adjacent Grand Narrows station alerted the divisional authorities in Sydney of their local predicament, and even danger. Two hours later a passenger train arrived at the Grand narrows station from Sydney with an IRC policeman on board. He proceeded to apprehend John the Grit at his boarding house and take him into custody back to the Sydney lock-up aboard the passenger train.

"In the meantime the local officials called upon the other tenderer to close the bridge and turn the safety lights so that the two freights could proceed on their way to Sydney....

"But that was not quite the end of the tale. John the Grit, being a very well-known local character and 'politician', his Ottawa and Halifax friends such as D. D. MacKenzie, M.P.; Dr. Kendall, M.L.A.; and especially George Murray, M.L.A., a native of Grand Narrows, and long-time Premier of Nova Scotia, spoke up on his behalf as character witnesses at the court hearing the next day in Sydney. 'John the Grit' MacKinnon was released from jail. But he lost his ICR job as bridge tenderer."

MacKenzie's account of "John the Grit" went on to note that "several years later he was rehired" as painting foreman for Intercolonial bridges, a post he held for several years. It seems reasonable to speculate that MacKinnon's return to the railway took place after the Liberals came to power in Ottawa under Laurier in 1896, perhaps during the period between the 1904 election and mid-1906 when D. D. MacKenzie was the Liberal MP for the riding of North Cape Breton-Victoria.

From Michael MacKenzie, *Glimpses of the Past*, 90-91. Reprinted by permission of Breton Books, Wreck Cove, NS.

recognition. In 1882, however, the Macdonald government intervened to permit the Brotherhood of Locomotive Engineers to represent IRC engineers and over the next few years other major unions were also given bargaining rights.[4] From the late-1880s on, relations between the IRC and the unions were relatively tranquil in contrast to many of the other big Canadian railways where strikes were fairly common.[5] The IRC led the way in introducing many types of employee benefits for railway employees in Cape Breton and the Maritimes. For example, a pension plan called "the provident fund" was established in 1907 with employees paying in 1.5 per cent of their earnings which was being matched by the railway.[6] Not all railway employees belonged to unions. Those without union membership often had problems in trying to negotiate independently. The story of "John the Grit" of Grand Narrows provides a touch of humour while reflecting several sides of the realities of life for many railway employees in the 1890s.

Most Canadian railway unions, both in the running trades and those for "non-operating" employees, were International unions attached to organizations based in the United States. One exception to this model was a union founded by Intercolonial employees in Moncton in 1908. The Canadian Brotherhood of Railroad Employees (CBRE) emerged to represent employees such as roundhouse workers, freight handlers and clerks whose job classes left them excluded from membership in other unions whose memberships were tied to specific occupation groups. The charter of CBRE Division 68 established at Point Tupper with sixteen members can be seen at the Port Hastings Museum and Archives. By the late 1920s, the CBRE had the largest membership of all Canadian railway unions.[7] As a passing illustration of the long-run trend in the history of Canadian railways and their unions, it seems appropriate to mention that the CBRE no longer exists as an independent union. In 1993, the organization merged with the Canadian Auto Workers union.

On railways that operated in conjunction with the mines, workers who tried to establish unions often had a more difficult time; this is in keeping with the stormy history of labour relations in Cape Breton's mines. In 1902, labourers on the Scotia railway tried to establish a union. Recognition was refused and the men were fired. A newspaper account reported that "others have taken their place and the work continues without any interruption."[8] On the Inverness and Richmond, employees were able to join the Provincial Workmens' Association (PWA) which was primarily a miners' union. Founded in Springhill in 1879, the PWA was a strong voice for labour in its early years, but by 1900 it had become so conservative that it was widely regarded as little more than a "company union."[9]

On the S&L, the railway workers achieved more and did so sooner than might have been expected given the long-running resistance of Dominion Coal and most of its associated companies to the labour movement. Running trades locals were established just after 1900. The charter of the Brotherhood of Railroad Trainmen, issued to local # 684 in Glace Bay in 1903, is on display at the S&L Museum in Louisbourg. The local was originally established with ten members. Other running trades unions were set up on the S&L at about the same time.[10]

Fig. 9.4 - This B.R.T. ribbon from the S&L Trainmen's union probably dates from the 1903 founding of the local or very soon after that date.

Sydney & Louisburg Railway Museum.

The differences between wage levels and working hours for employees on the government railway (by 1921 the CGR) versus those on the railways owned by Cape Breton's two steel and coal companies illustrates the differentials that tended to exist throughout the history of Cape Breton's railways. The unions on the mining and steel-related lines were never able to achieve wage or benefit levels for their members to match those on the national railway system.

Fig. 9.5 - A relatively recent membership card from the B.L.F.E. Many CNR engineers and firemen belonged to this union.

Sydney & Louisburg Railway Museum.

Table 9.2 - Wage Rates: Scotia, Disco and Canadian Government Railways, April 1921			
Employee Category	Scotia	Disco	CGR
Engineers	.57 /hr	.64 /hr	.88 /hr
Firemen	.44 /hr	.50 /hr	.70 /hr
Conductors	.50 /hr	.60 /hr	.88 /hr
Brakemen	.44 /hr	.60 /hr	.81 /hr
Overtime: Above 8 hrs/day	As above	As above	1.5 times above rates
Standard Work Day	12 hrs	12 hrs	8 hrs
Total Average Wage For 12-Hour Day	$5.85	$7.02	$11.45
Note: It is uncertain whether the "Disco" rates applied to all Disco railway employees including those on the S&L or if the rate schedule was specific to rail employees within the steel plant. Recall that at this time the S&L was a distinct company though it was owned outright by Disco. Data source: *Workers' Weekly*, Stellarton, NS, April 26, 1921: 1.			

Construction Workers and Sectionmen

The previous part of this chapter has dealt with "local" employees, those who went to work on Cape Breton's railways as job opportunities appeared nearby. Not all jobs, however, went to locals. This was particularly true at the construction stage and especially for the construction of the Intercolonial. Most of the IRC line was built through districts where few people lived. As a result, there was a shortage of labour for temporary work on the project. Partly related to this, the primary contractor—Reid and Isbester on the western section, and Sims and Slater on the section from Grand Narrows to Sydney—issued subcontracts to firms or individuals "from away" who had appropriate experience and could bring in their own workers. From the history of the Italian community in the Sydney area comes the story of one of those sub-contractors.

Running a Construction Gang at Boisdale, 1887

by Thomas Cozzolino

"While in Ottawa, we met someone hiring men to go to Cape Breton where the government was building a railway from Port Hawkesbury to North Sydney. I spoke to the contractor, and agreed to take a gang of men to Cape Breton on condition that the company pay our travel fare. He agreed. The men were to be paid $1.25 for each 10 hour day they worked. Our arrangement was for a six month work period.

"We travelled from Ottawa to Mulgrave, Nova Scotia by rail. From there we were to take a boat to St. Peter's Canal but the canal was blocked with ice. The railway manager told us to go to West Bay Road, about ten miles away, to wait for a boat. We hired a few teams to carry our baggage, and we started off on foot. We arrived at West Bay Road in late afternoon. The weather was cold along the seashore. We spent the entire night on the wharf waiting for the boat; we nearly froze. There was no accommodation in the little town for such a big crowd of men. The people were afraid of us, and would not allow us near their places.

"By the next night the boat still had not come. We decided that we could not spend another night outside; so we broke into the schoolhouse and lit the stove. The people of the place thought we were awful to have done this, but we did no damage. We just kept ourselves warm for the night. It is very cold at night along the seashore.

"In the morning, at about 9 am, the boat finally arrived, and we were able to continue our journey. We arrived in Grand Narrows that evening, and spent the night in a large barn. The next day we walked the remaining 20 miles to Boisdale. There we rented a large house for the men, and got the straw to make the beds. The men were comfortable there, so we made it our headquarters. I boarded at a place called MacIntyre's near the Post Office. They were nice people. The townspeople, however, were not aware that such a large group was coming to Boisdale. No one had made preparations to supply our food. We could not get any bread, so we lived on potatoes and eggs for a few days. Eggs were very cheap at that time—eight cents a dozen.

"I went to Sydney on horseback (no saddle) to try to get some provisions, especially bread, for the men, but I could not get any that day. So I bought lots of goods, a few barrels of hard crackers, and enough bricks to build an oven. In three days time we baked our own bread.

"I was in charge of a gang of men for over a month; then the contractor gave me full charge of a five mile section of the line. I was pretty young to have that charge, but I managed well. The local people were being paid 90 cents a day, while my men, being under contract for six months, were getting $1.25. The local men were good workers. When they found out that they were being paid less, they all went on strike. But, all along the line, the contractors were paying 90 cents per day; they did not get an increase. I was sorry for them. After our six months were up, the contractor told us that the men would have to accept 90 cents per day if they wanted to stay on the job. The men would not stay. The contractor wanted me to remain to finish the section, but I would not leave my men. So we all left at the end of October, 1887."

From "Memoirs of Thomas Cozzolino," in Migliore and DiPierro, eds., 49-50.[11]

In 1880, Thomas Cozzolino sailed from Naples for the United States at age fourteen. He found opportunities in railway construction, first as a labourer then as a foreman and then as a sub-contractor who organized and supervised work crews. In 1885, he came to Canada as a foreman on a Canadian Pacific line being built westward from Montreal. Following several other Canadian railway projects, he came to Cape Breton in 1887. His memoirs offer a first-hand account of the challenges faced by the men who built the Intercolonial toward Sydney.

Cozzolino's experience in Cape Breton in 1887 was only one part of his story. He came back to the IRC project in 1889, working on the western end of the line under construction. He married a New Brunswick girl and established a home there while continuing with railway contracts across eastern Canada. In 1899, he returned to Sydney on a contract on the new steel plant. In January of 1901, Cozzolino's family moved to Sydney where they lived for almost thirty years. Through the Nova Scotia Construction Company, which he established in 1905, he continued to undertake contracts in eastern and central Canada for railways, bridges and wharves. The family moved to Montreal in the late 1920s, but returned to Sydney after Cozzolino's retirement in the 1930s. He died in Sydney in 1949.

Once construction was completed on rail lines, permanent local employees were required for many jobs. One of the most critical was that of maintaining and repairing the track. These men made up section gangs responsible for short sections of line in the range of five to ten miles. As an extension of Thomas Cozzolino's account from 1887, Peter MacDonald of Big Beach, a short distance along the Intercolonial from Boisdale, wrote an account of his father's experiences as a sectionman soon after the IRC opened for traffic.

Over the years, one of the greatest changes in the lives of sectionmen was in how they moved about to do their jobs along the line. Peter MacDonald's account seems to suggest that his father's gang travelled on foot and that was quite likely the case. Before too long, a wonderful invention called the "pumper" appeared on the scene. It was light enough that just one man could move it on or off the track though that was quicker and easier as a two-man job. Powered by the up and down handles which controlled a set of gears, the pumper could travel fairly fast and easily handle four men. Equally important, attachment of one or more flat trolleys built with a similarly sized wheelbase gave the gang capacity to haul tools, wooden ties (which were heavy), barrels of spikes (which were

Fig. 9.6 - A S&L sectionman with his hammer, ca. 1920. Railways have always depended on their sectionmen to inspect and maintain the tracks that are the foundation for railway operations.

Sydney & Louisburg Railway Museum, #SL-00-587.

177 WORKING ON THE RAILWAYS

> ### Working on an Intercolonial Section Gang in the 1890s
> by Peter MacDonald
>
> "My late father was one of the first section-men when the road was completed for traffic. The wages for a section-man for ten hours work, at that time, was one dollar per day. There being very little ballast to keep the track from sinking into the mud and clay with the result that during winter the track was heaving which made very rough riding. The track had to be shimmed, owing to such heavy heaving almost all the time. The section-foreman used to buy poplar trees in order to make shims. On a stormy day or when raining, the section-men had to take this poplar wood to the toolhouse and make shims. They had to have an auger to bore holes in the wood where spikes were going through. The track used to spread considerable and the section-men had to make plugs out of cedar railway ties to plug holes where spreads occurred. And that was quite often. Through this means, they were taking the track to proper gauge. My father had to walk the distance of three miles each morning to the toolhouse and had to carry a bag on his back containing some spikes and bolts with a track hammer and a track wrench. On Sunday he had to patrol three miles of the section while the other section-man patrolled the other three miles."
>
> From "History of Cape Breton Railroad," Beaton Institute, Reports: Transportation, # 82-98-1568: 4-5. Date uncertain but believed written ca. 1948. An article by Peter MacDonald, "How the Railway Came to Cape Breton," appeared in the *Sydney Post-Record* of April 23, 1948. Reprinted with permission of the Beaton Institute, Cape Breton University

even heavier) and even rails. Hammers, crowbars, ties, spikes and rails formed the core of a section gang's stock in trade—and still do except in locations with more modern track where rails are welded rather than sectional.

The beautifully preserved pumper at the S&L Museum in Louisbourg calls out for a section of track for test runs by railroaders past and present—and those who, in the right time and place, had the opportunity to take a pumper out for a run, to go fishing, to a ball game or just for fun. Hopefully, memories of doing that will come back to more than one reader of this book as they did to Linden MacIntyre as he wrote his memoir of growing up in Port Hastings.

Fig. 9.7 - A restored S&L pumper that is as ready to roll as it was a century ago.

Author's photo courtesy of Sydney & Louisburg Railway Museum.

Boyhood Adventures on the Inverness Branch
by Linden MacIntyre

"On Sundays, when there were no trains, and before all the new construction, older boys would sometimes steal the pump-car from the railway shack. We'd travel the rails, pumping up and down at either end of a long handle that works like a see-saw. The summit of liberation—pumping slowly up and down, the little trolley skimming over the rails silently, heading northward where we wouldn't be noticed by the railwaymen. Rumbling along Ghost Beach, with the strait on the left and Long Pond on the right, dark and calm. Riding along with the breeze on my face, feeling like an outlaw."

From MacIntyre, *Causeway*, 46.

Pumpers came into general use early in the 20th century and were still around, particularly on branch lines, into the 1960s. By the 1930s, however, they had become second class technology with the arrival of gasoline-powered units usually called "speedies." They were heavier than pumpers and more difficult to get on and off the track but, on the plus side, they were faster and the engine provided the power. While the speedy shown here probably dates from the 1930s, modern-day versions are only cosmetically different from those from decades gone by.

Fig. 9.8 (left) - 1920s CNR section gang that worked out of Point Tupper. Left to right are Duncan Francis MacDonald (Section Foreman who was killed on the railway in 1930); Angus MacKinnon; Donald MacIsaac; Allie Nicholson.

Port Hastings Museum and Archives, #87.665/N.107.6.

Fig. 9.9 (right) - S&L section gang on a speedy, ca. 1945

Sydney & Louisburg Railway Museum.

Station Agents

To deal with most railway customers, station agents were the front line employees, the first level of contact with people travelling on the trains. For those who used freight or express services, for either a small parcel or a boxcar loaded with lumber, the agents made arrangements for shipments going out or being received. At most stations, money orders could be purchased, a useful service in earlier days when few people had bank accounts let alone debit or credit

The Ten Thousand Dollar Lesson

J. William Calder

The following is a first-person account by Calder's brother, Jamie, who served for decades as the CNR agent at St. Peter's.

"Many small packages of value were shipped by express; these I would place in the safe to be handed to the baggage man who doubled as express agent aboard the train. He was obliged to sign for any shipment, which relieved me of further responsibility. He had the loose habit of signing without checking. From time to time, I reminded him of the possibility of a misunderstanding; of a shortage and the dire consequences; but he merely laughed and would say, 'That's OK, I trust you'.

"The Royal Bank of the village would from time to time forward packages of paper currency consigned to their head office in Halifax. One afternoon, the manager, W. L. Wright, came to the station with a carefully wrapped package. It was glued and tied and the knots of the tough twine were encased with wax.

"'You'll be very careful with this', the manager said, 'there's ten thousand dollars in there; 'course you'd be in bad trouble if it disappeared.' He sort of laughed and peered over his glasses as if he wasn't quite sure. I gave Mr. Wright a receipt and immediately placed the package in the safe, tucking it far back into a corner.

"As the train was about to depart the following morning, the baggage man hurried into the office. The express voucher was made out and lay on my desk. He took his pencil and signed as I removed the packages from the safe. These he placed in a canvas bag and bidding me, so long, he quick stepped it to the waiting train.

"It was half an hour or more later I had occasion to open the safe and I discovered the bank package still tucked in a far corner. My first impulse was to ring the agent at Point Tupper and advise him about the oversight. He would certainly check carefully before releasing our agent. I decided against it; let our man call me.

"He did of course and he was quite cocky. 'Say, boy, you didn't give me that package with the ten thousand dollars'!

"His attitude and the tone of his voice riled me. 'You signed for it, fellow'! I hung up.

"The train at that time was on a three day schedule to St. Peter's so our man had a forty-eight hour period to sweat it out, and I was told he did just that. When the train arrived the next morning, the conductor hurried to the office and took me to one side. 'Say', he spoke quietly to me, 'do you know if our baggage man is in any trouble? God, he paced the floor all night; didn't shut an eye'.

"When the baggage man came to the office, he was pale and haggard. He flopped to a chair and when he learned the truth he was silent, and never once, as long as I knew him, did he refer to the episode. But he sure did, from that time on, check and recount the packages before signing a voucher."

From Calder, *All Aboard*, 134-35. reprinted by permission of Formac Publishing Company Limited.

cards. A related service was the railway's telegraph system. While sending or receiving telegrams was not as common or as widely available as the use of railway-issued money orders, the telegraph system provided a means of rapid communication until the ready availability of reliable telephone service.

At large stations such as Sydney, there would be a number of employees; duties would be divided into specialty service areas such as passenger ticket sales, baggage, express and freight. Across most of Cape Breton and the rest of the Maritimes, however, agents were responsible for all these functions and more. As a result they had to be familiar with the fare structure for passenger tickets and the rates for various categories of express shipments. At stations with telegraph service, agents had to be trained "on the key" as it was called. Handling freight shipments like a boxcar load of lumber required knowledge of the complex set of freight tariffs. By the 1950s, the freight tariffs filled a massive set of binders with thousands of pages of rate details covering all possible types of products to all possible destinations.

In addition to dealing with the public, the agents had close contact with train crews. They, or the signals they operated, served for many years as the source of orders to provide updated instructions to locomotive engineers and train conductors. They also relayed the orders about freight cars required for loading or loaded cars ready to be picked up. For small express or freight shipments, they were responsible for supervision of loading and unloading, for storage, and for delivery of goods arriving. Keeping accurate records of both shipments and cash was an important part of the job and station records were reviewed regularly by auditors. Sometimes formal procedures were not followed and the results could be interesting for those involved. William Calder's account of an incident involving a shipment of cash from the St. Peter's station provides an entertaining example.

While station hours and agents' work-schedules were generally set, in smaller communities they were often informal in practice. It was common for agents to make themselves available "out of hours" to people who needed to buy a money order or pick up an express shipment but could not do so in regular station hours. Smaller railway stations also often served as virtual community centres. People would often gather, especially at the time of arrival of evening passenger trains, to see who was travelling, have a cup of tea, share the news of the day, play a game of cards or make music. It was not unusual for a fiddle or two to be heard at small Cape Breton stations. In some locations, the fiddler might prove to be both a station master and a master of the instrument.

The *Flyer* and the Fiddler

In 1938, the young Buddy MacMaster took the *Judique Flyer* on his way home after playing his first dance at Troy, just outside Port Hastings. That dance was the launch of the public career of one of Cape Breton's greatest fiddlers. MacMaster also had a long career as an employee of the CNR.

His railway service lasted for forty-five years, beginning in 1943 when he trained as a telegrapher and station agent. One of his early assignments was at Valley, a short distance east of Truro, where he often worked the late shift. The train dispatcher in New Glasgow, Allan MacGregor, would contact Buddy and other agents through the railway phone system to exchange "good nights" and update them on any traffic moving. Sometimes he asked Buddy to play a tune and other agents up and down the line started to listen in on their headsets. Soon the Halifax and Moncton divisions were asking to be patched in and Buddy's tunes were being enjoyed by agents throughout the Maritimes.

When time was available between trains, Buddy would practice at his stations. He recounted that the stations built in the early part of the century, with their traditional plaster and lath combined with Douglas Fir panelling, had great acoustics. The smaller office rooms were great for dance music and the larger waiting rooms with their wooden ceilings complemented the slow aires. Buddy often played for waiting passengers and fiddlers such as Dan R. MacDonald and Dan Hughie MacEachern would visit to play with him.

Fig. 9.10 - Buddy MacMaster: stationmaster on duty at Mabou, 1949.

Reproduced by permission of Buddy MacMaster, Judique.

As he obtained seniority, MacMaster found himself doing lengthy stays in single stations in contrast to his early years on the "spare board" when he was frequently moved about from station to station for short periods. His first stay in the Mabou station, where the photo was taken in 1949, was for five years. While there, and in other posts, he continued to travel on the *Judique Flyer* on a regular basis until passenger service on the Inverness branch ended in 1959. His last post was at Havre Boucher where he spent fourteen years before retirement in 1988. Since then, from his home in Judique, Buddy was able to devote himself to music full time. Long before he left the railway, he had become internationally recognized as a superstar of the fiddle—though few of his listeners and fans have known that he was also a railroader for almost half a century.

Sources: liner notes from Buddy MacMaster: *The Judique Flyer*, 2000; MacInnes, *Buddy MacMaster*, 2007; interview with Buddy MacMaster, Judique, October 5, 2010.

The Roundhouse

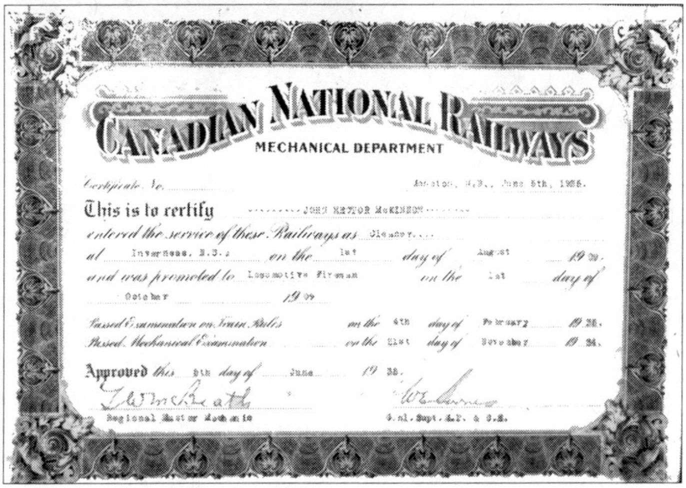

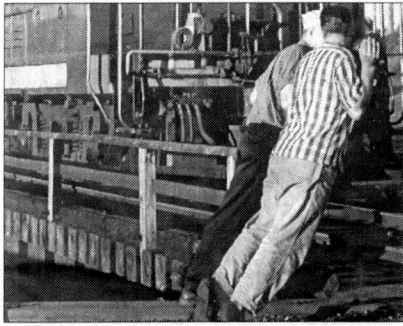

Fig. 9.11 - Turning the turntable at Inverness, 1957. While little of the locomotive is visible, it is clearly a diesel engine.

Inverness Miners' Museum, #1978, 52.

The aerial photo of the S&L facilities at Glace Bay makes it obvious why a roundhouse was called a roundhouse. Not clearly visible in the photo is the turntable in the open interior heart of the building. Whether in a roundhouse like that at Glace Bay or in a stand-alone setting like Inverness, a turntable was a device which permitted partial or full rotation of a locomotive. The "table" was delicately balanced so it could be turned on its inner and lower rail base with minimum effort. The photo from Inverness shows that table carrying a diesel engine that weighed more than 100 t could be rotated by two men. A table like the one at Inverness could even be turned by a group of boys—the sort of boys who might also go for rides on borrowed pumpers. In a roundhouse setting, always too secure and too busy for boys seeking railway adventures, the turntable would take locomotives from a single feeder track and permit them to move into any one of the many inner stalls in the building.

CANADIAN NATIONAL RAILWAYS
MECHANICAL DEPARTMENT

Certificate No. .... [illegible], N.B., June 5th, 19[illegible].

This is to certify .... JOHN HE[illegible]OR McKINNON ....

entered the service of these Railways as Cleaner...

at Inverness, N.S., on the 1st day of August 19[illegible].

and was promoted to Locomotive Fireman on the 1st day of October 1909

Passed Examination on Train Rules on the 4th day of February 19 3[illegible].

Passed Mechanical Examination on the [illegible] day of November 19 3[illegible].

Approved this 5th day of June 19 3[illegible].

Regional Master Mechanic — G[illegible].Supt. [illegible]

Fig. 9.12 - While McKinnon's certificate shows he had passed the two critical sets of examinations prior to being promoted to engineer, it suggests that his formal promotion had not yet been approved.

Port Hastings Museum and Archives.

Throughout the steam era and beyond, a roundhouse or a large engine shed was more than just a storage site for locomotives. It was also the centre for regular service and maintenance work: the cleaning, inspection and oiling of moving parts that kept engines running. A roundhouse site usually had machine shops where locomotives and other rolling stock could be repaired. During the steam era, a roundhouse site always had towers where locomotives could be "fed" coal for the firebox, water to convert to steam and sand to provide additional traction for the driving wheels when needed.

Work on a roundhouse crew was often a starting point for prospective firemen and engineers. The certificate for John Hector McKinnon documents his promotion from locomotive cleaner to fireman at Inverness in 1909. The 1934 examinations recorded on the certificate would have been steps preceding designation as an engineer. The memoir below (p. 188) by Harry Bulley records a similar career path.

Fig. 9.13 - The Inverness & Richmond roundhouse crew at Inverness, c. 1910.

Inverness Miners' Museum, #1978.51.

Train Crews

Today, except on those rare things called passenger trains, most train "crews" are made up of one person, the locomotive engineer. That marks a major change from the norm that applied during most of the railway era when a train crew had at least four men. It should be noted in passing that "four men" reflects the fact that for most of their history, railways had very few female employees. When women were employed, they were in positions other than as members of train crews.

The senior member of a traditional train crew was the conductor whose role was that of train supervisor. On passenger trains, the conductor played the primary role in dealing with passengers. On all trains, the conductor was responsible for keeping to schedule An indication of the conductor's role is found in the 1935 "special rules" of the S&L.[12] Rule # 8 stated

> No train will pass a time-table station or leave any station without a signal from its conductor. Drivers will receive the "Go Ahead" signal from the conductor immediately after blowing for station (if no stop is to be made). If stop is to be made, conductor will give stop signal.

In addition to indicating the conductor's authority over the engineer, the wording of this rule also indicates two aspects of communication between the engine cab and the conductor at a time before the appearance of on-train radios. In addition to its capacity to warn people of the approaching train, the locomotive's whistle was used by the engineer to send signals to the conductor. At this time, a steam-driven internal whistle system permitted the conductor to send signals to the engineer when the train was moving.

A conductor was almost always promoted to the position after service within the ranks of the brakemen. These were the men whose original duties had involved handling brakes on individual train cars before the development

Fig. 9.14 - Billie Burke, a brakeman on S&L passenger trains, ca. 1930.

Sydney & Louisburg Railway Museum, #SL-00-470.

of central air brake systems controlled from the locomotive. Their secondary duty was to deal with car couplers when cars were being picked up or dropped off. On passenger trains, brakemen also helped travellers getting on and off, assisted with luggage and worked with the conductor to deal with tickets and seating. Well before the appearance of passenger trains on Cape Breton, it had become standard practice for brakemen and conductors on passenger trains to

Dangerous Dagger Dan

Pat Meagher's book, *Scotia People*, the source of the "Jesse James story" in the previous chapter, also includes an account in verse about Dan Chisholm, "Dangerous Dagger Dan," a CNR conductor who worked out of Point Tupper for many years. Chisholm's railway career lasted forty-three years, from 1916 until his retirement at the end of 1959. For eight years in the 1930s, he was yard agent at Point Tupper, supervising loading and unloading of trains at the railway ferry dock. He then became a conductor on passenger trains, a post he held for two decades. After the Canso causeway was opened, he was a conductor on the mixed trains running out of Port Hawkesbury, one to St. Peter's and the other, the *Judique Flyer*, to Inverness. At the time of his retirement he said that he had experienced only one wreck in his long years of service. It happened at Judique Pond on the Inverness branch in late December of 1944 when Frank Philpott, the engineer, was killed. Chisholm was not the only member of his family to "go railroading." His brother, Christopher, was a CNR car inspector in Sydney and another brother, Alan, was an engineer.

See Halifax *Chronicle Herald*, January 5, 1960, for an account of Chisholm's career and retirement.

Fig. 9.14 (top) - CNR conductor Dan Chisholm, ca. 1955.

Port Hastings Museum and Archives.

Fig. 9.15 (bottom) - The Judique Pond wreck site, December, 1944. In the foreground is the overturned locomotive.

Chestico Museum & Historical Society, Port Hood.

wear rather formal uniforms. These are seen in the photos of Billie Burke of the S&L and Dan Chisholm of the CNR.

The reference above to Dan Chisholm's brothers being railway employees is a significant detail. From the years before 1900 until after the middle of the 20th century, it was very common to find that working on the railway was an occupation that often spanned families and generations. Jack Norris of Port Morien, whose S&L career began in 1908, had four sons who also worked for the S&L. Ralph and Graham were both car inspectors, Gerald worked on the section gang and Lawrence became a conductor like his father.[13] Another example is seen in a newspaper account of the retirement of Stephen McDonald of Port Hawkesbury, a member of another family with railway genes. McDonald's forty-six years of service and Dan Chisholm's forty-three years also show that it was common for railway employees to have long working careers. Recall the reference to Buddy MacMaster's 45 years of CNR service and note the length of Harry Bulley's career on the railway (p. 188). Their experiences provide a strong contrast with more recent norms for workers which see earlier retirement ages as well as the probability of frequent changes in employer.

Railroading as a Family Affair

"Stephen McDonald completing a 46-year career with the C.N.R. has retired. For the past seven years he was foreman at the Point Tupper roundhouse. Prior to that he was night foreman for 14 years. He was stationed at North Sydney when he first went with the C.N.R. He has a brother John T. McDonald, North Sydney, who was a conductor, a brother Dan, who used to be station master at Mahone Bay but is now in Windsor, Ontario, [and a son] Webb is with the C.N.R. between Sydney and Point Tupper. His father, Alexander McDonald, was car inspector for years at Point Tupper."

Excerpted from a newpaper clipping, Port Hastings Museum and Archives. The clipping is neither sourced nor dated, but appears to have been printed in the early 1950s.

In the locomotive at the front of the train was the engine crew: the fireman and the engineer. The "fireman" of course was so-named during the early days when the hungry firebox of a steam locomotive has fed by a man with a shovel. In later days, particularly after the advent of diesel engines, the fireman was in effect an assistant engineer. The engineer, known as the "driver" in the language of railroaders, was the senior man in the engine cab. While drivers were subordinate to their conductors, in the railway world, they enjoyed a status second to no one. As at the rear of the train, where there was a normal progression from brakeman to conductor, in the cab a driver had always spent his time in the junior role. Murdock McDonald became an S&L fireman at Glace Bay in 1916 and spent almost seven years in the fireman's seat before he was promoted to the rank of driver in 1923. Harry Bulley, whose memoir is found below, followed a similar path leading to a long career as a driver on the CNR.

Fig. 9.17 - Portion of the roster of S&L locomotive engineers in 1905. Muggah and Pushie were obviously the bosses, probably the Mechanical Superintendent and Assistant Superintendent.

Whitney Pier Historical Society Museum.

Fig. 9.18 - Another locomotive engineer's certificate. It is interesting to note that McDonald's promotion path on the S&L was much more rapid that that for John Hector McKinnon who had started as an employee on the Inverness & Richmond. McDonald had become an engineer seven years after being appointed fireman. McKinnon had become a fireman in 1909 and in the mid-1930s was still in the process of promotion to the driver's seat.

Glace Bay Heritage Museum.

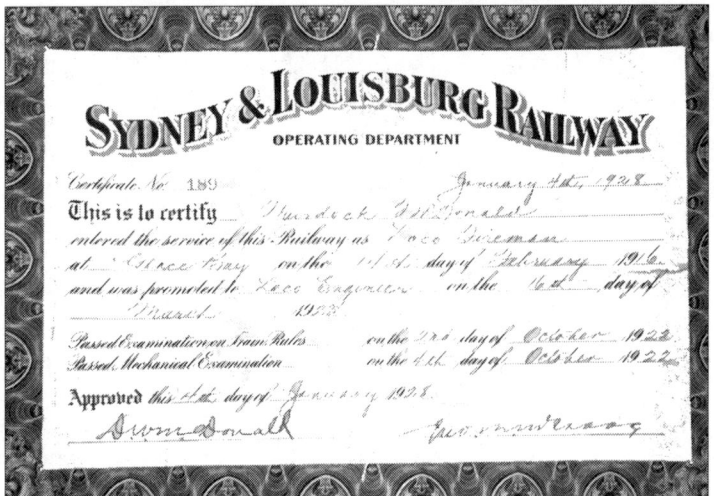

A Fireman's Secret
by Harry Bulley

Harry Bulley of Sydney joined the CGR staff at the Sydney roundhouse 1915 at age eighteen. Two years later he became a fireman and then was promoted to engineer. He worked as a "driver" out of Sydney until he retired in 1962. He was interviewed by *Cape Breton's Magazine* more than twenty years after his retirement.

"I worked in the roundhouse pretty near two years. I got out when I was 21 years old—firing on the road. This fireman took sick. And they got me out of the roundhouse, and I went on the engine. And I made a good run out on them…. That means you kept her hot for the driver, stuff like that. You kept the steam up. You knew your work hand-firing, see. You had a shovel there. And when you put a fire in the engine, you turned your shovel upside down. That would fan the flames, and that would show you where to put your coal. That would show you where the holes were in your firebox. And then if you wouldn't get the right smoke out of your stack, you didn't have the right fire in her. There's something wrong. You would have to get nice black smoke out of her stack to have a good fire. 'Cause you had different kinds of coal. This Sydney coal, it was very easy to fire her. But the Inverness coal was very hard to fire. It clinkered a lot.

"And I'll tell you, I was called a first-class fireman. I was no better than the others. But I'll tell you how. We'd leave before supper with this Inverness coal and go to Grand Narrows. And half the way it'd be clinkered. When I'd get to Iona, I'd go to work and clean my fire. They used to transfer mail at Iona. Well, I had time then to shake my grates; I'd clean my fire. And going over the Grand Narrows bridge, I'd get my engine pretty hot. When I'd get to Grand Narrows, I'd go to work. I'd get on top of the tender and fill my tender full of water. And the driver'd empty the ashes out of the ash pan. I'd have a real good fire in there. And they'd wonder how I was always making up my time. The others that'd come to work, they wouldn't bother cleaning their fire at Iona. They'd come to Grand Narrows, they'd lose time. That was my secret. I had my fire all clean, all ready. Lose no time there."

From Bulley "Accidents Averted," 21.

While all members of train crews carried responsibility for operational procedures and safety, the performance of the engineer was especially important. For each individual run, he and the conductor received what was called a train order. For short runs like those on the S&L, these were relatively simple and straightforward. For longer runs, on the Intercolonial and the CNR, they were more complex and more likely to be modified along the way.

Behind the orders for individual runs were the rule books plus additional special rules that might apply to specific locations or circumstances or that drew particular attention to standing rules. The S&L's "Special Rules" in 1935 provide good examples. Rule # 6 stated that "the absence of a signal, day or night, at a point where one is usually shown, will be regarded as a danger signal and trains must be stopped, cause ascertained and reported. Trains will not proceed until all doubt is removed." Rule # 16 indicated the legacy of the Mira bridge wreck in 1903. It stated "All trains or light engines approaching Mira Bridge must come to a full stop before crossing the same." Comparable running rules were found on all railways. For the Port Hastings coal pier, the CNR's special rule # 9 stated

"Great care must be exercised in handling Engines or Trains upon Port Hastings Pier. The speed must not exceed 3 miles per hour, and Engine ash pans must be securely closed as a precaution against fire. Engineers must maintain absolute control of Engines or Trains approaching the Pier."[14]

Even during its days as the Intercolonial, the national railway system had more complex sets of rules than the smaller lines. This remained the case after the evolution of the IRC into the CNR. Many subjects that had appeared in the IRC rule book before the railway expanded to Cape Breton remained in the CN rules into the modern era. Pat Meagher provides an amusing perspective on one such rule.

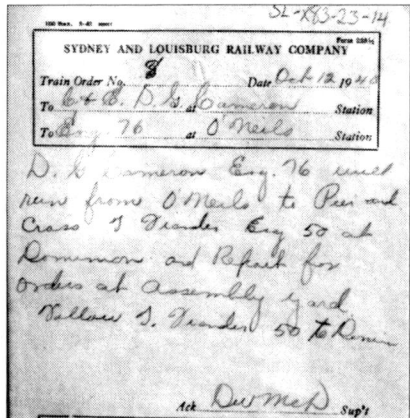

Fig. 9.19 - Written orders: a 1940 S&L train order.

Sydney & Louisburg Railway Museum, #SL-X83-23-14.

Fig. 9.20 (above left) - The fireman filling the water tank at the S&L yard in Glace Bay ca. 1950.

Sydney & Louisburg Railway Museum.

Fig. 9.21 (above right) - Heading home from work. An engineer and fireman with S&L #105 in the Glace Bay yard, probably mid-1950s.

Sydney & Louisburg Railway Museum, #SL-00-621.

Rule G

Pat Meagher, a long-serving CNR station agent at Point Tupper, returns to tell a story about the CNR rule book.

"If you were a train engineer, brakeman, conductor or telegrapher working for Canadian National you had to study the Company's Standard Rules and pass a test. When you worked on the CN, you lived by the rules.

"Rule G, one of the first rules in the Company's Standard Rules, states that no employee while on duty shall partake of intoxicating liquor or frequent places where it is sold.

"To keep employees on their toes and make sure they carried the rulebooks, CN officials put out a bulletin called 'The rule of the day'. Each day, dispatchers and superintendents asked us to recite a particular rule, designated in advance.

"Locomotive engineer Finn Geddes from Stellarton, N.S. ignored Rule G much of the time. While running on a freight extra between Stellarton and Pirate Harbour one night, Finn was caught partaking of good cheer. He was taken in for investigation, a euphusism for disciplinary action before the superintendent.

"Finn was demoted from the main line to yard service on a yard switcher (yard locomotive). Because he didn't have enough service to hold a yard job in Stellarton, he had to transfer to Mulgrave. Finn had enough whiskers to hold the day shift—7 am to 3 pm.

"The superintendent and his staff often made trips over the division in a private car coupled to the rear of passenger trains. Frank Ward, the superintendent at the time this story took place, was the very man who demoted Finn. On this particular day, Ward was eastbound for Sydney in the private rail car. While the express and baggage on the passenger train were being unloaded in Mulgrave, Ward ambled up to the liquor store, just up the hill from the station. The time was about 3:30 pm.

"Now Finn, who had finished his shift at 3 pm was in the liquor store. He was on his way out with a case of beer and some hard liquor when he met Ward in the doorway coming in.

"To cover his embarrassment, Ward said to Finn, 'What's the rule of the day'?

"Without a moment's hesitation, Finn replied, 'Rule G'.

"Liquor was the cause of Finn's demotion but it sure as hell didn't dull his quick wit."

From Meagher, *Scotia People*, 23-24.

Pat Meagher's Scotia People (2005) and *All Aboard* (1974) by William Calder, from which excerpts have been reprinted in this chapter and elsewhere, are two of the very best sources of accounts of the life of railway employees in Cape Breton.

There are two other sources that are too valuable to be left buried in the endnotes. In 1981, issues 28 and 29 of *Cape Breton's Magazine* carried a two part series called "Working on the S&L" with memories of veterans from that line. At the time of writing, these (and all other issues of the magazine) are available online at http://capebretonsmagazine.com/. The second source is from Newfoundland rather than Cape Breton but is a wonderful memoir of a station agent's half-century of service during the Golden Age of the railway. Much of the author's experience was similar to his peers in Cape Breton and elsewhere in the Maritimes.[15]

10 – Fading Away: The End of the Golden Age

The Golden Days of the 1950s

During the 1950s, Cape Breton railways reached the peak of their importance. The national economic boom following the Second World War continued unabated. Cape Breton coal and steel industries enjoyed a period of relative prosperity, especially in comparison with the economic collapse that had followed the First World War.

Out of Sydney, Canadian National was running three passenger trains a day to Halifax, one departing in early morning, one in late afternoon and the third leaving at 8:15 p.m. Freight traffic remained relatively high, strongly influenced by activity at the steel plant. The aerial photo showing the Sydney yards in the 1950s reflects the level of activity.

The rail connection to Newfoundland through North Sydney continued to operate in the traditional way with both freight and passengers being transferred via the ferries to the Newfoundland line's narrow gauge terminus in Port aux Basques. The Newfoundland ferries only started carrying rail cars from the mainland in 1968 when two new ships, *Frederick Carter* and *Patrick Morris*, went into service. Once rail cars were unloaded from the ferries at Port aux Basques, the standard gauge

Fig. 10.1 - Shipments of rails from the Sydney steel plant remained one of the most important types of CNR traffic westbound from Cape Breton in the years after the Second World War.

Whitney Pier Historical Society Museum.

Fig. 10.2 - The CNR rail yard in Sydney, ca. 1955. The roundhouse in the foreground had bays for over a dozen locomotives.

Author's collection.

wheel sets were replaced with narrow gauge sets so the cars could operate on the Newfoundland track. This process, called retrucking, was used until the Newfoundland railway was abandoned in 1988.

With Canadian National traffic moving at relatively high levels in the 1950s and 60s, the risk of accidents also continued. In the following excerpt from an interview, Harry Bulley, a CNR engineer from Sydney, focused on the many accidents he avoided during his decades of experience. When Bulley retired in 1962, without ever being involved in a wreck, he was a driver on the passenger Railiners that had gone into service between Sydney and Halifax in the mid-1950s. Following are Bulley's summaries of seven of his own "accidents that didn't happen," selected to illustrate the types of hazards that engineers encountered.

In the 1950s, the S&L continued to provide passenger service with rolling stock now well past its "best by" date while the little railway concentrated on its core purpose—moving coal. Coal trains powered by steam locomotives continued to pound their ways up and down the tracks, feeding the Sydney shipping wharf, the steel plant and the power plants that required growing volumes of coal to generate electricity.

Accidents Averted

by Harry Bulley

"Engineer on Railiner 602 coming into Sydney west of Townsend Street. There was a man asleep and drunk on the track. I stopped the train and got him off the track....

"Engineer on # 7 train one morning. An oil truck full of gasoline crossed in front of me and stalled on the track at Sydney River. I stopped the train just in time by using the emergency brake and saved a bad accident.

"Coming down on Way-Freight one morning for Hastings. We left early that morning from Havre Boucher and there was a crew welding the tracks. They had five or six tanks on the trolley and they did not flag me as they were not thinking. I was almost on top of them when I stopped the train.

"Coming down on # 7 train as engineer one morning in 1950, with 9 passenger cars. Looking ahead, I saw the switch was not in the right position. I stopped the train and found that the switch was run through. I spiked the switch and reported it, saving another wreck. This happened at Tupper Junction and would have been a bad wreck as a derailer is at the other end of the switch.

"I was engineer on an Extra leaving Sydney for Point Tupper on a double-header. We got orders at Sydney for our meets. They were all changed at North Sydney except our meet at Georges River for 691 Train. It was forgotten by the engineer on the leading engine and the crew. I was the only one who did not forget. I sent my fireman to flag and saved a bad wreck.

"Coming down as Engineer on 602 Railiner, one evening in late March in 1960. I had a lot of passengers. I left Stellarton late and by making up this time, I saved the passengers and Railiner from going over a steep cliff, about 50 feet deep, and into the water. A [later] train going west with two diesel engines struck the mud slide and went over the bank. Another accident averted by making up time."

From Bulley: "Accidents Averted," 24-26.

Fig. 10.3 - S&L coach # 4 is seen here as part of a mixed train at Louisburg station in the early 1950s, more than half-a-century after it was built by Rhodes, Curry of Amherst. This car can now be seen at the Canadian Railroad Historical Association Museum at St. Contant, QC.

Sydney & Louisburg Railway Museum, #SL-00-408.

Fig. 10.4 - S&L # 70 by the water tank in the Glace Bay yard, c. 1945. This engine was acquired new from Montreal Locomotive Works in 1926 and operated on the S&L until it was scrapped in 1961. The engine plus tender, fully loaded with coal and water, weighed almost 200 t. Note the section gang speedy and trolly beside the engineer's cab.

Sydney & Louisburg Railway Museum, #SL-04-25.

Fig. 10.5 - The S&L main line at Victoria Junction in the late 1950s. This photo dates from close to the end of the steam era on the S&L. Loco # 105 was one of the seven largest engines on the line, 2-8-2 Mikado-class locomotives that had all seen service on American railways when new. # 105 arrived on the S&L in 1955 and was the second last steam engine purchased.

Sydney & Louisburg Railway Museum, #SL-00-406.

In Cape Breton, as elsewhere in Canada, change was coming at the front of the trains. Though the CNR had acquired its first experimental diesel engines in 1929, the new technology waited in the wings for several decades. By the mid 1950s, however, diesels were taking centre stage and the "age of steam" ended very quickly. Despite the fact that the prime reason for its existence was to move coal, even the S&L was not immune. In May of 1960, the S&L acquired its first diesel locomotive, # 200, built by the Montreal Locomotive Works. Two identical engines, #s 201 and 202, arrived soon after. The arrival of these engines marked the beginning of the end of the age of S&L steam. The changeover happened very quickly and the last steam locomotives were taken out of service before the end of 1961. Purchase of the first diesel locomotives marked a short-lived change in the S&L policy of buying second-hand engines. The first three MLW diesels were new but the old policy was soon restored. The thirteen additional diesels purchased by the S&L were all "experienced engines."[1]

Fig. 10.6 (top) - The first S&L diesel locomotive, # 200, upon arrival in Glace Bay in 1960. At left is Alex MacDonald, S&L Superintendent; in center is Joseph Fisher, Mechanical Superintendent; the driver's name is unknown.

Sydney & Louisburg Railway Museum, #SL-04-200.

Fig. 10.7 (bottom) - Old Sydney Collieries # 25 en route to the Canadian Railroad Historical Association Museum at St. Constant, Quebec in 1961. At right is Dr. Robert Nichols, President of CRHA at the time; identity of the other man is unknown. The photo location is uncertain but it was probably taken in Sydney Mines.

Sydney & Louisburg Railway Museum, #SL-96-1380.

Decades of Decline

Railway work forces remained large into the 1950s. Campbell and Johnston's account of the S&L states that line had 400 employees in 1959.[2] No data have been found to illustrate long-term trends in railway employment in Cape Breton in the decades after the Second World War. As a substitute, some statistics from a study of the impact of technological change on the CNR in the Maritimes in the 1950s may be useful. Those numbers show that Canadian National was becoming much less labour intensive. The numbers were also an omen of things to come—on both the CNR and the S&L.

Changing Employment Trends, CNR, Maritime Region, 1948-1960

The first table provides index numbers to track trends using 1948 as a benchmark. The reference numbers in the table are those for car miles run within the Maritime region. It should be noted that data on car miles do not tell us anything about tons of freight moved or number of trains run. During this period, as a generalization, freight car sizes were increasing and the total tonnage moved per car mile was increasing. At the same time, freight trains were getting longer as larger locomotives came into use. The fourth column records the downward trend in the number of employees per car mile. The third column, the one of greatest significance to CNR employees, shows that the number of hours worked per car mile had declined more rapidly that the total number of employees.

Table 10.1

Year	Car Miles 1948 = 100	Employment Hours per Car Mile 1948 = 100	Total Number of Employees per Car Mile 1948 = 100
1948	100	100	100
1949	95.4	98.3	101.5
1950	98.8	98.3	98.7
1951	103.8	100.4	98.0
1952	103.6	106.4	97.5
1953	100.9	102.2	99.1
1954	95.5	102.3	102.1
1955	105.5	88.9	99.2
1956	116.9	86.4	88.6
1957	106.9	89.9	95.9
1958	98.4	88.2	90.7
1959	109.7	79.9	90.1
1960	113.7	73.6	88.4

Table 10.2 provides some very basic data on numbers of employees in several job categories in 1948 and 1960. Again, the data are for the CNR for the Maritime region and not just Cape Breton.

Table 10.2

Year	Sectionmen	Station Agents and Telegraphers	Engineers	Brakemen	Total # Employees
1948	1718	575	431	730	16,800
1960	1082	615	229	564	14,500
% Change	- 37 %	+ 7 %	- 47 %	- 23 %	- 12 %

Data sources for both tables: Canada Department of Labour, Ottawa, *Technological Changes in the Railway Industry; Maritime Region; Canadian National Railway*, 1965, cat L2-23/12, Tables 1-3 and 12, 30-36 and 52ff.

After the end of the Second World War, railways had entered a period of decline in relative importance across North America. Across Canada, between 1945 and 1975, the number of rail passengers dropped by almost 50 per cent during a period when the country's population doubled. During that period a closely related factor was the dramatic change in the ownership of automobiles. Prior to the war, cars were still luxuries, but by the 1960s car ownership was quite common. On the freight side of railway operations, tonnage hauled did increase significantly but became much more concentrated in long-haul bulk traffic in central and western Canada. Local freight traffic took to the highways. In the wake of these shifts in traffic patterns, between 1945 and 1975 the number of railway employees across Canada declined by 30 per cent.

Much of the public investment in highways and airports was at the expense of the railway network. This was especially true in Eastern Canada and the more rural areas of the rest of the country where investment in railway infrastructure was primarily from the CNR (i.e., from either the railway's own earning power or the federal public purse). As a result of declining investment in infrastructure, railways became less competitive in terms of service speed, quality and cost. As this happened, more customers, both freight and passenger, were lost to other forms of transportation on the highways and on airlines.

More localized factors came into play within Nova Scotia and other parts of the Atlantic region. Increasing freight rates, a long-standing political issue, continued to have an impact on the regional economy. Densities of population and business activity declined except in a small number of urban centres. At the same time, Ottawa's willingness to fund Canadian National's role in regions such as the Maritimes continued to weaken, a trend that had started in 1917 with the movement of the Intercolonial's head office from Moncton to Montreal and the first moves to dismantle the IRC system of preferential freight rates designed to assist Maritime businesses.

This combination of pressures led to the eventual abandonment of most of the CNR passenger and freight services that had existed in 1950. Over the next twenty-odd years rail lines along mainland Nova Scotia's South Shore, in the

Musquodoboit Valley and along Northumberland Strait disappeared, as did the local branches in Pictou County. Those events provide a provincial context for the abandonments that would take place in Cape Breton.

The 1955 opening of the Canso Causeway also had important impacts, some positive and some negative. The negative effects were felt first in the Strait communities where abandonment of the rail and automobile ferries meant the loss of many jobs. Even though it also carried a rail line, the Causeway made car and truck traffic to and from Cape Breton much more attractive at a time when both private automobile ownership and commercial trucking were in a boom period. It literally opened a bridge making it easier for highway transport to replace the railway for much of the freight and passenger traffic. The resulting long-term decline in the volume of rail traffic and revenue increased the vulnerability of the railway connecting Sydney to the mainland.

The ultimately negative effect of the causeway on rail traffic was not part of the original plan. While the causeway is now seen by most people as part of the highway system, when the crossing was being considered and planned, its railway component was seen as being

Fig. 10.9 (top) - The end of the railway ferry era at the Strait of Canso with the last run of *Scotia II* on May 14, 1955.

Port Hastings Museum and Archives.

Fig. 10.10 (bottom) - The crew of *Scotia II* on the ferry's last run in May 1955.

Port Hastings Museum and Archives, #AAQF00aa00fr.

The CNR Moves to the Causeway

by Martin Boston

Prior to his retirement in 1992, Martin Boston had been a CNR employee for thirty-six years. Many of those years were as station agent at Orangedale until the station was closed in 1988. Boston played a critical role in the efforts to protect the station and develop the railway museum there. He served as president of the Orangedale Station Association from 1997 to 2011.

"Saturday May 14th 1955 brought great changes to railway operations on the Strait of Canso. That was the day that Point Tupper and Mulgrave were closed as railway terminals. The line was diverted between Linwood (Linwood Jct) and Inverness Jct (Pt. Tupper) via the Canso Causeway, a distance of 20.79 miles. This change also brought to an end the service of the train ferries *Scotia* and *Scotia 2*, which had plied the waters of the strait for many years.

"On this nice fine Saturday morning my class mate and good friend Daniel MacDonnell and I made our way to Point Tupper railway station. Our intention was to catch No.6, the daily except Sunday westbound passenger train. This was to be the last passenger train to cross the strait on the ferry to Mulgrave, N.S. We went into the station and purchased our tickets from Pat Meagher the Operator on duty. Dan and I purchased the last two tickets sold for No.6

"Very soon No.6 arrived hauled by Pacific type steam locomotive number 5271 with a consist of six cars. After the station work was completed, the yard switcher pushed the cars down to the boat. The cars were pushed on the boat, three on each of the outside tracks. The middle track was left empty for locomotive number 5271. Under normal circumstances the locomotive would wait at Point Tupper to return to Sydney on train No 5.

"The ferry crossed the Strait to Mulgrave, where the train was unloaded. Leaving Mulgrave our Locomotive was number 6006, a Mountain type locomotive and the same size cars. Locomotive No 5271 did not leave Mulgrave on No 6. It would probably follow on a freight train or as a light engine as it went West. After backing out to Pirate Harbour (the freight yard) the switch was turned to allow us to proceed up the hill to Cape Porcupine and on westward. Along the route I noticed many people in the yards and along the streets waving and watching as the train passed.

"This was a very sad day for the town of Mulgrave. Their town would die with the loss of the railway, the looks on their faces told the story. Our train continued on to Monastery where we and quite a few other people detrained. After a short wait (perhaps thirty minutes) the eastbound train arrived, running as Passenger Extra 6014 east. Locomotive No. 6014 was the first Mountain type locomotive to run east of Mulgrave as they were too heavy for the ferries.

"The train consisted of locomotive No. 6014 and ten cars. We travelled over the new diversion from Linwood Jct to Harve [*sic*] Boucher, Aulde Cove and across the Causeway to Port Hastings Jct, Port Hastings, Port Hawkesbury, the train rejoined the main line again at Tupper after travelling over a diversion of 20.79 miles. Daniel and I got off the train in Port Hawkesbury after our excursion, ending up about a mile from where we started."

Reprinted by permission of Martin Boston and the Orangedale Railway Museum.

equally important. In 1943-1944, the Parliamentary "Special Committee on Reconstruction and Re-establishment" and then the Dawson "Royal Commission on Provincial Development and Rehabilitation" concluded that some kind of strait crossing was needed to deal with problems associated with the railway ferry system, especially to make Cape Breton's coal and steel industries more competitive. The earlier chapter on coal and steel traffic noted the increases in traffic moving across the Strait by rail during the war years, a pattern which continued after 1945. Engineering studies began during the war about options for the Strait of Canso and included significant input from the engineering staff of the CNR. These continued until the decision was made in 1951 to build a causeway rather than a bridge or tunnel.[3] When the causeway was opened in 1955, one of the keynote speakers was CNR President Donald Gordon. Gordon's speech made an impression on the memory of a boy who was there. Linden MacIntyre's recollection was that Gordon's speech "seemed to go on all afternoon."[4]

After the opening of the causeway, the next dramatic event for Cape Bretoners was the 1966-1967 decisions by Hawker-Siddeley, the British-based firm that controlled Dosco, to abandon its remaining coal and steel operations in eastern Cape Breton. Out of Dosco came two separate organizations, the federally owned Cape Breton Development Corporation (Devco) to operate the mines and the coal company's railway and the provincially owned Sydney Steel Corporation (Sysco) to operate the steel plant.

As examined in chapter 7, declining markets for rails and other steel products led to declining traffic on the Canadian National line to Cape Breton. Like Sysco and Devco in their respective areas of activity, the CNR became increasingly dependent on political will to support the continuation of rail service at a time when that will and the associated financial support from Ottawa were starting to fade.

Fig. 10.11 (opposite) - Martin Boston at his desk in the bay window of the Orangedale station museum. This bay window, visible in the chapter 11 photos that show the outside of the station, provided a view up and down the station platform. Note the array of telephone and telegraph equipment from the station's earlier days. The gears are part of the high semaphore signal visible in the photos showing the outside of the station. The metal pole with the loop on the end was used in the days before mobile phones or radios. If there was need to pass a train order to the engineer of a passing train that would not be stopping, the order was attached to the pole. The agent would hold the pole from the lower end so that the top loop was at the right height for the engineer to grab it as the locomotive went by.

Photo by Roger Cook, Oradell, NJ, USA. Reproduced by permission of Martin Boston and the Orangedale Railway Museum.

The Old S&L
by Helen C. MacDonald

You have often heard tell both in story and song
Of the old S&L that has served us so long,
Though ridiculed oft, now its virtues I'll tell,
And sing to the praise of the old S&L.

Her speed was the reason why many folks kicked,
Some said from its windows they blueberries picked,
But more seasoned travellers they learned to sleep well,
And were truly content on the old S&L.

Her departure was noted by some at the Bay
Who laughed in derision as she pulled away,
The scream of her whistle they all knew so well,
And they'd sneer, "There's the flyer, the old S&L."

But when smoke and town noises were all left behind,
A Welcoming mob at each station she'd find;
The young and the old who loved her so well,
Waiting patiently there for the old S&L.

With Morien past she's wander away
With a brief stop at Homeville if it was mail day,
Then straight on to Mira where more kiddies would yell,
And the dogs bark in greeting to the old S&L.

Then after a while she'd pull out with a groan,
And she'd huff and she'd puff till she reached Catalone,
Then once more she'd be greeted with bark and with yell,
From those waiting long for the old S&L.

On, on she'd steam to her long journeys end,
Cheering many a heart, greeting many a friend,
To the Fortress Town, where she's rest a spell,
From her hard day of toil, the old S&L.

Now the faithful old train has gone to her rest,
For times are a-changing, perhaps for the best,
But sometimes we yearn for the whistle and bell,
And a whiff of smoke from the old S&L.

Reprinted from O'Donnell, ed., 1975, by permission of Mayfair Music Publishing Company, Keswick, Ontario.

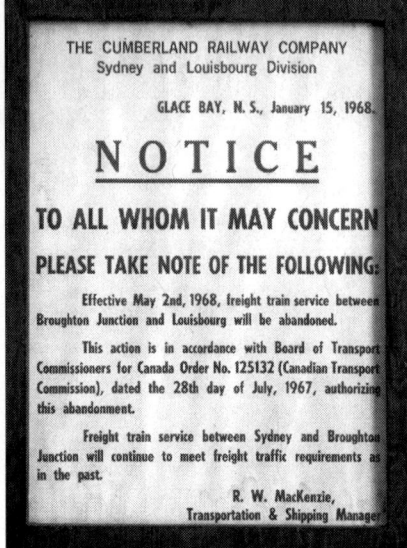

Fig. 10.13 - Formal notification of the end of the line to Louisbourg in 1968. The details in the notice reflect the fact that, some years before Dosco left Cape Breton, the S&L had been made a subsidiary of another Dosco company. This made the S&L eligible for federal railway subsidies because the Cumberland Railway Company was federally incorporated. After the abandonment of the Louisbourg end of the main line, the rest of the S&L was taken over by the Cape Breton Development Corporation and became the Devco Railway.

Fig. 10.14 - Alfred Tilley – the last agent at the S&L's Louisburg station.

Both: Sydney & Louisburg Railway Museum.

The pattern of railway abandonment that had begun on the Nova Scotia mainland continued on Cape Breton. Canadian National ended service on the St. Peter's branch in 1973 and the Inverness branch in 1986. In between those abandonments, the CNR got out of the passenger business on its remaining lines. Passenger services operated by both CN and the Canadian Pacific were turned over to a separate federal Crown Corporation, VIA Rail, in 1976. Under that name and using CNR track, passenger service continued for a time from Sydney to the mainland.

Fig. 10.12 - The St. Peter's station as it appeared after the end of railway service on the St. Peter's branch in 1973. The small roundhouse had been torn down and the rails would soon be taken up though the station survived. A photo of the building taken in 2011 appears in chapter 11.

Photo by George Parks, Moncton, NB. Reproduced by permission of Mr. Parks.

On the S&L, coal shipments through the Louisbourg pier had ended in 1962 and all passenger service was removed in 1963. With the formation of Devco, the historic name of the Sydney and Louisburg vanished and in 1968 the line became the Devco Railway. Almost simultaneously with the change of name, freight service to Louisbourg was ended, the Louisbourg branch officially abandoned and the rails were taken up.

Additional steps in the decline for Cape Breton's railways came in the early 1990s and completed the trend under way on the island and far beyond. Reference has been made previously in a general way to some specific events and some of the factors involved, both local and national. To see what happened in Cape Breton in a wider context, it is appropriate to return to the subject of the "political will" on which the CNR was dependent.

By the 1970s, changes were coming to reduce or eliminate unprofitable lines or services. This approach was seen as a business requirement on the privately-owned Canadian Pacific. On the CNR, the same policies were being pursued within the constraints of political pressures, since CN was ultimately responsible to Parliament. There was little doubt, however, about what way the winds were blowing for the railways. The strength of those winds increased throughout the 1980s; in the next decade, the federal government's role in transportation underwent many major changes.

Two key influences overshadowed the decisions that were made post-1980. One of these was the ideological shift that was reshaping the direction of government policy in Canada and beyond. There was a strong small-c conservative thrust toward a reduced role for governments in society. The direction taken by the Thatcher government in the U.K. and the Reagan administration in the United States through the 1980s was also followed by the Mulroney government in Ottawa. A second influence that came into play, particularly after the return of the Liberals to power in Ottawa under Jean Chrétien in 1993, was the state of the federal government's finances. Committed to dealing with the pressures of the government's deficits, the Chrétien government accepted the basic direction of transportation policies that had come into place over the previous decade. A continually diminishing role for Ottawa in transportation could make a financial contribution toward balancing the books.

Some examples of the changing federal roles in transportation under both the Mulroney and Chrétien governments provide a more complete context for developments that would affect the railways, nationally and in Cape Breton. Trans-Canada Airlines had been established in 1936 to operate as a Crown Corporation, an airline equivalent of the CNR. The airline, renamed Air Canada in 1965, was sold to private investors in 1988. During the 1980s and early 1990s, Ottawa abandoned responsibilities for most major Canadian port facilities. Originally administered under the National Harbours Board, they were "devolved" to local authorities that assumed the federal government's financial role. Over the same time period, the Department of Transport's responsibilities for airports were handed over to local boards or commissions. One partial exception to this trend has been Marine Atlantic, the 1986 successor to CN Marine which had been set up as a separate division of the CNR in 1977. Marine Atlantic has remained a federal Crown Corporation operating the ferry system from North Sydney to Newfoundland. Despite its continued role on that run, its routes on the Bay of Fundy and the Gulf of Maine as well as the Newfoundland coastal services were all abandoned in 1997.

The Rise and Decline of VIA Rail

VIA Rail, the Crown Corporation that took over rail passenger service in 1976, faced many problems from the outset. The post-1950 trend toward travel by car or airplane was continuing. In addition to difficulties retaining traffic or attracting new customers, VIA had to cope with its inheritance which had included a number of dubious blessings. The new passenger line was to use the track belonging to the railways that had run the passenger trains previously, but VIA had to pay for those running rights; VIA's rolling stock, at least at the outset, was that passed down by the CNR and the Canadian Pacific, and VIA had to pay for it too.

One indication of VIA's status from the outset was that the new operator's trains were second-class users of CN and CP tracks. On single-track main lines, VIA passenger trains were usually diverted to sidings when meeting CN or CP freight trains. VIA also had to cede the right-of-way to freight trains moving in the same direction at faster speeds. In addition, VIA had to pay to use or purchase existing railway stations and other facilities.

Assertions were made over the years that, in many cases, VIA was subjected to unfair and excessive financial demands by both Canadian National and Canadian Pacific, demands that CN and CP assumed would be covered by the federal government. In the case of the CNR, any excessive payments would have ultimately come from CN's own financial masters but, if such transactions made CN's books look better and VIA's look worse, that could have been seen as in CN's organizational interest.

The extent to which VIA's financial picture was shaped by its dependence on the other railways and the extent to which other factors, particularly its success (or lack of it), in attracting passengers have always been a subject for debate in the interpretation of VIA's financial accounts. As the 1980s progressed, several things were certain. The number of VIA passengers was declining and the deficits were rising. Despite the many suggestions that VIA's chances of being a financially successful railway operation were doomed from the outset, pressure on VIA reached the crisis point in the late 1980s and major cuts to services and staff were announced.

While isolated numbers may be deceptive, they can provide at least a sense of the situation to the extent that VIA's calculations of costs were realistic. In 1988, the Sydney-Halifax service was operating with only 17.9 per cent of its costs being covered by ticket revenue. The Halifax-Yarmouth service and Halifax-Moncton-Saint John ticket revenues as percentages of costs were equally low, 18.6 per cent and 13.8 per cent respectively. These low percentages were matched on short-haul regional services across the country, "regional" being those outside the Montreal-Ottawa-Windsor triangle with its much higher population density. The twelve regional routes, including the three in Nova Scotia, showed average ticket revenues bringing in 19.2 per cent of costs. The financial subsidy per passenger on the Sydney-Halifax run was recorded as $86.00 per ticket issued.[5] Based on these numbers, low rates of usage, and the assumption that drastic increases in fares would lead to equally drastic drops in ridership, decisions were made in 1989 to implement major cuts to services and staff. Nationally, VIA President Ron Lawless announced that employment was targeted for a reduction from 7,300 to 4,500, a cut of 38 per cent.[6] Virtually

Fig. 10.15 (right) - During the summer and autumn of 1989, newspapers in many parts of Canada were filled with notices about meetings to rally opposition to the proposed cuts to VIA Rail. There was widespread public participation in the movement but it had no impact on either VIA managers or the company's political masters.

Fig. 10.16 (below) - When the last VIA train left Sydney in January of 1990, the crowd at the station directed their hostility at Prime Minister Brian Mulroney. Many political factors were at work but the decisions about VIA certainly contributed to the results of the 1993 election when the governing Progressive Conservative party lost all but two of the 151 seats held before the election was called.

Raytel Photography. 90-22-19455. Beaton Institute, Cape Breton University.

all short-haul routes were to be abandoned. Inside VIA Rail, Lawless became known as "the slasher."

There were widespread protests and much debate, in and out of Parliament, but most of the proposed cuts were implemented.[7] The last VIA train left Sydney for the mainland on January 15, 1990.

At the same time, VIA service from Halifax to Yarmouth and the daily run from Halifax to Montreal via Saint John, NB, were both cancelled. The only passenger trains left running in the Maritimes were those following the original Intercolonial route, from Halifax to Moncton, north through Bathurst and Campbellton, on to the St. Lawrence shore at Mont Jolie, Quebec and from there to Montreal. In the wake of these reductions, the "national railway passenger system" was offering service only to the same communities served by the Intercolonial in 1876 when the Halifax-Montreal route was opened all the way. The cuts were not restricted to the east coast. An extensive list of other routes in Quebec, Ontario and Western Canada also lost their passenger trains at the same time.

CN Selling Truro-Sydney Freight Line

The *Scotia Sun*, Port Hawkesbury, September 17, 1991.

"In a move that caught employees and customers alike by surprise, Canadian National announced last week it plans to sell off its Truro to Sydney rail freight line. At meetings here, Sydney and Stellarton, company officials informed union members, major customers and local officials the crown-owned corporation hopes to have the sale complete by the end of 1992.

"At least one of the major customers, Stora Forest Industries in Point Tupper, has hinted that selling the rail line may mean the company has to curtail its plans for expansion of its newsprint operations with recycled content.

"CN vice-president Marvin Blackwell said the company is looking for 'expressions of interest' from the private sector to buy the 400 km route which employs 110 people. Although the line is not operating at a loss it is not particularly profitable and Mr. Blackwell said the line might better be operated as a short-line rather than as part of a national railway.

"Reaction was swift from politicians and the Nova Scotia government. Nova Scotia Premier Donald Cameron, coincidentally about to meet with Prime Minister Brian Mulroney at the time of the announcement, said he flatly opposed the move. Mr Cameron said the rail link between Nova Scotia and New Brunswick is part of Confederation and indicated he would make that point to Mulroney.[8] Mr Cameron suggested CN was not making enough effort to drum up new business for the rail line.

"Representatives of Stora Forest Industries were cautious in their estimation of the situation and said in a prepared statement the company is 'perfectly happy with the excellent service provided by CN Rail, but we are afraid we'll lose the reliable daily service if the line is privately operated. The question is, can CN guarantee that a private service will continue five or 10 years from now'? the statement wondered....

"Should CN find an interested operator for the rail line the change of ownership would have to be reviewed by government agencies, including the National Transportation Agency, which would have the power to veto any sale of the line."

The CNR Leaves Cape Breton

After handing over all responsibility for the passenger business to VIA Rail in 1976, the CNR remained under increasing political pressure to make regional and local freight services pay their own way. By the late 1980s, preparations were under way to privatize CN. Non-rail assets were sold off; for example the extensive chain of hotels was sold to Canadian Pacific Hotels in 1988. Routes that were unprofitable or uncertain were targeted for either the auction block or the chopping block. In 1991, CN announced that it wanted to dispose of the line from Truro through Cape Breton to Sydney.

The proposal was greeted by the same kinds of objections as had been offered when the VIA cuts, locally and nationally, had been announced two years earlier. The results, for the Sydney line and many others, were the same. Most of the reductions in CN service went ahead. The Canadian Transportation Agency (CTA), the federal regulator, gave approval to CN's request to try to sell the Sydney-Truro line and to a 1993 agreement for its sale. The last CNR freight train crossed the causeway to the mainland on October 1, 1993, with five diesel locomotives, thirty-five cars and the caboose. On this memorable last run, the engineer was Conrad Clark with Kevin Musgrave as brakeman and F. W. Ross as conductor.

The buyer of the CNR line was the Cape Breton & Central Nova Scotia Railway (CB&CNS). This company, established for the purpose of the purchase, was a subsidiary of an American firm, Rail-Tex Inc., which operated "short lines" across North America. The CTA document approving the sale provides an outline of the review process for the decision. It makes interesting reading in its entirety and is available online at the CTA website.[9] Two years after Canadian National's 1993 departure from Cape Breton, Canada's "National Railway" system was sold to private owners.[10] In 2000, Rail-Tex

Fig. 10.17 - A CB&CNS freight train leaving Cape Breton in 2006. At the time of writing, an extensive collection of CB&CNS photos, including many by Geoff Doane, is online at http://photos.greatrails.net. Another valuable source with fine colour photographs is David Othen's Cape Breton & Central Nova Scotia Railway: 1993-201. See http://www.blurb.com/bookstore/detail/2424188.

Photo by Geoff Doane, Halifax, NS. Reproduced by permission of Mr. Doane.

and its subsidiaries were purchased by RailAmerica Inc., another short-line operator. Since then, this firm, with headquarters in Boca Raton, Florida, has operated the CB&CNS under increasingly difficult circumstances.

The CB&CNS Struggle for Survival

During the latter part of its first decade of operation on the Sydney-Truro line, the CB&CNS began to encounter major problems. Shipment of Newfoundland-bound freight by rail to North Sydney had started to decline as the Newfoundland railway faced closure. After that closure in 1988, more and more Newfoundland freight shifted to the trucking industry. Transshipment of containers for and from Newfoundland was relocated by CN from North Sydney to Halifax. Then, in 2001, came two much more important events. Both the Sysco steel mill and the last Devco mine were closed.

In response to the earlier decline in traffic and the implications of the Devco/Sysco closures, the CB&CNS quickly applied to abandon the line east of Point Tupper. The railway proposed retaining only the short stub between Point Tupper and the Canso Causeway. Both hard facts and opinions about the rationale for and potential impact of the closure of the line went on the record on May 7, 2002, in the Nova Scotia legislature's Standing Committee on Economic Development. Before the Committee, Peter Touesnard, the railway's general manager, described the Devco/Sysco closures as "the loss of our anchor business east of Port Hawkesbury."[11] The lengthy transcript of the Committee hearing provides an insightful account about the wide range of issues that surround the fate of the CB&CNS line.

Despite a wide level of agreement about the theoretical desirability of saving the railway, the first level of the formal process led to approval for the proposed abandonment by the Nova Scotia Utility and Review Board in November of 2002. The Board's decision report[12] provides a more detailed version of the company's case, the positions taken by opponents and a wealth of detail about the line's activity and finances above and beyond what had been presented to the committee of the legislature.

The approval led to promises for subsidies from the Province and the federal government. The Province also arranged a short-run contract to move coal landed in Sydney to power plants outside the Sydney area. The application for abandonment was withdrawn and the railway continued to operate. In 2011, a new three-year subsidy of $2 million per year was put in place by the Province and followed by a 2012 grant of $3.3 million for infrastructure improvements.

Despite this government support, future prospects are not good. Coal imports for the Point Tupper power plant are now being landed by ship near the plant and there are no other major customers for the railway in sight. It would seem that it is only a matter of time before the island's main line carries its last train and that all that might be left of the CB&CNS on Cape Breton would be service across the Canso Causeway to the Point Tupper paper mill. Uncertainty about the future of that mill jeopardizes even that short island section of what was originally the Intercolonial and later the CNR main line to Sydney.

The Writing on the Wall

At the time of its 2002 application to abandon operations between Point Tupper and Sydney, the CB&CNS indicated its breakeven level for this section was approximately 5,000 carloads per year. The table below shows the trend in freight traffic moving between Cape Breton and the mainland before and since that application with biannual data. Though data on local traffic between Sydney and Point Tupper and from the mainland to Point Tupper are not included, the table clearly indicates the pattern of decline in rail traffic crossing the Canso Causeway. The 5,000 per year target has not been achieved in over a decade and the gaps between that 5,000 and actual traffic have been widening.

Table 10.3 - CB&CNS Carloads Terminating and Originating East of Point Tupper, 1996-2011								
Two-Year Period	1996-97	1998-99	2000-01	2002-03	2004-05	2006-07	2008-09	2010-11
Inbound	2700	1906	1790	1307	1592	1405	1118	1054
Outbound	22560	10766	4436	584	6106	761	693	470
Total	25260	12672	6226	1891	7698	2166	1811	1524
Ann Avg	12630	7337	3113	946	3849	1083	906	762
Data Sources: for 1996-2002: KPMG LLP, Cape Breton Island: Transportation Services and Infrastructure Market Analysis, Halifax, 2003, Exhibits II-6 and II-7: 12-13; for 2003-2011: Cape Breton & Central Nova Scotia Railway.								

Fig. 10.18 - While the real Devco Railway passed into history with the Cape Breton Development Corporation over a decade ago, it lives on in other scales on model railroads. At work here on the Fall River and Eastern Railroad of Dave McMahon, Fall River, NS, is an HO scale model of Devco # 209 built by Halifax modeller, Jim Simmons. The engine won a 1st in its class in the 2011 competition of the Maritime Federation of Model Railroaders (MFMR). In the real world, # 209 was one of two Devco diesels that went to the Salem & Hillsborough Railway and Museum in southern New Brunswick only to be lost when a fire destroyed the S&H roundhouse in 1994. For notes and photos by Simmons on the real-world Devco line, see his column, "Nova Scotia's Branchline Jewel," *The Maritime Branchline*, MFMR, 2011-12: 13-14.

Photo by Dave McMahon, courtesy of Jim Simmons. Reproduced by permission of Mr. Simmons and Mr. McMahon.

Fig. 10.19 - Locos 222 and 228 take a Sydney Coal Railway train out of the pier in February of 2006 with imported coal destined for the Lingan power plant. The SCR pier is close to the site of the International Company's wharf built in 1870 and the series of later docks that handled coal for export.

Photo by Geoff Doane, Halifax, NS. Reproduced by permission of Mr. Doane.

The Latest Heir to the S&L: The Sydney Coal Railway

The future of the remaining fragment of the S&L is also insecure. When the mines were taken over by Devco in 1968, the S&L had become the Devco Railway. Over the next three decades, as coal output declined and mines were closed, rail traffic decreased and branches were abandoned. The roundhouse and shops at Glace Bay were shut and torn down and a new, smaller complex for diesel locomotives built at Victoria Junction adjacent to a new coal-washing plant. The wind-up of Devco in 2001 included the sale or scrapping of the Devco Railway's remaining assets.

In 2002, the Sydney coal pier, a short section of the S&L/Devco track between the pier and the Lingan power plant, and a small amount of rolling stock were purchased by a new company connected to the Nova Scotia Power Corporation.[13] Since then, the Sydney Coal Railway has operated the pier and carried imported coal to Lingan. This line now runs with five locomotives and slightly fewer than 100 hopper cars, all purchased from the Devco Railway. Staff complement is fewer than twenty, a far cry from the hundreds of employees on the S&L as late as the 1960s.

The uncertain future of the CB&CNS makes it seem likely that the operating railway system in eastern Cape Breton will revert to this single tiny coal-hauling line. Survival of even this much activity, however, will be dependent on the continued use of coal to generate power at Lingan or the development of new mining projects such as the long-touted but still unrealized reopening of a major mine at Donkin, a project abandoned by Devco in the late 1980s. Even if it is goes into production, the Donkin mine may not have an impact on railway activity. At the time of writing, the company is proposing use of a conveyor system to load ships anchored offshore as an alternative to the traditional Cape Breton model of coal shipping piers that were fed by railways. Prediction of the future is a dangerous game but neither the long-run survival of coal-generated electricity nor the reopening of the Donkin mine appears to be a good bet.

Both pessimists and realists have reason to expect that most and perhaps all remaining railway activity on Cape Breton will come to an end in the not-too-distant future and that most of the few remaining rails will be taken up. Once upon a time, they might have gone to the steel plant in Sydney as scrap but that plant has vanished too.

In 1969, Kenneth Bagnell, a native of Glace Bay, published a poignant commentary triggered by the demise of the name of the "Sydney & Louisburg." At that time, save for the name change, the end of passenger service, and the closure of the Louisbourg branch, most of the island's railways were still operating more or less as they had years and decades before. Now, more than forty years later, with the changes those years have brought, Bagnell's words carry even more significance than they did in 1969.

The trains have spoken to me and I have not forgotten
by Kenneth Bagnell

"It is at night that I remember the trains. They come before sleep, up out of the dark, always coming, always going, and always taking me with them. We go where we have gone before and see what we have always seen: little towns where men sit, silent and staring, on back porches; trees, leafless and lean from winter winds; and always the fields, the never-beginning, never-ending fields. I know the trains. They have spoken to me and I have not forgotten. One of them, a circus train, a long serpent with its name in great letters of red, came to my town just once; but once was a thousand times. I went in the shivering morning and my father held my hand and I watched horses jangling their bells, zebras quivering in the chill, men cursing, and lions roaring. It was 20 years ago, but it was yesterday. I remember the trains for it was on the trains that my world first looked at me and told me never to forget it. I was 6, and the train was tired and slow and it ran not across a continent but part of a county. To me that county was the world. I would board it in Glace Bay, N.S., the old S&L, the Sydney & Louisburg Railway. It went so slowly that people said you could pick berries as you rode. But what mattered to a boy of 6 was that through the window his world stared at him, and he would remember forever where he began. I remember the S&L for it took me past the coal mine, No. 11, where almost everyone I knew worked—my father, my uncle, and all their friends.

"The S&L moved slowly past the mine, and a child could look out and see the men and the mountains of coal and slag; and they stared back at him and said, you are not a son of the palace but a son of the pit, and you must never forget it. The S&L is gone now, and the tracks are rusted and the stations along the way are fallen and alders cover where it ran. But it was a great train, and it died not on the tracks but in the boardrooms where men with sharp pencils added and subtracted and cut away a part of the nation.

"Now of course I fly. I cannot wait for the train to take me; I must hurry, I cannot wait, I must go and return. And only when the planes cannot fly will I take the train and let the land speak to me and me to it. Yet we need the train, all of us; for the train, not the car, not the plane, but the train, gives us a snatch of time, a stream of solitude to look at the little towns and to wonder if the men within them have pride or pain or both. Some of my most moving moments have been on trains when I have looked out and wondered about people behind lighted windows, children swing in the duck, mothers saying good-bye to fathers. Once I went to India and made the error of travelling always by plane, until someone put me on a train and it was the train that showed me the face of India. Someday the trains may all be gone. But then I shall be gone too. For the trains will not leave me behind."

Originally published in the *Globe & Mail*, Toronto, June 6, 1969; reproduced here by courtesy of Kenneth Bagnell.

11 – Cape Breton's Railway Heritage

As railways in Cape Breton and the rest of the Maritimes were evolving from transport backbones to the edge of extinction, most people ignored the fact that an important part of our region's history was fading away very quickly. The 1960 photo of the three boys beside a S&L locomotive makes the viewer wonder if the photographer had any sense that this locomotive and the rest of the S&L's roster of steam engines would be turned into scrap and fed into the Sydney steel plant in only a few years.

In some parts of the world, many small railways have made the transition from operating transport systems to heritage and tourism sites. In the U.K., for example, there are dozens of operating heritage lines. Many use steam locomotives, some of which date from the 19th century. The heritage of the age of British steam is not limited to small engines or preservation of locomotives from past decades. Recently, a new steam locomotive, *Tornado*, went into service. Built to original plans for one of the last series of large high-speed engines which handled passenger trains from London to Scotland on the London and North Eastern Railway in the 1950s, *Tornado* is a symbol of the strength of the railway heritage movement in the U.K. and beyond.[1] In addition to operating trains, there

Fig. 11.1 - A big toy for small boys. In the days of steam, locomotives were objects of fascination for boys – especially if they were accessible for close inspection.

Sydney & Louisburg Railway Museum, #SL-00-601.

are many U.K. museums, archives and societies with a railway focus. As in the rest of Canada, some moves have been made in this direction in Cape Breton but with mixed results.

In 1973, twelve years after the last S&L steam locomotives were retired, the Cape Breton Steam Railway was established as a joint venture of the recently-established S&L Historical Society and the Cape Breton Development Corporation. The line used a rebuilt locomotive, # 42, that had worked on the S&L for many years; a British engine, *Repton*, on loan from an American museum; and a number of vintage S&L and CNR passenger cars. Steam-powered excursions ran from Glace Bay or Victoria Junction or Port Morien with occasional specials run westward on the CN line to Iona. At the end of the 1970s, however, subsidy funding from Devco was cut off. Local attempts to save the Cape Breton Steam Railway were unsuccessful and the last run took place on September 7, 1979.

Repton, usually referred to in Cape Breton by its number, 926, went back to the United States, returned home to England in 1989, and is now running on the highly successful North Yorkshire Moors Railway. Built in 1934 and retired for the first time from main line duty on the Southern Railway in 1962, *Repton* is a good illustration of the potential operational longevity of a steam locomotive if it receives lots of oil and grease and tender loving care.

The fate of the Steam Railway concept was captured in a later front-page *Cape Breton Post* photo. It recorded Devco's eventual decision about what to do with the remaining passenger cars that had not gone to the S&L museum in Louisbourg. They were burned by Devco staff in 1987.[2] Wanton destruction was of course not unique

Fig. 11.2 (above) - Victoria Junction, 1973 - Cape Breton Steam Railway opening day.

Photographer unknown. 77-1426-1560. Beaton Institute, Cape Breton University.

Fig. 11.3 (left) - The cover of a CBSR brochure from the 1970s. In the photo, *Repton* is at the front of a double-header with # 42 in second place.

Author's collection.

Fig. 11.4 (right) - Crew for the last run of the CBSR, September 7, 1979.

Glace Bay Heritage Museum.

Fig. 11.5 (below) - A rally in Glace Bay in 1979 after the Devco decision to cancel funding for the Steam Railway.

Glace Bay Heritage Museum.

to railway heritage. At this time, Coast Guard staff and ships were sent out to pull down and burn the rubble of many abandoned lighthouses along the coast of Nova Scotia.

A similar fate was met by the single steam locomotive that had survived on Cape Breton Island. This engine, locally known as # 17, was preserved for a time outside the Glace Bay Miners' Museum. Though it was generally thought of as an S&L engine, that was not the case. Built in 1903, # 17 had originally belonged to the Scotia company, become an "Old Sydney Collieries" engine in 1921 and was later sold to the Bras d'Or Coal Company. This firm eventually transferred the locomotive to the Four Star mine that was opened to attempt to revive the coal property at Broughton. While at this site, # 17 ran only on the Broughton branch from the mine to a junction with the S&L track.

In the mid-1960s, after the last S&L steam loco had been scrapped and the Four Star mine closed, # 17 went back to the Bras d'Or colliery and worked there for a few more years. In 1970, the engine was donated to the new Miners' Museum at Glace Bay. In 1980, the museum suffered a catastrophic fire. In the years following, financial pressures faced by the museum in the wake of reconstruction had an impact on # 17. Lack of maintenance led to deterioration of the engine. To this was added the effect of vandalism, a result of # 17's location outside the museum building. The locomotive's condition reached the point where neither the museum nor other potential protectors were able to undertake the costs of restoration. In 1996 # 17 was converted to scrap.

There are only three surviving steam locomotives with connections to Cape Breton. One of these is known as Old Sydney Collieries # 25 though it has an interesting history that predates the 1921 Besco merger that established the "Old Sydney" corporate name. The engine was built in 1900 by the Baldwin company of Philadelphia for the General Mining Association, just before that firm sold its assets to Nova Scotia Steel & Coal, and # 25 was apparently originally named the *E. E. Bigge* after the man who was GMA Board Secretary in

1900. The Bigge surname goes back to the beginning of this book and the very beginning of Cape Breton's railways—see the reproduction of the 1830 GMA Board of Directors list in chapter 1.

When # 25 was taken out of service after a working life of sixty years, the locomotive was donated to the Canadian Railroad Historical Association Museum at St. Constant, Quebec, and has been on display there for the past half century.[3] The CRHA collection of rolling stock also includes S&L passenger car # 4 which was described toward the end of its working days in the previous chapter.

The other two surviving steam engines are at the Nova Scotia Museum of Industry in Stellarton. One is a relatively modern engine. Dosco # 151, a 36-in gauge tank locomotive built in 1942 by the Montreal Locomotive Works, operated within the Sydney steel plant.

The oldest survivor, built one year before OSC # 25 and certainly the best known to Cape Bretoners of the three engines, is S&L # 42.[4] After the demise of the Cape Breton Steam Railway in 1979, this engine went to New Brunswick and ran for five years on the Salem & Hillsborough heritage line. When it was no longer in operating condition, the engine was brought back to Nova Scotia to the Museum of Industry (NSMOI) in Stellarton. Photos of both # 42 and Dosco # 151 can be seen, as at the time of writing, on the NSMOI website.

Fig. 11.6 (left) - # 17 and the author's son Sean at the Glace Bay Miners' Museum, 1969.

Author's photo.

Fig. 11.7 (below) - Old Sydney Collieries # 25 on display at the Canadian Railroad Historical Association's museum, St. Constant, Quebec, in 2011.

Author's photo.

Two other engines have survived from the diesel era. Devco # 20, also at NSMOI, is one of the oldest preserved diesel locomotives in Canada. It was built in Chicago in 1940 though it only came to Cape Breton, to the Four Star Colliery, in the 1960s. Four Star was closed shortly after its arrival and the engine was transferred to the Devco Railway where it worked until it was retired in 1991. The second surviving diesel is one used at the Georgia Pacific Company gypsum terminal at Port Hawkesbury and later donated to the Orangedale Station Museum. A photo of this engine is in chapter 8.

A later attempt to link railway passenger service and tourism was launched by VIA Rail in 2000. For four years, VIA ran a weekly summer excursion train called the *Bras d'Or* from Halifax to Sydney. The excursion trains were abandoned, however, in the wake of uncertainty about the continued use and

maintenance of the Truro to Sydney section of the line. The Cape Breton and Central Nova Scotia had made application to abandon the line from the Strait of Canso to Sydney in 2002 and VIA stopped running the *Bras d'Or* at the end of the 2003 summer season.

In contrast to attempts to operate trains or protect locomotives, preservation and use of railway stations has been more successful in Cape Breton. The small St. Peter's station, where Jamie Calder served as agent for decades, is now the Bonnie Brae Senior Citizens Club. At Inverness, the station which served as the northern terminal for the *Judique Flyer* has been converted into a museum. Within its holdings, the Ned MacDonald Historical Complex collection includes an extensive array of material dealing with the Inverness railway line from its days as an inde-

Fig. 11.9 (top) - A VIA Rail passenger extra westbound at the Orangedale station on April 23, 2000. This was a single-run, chartered train that used the same equipment that went into service on VIA's *Bras d'Or*.

Photo by Bill Linley, Port Lorne, NS. Reproduced by permission of Bill Linley and the Orangedale Railway Museum.

Fig. 11.10 (middle) - The St. Peter's station in its new role in 2011.

Author's photo.

Fig. 11.11 (bottom) - The Inverness station in 2011.

Author's photo.

pendent through the years when it was part of the Canadian National system.

The Sydney Mines station, built by the Intercolonial Railway ca. 1906, is now the Sydney Mines Heritage Museum. The collection on display, which includes an S&L caboose in its later Devco Railway paint scheme, concentrates on railways and mines and their roles in the development of the community. Facing the Sydney Mines museum complex is a magnificent mural portraying the station in its operating years.

The S&L Historical Society was established in Louisbourg in 1971 and the Society's museum, built around the 1895 S&L station, has become an active tourist attraction in the town. The museum includes a number of pieces of rolling stock including several passenger cars acquired before Devco destroyed the others. The Society has continued a major effort to collect S&L memorabilia and has built up a major collection of photos of the S&L in operation. The number of photos in this book from the museum speaks to the scope of the collection.

Fig. 11.12 (above) - Jim Tobin of the Sydney Mines Heritage Museum and DR # 20. This caboose was one of the last two acquired by the S&L before that line became the Devco Railway in the mid-1960s.

Author's photo courtesy of Jim Tobin and the Sydney Mines Heritage Museum.

Fig. 11.13 (below) - Allen Hilgendorf's large mural that shows the Sydney Mines station as a working CNR railway station.

Author's photo courtesy of Sydney Mines Heritage Museum.

In 1986, a group of Orangedale residents formed an organization to try to prevent the demolition of the local station, built by the Intercolonial Railway a century previously. The attempts were successful and the building was given a reprieve. The Orangedale Station Association emerged to take ownership of the station, restore it and convert it into a museum. More than twenty years of work by Association members has turned the Orangedale Station into a site

Fig. 11.14 - At the S&L museum, 2011.

Author's photo courtesy of Sydney & Louisburg Railway Museum.

Fig. 11.15 - A S&L Museum volunteer section gang ca. 1975; from left, Neil MacLean, Freeman MacKenzie and Bill Barter.

Sydney & Louisburg Railway Museum, #SL-00-464.

Keeping a Railway Museum on Track

For many years, Bill Bussey has been one of the most public faces associated with the Sydney and Louisburg Railway Museum. To many visitors during the museum's four-month summer season, Bussey may appear as station agent, bridge and building superintendent, section foreman, or just an always-genial host—or all rolled into one. For researchers like your author, he is an invaluable aide. He of course has counterparts in the S&L Museum Society and at similar museums across Cape Breton, the province and the country. But, as a result of an association with him that predates even the idea of this book, he was an obvious candidate for an interview about a railway museum and a volunteer's involvement with it. The interview took place in the autumn of 2011 when his official title was Secretary-Treasurer of the museum society.

HM: Bill, just how far back does your connection with the museum go?

BB: Somehow I've built up a bit of seniority, as railroaders called it, 35 years to be exact. I signed on in 1976, just after we moved back from Newfoundland. The museum had opened just a couple of years before that. I never thought I'd be active for 35 years—enough service for a pension if there was a pension plan for volunteers.

HM: What got you to sign on and stay involved for so long? Family connection to the S&L, community involvement, or a hope for a long-service pension?

BB: It was the family link to the S&L for sure, at least for the sign-on. My grandfather, Charlie Bagnell, worked on the S&L all his life. He started as a brakeman and became a conductor—the regular path. He worked for the S&L for fifty years. He was retired when the museum opened and became one of the three original tour guides. My involvement was just a natural thing. As for the long haul, it's been well worth doing and it's been fun—at least most of the time.

Feb. 11.16 - Bill Bussey – a railway heritage veteran.

Author's photo courtesy of Bill Bussey and the Sydney & Louisburg Railway Museum.

HM: It's a long time since the S&L, the real S&L, became the Devco Railway. Does the society have any members left who are veterans of the real S&L?

BB: Believe it or not, we do have one—Harvey MacLeod who was a fireman when the S&L became Devco in 1967.

HM: What about the rest of the crew, society members and supporters? How many people are involved?

BB: Now we have about fifty people between active formal members and others, individuals and businesses, who will pitch in to help. But it's a much smaller base of support now than back in the 1970s. That's a big concern but it's a common problem for community organizations. And it's especially true in smaller communities like Louisbourg.

HM: Tell me a bit about your visitors, how many, where they're from, what brings them in to the S&L museum.

BB: Our count this year is about 3500—down a bit like last year was—and reflecting a general drop in the number of people travelling. We do keep records on where our visitors are from and that pattern is fairly stable. About 25 per cent are local, folks from Cape Breton County. Another 25 per cent are from elsewhere in Nova Scotia and the Maritimes so roughly half our visitors are from the Maritime region. Another 30 per cent are from west of New Brunswick, mostly from Quebec and Ontario. The remaining 20 per cent from outside Canada with most from the USA. We don't try to record what brings them to the museum but from conversation with people, I think that the majority don't come because of a specific interest in railways.

HM: What reactions do you get from people? What do they seem to find most interesting?

BB: From comments and questions, I'd say the top three things are our rolling stock, the model railway, and the station building itself. For older people, the rolling stock and the station bring back memories. For many younger people, those may both provide first-time up-close experiences. You know, a lot of young people have never been inside a railway station, new or old. And our station is a working time machine that carries you back to a different world. The model railway is a draw for everyone. I suspect those reactions are much the same at other railway museums. The specific S&L and Cape Breton sides of our displays have special appeal for people from the area or who have roots here – and we do see a lot of them over a summer.

HM: The museum has been open a long time now. Do you ever have S&L artifacts or photos or other things being added to the collection these days?

BB: It's surprising but we still do. Just recently the bell of loco # 23 came in the door. There had been stories that it was in service as a church bell in Glace Bay or that it had gone for scrap. But it had been with a family with S&L roots and they donated it to us. (See chapter 5 for a photo of # 23 with a passenger train at Sydney station.)

HM What are the big challenges the museum faces now?

BB: How long a list would you like? I guess the biggest is being able to do a good job of maintaining what we have. Doing that requires work hours and money and skills in various combinations for various things that have to be done. I mentioned before about our active roster. Finding ways to get it growing again is probably the key to long term success. It's more than that; it's the key to the very survival of organizations like ours.

HM: That's a concise mix of optimism and realism, true in Louisbourg, and just as true across the country, and an appropriate note on which to end. Thank you, Bill. As always, it's been a pleasure.

that draws visitors from across North America and beyond. As at Louisbourg, the station's collection ranges from rolling stock to office records and almost everything imaginable in between. Also like Louisbourg, one of the most valuable parts of the collection is the array of photos of railway life between the Strait of Canso and the Sydneys.

A Wish List for Future Discoveries

There have been numerous references in this book to the absence of documents, photos, artifacts or other material that could provide answers to questions or at

Fig. 11.17 (right) - Martin Boston on duty at Orangedale, 2011.

Author's photo courtesy of Martin Boston and the Orangedale Railway Museum.

Fig. 11.18 (below left) - In 2005, the Orangedale Station Association received a prestigious national award from the Canadian Railroad Historical Association for the society's restoration and preservation efforts.

Author's photo courtesy of Orangedale Railway Museum.

Fig. 11.19 (below right) - The Orangedale station is ready for snow. This large CNR plow dates from the 1950s.

Author's photo courtesy of Orangedale Railway Museum.

least a basis for making better guesses about possible answers. Within a chapter that deals with Cape Breton's surviving railway heritage, it seems appropriate to record a short "wish list" that identifies some of the more potentially significant materials that might be waiting for rediscovery in attics, photo albums or personal collections of family documents.

The hope that more important material may reappear may be naively optimistic. However, during fifteen years of research on the history of railways in Eastern Canada, I have had a number of experiences when totally unexpected items appeared from unexpected locations and I am sure that much more exists and is waiting to be found. It seems reasonable to think that some readers of the book may have or know about material related to Cape Breton's railway history that could provide valuable aid to future researchers. As a result, I would like to ask if you, the reader, have or know about items like the following:

General types of material:
- diaries, memoirs, letters or work-related documents of railway employees
- railway company documents of any type, for example railway station records
- descriptions of railway construction or operations, especially from the 19th century
- memoirs or letters about trips made by train, especially from pre-1939
- Photos: notably "missing" at the time of writing are:
  GMA locomotives Sydney and Halifax
  GMA train and wharf operations
  Cape Breton Company: Governor General's train, 1880
  Intercolonial opening: Governor General's train 1890
  Gowrie coal company mine and railway photos
  New Campbellton mine and railway photos
  Other photo subjects that are in very short supply include:
  G&CB and other narrow gauge locomotives, train and wharf operations
  Halifax & Cape Breton Railway other than the photo in chapter 3
  Mabou & Gulf Railway other than the photo in chapter 4
  Cape Breton Railway / St. Peter's branch of CNR photos,
  "special train" and "work train" operations
  station platform scenes
  passenger car interior scenes
  activity at coal wharves or other freight handling settings
  railway construction activity

If you or someone you know can make a personal contribution toward expanding the existing body of resources for Cape Breton's railway history, please contact the Beaton Institute at Cape Breton University with information about the documents or photos.

With railway heritage becoming a stronger tourist draw across North America, museums and archives can serve as catalysts for the growth of tourism as well as centres for the promotion of local history. In the latter role, they are positioned to continue to play the vital roles in preserving the story of Cape

Breton's railways.[5] Hundreds of dedicated volunteers have already invested thousands of hours of effort in that cause, a cause that will continue to be important until the date, sometime in the future, when Cape Breton's railways may rise again.

Though Jimmy Rankin's tribute refers specifically to Orangedale, it really applies to all of Cape Breton's stations and other railway facilities and to all those who have worked on the island's railways or for the preservation of their history.

Orangedale Whistle

The stationmaster looked all around
Along the track both up and down
But the train could not be found
For there was neither sight or sound
There was neither sight or sound

He walked on slowly to the station door
like so many times before
He looked outside into a sunshine beam
Closed his eyes and dreamed a dream
Drifted off into a dream

The winds of change forever blow
Some things stay and some things go
The falling rain must melt the snow
The Orangedale whistle will always blow

Years ago throughout this land
That line was laid by able men
But things saw change as time went by
People drive and people fly
People drive and people fly

The stationmaster is long since gone
He faded off into the sun
But the whistle shrill still lingers on
In the hearts of everyone
Everyday from dusk till dawn

The winds of change forever blow
Some things stay and some things go
The falling rain must melt the snow
The Orangedale whistle will always blow

Source: http://www.lyricsdownload.com/rankin-family-orangedale-whistle-lyrics.html
Reprinted by permission.

Notes

Introduction

1. On the development of British railways from the 1600s to the early 1800s, the definitive study is still Lewis, *Early Wooden Railways*. A concise and reliable review more easily found in Canada is in Flinn, *The History of the British Coal Industry*, see chapter 5, "The Transport of Coal."

2. On the two best-known landmark English railways, the Stockton and Darlington, and the Liverpool and Manchester, see Kirby, *The Origins of Railway Enterprise: the Stockton and Darlington Railway*, and Carlson, *The Liverpool and Manchester Railway Project*. For a wide-ranging look at the impact of the railway in the U.K. in the decades after 1830, see Freeman, *Railways and the Victorian Imagination*.

3. Pigott and Lewis, "The Pre-History of Britain's Railways," 9.

4. On the importance of this set of drawings, only part of which is reproduced, see Herb MacDonald, "The Rideau Railway Idea: 1816-1825."

Chapter 1

1. Details in this sidebar come from documentary and secondary material generally unknown to or ignored by those who have done work on the origins of the GMA: Prospectus of the General South American Mining Association; Deed of Settlement of General Mining Association (the Deed includes a list of shareholders and their holdings as at April 4, 1829, the Deed's date of record); *Quarterly Mining Review* (*QMR*), vol. 1, 1830. (The first four issues of this journal include extensive coverage of company activity in both Nova Scotia and South America. The 1829 Board list, reproduced from *QMR*, vol. 1, no. 1, identifies the firm as the "General Mining Company." I suspect this was because the report was dated March 20, 1829, and the provisions of the Deed of Settlement of 1829, including the change of the company's name, were not effective until 4 April); manuscript material on Philip Rundell; George Fox Manuscript; Culme, "A Devoted Attention to Business: An Obituary of Philip Rundell"; Bury, "A Tale of Two City

Firms"; *The Dictionary of National Biography, Missing Persons*, 87-88 and 575-76. Pressures of space preclude documentation of the range of the external connections of GMA Directors and shareholders. The one author who has captured some of the details and documentation noted here is Samson, *The Spirit of Industry and Improvement*, chapter 5.

2. The website for the Royal Collection illustrates the nature of Rundell's output for the Royal Family. As at the time of writing, see http://www.royalcollection.org.uk/eGallery/ and enter "Rundell" in the internal search engine. One item of particular interest in a GMA context is the "Shield of Achilles." The original went to George IV. Three other copies were made, one of which was purchased by the Duke of York. It was the Duke's taste for buying such items on credit that ultimately brought the GMA to Nova Scotia. The scope of Rundell's output for the Royal Household is demonstrated in a 227-page, 1832 report, "Descriptive inventories....". The report was prepared by "Rundell, Bridge & Co, Goldsmiths to their Majesties."

3. Brown, *The Coal Fields and Coal Trade of the Island of Cape Breton*.

4. The core source is the collection of GMA papers from Cape Breton, Beaton Institute, MG 14,19. This collection is extensive but far from complete. Among critical missing papers are the flows of correspondence between local collieries and head office in London. For a more detailed account of GMA horse-powered railways and the documentary record in Canada and England, see Herb MacDonald, "The Early Horse-Powered Mining Railways of Cape Breton."

5. *QMR*, vol. 1, no 3, September, 1830: 347.

6. At Albion Mines, the first 200 yards (185 m) of rails were laid at the end of April, 1830 suggesting that work on the roadbed had started very early that year if not before the end of 1829, ibid. 348.

7. For details, see Herb MacDonald, "The Early Horse-Powered Mining Railways of Cape Breton," 12.

8. Beaton Institute (BI), GMA papers, D-8-a, Manager's Letter Book, 1827-1833, R Brown to Belcher & Co, Halifax, January 6, 1833, and to William Fairclough, Liverpool, January 12, 1833.

9. BI, GMA papers, B-1-k; detail in the 1837 Stock Book is extended by the content of the 1838 volume, BI, GMA papers, B-4.

10. Assuming a weight of no more than 30 lb/yd (14 kg/m), this "light rail" inventory is compatible with the 1560 yards (1.426 km) reported in the *QMR* letter of January 15, 1830, if provision is made for additional track in sidings and on the wharf. This assumption is based on the record in the 1838 Stock Book of loose rails at Little Bras d'Or with a reported weight of 28 lb/yd (13 kg/m). The 75 t of "light rail" recorded in the 1837 Stock Book did not appear in 1838. I speculate this indicates the rails went into use in one of the pits, something that further suggests these were old rails, the only logical source of which would have been leftovers from the first Sydney Mines railway.

11. The Winchester (or London) chaldron was equal to half a Newcastle chaldron. Though both were primarily measures of volume rather than weight, a "Newcastle wagon" carried close to 6000 lb (2,721 kg) and the original Sydney Mines ½ Winchester wagons almost 1500 lb (680 kg). GMA reports to the Nova Scotia government relating to sales, the base for royalties payable to Halifax, used the Newcastle measure as a result of an arrangement negotiated by the GMA with the British government. That agreement was regarded by the Nova Scotia government as a case of "sharp dealing" since pre-GMA royalties on coal had been paid based on the Winchester measure. On the origin of this and other legal and political disputes between the GMA and the government in Halifax, see Muise, "The General Mining Association and Nova Scotia's Coal."

12. BI, GMA papers, D-8-a, Manager's Letter Book, 1827-1833, R. Smith to J. Smith, June 12, 1833.

13. *The Cape-Bretonian and General Reporter*, January 25, 1834. The timing of Foord's second trip suggests a sense of urgency since a winter voyage would have been much more dangerous.

14. For additional detail on Buddle's influence on events at Sydney Mines, see Herb MacDonald, "The Early Horse-Powered Mining Railways of Cape Breton." On Buddle's involvement in GMA railway construction in Pictou County in the late 1830s, see Herb MacDonald, "The Albion Railway of 1839-40." Flinn provides considerable detail on Buddle's activity in England in the fields of transportation, engineering and colliery management.

15. Nova Scotia Archives and Records Management (NSARM), Mines & Minerals Papers, RG 21A, vol 39, #32, George Duval, GMA, London, to Buddle, March 12, 1834.

16. The new mine was identified as "Biggs Main" in the 1837 and 1838 Stock Books and obviously named after Thomas Bigge despite the missing "e." It became known locally as "Jacob's Pit." While the Bridge and Rundell names disappeared from the GMA during the 19th century, the Bigge family connection continued. Edward Bigge was Secretary of the GMA Board when the firm was wound up in 1900.

17. Copies that came to Nova Scotia are at NSARM, RG 21A, vol. 39, # 32-33. Buddle's file copies are at the Northumberland County Record Office (NCRO), John Buddle papers, Reports Volume, BUD/19.

18. Unless otherwise noted, all details about the second Sydney Mines line are based on Buddle's two reports and several letters attached to the NSARM copy of the "Railway Report"; the Sydney Mines Stock Books of 1837 and 1838; and one letter from the Buddle papers at the Durham County Record Office (DCRO), NCB1/JB/717, Daniel Hoard, Sydney Mines, to Buddle, August 4, 1834.

19. Buddle's "Railway Report" identifies these as "Mr. Smith's plan." Richard Smith was the Albion Mines manager. He was also identified as the "Mining Engineer" for the firm in both the GMA 1829 Deed of Settlement and the 1829 Board list in *QMR*. In that capacity, he would have been Richard Brown's superior. The 1827-1833 Manager's Letter Book shows that Smith was in Sydney Mines most of the time during 1833 and early 1834. On Smith, see *Dictionary of Cana-*

dian Biography (*DCB*), IX, 1976: 730-31. Numerous footnotes will be found to entries in *DCB* with details on the hard copy editions. The complete texts of all biographies are available online.

20. No evidence has been found about how coal was loaded at the original Sydney Mines wharf but an "old frame" was included in the inventory reported at Little Bras d'Or. Use of a frame there likely preceded the recommendations in Buddle's "Railway Report" and suggests that a frame might have also been used on the first Sydney Mines wharf.

21. North England Institute of Mining & Mechanical Engineers (NEIMME), Newcastle, Buddle papers, vol. 64: 27. Rayne was also involved through Buddle in the supply of boiler parts and other pit machinery to Cape Breton, DCRO, NCB1/JB/1761; iron work for wagons for the Albion Railway in 1838, DCRO, NCB1/JB/1733-5 and NCRO, BUD/60/2/Folio 31; and shipments of locomotives to the GMA at Sydney Mines in 1853 and Albion Mines in 1854.

22. The self-acting incline at Sydney Mines was a late arrival in a North American context. Gamst documents the continent's first self-acting model on a line on Boston's Beacon Hill in 1805 in his study, "The Context and Significance of America's First Railroad." On our side of the border, the first double track incline appears to have been one used by the Royal Engineers during reconstruction work on the Citadel at Quebec City in the 1820s though it may have been powered by a stationary steam engine.

23. At the time of writing, two 1835 engravings of Seaham on the University of Newcastle website show how this kind of incline worked; see http://sine.ncl.ac.uk/search.asp. In the search engine, under "general search" enter "seaham incline" to locate the drawings. Within a five-mile radius (8 km) of the Rainton and Seaham line, nine other self-acting engines were in operation on the Lambton waggonway and the two branches of the Hetton Colliery line. An excellent recent study of inclines is Mountford's, "Rope Haulage: The Forgotten Element of Railway History."

24. For example, see Jackson, *Windows on the Past*, 5; Town of Sydney Mines, *The History of Sydney Mines*, 121; and most recently, Gillis, *Historic North Sydney*, x. These, I suspect, probably all have roots in a reference in Brown, "Canada's Earliest Railways," 60.

25 BI, Michael Dwyer Papers, MG 12, 40; C-1-38; Dwyer to Thomas Cantley, January 11, 1933.

26. For 1832, BI, GMA papers, E-1-a-4, Workmens' Time Book, June 1832; for 1835 and 1836, NSARM, RG 1, vol. 464, # 7, Statement of Men, Horses & Machinery Employed at Sydney Mines in 1835-36; for 1838, NSARM, RG 1, vol. 463 # 32, Statement of Men, Horses & Machinery at Sydney Mines in September, 1838.

27. BI, GMA papers, C-1-n, Surface Labour Accounts, 1838.

28. A sampling of GMA shipping documents at the Beaton Institute indicates a season generally running from mid/late April to mid/late December during the 1830s and 1840s.

29. See Longridge's 1821 letter quoted in Martin, *The Bedlington Engine and Iron Works*, 10.

30. "A. Somers Drove Noted Locomotives," *Halifax Herald*, May 29, 1930, 13.

31. At the time of writing, a good side-on photo of Albion that clearly shows the cylinder position is available on the website of the Nova Scotia Museum of Industry.

32. All photos from this very extensive collection except those identified with a negative number come from a single Merrilees box catalogued # 1980-149, Group D, subseries 1, Box # 2000725251. This box has c.400 photos from Nova Scotia mining company railways, most of them from Cape Breton.

33. For an account of the rewriting of this engine's history, see Bailey and MacDonald, "Tracking a Canadian Stephenson—A Transatlantic Quest."

34. Richard Brown papers, NSARM, MG1 vol. 157, # 72; General Mining Association Annual Report for 1888: 8. This collection is made up of the papers of Richard Brown Jr. who assumed his father's position in 1864. The younger Brown became the first Mayor of Sydney Mines in 1898.

35. Richard Brown papers, NSARM, MG1 vol. 157, # 35-36. On the full scope of Scotia's history, see Cameron, "The Scotia Steelmasters."

Chapter 2

1. Library and Archives Canada (LAC), Sir John A Macdonald papers, MG 26-A, vol 282: 129105; Tupper to Macdonald, April 30, 1868.

2. Nova Scotia Department of Mines Report for 1870, *Journals of House of Assembly of Nova Scotia* (*JHANS*), 1871, Appendix 14: 17.

3. As with many British engines that came to Cape Breton, previously published sources have demonstrated confusion and uncertainty about the origins of the International locomotives. The best example is seen in Campbell and Johnston's book on the Sydney & Louisburg, *Tracks Across The Landscape*, Sydney: UCCB Press, 1995, where the two locomotive rosters, contain internal contradictions in addition to factual errors (95-95). In the absence of original contracts or correspondence found in Canada about locomotives imported from Britain, studies done in the U.K. (usually based on manufacturers' records) are consistently much more reliable than Canadian secondary sources. For the International engines, the British evidence is clear. Baker, *Black, Hawthorne and Co. Works List*, 1988, quotes Black, Hawthorne documents for orders for *Henry Day* and *Alfred MacKay*, company works #s 113 and 114, in May of 1869. The *Hunslet Engine Company Engine Book No 1*, Hunslet Archives, Armley Mill, Leeds, U.K., shows shipment of *A. C. Morton*, company works # 44, in July of 1870. The records show the orders for these engines were both placed by James Livesey, a London-based agent and broker, on behalf of the International Company.

4. Mines Report for 1883, *JHANS*, 1884, Appendix 6: 9.

5. *DCB*, XIV, 1998: 939-47.

6. *Neilson & Co Order Book, 1863-c.1880.*

7. In its summary of activity at the Little Glace Bay colliery, the Mines Report for 1867 refers to "a locomotive engine which has recently been substituted for the horses previously employed," *JHANS*, 1868, Appendix 12: 3.

8. Often misnamed as "Archibald" but the engine nameplate is quite clear in photos and the name is spelled "Archbold" in Glace Bay Mining's Act of Incorporation, *Statutes of Nova Scotia* (*SNS*), 1862, ch. 72.

9. A tank locomotive, built for this line in 1942, is preserved at the Nova Scotia Museum of Industry in Stellarton. See reference to this engine in chapter 11.

10. The 1871 prospectus indicated a change of name to "Glasgow and Cape Breton (Nova Scotia) Coal & Railway Company Limited." This renamed firm, incorporated in Nova Scotia in 1872, (*SNS*), 1872, ch 71, merged the original railway company with the separate firm that owned the Reserve colliery.

11. Summaries of Avonside records at the Hunslet Archives, Armley Mill, Leeds, U.K. show three Patents built for "Cape Breton" in 1871-72, works numbers 907-912. Avonside records of Patents have two works numbers per locomotive, one for each boiler. Some sources have suggested the order was for four or six locomotives. A list of Patents "completed or in the course of construction" in the London-based journal *Engineering,* November 10, 1871: 303, includes four for the G&CB. Perhaps an order for one was cancelled; perhaps the number quoted was incorrect. No evidence has been found to explain the variance. References to six Patents on the G&CB appear to have been based on a failure to realize that each of these engines carried two works numbers.

12. Mines Report for 1872, *JHANS,* 1873, Appendix 11: 13; Parliament of Canada, *Sessional Papers*, 1876, vol 8, Sessional Paper # 78, Canada Customs Report: 2.

13. The rarity of Fairlie Patents in Canada was a result of the fact that narrow gauge railways were rare in North America. Patents were designed for narrow gauge lines and widely used in the U.K. and other locations where narrow gauges were common. On Fairlie and his locomotive design, see Abbott, *The Fairlie Locomotives*, 1970; and Binns, *Fairlie Articulated Locomotives*, 2001.

14. See Clarke, "The Ontario Narrow Gauge."

15. See for example, Omer Lavallee, *Narrow Gauge Railways in Canada*, 1972 and 2005.

16. *DCB*, XII, 1990: 373-76; a letter by Gisborne in *The Times*, London, March 20, 1871, shows that he was still in London and acting as the Nova Scotia "Government Agent for Mines" on that date.

17. The possibility of a broker's involvement is demonstrated by James Livesey's role as agent for the International Company's 1869-70 locomotive purchases from Black, Hawthorne and Hunslet. In 1872, Livesey acted as agent for the Prince Edward Island Railway in the purchase of engines from Black, Hawthorne.

18. Locomotive manufacturers sometimes split or shared orders to cope with incapacity of the order recipient to meet a customer's need. Fox, Walker is identified

as the source of the first G&CB locomotive in 1871 in a works list compiled from Fox records by Terrence King, Stephenson Locomotive Society Library, Hersham, Surrey, U.K., cat WL 10313. Canada Customs records show the G&CB took delivery of one engine in 1871 and three in 1872 though no details are included about their origins. The 1871 locomotive was valued at $9733 and the 1872 shipment at $24,333. Duty was paid at the rate of 15 per cent; Parliament of Canada, *Sessional Papers*, 1876, vol 8, Sessional Paper # 78: 2.

19. Bailey, "James Samuel."

20. *The Engineer*, London, July 16, 1869: 40.

21. *Engineering*, London, August 21, 1874, 144. The two-page plate, the source of the drawing of the G&CB Patent found in figure 2.10, includes profiles of 17 other models of Patents with dimensions and mechanical specifications for each. That plate, a virtual "infomercial" for Fairlie, is an invaluable resource regarding Patents built for various railways.

22. Numeric codes such as this are often used to classify locomotives. The first number refers to the number of wheels on a leading wheel set at the front of the engine. A Patent did not have a leading wheel set or "truck" so the first number in the code was a 0. The second number refers to the number of driving wheels, those powered by rods that were controlled by the steam generated by the engine. Most locomotives had only one set of driving wheels but the Patents had two sets, each with four wheels. This produced the second and third numbers, the 4-4. Since there was no set of non-driving support wheels at the back of a Patent, the last number in the code was another 0. Tank engines, those without a separate tender to carry fuel and/or water, had a T added to the numeric code. This produced the 0-4-4-0T designation for the G&CB Patents. The coding system can be readily understood by looking at the locomotive photos in the earlier part of the chapter as examples. *Henry Day* was an 0-6-0T with no leading wheels, six connected drivers, no trailing wheel set under the engineer's cab and no tender. *Sir Donald* was a 2-6-4T. *Pinkie* was an 0-4-0T. Since the codes reflect the total number of wheels on the engine, the numbers in the code must be reduced by half when counting the number of wheels visible in a profile photo that shows only one side of a locomotive. In the case of a locomotive with a separate tender, the wheels on the tender were not included in the code. As an illustration, look at figure 3.2. The Halifax & Cape Breton engine would be coded as a 4-4-0.

23. One original Patent built in 1879 plus two modern working replicas run on the Ffestiniog Railway in North Wales. Photos of these working Patents can be easily found through an internet search.

24. The 200 original G&CB wagons were reported as having 4 t capacity; see Mines Report for 1872, *JHANS*, 1873, Appendix 11: 14. The total weight of Young's forty-car train would have approached 200 t.

25. Quoted in Binns, 2001: 51. No source is given for this letter and there is no indication of its recipient though the quote suggests it went to either Avonside or G&CB principals in England. The quote indicates that Binns had access to rel-

evant archival papers from some source other than the collections I have been able to trace. Attempts to contact Binns to pursue his source(s) have been unsuccessful.

26. The Cape Breton Company was the result of the 1874 merger of three firms, the 1872 G&CB and two of Gisborne's mining companies, the Schooner Pond Coal Company and the Lorway Coal Company. See *SNS*, 1874, ch 73. Gisborne appears to have left Cape Breton soon after the reorganization and he was involved in an extended legal battle with the new company; see NSARM, Scotian Railroad Society Papers, MG 28S, vol 189: 1. After leaving Cape Breton, Gisborne went back to the field of telegraphy as Superintendent of the Canadian Government's new Telegraph and Signal Service.

27 In addition to Kennelly's involvement with railways and mines, in the latter years of his life Kennelly was very active in promoting the preservation of the ruins of the French fortress and townsite at Louisbourg; see Johnston, "Preserving History…," 61-64. Obituaries for Kennelly can be seen in the Sydney newspapers of August 28, 1907.

28. "Henry Alfred Gray," in Rose, *A Cyclopaedia of Canadian Biography*, 362-63.

29. LAC, Sandford Fleming Collection, negative # PA-027635.

30. *Evening Reporter*, Halifax, October 25, 1877:2. Reports such as this indicating first operations in late October of 1877 cannot be reconciled with evidence such as the Cape Breton Company document, the source of the map in this chapter, or the coverage in the *Canadian Illustrated News* of June 5, 1875, that the Louisbourg line was ready to open in the summer of 1875. Perhaps a decline in business or shortage of cash delayed the opening; perhaps it did open, at least for partial service, in 1875. Perhaps what happened is something else again. There are no answers to the obvious question about what transpired on the Louisbourg branch during this period.

31. *SNS*, 1881, ch 73.

32. *Halifax Herald*, April 19, 1930: 10.

33. *Railway and Shipping World* (*RSW*), January, 1903: 15.

34. For an award-winning biography, see Knowles, *From Telegrapher To Titan*.

35. See MacGillivray, "Henry Melville Whitney Comes To Cape Breton."; *DCB*, "Henry Melville Whitney," XV, 2005: 1073-75; *DCB*, "Benjamin Franklin Pearson," XIV, 1998: 827-30.

36. Donkin's name reappears on several occasions in the next two chapters. For a concise biography, see an account in the *Daily News*, Amherst, April 23, 1932:2, published on the occasion of his 85th birthday.

37. *SNS*, 1910, ch 171.

38. Parliament of Canada, *Sessional Papers*, 1876, vol 8, Sessional Paper # 51, "Railway Statistics," Table 9, "Lines of Railway owned by Coal Mines."

39. A photo of one of the PEI engines when new has been widely reproduced; see for example either edition of Lavallee's book on narrow gauge. This is considered the standard work on the subject but his coverage of Nova Scotia lines contains

some problems. For example, he states that the Gowrie line was opened in 1877, missing the correct date by four years.

40. The 1865 and 1874 reports are both included in Canadian Institute for Historic Microreproduction (CIHM), microfiche # 36058, "Reports on the New Campbellton Coal Mines."

41. CIHM, "New Campbellton Coal Mines," Nova Scotia Printing Company, 1880, microfiche # 34830. This document also included the 1864 and 1874 reports plus a detailed map of the site.

Chapter 3

1. During the 1840s, the *Journals of the Nova Scotia House of Assembly* were filled with documents dealing with the Halifax and Quebec project. At the time of writing, a handy collection of these from 1846 is available online at http://alts.net/ns1625/railway1846.html. Complete volumes of *JHANS* up to 1867 are online at Early Canadiana Online http://www.canadiana.org/ECO.

2. The extent of Poor's influence on the development of railways in this country warranted his inclusion in the *Dictionary of Canadian Biography (DCB)*, X, 1972: 590-93.

3. *DCB* XII, 1990: 348-56.

4. For an insightful examination of the conflicting pressures between east-west and north-south railway projects, see den Otter, *The Philosophy of Railways*.

5. "Prospectus of the European and North American Railway Company," [Portland, 1851], CIHM microfiche # 22291.

6. A. C. Morton, "Report on the Survey of the European and North American Railway," [Portland, 1851], CIHM microfiche # 22278.

7. *Cape-Breton News*, March 1, 1851.

8. For more about the Sydney meeting, see *Cape-Breton News*, March 14, April 5 and April 19, 1851. Details on the Committee report appeared in the *News* of May 3, 1851. Original copies of the report, *European and North American Railway Terminus*, Sydney, 1851, are rare but the document is available in CIHM, microfiche # 63539.

9. See Beck, *Joseph Howe*, vol. II, 34-52.

10. Chisholm, vol. II, 170.

11. *JHANS*, 1852, Appendix 10; Grey (Colonial Secretary) to Harvey (Governor of Nova Scotia), November 27, 1852.

12. See Underwood, *Built For War*. This study assesses the military considerations that shaped the debates and the ultimate decision for a route for the first railway that would link the colonies.

13. Howe had been promoting a railway to Windsor and beyond to the Annapolis Valley as early as 1835. See *The Novascotian*, then being published by Howe, Octo-

ber 1, October 8 and October 14, 1835. For a wider perspective, see Chard, "Joseph Howe and the Struggle for Railways in Nova Scotia, 1830-1858."

14. See Underwood, *From Folly to Fortune*. While its focus is on the fate of the NSR's chief civil engineer, James Richardson Forman, when the Conservative party regained office in 1858, this book provides an excellent look at the personalities and politics of railway-building in Nova Scotia in the 1850s.

15. LAC, Sir John A Macdonald Papers, MG 26-A, vol. 282: 129104; Tupper to Macdonald, April 30, 1868.

16. See Tibbetts, "The Pictou Branch." Fleming went on to be Chief Engineer for the construction of the Intercolonial. His book, *The Intercolonial Railway*, is one of the classic works in Canadian railway history. Fleming later played a prominent role in the later construction of the Canadian Pacific and is the subject of numerous biographies.

17. In 1880, Schreiber became General Manager as well as Chief Engineer. From 1892 until his retirement in 1905, he also held the position of Deputy Minister of Railways and Canals. See *DCB* XIV, 1998: 910-11.

18. *SNS*, 1872, ch. 63.

19. *Daily News*, Saint John, August 28, 1876: 1.

20. *DCB*, XI, 1982: 5-15.

21. See Stevens, *Canadian National Railways*, vol. 2, 1962, 287-90.

22. Parliament of Canada, *Sessional Papers*, 1885, vol. 7, Sessional Paper # 11, Annual Report, Department of Railways and Canals, Appendix 4; Canadian Government Railways Annual Report, 1883-84: 18.

23. See Stevens, vol. 2, 1962, 290-95; the volumes of *JHANS*, 1880-84, contain a massive collection of documents dealing with the H&CB project.

24. *JHANS*, 1885, Appendix 14, Eastern Extension Transfer, 4.

25. *JHANS*, 1882, Appendix 7, Provincial Engineer's Report, 4-7.

26. See McQueen and Thompson, *Constructed in Kingston*.

27. The Intercolonial's original western terminus was at Riviere du Loup; the track west of Riviere du Loup was part of the Grand Trunk. IRC service was extended westward in two stages, by the purchase in 1879 of Grand Trunk track from Riviere du Loup to Chaudiere, near Levis and Quebec City, and by an 1898 arrangement to give the IRC running rights on Grand Trunk track into downtown Montreal. Until 1898, Montreal-bound passengers had to change to a Grand Trunk train for the last leg of the journey.

28. *Statutes of Canada*, 1886, ch. 14.

29. Some sources have suggested that the name honoured Charles Tupper, by this time Minister of Railways in Macdonald's government. However, Hamilton's *Place Names of Atlantic Canada* states that the name came from another Tupper who received a land grant in the area in 1824. Though the former Nova Scotia Premier

did not receive railway recognition, an automobile ferry called *Sir Charles Tupper* operated at the Strait for many years after it was launched in 1928.

30. Parliament of Canada, *Sessional Papers*, 1886, vol. 13, Sessional Paper # 67.

31. Peter MacDonald, "How The Railway Came To Cape Breton," 13.

32. For an account of the work on the piers, see "Building the Grand Narrows Bridge," *Cape Breton's Magazine*, # 23, 1979: 15-17. On Reid, see *DCB* XIII, 1994: 859-62; on Isbester, see Jay Underwood's study, *The Inside Man: The Life and Times of James Isbester* (forthcoming).

33. *Morning Chronicle*, Halifax, October 18, 1890: 3 and October 20, 1890: 3.

34. Colleagues knowledgeable about locomotives of this era are confident the smokestack visible in the photo identifies the engine as built for burning wood rather than coal. That assumption and comparison of the photo with others from the period suggest this engine was the first IRC #41, a broad gauge wood-burning locomotive built by Dubs of Glasgow, Scotland, as one in a set of eight engines delivered in 1871. But IRC records show that # 41 was renumbered to # 26 in 1875 and subsequently sold to the Caraquet Railway in northern New Brunswick still carrying # 26. The second IRC # 41 was received from the Manchester Locomotive Works of Manchester, New Hampshire, in 1875. It was one of a large order of coal-burning 4-4-0 engines built for the IRC in 1874-75. No photo has been found of the second # 41 but photos of several other Manchester engines in this series show a number of differences from the locomotive in the photo. No explanation can be offered for the note's reference to the locomotive as a "Hoag Engine." A company by that name in Brantford, Ontario, made small gasoline engines in the first decades of the 20th century but no basis has been found to suggest any connection between that firm or its products with Intercolonial Railway locomotives. The only guess that can be offered is that an engineer by name of Hoag was the driver on # 41 at some time.

35. Stevens, vol. 1, 1960: 218.

36. LAC, Sir John A Macdonald Papers, MG 26-A, vol. 137: 56919; Schreiber to Macdonald, May 19, 1891.

37. LAC, Sir John A Macdonald Papers, MG 26-A, vol. 286: 131206-07; Tupper to Macdonald, September 17, 1888.

Chapter 4

1. *SNS*, 1872, ch. 63.

2. *SNS*, 1872, ch. 17, section 2.

3. See Annand-Kennelly correspondence, NSARM, Railway Papers, RG 28, vol 8; the *Act* to reincorporate the Extension company, *SNS*, 1875, ch. 66; and the *Act* outlining potential aid to railways, *SNS*, 1875, ch 30.

4. NSARM, RG 28, vol 8, # 3, Kennelly to Annand, 11 June, 1874.

5. NSARM, RG 28, vol 8, # 29.

6. NSARM, RG 28, vol 8, # 14.

7. NSARM, RG 28, vol 8, # 30.

8. This "Twenty Years" section is based on a small collection of correspondence in the NSARM Railway Papers, RG 28, vol 8, newspaper reports and statutes. All *Acts* of incorporation referred to are Nova Scotia statutes unless identified as federal *Acts*.

9. *Daily Record*, Sydney, 1 October, 1901: 2.

10. *Railway and Shipping World* (*RSW*), December, 1899: 351.

11. Most of Pearson's ventures involved electricity and tramway companies in major cities in the West Indies and Latin America, but some were closer to home. In 1902, he headed a Halifax group that purchased the Petitcodiac and Elgin Railway, a small branch line near Moncton, New Brunswick. Nason, *Railways of New Brunswick*, 75.

12. *SNS*, 1899, ch. 126.

13. The Americans named in the 1899 *Act* were Lorenzo Shute and Herbert Dix of Stanwick, NJ, Joseph Shute of Atlantic City, NJ, Charles Corfield of Philadelphia, PA, and John Crump of New York City. Crump was identified as Superintendent of Docks in New York. "L. M. Shute" had been included in an 1895 list of shareholders in the Alton group's version of the Extension Company, NSARM, RG 28, vol 8, # 47. It is assumed L. M. was the Lorenzo Shute of 1899.

14. NSARM, Provincial Secretary's Papers, RG 7, vol 383, # 175 (1). This document was issued in conjunction with meetings of the railway company shareholders that approved a $2.4 million bond issue.

15. Nova Scotia House of Assembly, *Debates and Proceedings*, 1899: 122 and 139.

16. From Cape Breton, see for example *Daily Record*, October 1, 1901: 2

17. All *New York Times* references are taken from the paper's online archive system which provides full texts of articles and dates but does not include original page numbers.

18. *Daily Post*, Sydney, June 21, 1901: 4; June 22, 1901: 8; and June 26, 1901: 1.

19. NSARM, RG 28, 8, # 60(1). Webb to Murray, June 9, 1901. This appears to be the only surviving letter to or from Webb about the CBR project. A front page story in the *Daily Post* of August 23, 1901, reported that Leonard had most recently been chief engineer on the St. Lawrence and Adirondack Railroad. Webb was president of that company that then operated a short line railway from Malone Junction, New York, across the border to Valleyfield, Quebec. In 1907-1908, Leonard struck it rich in the silver boom in Cobalt, Ontario, and became a millionaire. For a biography of this interesting man, see the first chapter in Ziff, *Unforeseen Legacies*. It should be noted that Leonard's CBR connection draws only passing reference by Ziff and with an inaccurate date attached.

20. *New York Times*, June 12, 1901. The company was incorrectly identified as "incorporated in Canada"; it was actually incorporated in New Jersey. There was a

firm in Toronto called Dominion Securities, but it had no connection with Webb's New Jersey company.

21. *The Royal Gazette*, Halifax, August 7, 1901: 350.

22. *Daily Post*, August 24, 1901: 1.

23. *Daily Record*, October 5, 1901: 5; and October 5, 1901: 7; *Daily Post*, October 7, 1901: 1.

24. *RSW,* February 1902: 55.

25. *Evening Telegram*, St. John's, January 15, 1902: 1.

26. *Sydney Record*, November 24, 1902: 5; the *Daily Record* had changed its name during the summer of 1902. By this time, Dominion Bridge was headed by James Ross of Montreal who had assumed a major role in the Cape Breton economy that lasted for ten years. In 1901, Ross led a group in Montreal businessmen in gaining control of both the Dominion Coal Company and Dominion Iron and Steel Company from H. M. Whitney.

27. *Sydney Record*, November 28, 1902: 4.

28. *New York Times*, December 8, 1902; *New York Tribune*, December 8, 1902: 12.

29. A further illustration of the potential unreliability of the printed word can be seen by comparing the *Post* report on September 18, 1903: 8, with J. William Calder, *All Aboard*, 21. The second half of Calder's quote attributed to the *Post* is quite different from what actually appeared in the paper.

30. Almost all sources noted for this section have come from the *New York Times* because of the ready online accessibility of the *Times* and the completeness of its coverage from a New York perspective. Targeting the *Times* archive search engine on Webb and Webb-Meyer will generate a rich collection of relevant reports from the paper. Sydney and Halifax newspapers reprinted much of the ongoing story, sometimes with more focus on the implications for the CBR. The *Daily Sun* of Saint John, New Brunswick, is another particularly valuable source for the story from a Maritime perspective.

31. *RSW*, February, 1902: 55; April 1902: 122

32. In addition to Dominion Securities, other companies with Webb-Meyer connections included the Rutland Railroad, the St. Lawrence and Adirondack Railroad, the Hackensack Meadows Company, the Manhattan Contracting Company (which appears to have been set up to act as general contractor for the CBR), the North American Lumber and Pulp Company (to develop timber properties in Cape Breton), and the North American Coal and Development Company, *SNS*, 1902, ch 139, (to develop mining properties in Cape Breton). North American Lumber and North American Coal both appear to have been only shell companies, firms that had legal existence but nothing more.

33. *New York Times*, August 15, 1901; October 9, 1901; January 25, 1902; April 15, 1902.

34. *New York Times*, May 15, 1902.

35. *New York Times*, May 4, 1902.

36. The cut and thrust of Canadian political debate may have played a role. In late April, during the Parliamentary debate on government railway spending, John Haggart, Minister of Railways in several of the Conservative administrations after John A. Macdonald's death, raised numerous questions about the Webb-Meyer syndicate in the House of Commons. In addition to presenting Dominion Securities in a very unflattering light through the entry of stock-promotion documents into the parliamentary record, the debate led to denials by Andrew Blair, the Minister of Railways, that any commitments for federal or provincial construction subsidy funds had been made to the CBR project. This clearly contradicted claims by Campbell and Webb that had been appearing in the press. See *House of Commons Debates*, April 24, 1902: 3469-3483 and April 25, 1902: 3535-3547.

37. *New York Times*, May 8, 1902.

38. *New York Times*, May 29, 1902.

39. *New York Times*, August 29, 1902.

40. *New York Times*, May 27, 1902.

41. *New York Times*, May 27, 1902. Only two price quotes have been seen for CBR bonds. On May 6, 1902, the Saint John *Daily Sun* quoted the *New York Herald*'s report that they were "being peddled around the street were few takers at 69," that is at a price of $69 per $100 par value. Several weeks later, the *New York Times* of May 22, 1902, noted the sale of a $30,000 par value lot for $1610 or $5.36 per $100 par value—a dramatic drop from the price in early May. No quotes for either bid or sale prices for CBR common shares have been found.

42. Creighton, *John A. Macdonald: The Old Chieftan*, 163.

43. NSARM, Railway Papers, RG 28, 8, # 57, Guerin to Murray, December 22, 1899: 5.

44. *Daily Record*, May 13, 1902: 1.

45. *Sydney Record*, December 8, 1902: 5. The *Daily Record* had changed its name during the autumn of 1902.

46. See for example the federal *Act* regarding railway subsidies, *Statutes of Canada*, 1903, ch. 57, section 2, subsection 64, which authorized possible doubling of the normal federal subsidy of $3,200 per mile (per 1.6 km) for "a line of railway from St. Peter's to Louisburg" and *SNS*, 1905, ch. 2, *An Act To Authorize The Granting Of Aid To The Construction Of A Railway From St. Peter's to Louisburg*.

47. Stevens, vol 2, 298. Such comments about the Maritimes are fairly common in Stevens's two volumes. They are rather amusing to find written by a man who was born in the railway station living quarters at Tatamagouche, NS, where his father was station agent.

48. NSARM, Railway Papers, RG 28, vol 14, # 1-4; the projected cost for the proposed 64 miles (103 km) was $1.17 million, a total quite close to the cost when the line was built twenty-five years later.

49. Data can be found in the Department of Mines Annual Reports, *JHANS*, 1895-1898 and 1900; MacDonald, *The Coal and Iron Industries of Nova Scotia*; and Drummond, *Minerals and Mining, Nova Scotia*. While these sources are inconsistent at a detailed level, they are in agreement that Hussey's output seldom exceeded 1000 t per year. Campbell's *Banking on Coal*, 31, states that in 1899 Hussey "was producing 4,000 t of coal per week." This figure is not documented and does not appear to be even close to realistic.

50. J. L. MacDougall's *History of Inverness County*, 117, suggests Hussey's departure was simply a matter of taking his profits and retiring back to Boston.

51. *SNS*, 1893, ch. 147.

52. *SNS*, 1887, ch. 57.

53. *RSW*, November, 1898: 238.

54. *RSW*, March, 1899: 82.

55. Stevens, vol. 2, 81.

56. *RSW*, May, 1899: 143; June, 1899: 175; July, 1899: 209; October, 1899: 295.

57. NSARM, Railway Papers, RG 28, vol 14, # 57, Mann to Murray, 20 March, 1899.

58. NSARM, Railway Papers, RG 28, vol 14, # 80, M Murphy to Murray, 20 December, 1901.

59. The complete contract was printed in the Public Works Report for 1899, *JHANS*, 1900, Appendix 7: 14-21.

60. Samson, "The Making of a Cape Breton Coal Town," 88.

61. Ibid., 40-42.

62. See for example, NSARM, Railway Papers, RG 28, vol 14, # 65, Alex McDonald to Murray, April 10, 1900. McDonald, a Port Hood lawyer, stated that work on the rail line at Broad Cove suggested there was no intention of continuing it further north.

63. See for example, Vernon, *Cape Breton at the Turn of the Century*: 332.

64. *SNS*, 1902, ch. 132.

65. *SNS*, 1902, ch. 134.

66. The beginning of work received a glowing report in the *Daily Record*, November 15, 1902: 4. The *Record*, reprinting details from the Hawkesbury *Journal*, optimistically described the M&G as "now an assured fact," the same phrase that headlined the Cape Breton Railway story in the *New York Times* in August of 1900.

67. *JHANS*, 1905, Appendix 7: 7.

68. The railway and the Mabou mine reappear in the statutes of 1908 (ch. 135) and 1910 (ch. 153) under a revised name and with different principals in each of those two years. These presumably marked attempts to salvage the company though no indication has been found of mining activity after August of 1908.

69. *Statutes of Canada*, 1902, ch. 104.

70. *DCB*, XIV, 1998, 375-78.

71. On Stairs's interests and connections, see James Frost, *Merchant Princes*, 192-95; see also *DCB*, XIV, 1998: 978-82.

72. See for example the *New York Times* stories of June 21 and November 2, 1902.

73. *Statutes of Canada*, 1904, ch. 127.

74. *The Gazette*, Montreal, May 23, 1904: 7.

Chapter 5

1. See Ron Crawley, "Off to Sydney: Newfoundlanders Emigrate to Industrial Cape Breton, 1890-1914."

2. Provincial Engineer's Reports, *JHANS*, 1896, Appendix 7, 48a-50 and *JHANS*, 1915, Part 2, Appendix 7B: 59-64.

3. On the role of Max Aitken, the future Lord Beaverbrook, in Maritime finance in the pre-First World War era, see Frost, *Merchant Princes*, chapter 8; for a much more detailed study in a national context, Marchildon, *Profits and Politics*, 1996. On the rise and fall of Rhodes Curry in a community context, see Reilly, "The Rise and Fall of Industrial Amherst."

4. See *RSW*, March, 1899: 85.

5. *House of Commons Debates*, June 21, 1900: 7972-88.

6. Parliament of Canada, *Sessional Papers*, 1916, vol. 14, Sessional Paper # 20, Annual Report, Department of Railways and Canals, 1913-14: 179; vol. 15, Sessional Paper # 20, Annual Report, Department of Railways and Canals, 1914-15, Appendix 1, Part III: 127.

7. At the time of writing, a good concise history of the Newfoundland Railway is found online at http://www.heritage.nf.ca/society/railway.html. Two good print sources are Hiller, "The Newfoundland Railway, 1881-1949," and Cramm's MA thesis, "The Construction of the Newfoundland Railway, 1875-1898."

8. For an early account of the Newfoundland ferry service, see *Railway and Shipping World*, September, 1898: 187. In its issue of February, 1899, that journal reported the *Bruce* was "taking 8 to 10 carloads [of freight] each trip," 45.

9. See the S&L summer timetable for 1903 reproduced in figure 6.3.

10. On *Scotia*'s exciting transatlantic crossing in 1901 as well as virtually all other aspects of the Strait's rail ferry system, see Rafuse, *A Railway To The Isle*. See also "Ferries in the Strait of Canso," *Cape Breton's Magazine*, # 20, 1978: 22-28.

11. On William Mackenzie, see *DCB*, vol. XV, 2005: 663-68; Donald Mann will almost certainly appear in *DCB*, vol. XVI when it is published; on the partners, see Stevens, vol. 2, chapters 1-5; and Regehr, *The Canadian Northern Railway*. Regehr provides an excellent analysis of the CNoR in central and western Canada but

only passing reference to the Inverness and Richmond and little more than that to the Halifax and South Western, Mackenzie and Mann's other Nova Scotia railway.

12. Parliament of Canada, *Sessional Papers*, 1920, vol 6, Sessional Paper # 20, Annual Report, Department of Railways and Canals, 1918-19: xxxiv;

13. Stevens, 1962: chapters 9, 10, 17 and 18.

14. NASARM, RG 28, vol 62, # 4, "Report on Property of Inverness Railway and Coal Company," 1919.

15. Quoted from the *New York Herald* in the *Daily Sun*, Saint John, NB, May 6, 1902: 4

16. *The Gazette*, Montreal, January 15, 1909: 5

17. Between the years ending in 1906 and 1920, CBR passenger counts rose from ca. 7500 to more than 15,000; freight tonnage went from ca. 5000 to just more than 14,000. Provincial Engineer's Reports for 1906 and 1920, *JHANS*, Appendix 7, 1907 and 1921.

18. This cumulative total is based on the annual operating results from the Provincial Engineer's Reports 1904-1920 inclusive.

19. See *Railway and Shipping World*, September, 1899: 254.

20. Parliament of Canada, *Sessional Papers*, 1915, vol. 14, Sessional Paper # 20, Annual Report, Department of Railways and Canals, 1913-14: 224-33.

21. Provincial Engineer's Report, *JHANS*, 1915, Part 2, Appendix 7B, 33 and 72-73.

22. "Yet" has been as recent as the autumn of 2010 when a man was hit and killed by a Cape Breton and Central Nova Scotia Railway train near downtown Sydney.

23. Parliament of Canada, *Sessional Papers*, 1916, vol. 15, Sessional Paper # 20, Annual Report, Department of Railways and Canals, 1914-15, Appendix 1, Part III: 141.

24. Details are from Campbell and Johnston, *Tracks Across The Landscape*, 57-60.

25. Details are from MacBean, *The Inverness and Richmond Railway*, 46-47.

26. *SNS*, 1873, ch. 39; 1904, ch. 141; 1909; ch. 179; 1911, ch. 156.

27. *SNS*, 1911, ch 156; the founders were Daniel McQuaig, a broker; John P. Joy, a "trader," Joseph B, McCormack, Deputy Chief of Police; and Daniel A. Cameron, a lawyer.

28. See Boyes, "An Alternate Railway Technology: Early Monorail Systems."

29. *SNS*, 1895, ch. 110.

Chapter 6

1. For the Cape Breton Company Railway, this is confirmed in a recollection of a trip from Sydney to Reserve in the early 1880s when "the passenger car was coupled to the rear of a string of 20 or 30 empty coal hoppers." See MacAulay, "Sydney in the 1880s," 8.

2. See A. H. MacDonald, "The Albion Railway," 152-59.

3. *Morning Chronicle*, Halifax, August 20, 1880: 3.

4. The most reliable published roster of S&L locomotives and other rolling stock is in Donaldson, *Sydney And Louisburg Ry*, 28-30.

5. For accounts of the hobo trains, see Campbell and Johnston, 71-72; and MacDonald, *Port Morien: Pages From The Past*, 44-46.

6. For a recent article on the *Ocean*, published on the occasion of the 100th anniversary of the train, see Underwood, "History Follows the Ocean to the Ocean."

7. See Monica MacDonald, "Railway Tourism in the Land of Evangeline"; Marguerite Woodworth, *History of the Dominion Atlantic Railway*; McKay and Bates, *In The Province of History: the Making of the Public Past in Twentieth-Century Nova Scotia*.

8. See for example, Hart, *The Selling of Canada*.

9. See Hanington, *The Lady Boats: The Life and Times of Canada's West Indies Merchant Fleet*.

10. Intercolonial Railway, "Tours to Summer Haunts by the Sea," May, 1910. The $33 fare in 1910 would have been equivalent to about $600 in 2012 dollars.

11. For advertising for a 1905 IRC picnic special to Iona, with connecting special runs in the new streetcar systems, see *The Daily Post*, Sydney, July 15, 1905.

12. On the opening day special, see Campbell and Johnston, 44-47.

13. See for example, Brodie, "The Harvest Excusion." Brodie's account of his participation in an excursion in 1923 differs from Mackenzie's overview in one notable way. Mackenzie's details suggest there was a basis for what he calls the "legend of the wild Cape Bretoners raising hell across the country." Brodie noted that "there had always been a good deal said about the rowdyism of the harvest trains," but stated that he "saw very little of it" when he went west in 1923.

14. For a fairly detailed look at the involvement of Whitney and his family in street railways in the Boston area, see MacGillivray, 47-51.

15 For a national survey, see Due, *The Intercity Electric Railway in Canada*. An excellent online source is David A. Wyatt's website, "Canadian Street Railways," http://home.cc.umanitoba.ca/~wyatt/streetcar-list.html. A good study of the Halifax system, covering the years of both horse-powered and electric-powered operations, is Cunningham and Artz, *The Halifax Street Railway, 1886-1949*.

16. *The Daily Post*, Sydney, July 12, 1905: 6.

17. A report in the *Daily Post*, October 1, 1901, stated that Dominion Coal was then considering establishing a "fast and up to date passenger service" between Sydney and Glace Bay on a new line to be laid along the route of the original narrow gauge G&CB track. Perhaps Dominion Coal did have something to do with Stone and Webster's appearance within a few years and on this route.

18. MacGillivray, 68.

19. See "When the Employees Owned the Trams," *Cape Breton's Magazine*, # 24, 1979: 1-8.

Chapter 7

1. For concise histories, see Earle, "Coal in the History of Nova Scotia"; and Millward, "Mine Locations and the Sequence of Coal Exploitation on the Sydney Coalfield, 1720-1980."

2. See *DCB*, XIV, 1998: 896-99.

3. For one account, in the contexts of Ross and Van Horne (who had been colleagues in their Canadian Pacific roles as well as in a number of other business ventures), see Knowles, 380-83. Van Horne's correspondence shows he had been an active director at Dominion Coal from the outset and was not just a decorative name on the board. For example, an 1898 letter demonstrates his close involvement in the selection of "a suitable person to examine and report upon the iron properties in Newfoundland" in preparation for the coal company's expansion into steel production. Van Horne personal letterbook, vol 52, 1897-98, LAC, Ottawa, MG 29, A60: 448-48; Van Horne to H. M. Whitney, September 1, 1898.

4. In 1909, Max Aitken and his Royal Securities associates were trying to bring about a merger of various steel companies from Ontario and Quebec, the end result of which was the creation of the Steel Company of Canada (Stelco) of Hamilton. Unsuccessful attempts were made to bring Dominion Coal and Disco into the deal and also to gain control of Scotia. See Marchildon, 186-201.

5. Acquisition of control of major companies by owners outside the region or the country has frequently been offered by historians and economists as an explanation for subsequent problems and the long-term decline of industries such as steel and coal in Nova Scotia. Some interpretations, however, suggest those explanations inversed what had actually happened. Inwood's study, "Local Control, Resources and the Nova Scotia Steel Company," concludes that serious production problems and low profitability had emerged during the period of local control of the company. He maintains that these difficulties led to the sale of Scotia to American owners and were not the result of management practices during the post-1915 period of American control. Inwood's paper is an important illustration of the fact that there are different and conflicting approaches to explaining the economic history of Cape Breton and the Maritimes.

6. Frank, "The Cape Breton Coal Industry and the Rise and Fall of the British Empire Steel Corporation."

7. See Crawley, "Class Conflict and the Establishment of the Sydney Steel Industry, 1899-1904"; Frank, "The Cape Breton Coal Miners, 1917-26"; Earle and Gamberg, "The United Mine Workers and the Coming of the CCF to Cape Breton"; Earle, "Down With Hitler and Silby Barrett: The Cape Breton Miners' Slowdown Strke of 1941."

8. OSC was established as a separately incorporated Dosco subsidiary in 1938; *Report of the Royal Commission on Coal*, Ottawa, King's Printer, 1946: 114.

9. See Bruce, R.A.: *The Story of R. A. Joudrey*, chapters 9-12; and Bruce, *Frank Sobey*, chapter 7.

10. The *Arrow* has been the subject of numerous books. One study that provides considerable background on A. V. Roe in Canada and its British parent, Hawker Siddeley (builder, during the Second World War, of Hawker Hurricanes and Lancaster bombers), is Stewart, *Shutting Down the National Dream*.

11. This topic will be dealt with in some detail in chapter 8.

12. For one snapshot view as at 1946, see the assessments in the 1946 Royal Commission *Report*: 590-94.

13. On the structure of tariffs on American coal coming into Canada up to the early 1940s, see the 1946 Royal Commission *Report*: 574-94. On the increasing role of American coal in the central Canadian market, see Frank, "The Cape Breton Coal Industry," 6-8.

14. See data in the 1946 Royal Commission *Report*: 64-65 and 567-68.

15. Dominion Coal Company, "Submission to the Royal Commission on Coal," 1960: 50. The end of the age of steam on Canadian railways was no surprise. The fast-growing importance of diesel locomotives on American lines had been noted fourteen years earlier in the *Report* of the 1946 Royal Commission on Coal: 470.

16. See MacEwan, *Miners and Steelworkers*, 1976. This book covers the period from before the First World War into the 1970s but is particularly valuable for its account of Dosco's departure from Cape Breton. MacEwan was very active in the revival of the political fortunes of the NDP on Cape Breton. In 1970 he was elected to the Nova Scotia Legislature where he would represent his constituency for thirty-three years.

17. For two early interpretations of the projected role of Devco, see Tupper, "Public Enterprise as Social Welfare"; and George, "The Cape Breton Development Corporation."

18. See the 1946 Royal Commission *Report*: 64-65.

19. See Arseneau, "Science and Technology in Old Sydney," 12-13.

20. One assessment suggested that federal policy during and immediately after the Second World War was critical. To meet wartime needs and prepare for the post-war period, Ottawa poured large amounts of money into some Canadian steel companies for plant modernization and expansion. Virtually all of it went to Stelco and Dofasco in Hamilton, and Algoma in Sault Ste. Marie. Ernest R. Forbes suggests this was a conscious policy driven by C. D. Howe. As Minister of

Munitions and Supply and then Minister of Reconstruction, Howe played a leading role in shaping federal industrial policies in the King and St. Laurent governments. See Forbes's study, "Consolidating Disparity," 172-99 in *Challenging the Regional Stereotype*.

21. See Boyce, "Steel making in Atlantic Canada."

22. Atlantic Provinces Economic Council, *Steelmaking in the Atlantic Provinces*, 19-25.

23. Quoted from Sysco documents in Matheson, "An Examination of the Operations of the Sydney Steel Corporation," 58.

24. An excellent collection of photos and accounts by steel plant employees is found in Caplan, *Views from the Steel Plant*. See also the website of the Sydney Steel Museum Society, http://sydneysteelmuseum.com/.

25. At the time of writing, photos of rolling stock built in Trenton during the plant's final years are available online on the "Freight Cars Illustrated" website; see http://fcix.info/ref_sheets/ref004_tw.pdf.

26. See Underwood and Smith, "History of the Eastern Car Company."

27. See chapter 10 in Savoie, *Visiting Grandchildren*. The focus of the chapter is well summarized by one sentence within it: 304-05. "Big dogs not only eat first, they also have a large appetite to satisfy when it comes to national economic development policies, federal investment, and the location of federal government activities."

Chapter 8

1. The most extensive collection in Nova Scotia is a set of inbound and outbound freight registers from Brookfield, Colchester County, from the mid-1950s now in the Scotian Railroad Society collection, NSARM, MG 20(S), vols 51 and 54-57.

2. On the changes in retailing and other sectors of the economy of the Maritimes, see McCann, "Metropolitanism and Branch Businesses in the Maritimes." On Eaton's, see Stephenson, *The Store That Timothy Built*. It's a fine study of Canadian social history in the century after Confederation, the period that corresponded to the rise of the firm that became Canada's dominant retailer with a national reach. After Eaton's 1969 centennial, the company was affected by competition, changing demographics and management problems that all contributed to the firm's bankruptcy in 1999. What has survived under the Eaton name is now owned by the American-based Sears retail empire.

3. For an important assessment of the impacts on Maritime businesses of increased access to central Canadian markets by the Intercolonial and the tariffs, see Acheson, "The National Policy and the Industrialization of the Maritimes."

4. See Reilly on the rise and fall of Amherst.

5. On New Glasgow and adjacent towns, see McCann, "The Mercantile-Industrial Transition of the Metals Towns of Pictou County."

6. On the initial rationale for the IRC approach to rates, see the comments of Sir Charles Tupper, then Minister of Railways and Canals, in *House of Commons Debates*, 1879: 157-59.

7. For an excellent single-source assessment, see Savoie, chapter 2, "History Matters." As an alternative to print, a 1979 documentary from the National Film Board merits reference. *Empty Harbours, Empty Dreams: The Story of the Maritimes in Confederation* is, at the time of writing, available on video and may appear in DVD format.

8. See Cruikshank, *Close Ties: Railways, Government and the Board of Railway Commissioners,"* 1991.

9. Forbes, "Misguided Symmetry," in *Challenging the Regional Stereotype*, 119. Borden was a native of Nova Scotia and had a Halifax seat in the House of Commons.

10. As illustrations, though none of the data refer to rates from Cape Breton, see Cruikshank, "The Intercolonial Railway," tables 2-4.

11. Forbes, *The Maritime Rights Movement*; for an abbreviated account, see Forbes's paper, "The Maritime Rights Movement" in *Challenging the Regional Stereotype*, 100-13.

12. On McRitchie, see Conrad, "The Art of Regional Protest," 1979. An interesting account of the role of the *Herald* is found in March, *Red Line*, 1986.

13. It should be noted that the provincial Conservatives were led to victory by Edgar Nelson Rhodes, son of the co-founder of Rhodes Curry and Company, the Amherst railway rolling stock company sold to Montreal interests in 1909. The remains of the Amherst plant had been closed down two years before the younger Rhodes was recruited to abandon his seat in the House of Commons and come back to Nova Scotia to lead the party. Rhodes's conversion to the "Maritime Rights" cause in 1925 is a subject that has yet to be examined in depth. Some sources, both at the time and later, have suggested the conversion was based on political expediency rather than conviction.

14. See for example, *Daily Post*, April 24, 1923: 3.

15. *Report of the Royal Commission on Maritime Claims*, Ottawa, King's Printer, 1927; on freight rates and related transportation issues, see pp. 20-28.

16. See Forbes, "Misguided Symmetry," 129-35; and Savoie, 36-40.

17. The application of the rates to coal shipped by rail became significant by the 1930s. On the early years of coal traffic subsidies, see Wallace, "Nova Scotia Coal Industry and Freight Rate Subvention"; and the *Report of the Royal Commission on Coal*, 1946: 64-65 and 567-69.

18. As an illustration, see *The Chronicle-Herald*, Halifax, August 27, 1989, 7, for a full-page report, "Freight Rates and Regional Equality: Royal Commission Needed on Maritime Benefits." The title and the date indicate that the problems of the 1920s were alive and well sixty years later.

19. See for example the two-volume submission of the Commission to the 1960 Royal Commission on Transportation (the "MacPherson Commission"). This par-

ticular document provides a valuable summary of freight rates issues and decisions from the 1920s to 1960.

20. In addition to their works cited above, see Cruikshank, "The People's Railway," 1986; Forbes, "The Intercolonial Railway and the Decline of the Maritime Provinces Revisited" and Cruikshank, "With Apologies to James: A Response to E. R. Forbes," 3-34.

21. Inwood, "Maritime Industrialization from 1870 to 1910"; and Darling, *The Politics of Freight Rates*, chapters 4 and 5.

22. For a short Canadian Press account of other Canadian train robberies, see *The Chronicle-Herald*, August 19, 1958: 1, 6.

23. *Daily Post*, August 1, 1914: 7.

24. The events of August 1914 are covered in detail in a comprehensive study of Sydney and eastern Cape Breton during wartime; see Tennyson and Sarty, *Guardian of the Gulf*, 2000.

25. See Cuff, "The Newfoundland Railway At War."

26. On the naval war in the Gulf and the record of ships lost, see the Department of Veterans Affairs website, http://www.veterans.gc.ca/eng/history/secondwar/battlegulf. In print form, see Hadley, *U-boats Against Canada*; and Greenfield, *The Battle of the St. Lawrence*.

27. See http://sydneysteelmuseum.com/history/sinking.htm; see also first-hand accounts by two merchant seamen who survived the Bell Island sinkings in Parker, *Running The Gauntlet*, 108-118.

28. How, *Night of the Caribou*, 1988.

29. See McGillivray, "Cape Breton in the 1920s: A Community Besieged." Also see David Frank, *J. B. McLachlan: A Biography*. Frank's book, pp. 305-10, includes an account of another railway sidebar to the events of July, 1923. McLachlan and Livingstone were released on bail on July 13 and on the way back to Cape Breton they arranged a meeting with the Governor General, Viscount Byng of Vimy, who was in his private railway car in Pictou on a tour of the Maritimes. The meeting might have led to a resolution of the 1923 strike but for the intervention of John L. Lewis, the International President of the Mineworkers of America, who revoked the charter of the Cape Breton local, District 26, and removed the officers. Byng's involvement in the strike, which had angered Prime Minister Mackenzie King, set part of the stage for the showdown between King and Byng that came in 1926.

30. The website http://www.circushistory.org contains a wealth of information about the circuses that travelled North America by rail. The site includes many articles and "routebooks" from the journal *Bandwagon* that provide detailed records of individual circuses. The most interesting event related to a railway circus in Nova Scotia comes from the mainland rather than Cape Breton. On August 1, 1876, P. T. Barnum's "Great Travelling World's Fair" arrived in Halifax and mounted a grand parade through the downtown area. While the parade was passing, the Bank of Nova Scotia on Hollis Street was robbed of $22,000, a very large

sum at that time. At almost the same time, a cash box containing about $2,000 disappeared from the Treasury Office at Province House, a short distance along the street from the bank. See Jobb, "Three-ring Robbery."

31. The adventures of Daily Bros. in eastern Canada were recorded in the entertainment industry journal, *The Billboard*, August 27, 1949: 60 and 77.

32. *SNS*, 1910, ch. 142.

33. Considerable detail on quarrying and processing operations in the early years is found in L. H. Cole, *Gypsum in Canada*, 30-35

34. See "La Mine de Platre a Cheticamp," *Cape Breton's Magazine*, # 24, 1979: 28-33; a photo of the locomotive *Louise* appears on page 30.

35. *DCB*, XIII, 1994, 341-43.

36. *SNS*, 1890, ch 165. a small collection of McCurdy papers is at the Beaton Institute, MG 14, 111.

37. Cole, 1913: 36; also see "The Plaster Quarry at St. Ann's," *Cape Breton's Magazine*, # 15, 1976: 1-7.

38. See Underwood, *Ketchum's Folly*, 1995; for more technical accounts of the proposed railway, see Ircha, "The Chignecto Ship Railway"; and John G. McKay, *The Chignecto Marine Transport Railway*; on Ketchum, see *DCB*, vol XII, 1990: 484-85.

39. An "open for business" advertisement for the Strait of Canso Maine Railway is found in the Halifax *Morning Chronicle*, September 22, 1864: 3. On post-1920 operations at Point Tupper, see "A Visit With Art Langley Sr.," *Cape Breton's Magazine*, # 22, 1979: 37-44. The wartime roles of marine railways at North Sydney and Sydney are discussed in Tennyson and Sarty, 2000.

40. Fraser, *Folklore of Nova Scotia*.

41. Underwood, *Ghost Tracks*.

42. Michael MacKenzie, *Tracks Across The Maritimes*, 83-84.

43. Jessome, *Maritime Mysteries and the Ghosts Who Surround Us*, 41-42; also see Underwood, *Ghost Tracks*, 98-102.

Chapter 9

1. For a concise review of Canadian railway unions over their first seventy-five years, see Logan, *Trade Unions in Canada*, 135-57.

2. "Working on the S&L," part 1, *Cape Breton's Magazine*, # 28, 1981: 1.

3. The train to Boston was for many decades a unique railway experience for Maritimers. *The Gull* was a "pool train." Southbound, it ran from Halifax to Saint John on the CNR lines. From Saint John to Vanceboro,. Maine, it ran on Canadian Pacific track with CPR engines. From Vanceboro to Portland, the Maine Central took over and the Boston and Maine operated the final leg of the 24-hour run into Boston. The coaches, sleepers and dining car were usually CNR stock, but a traveller might encounter cars from any of the other railways. Boston's North Station,

the B&M terminal where Dan MacKinnon tried to get his B&M pass, was also unique. From 1928 until 1997, the very large station had an equally large upstairs tenant, the Boston Garden, home of the Boston Bruins hockey team.

4. Tuck, "Canadian Railways and Unions in the Running Trades, 1865-1914," 113.

5. On the Grand Trunk strike of 1910, see Tuck, "Union Authority, Corporate Obstinacy, and the Grand Trunk Strike of 1910." On a major railway strike much closer to Cape Breton, see McInnis, "All Solid Along The Line: The Reid Newfoundland Strike of 1918."

6. Parliament of Canada, *Sessional Papers*, 1915, vol. 14, Sessional Paper 20, Annual Report of Department of Railways and Canals: 15-16.

7. Logan, 1948, 137, table XII.

8. Quoted in McKay, "Strikes in the Maritimes," 25.

9. McKay, "By Wisdom, Wile or War."

10. The Beaton Institute's manuscripts collection includes material from the Brotherhood of Railroad Trainmen's S&L lodge at Glace Bay for the period 1903-1960 and the Brotherhood of Locomotive Firemen and Enginemen's IRC/CGR/CNR Lodge at Sydney for the period 1907-1979. A smaller collection of documents from various Cape Breton locals of the Canadian Brotherhood of Railway, Transport and General Workers, 1961-1981, is also in the Beaton collection.

11. The original Cozzolini memoir is found in two manuscripts at the Beaton Institute, MG 7E, 2. The original was completed in 1935 and a second, edited version was prepared by Cozzolini's daughter some time after her father's death in 1949. A brief biography of Cozzolini is in *Prominent People of the Maritime Provinces*, 43.

12. Sydney and Louisburg Railway, Time Table # 52, September 30, 1935.

13. Campbell and Johnston, 64.

14. MacBean, 80.

15. See Chafe, *I've Been Working on the Railroad* for an entertaining read.

Chapter 10

1. The most reliable published roster of S&L locomotives and other rolling stock is in Donaldson, 28-30.

2. Campbell and Johnston, 105.

3. On the background to the causeway's construction as well as its impact, see Beaton, "The Canso Causeway," 2001. Another excellent source that focuses on the role of Angus L. Macdonald, is Stephen Henderson's biography.

4. MacIntyre, *Causeway*, 222.

5. Data generated during the VIA debates filled the pages of newspapers and the proceedings of both federal and provincial legislative bodies. The data quoted come

from a report on VIA performance provided to the author by Ron MacDonald, MP, in October 1989.

6. Ron Lawless, President, VIA Rail Canada, Letter to all VIA Employees, October 4, 1989.

7. For a national perspective, very critical of the cuts in VIA services, see Davis, ed., *Not a Sentimental Journey*. The full text of the Order in Council ending VIA's service to Sydney is available online at http://laws.justice.gc.ca/eng/SOR-89-488/FullText.html; see section 2, schedule IV.

8. Premier Cameron was not the only provincial or regional politician to have ignored or not been aware of the fact that Section 145 of the *British North America Act* (reproduced in chapter 3) had been repealed in London in 1893 (*Statute Law Revision Act*, 1893, 56-57 Vict., Ch 14). Since that repeal, despite the widely held view that Section 145 is still in effect, the federal government's railway responsibilities to the Maritimes have been limited to operating such railway companies as it wished to continue to own, over routes it chooses to serve, and for only as long as it chooses to continue those operations. The "constitutional guarantee" has not meant anything for more than a century.

9. Canadian Transportation Agency, Decision No 498-R-1993, 1993; http://www.otc-cta.gc.ca/decision-ruling/decision-ruling.php?id=3241&lang=eng.

10. On the preparation for and the privatization of the CNR, see Harry Bruce, *The Pig That Flew*.

11. http://www.gov.ns.ca/legislature/hansard/comm/ed/ed_2002may07.htm, 1.

12. Nova Scotia Utility and Review Board, Decision RAIL-A-02, RAIL-D-02, 2002; http://www.canlii.org/en/ns/nsuarb/doc/2002/2002nsuarb62/2002nsuarb62.html.

13. Canadian Transportation Agency, Decision No 657-R-2002, 2002; http://www.otc-cta.gc.ca/decision-ruling/drv.php?id=19993&lang=eng.

Chapter 11

1. The official *Tornado* website is http://www.a1steam.com/. For a portal leading to websites for UK heritage railways and museums, see http://ukhrail.uel.ac.uk/. For anyone interested in railways, the prime place to visit in the U.K. is the National Railway Museum in York, see http://www.nrm.org.uk/.

2. *Cape Breton Post*, Sydney, August 28, 1987: 1.

3. For details on the Association and its museum near Montreal, see http://www.exporail.org/public/index.asp.

4. # 42 came to Cape Breton in 1899 and ran on the S&L for over 50 years. In 1955, it was transferred to the Dosco-owned Acadia Coal Company at Stellarton. When Acadia Coal converted to diesels, # 42 was purchased by Robert Tibbett of Trenton. While the Cape Breton Steam Railway project was in the planning stage, Devco leased the locomotive and brought it back to Glace Bay to go back into service.

5. For links to railway heritage sites in Cape Breton and the rest of Nova Scotia as well as other resources dealing with the province's railway history, visit the website of the Nova Scotia Railway Heritage Society, http://www.novascotiarailwayheritage.com/index.htm.

Bibliography

Primary Sources

Brown, Richard. Papers. Nova Scotia Archives and Records Management (NSARM), MG 1 vol. 157.

Buddle, John. Papers. Durham County Record Office, Durham, U.K., NCB1/JB.

Buddle, John. Papers. Northumberland County Record Office, Newcastle upon Tyne, U.K.

Buddle, John. Papers. North England Institute of Mining & Mechanical Engineers, Newcastle upon Tyne, U.K., vol. 64.

"Descriptive inventories of the various services of plate, &c Belonging to the Crown," British Library, ms C.21.e.15.

Dosco Papers. Beaton Institute, Cape Breton University, MG 24, 16.

Dwyer, Michael. Papers. Beaton Institute, MG 12, 40.

Fox, George. Papers. Harvard Business Archives, Baker Library, Harvard University, Boston.

General Mining Association (GMA) Papers. "Deed of Settlement of General Mining Association." Guildhall Archives, London, ms 24, 532.

GMA Papers. "Papers from Cape Breton." Beaton Institute, Cape Breton University, MG 14, 19.

GMA Papers. "Prospectus of the General South American Mining Association." British Library, London, ms 8223.e.10 (47).

Government of Canada. *House of Commons Debates.*

Hunslet Engine Company Papers, Hunslet Archives, Armley Mill, Leeds, U.K.

Journals of House of Assembly of Nova Scotia.

Macdonald, Sir John A. Papers. Library and Archives Canada (LAC), MG 26-A.

Neilson & Company Papers, National Railway Museum, York, U.K.

Nova Scotia House of Assembly, *Debates and Proceedings*.

Nova Scotia Mines & Minerals Papers. NSARM, RG 1 and RG21A.

Nova Scotia Provincial Secretary's Papers, NSARM, RG 7

Nova Scotia Railway Papers, NSARM, RG 28

Parliament of Canada, *Sessional Papers*.

Report of the Royal Commission on Coal. Ottawa: King's Printer, 1946.

Report of the Royal Commission on Maritime Claims. Ottawa: King's Printer, 1927.

Report of the Royal Commission on Transportation. Ottawa: Queen's Printer, 1960.

Rundell, Philip. Papers. Goldsmiths' Company Library, London, cat 3035/G31.

Scotian Railroad Society Papers. NSARM, MG 28 S.

Statutes of Canada.

Statutes of Nova Scotia.

Sysco Papers, NSARM

Van Horne, William Cornelius. Papers. LAC MG 29.

Periodicals (newspapers, serials, etc.)

The Billboard, New York, NY.

Canada Yearbook, Ottawa, ON.

Canadian Mining Review.

Canadian Illustrated News, Montreal, PQ.

The Cape-Bretonian and General Reporter, Sydney, NS.

Cape Breton's Magazine, Wreck Cove, NS.

Cape Breton Mirror, Glace Bay, NS.

Cape Breton Post, Sydney, NS.

Daily News, Amherst, NS.

Daily News, Saint John, NB.

Daily Post, Sydney, NS.

Daily Record, Sydney, NS.

Daily Sun, Saint John, NB.

Daily Tribune, New York, NY.

Dictionary of Canadian Biography, Toronto, ON.

The Engineer, London, U.K.

Engineering, London, U.K.

Evening Reporter, Halifax, NS.

Evening Telegram, St. John's, NL.
Halifax Herald, Halifax, NS.
Journal, Port Hawkesbury, NS.
Mail and Empire, Toronto, ON.
The Morning Chronicle, Halifax, NS.
New York Herald, New York, NY.
New York Times, New York, NY.
New York Tribune, New York, NY.
Nova Scotia Royal Gazette, Halifax, NS.
The Novascotian, Halifax, NS.
Quarterly Mining Review, London, U.K.
Railway and Shipping World, Toronto, ON.
The Royal Gazette, Halifax, NS
Scotia Sun, Port Hawkesbury, NS
Sydney Record, Sydney, NS
Workers' Weekly, Stellarton, NS

Secondary Sources

Abbott, Rowland. *The Fairlie Locomotive*. Newton Abbot, U.K.: David and Charles, 1970.

Acheson, T. W. "The National Policy and the Industrialization of the Maritimes, 1880-1910." *Acadiensis* I, no. 2 (1971): 3-28.

"A. Somers Drove Noted Locomotives." *Halifax Herald* 29 March 1930: 13.

Arseneau, D. F. "Science and Technology in Old Sydney." In *More Essays in Cape Breton History*, edited by R.J. Morgan, 12-20. Windsor, NS: Lancelot Press, 1977.

Bailey, Michael R. "James Samuel." In *A Biographical Dictionary of Civil Engineers*, edited by Peter Cross-Rudkin and Mike Chrimes, vol. 2, 684-86. London: Institution of Civil Engineers, 2008.

Bailey, Michael R. and Herb MacDonald. "Tracking a Canadian Stephenson - A Transatlantic Quest." *Journal of the Stephenson Locomotive Society* 862 (March/April 2010): 77-81.

Baker, Allan C. *Black, Hawthorne & Co Works List*. Richmond, U.K.: Industrial Locomotive Society, 1988.

Beaton, Elizabeth. "Interview with Peter Willy Murphy, New Waterford." *Cape Breton's Magazine* 15 (1976): front cover verso.

Beaton, Meaghan. "The Canso Causeway: Regionalism, Reconstruction, Representations, and Results." MA thesis, Saint Mary's University, Halifax, 2001.

Beck, J. Murray. *Joseph Howe*. 2 vols. Kingston and Montreal: McGill-Queens University Press, 1983.

Bell, B. T. A., ed. *Canadian Mining, Iron and Steel Manual*. Ottawa: [n.p.], Annuals, 1890-1903.

Binns, Donald. *Fairlie Articulated Locomotives Vol. 1: On the American Continent*. Skipton, U.K.: Trackside Publications, 2001.

Boyce, Gordon. "Steel Making in Atlantic Canada." In *Political Economy of Atlantic Canada*, edited by M. A. Choudhury, 159-70. Sydney, UCCB Press, 1988.

Boyes, Grahame. "An Alternate Railway Technology: Early Monorail Systems." In *Early Railways*, edited by Andy Guy and Jim Rees, 192-207. London: The Newcomen Society, 2001.

Brodie, D. N. "The Harvest Excursion." *Cape Breton Mirror* 2, no. 8 (July 1953): 9-12.

Brown, Richard. *The Coal Fields and Coal Trade of the Island of Cape Breton*. London: Samson, Low, Marston, Low and Searle, 1871.

Brown, Robert. "Canada's Earliest Railways." *Bulletin of the Railway and Locomotive Historical Society* 78 (1949): 49-63.

Bruce, Harry. *Frank Sobey: The Man and the Empire*. Halifax: Nimbus, 1985.

———. *The Pig That Flew*. Vancouver, BC: Douglas and McIntyre, 1997.

———. *R. A.: The Story of R. A. Joudrey*. Toronto: McClelland and Stewart, 1979.

Bulley, Harry Albert. "Accidents Averted." *Cape Breton's Magazine* 37 (1984): 21-26.

Bury, Shirley. "A Tale of Two City Firms." *Goldsmiths Review* (1991): 22-27.

Calder, J. William. *All Aboard*. Antigonish, N.S.: Formac, 1974.

Cameron, J. M. "The Scotia Steelmasters," *Collections of the Nova Scotia Historical Society*, vol. 40, 1980: 31-56.

Campbell, Brian, and A. J. B. Johnston. *Tracks across the Landscape: The S&L Commemorative History*. Sydney, N.S.: UCCB Press, 1999.

Campbell, Douglas. *Banking on Coal*. Sydney, NS: UCCB Press, 1997.

Camu, Pierre. "The Strait of Canso and Cape Breton Island." *Geographical Bulletin* 3 (1953): 50-69.

Caplan, Ronald, ed. *Views from the Steel Plant*. Wreck Cove, NS: Breton Books, 2005.

Carlson, R. E. *The Liverpool and Manchester Railway Project*. New York: Augustus Kelley, 1969.

Chafe, W. J. *I've Been Working on the Railroad: Memoirs of a Railwayman, 1911-1962*. St John's, NL: Harry Cuff Publications, 1987.

Chard, D. A. "Joseph Howe and the Struggle for Railways in Nova Scotia, 1830-1858." *Nova Scotia Historical Quarterly* 8, no. 4 (1978): 289-97.

Chisholm, Joseph Andrew. *The Speeches and Public Letters of Joseph Howe.* 2 vols. Halifax: Chronicle Publishing, 1909.

Clarke, Rod. "The Ontario Narrow Gauge." *Canadian Rail* 518 (May-June 2007): 99-106.

Cole, L. H. *Gypsum in Canada.* Ottawa: Canada Department of Mines, 1913.

Conrad, Margaret. "The Art of Regional Protest: The Political Cartoons of Donald McRitchie, 1904-1937." *Acadiensis* 21, no. 1 (1979): 5-29.

Cramm, Frank. "The Construction of the Newfoundland Railway, 1875-1898." Master's thesis, Memorial University, 1961.

Crawley, Ron. "Class Conflict and the Establishment of the Sydney Steel Industry, 1899-1904." In *The Island*, edited by Kenneth Donovan, 145-64. Fredericton, N.B. and Sydney, N.S.: Acadiensis Press and UCCB Press, 1990.

———. "Off to Sydney: Newfoundlanders Emigrate to Industrial Cape Breton, 1890-1914." *Acadiensis* 17, no. 2 (1988): 27-51.

Creighton, Donald. *John A. Macdonald: The Old Chieftain.* Toronto: Macmillan, 1955.

Cruikshank, Ken. *Close Ties: Railways, Government and the Board of Railway Commissioners.* Montreal and Kingston: McGill-Queens University Press, 1991.

———. "The Intercolonial Railway: Freight Rates and the Maritime Economy." *Acadiensis* 22, no. 1 (1992): 87-110.

———. "The People's Railway: The Intercolonial Railway and the Canadian Public Enterprise Experience." *Acadiensis* 16, no. 1 (1986): 78-100.

———. "With Apologies to James: A Response to E. R. Forbes." *Acadiensis* 24, no. 1 (1994): 3-34.

Cuff, Robert. "The Newfoundland Railway at War." In *God Guard Thee, Newfoundland*, edited by Paul J. Johnson, 77-104. St. John's: Flanker Press, 2009.

Culme, John. "A Devoted Attention to Business: An Obituary of Philip Rundell." *The Silver Society Journal* (Winter 1991): 91-102.

Cunningham, Don and Don Artz. *The Halifax Street Railway, 1886-1949.* Halifax, NS: Nimbus, 2009.

Darling, Howard. *The Politics of Freight Rates: The Railway Freight Rate Issue in Canada.* Toronto: McClelland and Stewart, 1980.

Davis, Jo, ed., *Not a Sentimental Journey*. Waterloo, ON: Gunbyfield Publishing, 1990.

den Otter, A. A. *The Philosophy of Railways: The Transcontinental Railway Idea in British North America.* Toronto: University of Toronto Press, 1997.

The Dictionary of National Biography: Missing Persons. Oxford: Oxford University Press, 1993.

Donaldson, Ian. *Sydney and Louisburg Ry: Carrying Coals to Tidewater*. Calgary, AB: British Railway Modellers of North America, 2000.

Drummond, Robert. *Minerals and Mining, Nova Scotia*. Stellarton, N.S.: Mining Record Office, 1918.

Due, John F. *The Intercity Electric Railway in Canada*. Toronto: University of Toronto Press, 1966.

Earle, Michael. "Coal in the History of Nova Scotia." In *Industry and Society in Nova Scotia: An Illustrated History*, edited by James E. Candow, 57-80. Halifax, NS: Fernwood Publishing, 2001.

———. "Down With Hitler and Silby Barrett: The Cape Breton Miners' Slowdown Strike of 1941." *Acadiensis* 18, no. 1 (1988): 56-90.

Earle, M. and H. Gamberg. "The United Mine Workers and the Coming of the CCF to Cape Breton." *Acadiensis* 19, no. 1 (1989): 3-26.

Empty Harbours, Empty Dreams: The Story of the Maritimes in Confederation. Montreal: National Film Board, 1979.

"Ferries in the Strait of Canso." *Cape Breton's Magazine* 20 (1978): 22-28.

Fleming, Sandford. *The Intercolonial Railway*. Montreal: Dawson Brothers, 1876.

Flinn, Michael. *The History of the British Coal Industry*. Vol. 2, *1700-1830*. Oxford: Clarendon Press, 1984.

Forbes, Ernest R. *Challenging the Regional Stereotype: Essays on the 20th Century Maritimes*. Fredericton: Acadiensis Press, 1989.

———. "The Intercolonial Railway and the Decline of the Maritime Provinces Revisited." *Acadiensis* 24, no. 1 (1994): 3-34.

———. *The Maritime Rights Movement, 1919-1927*. Montreal: McGill-Queens University Press, 1991.

Frank, David. "The Cape Breton Coal Industry and the Rise and Fall of the British Empire Steel Corporation." *Acadiensis* 7, no. 1 (1977): 3-34.

———. "The Cape Breton Coal Miners, 1917-26." PhD diss., Dalhousie University, 1979.

———. *J. B. McLachlan: A Biography*. Toronto: James Lorimer, 1999.

Fraser, Mary. *Folklore of Nova Scotia*. Toronto: Catholic Truth Society, 1932.

Freeman, Michael. *Railways and the Victorian Imagination*. London/New Haven: Yale University Press, 1999.

Frost, James. *Merchant Princes*. Toronto: James Lorimer, 2003.

Gamst, Fred. "The Context and Significance of America's First Railroad." *Technology and Culture* 33, no. 2 (January 1992): 66-100.

George, Roy. "The Cape Breton Development Corporation." In *Public Corporations and Public Policy in Canada*, edited by Allan Tupper and G. Bruce Doern, 365-88. Montreal: Institute for Research on Public Policy, 1981.

Gillis, Rannie. *Historic North Sydney.* Halifax, NS: Nimbus, 2005.

Gow, John M. *Cape Breton Illustrated.* Toronto: William Briggs, 1893.

Grant, George Monro. *Picturesque Canada.* 2 vols. Toronto: Belden, 1882.

Greenfield, Nathan M. *The Battle of the St. Lawrence: The Second World War in Canada.* Toronto: HarperCollins, 2004.

Hadley, Michael L. *U-boats Against Canada: German Submarines in Canadian Waters.* Montreal/Kingston: McGill-Queen's University Press, 1990.

Hamilton, William B. *Place Names of Atlantic Canada.* Toronto: University of Toronto Press, 1996.

Hanington, Felicity. *The Lady Boats: The Life and Times of Canada's West Indies Merchant Fleet.* Halifax, NS: Canadian Marine Transportation Centre, Dalhousie University, 1980.

Harrison, Mitchell C. *Prominent and Progressive Americans: Vol. I.* New York, NY: Tribune, 1902.

Hart, E. J. *The Selling of Canada: The CPR and the Beginnings of Canadian Tourism.* Banff, AB: Altitude Publishing, 1983.

Henderson, Stephen. *Angus L. Macdonald: A Provincial Liberal.* Toronto: University of Toronto Press, 2007.

Hiller, James K. "The Newfoundland Railway, 1881-1949." [St. John's]: Newfoundland Historical Society, 1981.

How, Douglas. *Night of the Caribou.* Hantsport, N.S.: Lancelot Press, 1988.

Inwood, Kris. "Local Control, Resources and the Nova Scotia Steel Company." *Canadian Historical Association Historical Papers* 21, no. 1 (1986): 254-82.

———. "Maritime Industrialization from 1870 to 1910: A Review of the Evidence and Its Interpretation." *Acadiensis* 21, no. 1 (1991): 132-55.

Ircha, C. M. "The Chignecto Ship Railway." *Canadian Journal of Civil Engineering* 19, no. 1 (1992): 164-77.

Jackson, Elva E. *Windows on the Past: North Sydney, Nova Scotia.* Windsor, NS: Lancelot Press, 1974.

Jessome, Bill. *Maritime Mysteries and the Ghosts Who Surround Us.* Halifax, NS: Nimbus, 1999.

Jobb, Dean. "Three-ring Robbery." *Canadian Banker* 96, no. 5 (1989): 38-42.

Johnston, A. J. B. "Preserving History: The Commemoration of 18th Century Louisbourg." *Acadiensis* 13, no. 1 (Autumn 1983): 53-80.

Kirby, M. W. *The Origins of Railway Enterprise: The Stockton and Darlington Railway.* Cambridge: Cambridge University Press, 1993.

Knowles, Valerie. *From Telegrapher to Titan: The Life of William C. Van Horne.* Toronto: Dundurn, 2004.

Lavallee, Omer. *Narrow Gauge Railways in Canada.* Montreal: Railfare Books, 1972 and 2005.

Lewis, Michael J. T. *Early Wooden Railways.* London: Routledge, 1970.

Logan, H. A. *Trade Unions in Canada.* Toronto: University of Toronto Press, 1948.

MacAulay, John A. "Sydney in the 1880s." In *More Essays in Cape Breton History*, edited by R. J. Morgan, 6-9. Windsor, NS: Lancelot Press, 1977.

MacBean, Allister W. D. *The Inverness and Richmond Railway.* Halifax, NS: Tenant Publishing, 1987.

MacDonald, A. H. "The Albion Railway: A Study of an Early Nova Scotia Experience with the Industrial Revolution." MBA thesis, St. Mary's University, Halifax, 1999.

MacDonald, C. O. *The Coal and Iron Industries of Nova Scotia.* Halifax, NS: Chronicle Publishing, 1909.

MacDonald, Herb. "The Albion Railway of 1839-40." *Canadian Rail* 474 (January-February 2000): 3-12.

———. "The Early Horse-Powered Mining Railways of Cape Breton." *Canadian Rail* 535 (January-February 2010): 10-17 and 27-36.

———. "The Rideau Railway Idea: 1816-1825." *Canadian Rail* 545 (November-December 2011): 263-73.

MacDonald, Ken. *Port Morien: Pages from the Past.* Sydney, N.S.: UCCB Press, 1995.

MacDonald, Monica. "Railway Tourism in the Land of Evangeline." *Acadiensis* 35 (Autumn 2005): 158-80.

MacDonald, Peter. "How the Railway Came to Cape Breton." *The Post-Record*, Sydney, April 23, 1948: 13.

MacDougall, J. L. *History of Inverness County.* Truro, N.S.: News Publishing Company, 1922.

MacEwan, Paul. *Miners and Steelworkers: Labour in Cape Breton.* Toronto: Hakkert, 1976.

MacInnes, Sheldon. *Buddy MacMaster: The Judique Fiddler.* East Lawrencetown, N.S.: Pottersfield Press, 2007.

MacIntyre, Linden. *Causeway.* Toronto: HarperCollins, 2006.

MacKenzie, A. A. "Cape Breton and the Western Harvest Excursions, 1890-1928." In *Cape Breton at 200*, edited by Kenneth Donovan, 71-83. Sydney, NS: UCCB Press, 1985.

MacKenzie, A. A. *The Harvest Train.* Wreck Cove: Breton Books, 2002.

MacKenzie, Michael. *Glimpses of the Past.* Christmas Island, NS: MacKenzie Books, 1984.

———. *Tracks across the Maritimes.* Christmas Island, NS: MacKenzie Books, 1985.

MacMaster, Buddy. *The Judique Flyer*. Atlantic Artists, 2000.

March, William. *Red Line: The Chronicle-Herald and the Mail-Star, 1875-1954.* Halifax, NS: Chebucto Agencies, 1986.

Marchildon, Gregory. *Profits and Politics: Beaverbrook and the Gilded Age of Canadian Finance.* Toronto: University of Toronto Press, 1996.

Martin, Evan. *The Bedlington Engine and Iron Works.* Newcastle: Frank Graham, 1974.

Matheson, Scott MacKenzie. "An Examination of the Operations of the Sydney Steel Corporation." BA thesis, Acadia University, 1985.

McAlpine's Nova Scotia Directory, 1907-1908. Halifax: McAlpine, 1908.

McCann, Larry. "The Mercantile-Industrial Transition of the Metals Towns of Pictou County, 1857-1931." *Acadiensis* 10, no. 2 (1981): 29-64.

———. "Metropolitanism and Branch Businesses in the Maritimes, 1881-1931," *Acadiensis* 13, no. 1 (1983): 1983: 112-25.

McGillivray, Don. "Cape Breton in the 1920s: A Community Besieged." In *Essays in Cape Breton History*, edited by Brian Tennyson, 49-67. Windsor, N.S., Lancelot Press, 1973. Revised and with a different title, in *Acadiensis* 3, no. 2 (1974): 45-64.

———. "Henry Melville Whitney Comes to Cape Breton." *Acadiensis* 9, no. 1 (Autumn 1979): 44-70.

McInnis, Peter. "All Solid Along The Line: The Reid Newfoundland Strike of 1918," *Labour/Le Travail* 26 (1990): 61-84.

McKay, Ian. "By Wisdom, Wile or War." *Labour/Le Travail* 18 (1986): 13-62.

———. "Strikes in the Maritimes." *Acadiensis* 13, no. 1 (1983): 3-46.

McKay, Ian and Robin Bates. *In the Province of History: The Making of the Public Past in Twentieth-Century Nova Scotia.* Montreal and Kingston: McGill-Queens University Press, 2010.

McKay, John G. *The Chignecto Marine Transport Railway.* Amherst, NS (privately printed), 2002.

McQueen, Donald R. and William D. Thompson. *Constructed in Kingston: A History of the Canadian Locomotive Companies, 1854-1868.* Kingston, ON: Canadian Railroad Historical Association, 2000.

Meagher, Pat. *Scotia People: Tales from the Strait.* Kemptville, ON: Veterans Publications, 2005.

Migliore, Sam and A. Evo DiPierro, eds. *Italian Lives, Cape Breton Memories.* Sydney, N.S.: UCCB Press, 1999.

Millward, Hugh. "Mine Locations and the Sequence of Coal Exploitation on the Sydney Coalfield, 1720-1980." In *Cape Breton at 200*, edited by Kenneth Donovan, 183-202. Sydney, N.S.: UCCB Press, 1985.

Mountford, Colin. "Rope Haulage: The Forgotten Element of Railway History." In *Early Railways*, edited by Andy Guy and Jim Rees, 171-91. London: The Newcomen Society, 2001.

Muise, Del. "The General Mining Association and Nova Scotia's Coal." *Bulletin of Canadian Studies* (Autumn 1983): 71-87.

Nason, David. *Railways of New Brunswick*. Fredericton, NB: New Ireland Press, 1992.

O'Donnell, John C., ed. *The Men of the Deeps: Melody Edition*. Waterloo, ON: Waterloo Music Company, 1975.

Othen, David. *Cape Breton & Central Nova Scotia Railway: 1993-2001*. Self published. http://www.blurb.com/bookstore/detail/2424188.

Parker, Mike. *Running the Gauntlet*. Halifax, NS: Nimbus, 2003.

Pigott, Nick and Michael J. T. Lewis. "The Pre-History of Britain's Railways." *The Railway Magazine*, London (March 2004): 9.

Prominent People of the Maritime Provinces. Montreal: Canadian Publicity Company, 1922.

Rafuse, Ted. *A Railway to the Isle*. Port Hope, ON: Steampower Publishing, 2005.

Regehr, T. D. *The Canadian Northern Railway*. Toronto: Macmillan, 1976.

Reilly, Nolan. "The Rise and Fall of Industrial Amherst, 1860-1930." In *Industry and Society in Nova Scotia: An Illustrated History*, edited by James E. Candow, 129-58. Halifax: Fernwood Publishing, 2001.

Rose, George MacLean, ed. "Henry Alfred Gray." *A Cyclopaedia of Canadian Biography: Vol. 1*. Toronto: Rose Publishing, 1886: 362-63.

Samson, Daniel. *The Spirit of Industry and Improvement*. Montreal and Kingston: McGill-Queens University Press, 2008.

Samson, Danny. "The Making of a Cape Breton Coal Town." MA thesis, University of New Brunswick, 1988.

Savoie, Donald J. *Visiting Grandchildren: Economic Development in the Maritimes*. Toronto: University of Toronto Press, 2006.

Steelmaking in the Atlantic Provinces. Halifax: Atlantic Provinces Economic Council, 1974.

Stephenson, William. *The Store that Timothy Built*. Toronto: McClelland and Stewart, 1969.

Stevens, G. R. *Canadian National Railways*. 2 vols. Toronto: Clarke Irwin, 1960-62.

Stewart, Greig. *Shutting Down the National Dream*. Toronto: McGraw-Hill Ryerson, 1988.

Tennyson, Brian and Roger Sarty. *Guardian of the Gulf: Sydney, Cape Breton, and the Atlantic Wars*. Toronto: University of Toronto Press, 2000.

Tennyson, Brian. *Cape Bretoniana: An Annotated Bibliography*. Toronto: University of Toronto Press, 2005.

Tibbetts, R. C. "The Pictou Branch." *Canadian Rail* 205 (December 1968), s 262-72.

Town of Sydney Mines. *The History of Sydney Mines*. Sydney Mines, NS: Princess Print, 1990.

Tuck, J.H. "Canadian Railways and Unions in the Running Trades, 1865-1914." *Industrial Relations* 36, no. 1 (1981): 106-31. http://id.erudit.org/iderudit/029128ar

———. "Union Authority, Corporate Obstinacy, and the Grand Trunk Strike of 1910." *Historical Papers* 11, no. 1 (1976): 175-92.

Tupper, Allan. "Public Enterprise as Social Welfare: The Case of the Cape Breton Development Corporation." *Canadian Public Policy* 4, no. 4 (1978): 530-46.

Underwood, Jay. *Built for War: Canada's Intercolonial Railway*. Montreal: Railfare Books, 2005.

———. *From Folly to Fortune*. Montreal: Railfare Books, 2007.

———. *Ghost Tracks*. Montreal: Railfare Books, 2009.

———. "History Follows the Ocean to the Ocean." *Canadian Rail* no. 536 (2010): 95-106.

———. *The Inside Man: The Life and Times of James Isbester*. Forthcoming.

———. *Ketchum's Folly*. Hantsport, N.S.: Lancelot Press, 1995.

Underwood, Jay and Douglas N. W. Smith, "History of the Eastern Car Company." *Canadian Rail* no. 524 (2008): 87-101 and 112-17.

Vernon, C. W. *Cape Breton at the Turn of the 20th Century*. Toronto: Nation Publishing, 1903.

Wallace, Donald R. "Nova Scotia Coal Industry and Freight Rate Subvention." *Public Affairs* 2, no. 4 (1939).

Woodworth, Marguerite. *History of the Dominion Atlantic Railway*. [Kentville, N.S.: Kentville Publishing], 1936.

Ziff, Bruce. *Unforeseen Legacies*. Toronto: University of Toronto Press, 2000.

Index

Abbott, Harry 52-53, 58, 66, 69, 76, 120, 227
A. C. Morton 33, 226
Air Canada 202
Albion 26-27
Albion Mines 17, 26-27, 29, 112, 223-26, 239
Albion Railway 112
Alfred MacKay 32-33, 226
Algoma Steel Corp 142, 146
Allan, Hugh 52-53, 66, 69
Amherst 35, 92, 115, 193, 229, 237, 243
Antigonish 9, 53-55, 126
Avonside Co. 37-38, 227-28
A. V. Roe (Avro) 133, 241

Baddeck , 47, 63, 80, 85, 96, 165
Baddeck & North Sydney project
Baldwin and Co. 36, 212
Barrachois 167-68
Bedlington Iron Works 25, 226
Bell Island 160-61, 244
Bigge, Thomas 16, 20, 212-13, 224
Black, Hawthorne and Co. 29, 32-33, 42, 226-27
Borden, Robert 102, 153, 243
Boston and Nova Scotia Coal Co. 80
Boston, Martin 124, 198-99, 219
Boularderie
Bras d'Or 214
Bras d'Or Coal Co. 212
Bridgeport 18, 24-25, 31-32, 34, 36, 45-46, 111
British Empire Steel Corporation (Besco) 132, 240
Broad Cove, Baddeck and North Sydney project (BCB&NS) 85
Broad Cove Coal Co. 79-80
Broad Cove (Inverness) 79-80, 82-84, 236

Brotherhood of Locomotive Engineers (BLE) 171, 174
Brotherhood of Locomotive Firemen and Enginemen (BLFE) 171, 246
Brotherhood of Railroad Trainmen (BRT) 171, 174, 246
Broughton 107-108, 212
Brown, Richard 17-18, 23, 27, 49-50, 223-26
Brown, Richard Jr. 226
Buddle, John 12, 19-22, 24, 26, 224-25
Burn, J. H. 30
Bussey, Bill 217-18

Calder, William 77-78, 101-103, 148, 157, 180-81, 190, 215, 234
Caledonia Coal Co 34-35
Campbell, Brian 124, 195, 226, 239
Campbell, Charles 47
Campbell, Robert 71, 72, 74, 236
Canadian Brotherhood of Railroad Employees (CBRE) 174
Canadian Government Railways (CGR) 52, 54, 57, 100, 102, 121, 124-25, 138, 148, 152-53, 175, 188, 231, 246
Canadian National Railway (CNR) 9, 43, 58, 99-101, 108-109, 118-23, 134, 136, 138, 140-42, 144, 148-51, 154, 157-61, 163-65, 168-69, 171-73, 175, 179-80, 182, 185-86, 188-89, 190-92, 194-96, 198-99, 201-202, 205-206, 211, 215, 219-20, 245-247
Canadian Northern Railway (CNoR) 100, 237-38
Canadian Railroad Historical Association (CRHA) 115-16, 135, 193-94, 213, 219
Canso and Louisburg project 51, 55, 63, 69-70

Canso crossings *See* chapter 4 and 51-53, 55, 58, 63-64, 96-97, 99, 107-108, 122-23, 136, 140, 149-50, 160, 162-63, 166, 169, 197-98, 206-207, 237, 245-46
Cape Breton and Central Nova Scotia Railway (CB&CNS) 108, 205-208, 214, 238
Cape Breton Coal, Iron and Railway Co. 68, 107
Cape Breton Co. Railway 40-41, 52-53, 64, 66, 111-13, 220, 229, 239
Cape Breton Development Corp (Devco) 9, 108, 137-38, 199-201, 206-208, 211-13, 215-17, 241, 247
Cape Breton Electric Railway (CBE) 128-29
Cape Breton Northern project 85
Cape Breton Railway and Coal Co. 120
Cape Breton Railway (CBR) 65, 71-79, 84, 98-99, 101-103, 117, 157, 169, 220, 236
Cape Breton Railway Extension Co. 68-70, 76, 77
Cape Breton Steam Railway 211-13
Cape Breton Tramways 127, 129
C. G. Swann 28, 30
Champlain and St. Lawrence Railway 48
Chéticamp 79, 84-85, 165
Chrétien, Jean 201-202
Christmas Island 62, 168
circus trains 162-63, 209
CN Marine 202
common carrier railway 48, 164
Converse, J. H. 34
Crowsnest Pass freight rates 156
Cruikshank, Ken 156, 244
Cumberland Railway Co 115, 200
Cunard, Samuel 21-23

dandy cars 22
Darling, Howard 156, 244
den Otter, A. A. 230
Devco Railway (DR) 9, 108, 137-38, 200-201, 207-208, 213, 215, 217
diesel locomotives 10, 138, 183, 186, 192, 194, 205, 207-208, 213, 241, 247
Dominion Atlantic Railway (DAR) 124, 239
Dominion Bridge Co 58, 73, 87, 234
Dominion Coal Co (Domco) 30, 33-35, 40-47, 55, 70-71, 78, 81, 85, 87-88, 108, 112-13, 127-28, 131, 134, 136, 174, 234, 240-41
Dominion Foundaries and Steel (Dofasco) 146

Dominion Iron and Steel Co (Disco) 44, 88, 131, 142-43, 234
Dominion Securities Co. 72, 74-76, 234-35
Dominion Steel and Coal Co (Dosco) 90, 108, 132-33, 137, 143
Donkin 37, 44, 46, 115, 208, 229
Donkin, Hiram 44-45, 55, 57, 80, 85, 87-89
dual gauge 37, 41-42
Duncan, Andrew Rae 155
Dwyer, Michael 22, 225

Eastern Car Co. 116, 133, 135, 146-47, 242
Eastern Extension Railway 52-54, 68, 120, 231
E. E. Bigge 212
E. P. Archbold 36
European and North American project 51
European and North American Railway 49, 230

Fairlie Patent 37-40, 42, 112, 227-28
Fletcher, Jennings and Co. 30
Florence 94, 120
Foord, J. B. 20, 224
Forbes, Ernest R. 156, 241-44
Four Star Colliery 212-213
Fox, Walker and Co 38
Fraser, Graham 86, 88
freight rates as political issue 137-38, 151, 153, 155-56, 196, 243-44

General Mining Association (GMA) 5, 14-31, 33-34, 47-49, 67, 88-89, 112, 131, 164, 212-13, 220, 222-26
Gisborne, Frederick 38, 40, 52, 65, 107, 227, 229
Glace Bay 34-36, 45-46, 79, 87, 89-90, 105, 107, 111, 113-17, 120, 128-29, 132, 134, 137, 144, 159, 161-62, 168-71, 174, 183, 186-87, 189, 193-94, 208-209, 211-13, 218, 227, 240, 246-47
Glace Bay Mining Co. 34-37
Glasgow and Cape Breton Railway (G&CB) 36-39, 52, 65, 107, 112, 128, 227
Glendyer 106-107, 119
Gowrie Co. Railway 45-47, 166, 220, 230
Grand Narrows 56-60, 62, 66, 73, 85, 96-97, 100, 173-76, 188, 232
Grand Trunk Railway 49, 100, 153-54, 172, 231, 246
Great Northern Mining & Railway Co 165

Hackworth, Timothy 26
Halifax 24-26, 29-30
Halifax and Cape Breton Railway and Coal Co
    (H&CB) 53-54, 64, 120, 220
Halifax and Quebec project 16, 48-52
Halifax and Southwestern Railway (H&SW) 77, 84
harvest excursions 125-26, 239
Harvey Graham 131
Hawker Siddeley Co. 133, 241
Henry Day 32-33, 42, 226, 228
Hoard, Daniel 20-21, 224
hobo trains on S&L 116-17, 239
horse-powered railways 9-11, 17-25, 34, 47
Howe, Joseph 31, 49-51, 230
Hubbard, Gardiner 34
Hunslet Engine Works 33, 47, 226-27
Hussey, William 79-80, 236

incline 18, 21-22
Intercolonial Railway of Canada (IRC) 5, 9, 13, 27,
    30, 40, 44, 48, 51-52, 55-56, 58, 60-66, 70,
    72-73, 79-80, 82, 85, 87, 89-91, 93-97, 99-100,
    102-103, 105, 119-21, 124-25, 128, 131, 134,
    138-39, 141, 148, 150-57, 159, 162, 164, 167-
    69, 171-75, 177-78, 188-89, 196, 204, 206, 215,
    219-20, 231-32, 239, 242-44, 246
International Coal and Railway Co 31-34, 38, 42, 43-
    45, 51, 91, 111-13, 134, 157, 208, 226-27
Inverness 56, 61, 65, 78-81, 84-85, 99, 101, 107, 117-
    19, 124, 140, 171, 179, 182-83
Inverness and Richmond Railway and Coal Co (I&R)
    65, 75, 77, 79-80, 82-84, 96, 99-100, 101, 106-
    107, 117, 119, 126, 139, 165, 167, 169, 174,
    184, 238
Inverness and Victoria project 80, 84
Inverness Miners' Museum 82, 101, 183-84, 214
Inwood, Kris 156, 240, 244
Iona 56, 58, 66, 96, 124, 151-52, 165, 173, 188, 211,
    239
Iona Gypsum Co 151-52
John Bridge 16, 26, 28, 30
Judique 118-19, 123, 182, 185, 215
Judique Flyer 118-19, 123, 182, 185, 215

Kennelly, D. J. 40, 41, 66, 68-69, 229, 232
King, Mackenzie 153, 155, 242, 244

Laurier, Wilfrid 69, 93, 102, 153, 173
Lavallee, Omer 41, 227, 229
Lawless, Ron 203-04, 247
Leonard, Reuben 72-73, 233
Lingan 27, 29, 47, 208
Little Bras 24-25, 94-95, 120, 158, 223, 225
Longridge, Michael 25-26, 226
Louisbourg 37, 39-41, 45-46, 49, 52, 65-67, 69, 72,
    74, 77, 79, 91, 96, 101, 105, 111-13, 116-17,
    124, 134, 171, 174, 178, 200-201, 209, 211,
    215, 217-19, 229
Louisburg Extension project 52, 65

Mabou 63, 79, 85-86, 119, 167, 182, 220, 236
Mabou and Gulf Railway (M&G) 85-86, 236
MacBean, Allister 119, 124, 238, 246
Macdonald, John A. 31, 51-53, 55, 56, 58-62, 100,
    137, 150, 171, 226, 231, 235
MacKay, Alfred 32-33
MacKenzie, A. A. (Tony) 125-26, 239
Mackenzie and Mann 77, 80-81, 83-84, 88, 96, 100-
    101, 238
MacKenzie, Michael 151, 168, 173
Mackenzie, William 75, 80-81, 237
MacMaster, Buddy 182
Mann, Donald 75, 77, 80-84, 88, 96, 100-101, 236-38
Marine Atlantic 202
Maritime Freight Rates Act 155-56
Maritime Rights 154-55, 243
Mayhew, Horace 107-108
McLachlan, J. B. 132-33, 161, 244
Meagher, Pat 163, 190
Mira 96, 115, 124, 200
Mira River 40, 46, 105-106, 188
Mira River Co. 96
model railway 60, 207, 218
Montreal Locomotive Works Ltd 193-94, 213
Mulgrave 53-55, 64, 83, 96-97, 99, 120, 141, 163, 169,
    176, 190, 198
Mulroney, Brian 201-204
Murray, George 72, 76, 81-82, 108, 173
MV Frederick Carter 191
MV Patrick Morris 191

narrow gauge 29, 37-38, 40-45, 47, 66, 79, 94, 96,
    107, 111-12, 128, 134, 157, 165, 191-92, 220,
    227, 229, 240

"National Policy" 137, 150, 242
Neilson and Co. 26, 30, 34-35
New Campbellton 47, 85, 220, 230
Newfoundland ferries 21, 29, 58, 95, 120, 149-50, 159, 161, 191, 237, 244
Newfoundland Railway 58, 68, 94, 96, 159, 161, 191-92, 206, 237
New Waterford 107, 114-15, 127, 162
North Sydney 18, 21, 25, 27, 29-30, 56-58, 61-62, 69, 74, 80, 85-86, 89-90, 93- 96, 108, 120, 122, 126, 128, 134, 149, 150, 157, 159, 161-62, 166-67, 169, 171, 176, 186, 191-92, 202, 206, 225, 245
North Sydney Junction 62
North Sydney Marine Railway 166-67, 245
Nova Scotia Railway (NSR) 51, 231
Nova Scotia Steel and Coal Co (Scotia) 22, 85-86, 88-90, 94, 131-34, 138, 146, 164, 174-75, 212, 240

Ocean Limited 121
Old Sydney Collieries Ltd (OSC) 132, 135, 164, 194, 212-13
Old Sydney Collieries Railway (OSC) 132-34, 138, 164
Orangedale 62, 85, 123, 127, 158, 198, 214, 219, 221
Orangedale Railway Museum 122-24, 148, 166, 199, 213, 219
Order of Railway Conductors 171
OSC # 25 213
Othen, David 205

Pearson, Benjamin 44, 70, 128-29, 233
Pictou Branch 33, 51-54, 66, 150, 231
Pinkie 34-36, 42, 228
Point Tupper 55-56, 58, 64-65, 70, 73-74, 77, 80, 82-83, 96-99, 119, 149, 162-63, 166-67, 169, 174, 179-80, 185-86, 190, 192, 198, 204, 206-207, 245
Poor, John A. 48-49, 230
Port aux Basques 58, 95-96, 161, 191
Port Hastings 65, 73, 77, 82-83, 86, 96, 101, 107, 118-19, 141, 149, 163, 172, 174, 178-79, 182-83, 185-86, 188-89, 197-98
Port Hawkesbury 4, 60, 69, 80, 96-97, 118-19, 124, 158-59, 165-66, 176, 185-86, 198, 204, 206, 213

Port Hood 63, 79, 82, 118-19, 139
Port Morien 43, 46, 67, 114-15, 133-34, 186, 211
Pottinger, David 61, 172
Prince Edward Island Railway 47, 100, 227, 229
Provincial Workmens' Association (PWA) 174

Railiners 121-23, 192
rail manufacturing in Sydney 142-45
rails: cast iron 11, 24; malleable/rolled iron 12, 17-18, 24-26, 47; steel 30, 33, 46, 54; wooden 11, 25, 47
rail traffic: coal and steel 10-11, 23-24, 29, 37, 45, 84, 91-92, 133-44, 199-201, 207-208; containers 206; express 46, 78, 148-50, 180; freight 46, 64, 78, 96, 148-56, 204-207; mail 46, 61, 78, 93, 107, 157-58; passengers 46, 64, 92-93, 96, 111-29, 191-92, 195, 202-204
railway ferries 21, 29, 52, 57-58, 64, 83, 95-97, 99, 122, 128, 136, 140-41, 147, 149-50, 159-62, 185, 191, 197-99, 202, 237
railway ghosts and forerunners 167-68
railway stations 57, 61, 123-24, 149, 158, 169-70, 179, 181-82, 184, 190, 196, 202, 214; Black River 119; Christmas Island 62; Creignish 119; Estmere 62; Glace Bay 114; Glencoe 119; Glendyer 119; Grand Narrows 62, 173; Inverness 119, 214-15; Inverness & Richmond 119; Little Bras d'Or 95; Louisbourg (Louisburg) 116, 123, 193, 200; Mabou 119, 182; Mira Gut 115; Mulgrave 198; North Sydney 62, 93, 95, 159; Orangedale 62, 123, 166, 198, 199, 214, 219; Point Tupper 73, 98, 119, 149, 163, 198; Port Hastings 119; Port Hawkesbury 119; Port Hood 118, 119; S&L 114, 115, 216, 217, 218; St. Peter's 103, 181, 201, 214, 215; Sydney 91, 113, 123, 159, 218; Sydney Mines 90, 215; West Bay 62
railway wrecks 103, 106-107, 185, 188
Rayne and Burn 26, 30
Rayne, Robert 21, 225
Reid and Isbester 58, 85, 175
Reid, Robert 58, 85, 96, 232
Reserve 37-46, 65, 111, 128-29, 134, 227, 239
Rhodes, Curry and Co. 35, 42, 92, 115, 193, 237, 243
Robert Stephenson & Co 30
Ross, Alexander 69-70, 80, 85, 87
Ross, James 81, 88, 128, 131, 234

roundhouses 86, 115, 163, 168-70, 183-84, 186, 188, 191, 201, 207-208
Rundell, Bridge and Rundell 15, 16, 223

Samuel, James 39, 228
Schooner Pond 37, 41, 45, 111, 229
Schreiber, Collingwood 52, 56-59, 61, 100, 231-32
Scotia Steel and Coal Railway 131-34, 138, 164, 174-75
self-acting engine 18, 21-22
Sir Donald 33-34, 43, 228
S&L # 42 211, 213, 247
Smith, Donald 33, 42
Smith, Richard 224
special trains 58, 83, 103, 107, 124-25, 157, 159, 161-62, 211, 239
Springhill 116, 136, 140, 174
SS Alameda 105
SS Blue Hill 96
SS Bruce 95-96, 237
SS Caribou 161, 244
SS Scotia 64, 97-99, 198
SS Scotia II 99, 197-98
Stairs, John F. 86, 131, 237
St. Ann's 165, 245
Stellarton 17, 26, 136, 162, 175, 190, 192, 204, 213, 227, 247
Stephenson 26-27, 29-30
Stephenson, George 10
Stevens, George 58, 81, 102
Stewart Fish Co. 78
Stone and Webster 128, 240
St. Peter's 9, 52, 65, 67-69, 72-74, 77, 84, 98-99, 102-103, 117-19, 157-58, 176, 180-81, 185, 201, 214-15, 220, 235
Strait of Canso 5, 44, 51-53, 55, 58, 63-66, 68, 70, 72, 85, 87, 97, 107-108, 117, 122, 136, 140, 147, 149,-50, 160, 162, 166, 169, 197-99, 214, 219, 237, 245
Strait of Canso Bridge Co 85
Strait of Canso ferries 96-97, 99, 122, 136, 140-41, 147, 149, 160, 162, 185, 197-98
Strait of Canso Marine Railway 166
street railways 81, 127-29, 239
Sydney 25-26, 29-30
Sydney 16, 30-32, 34, 36, 38, 40, 43-46, 49-52, 55-58, 63-67, 69, 71, 74, 78-79, 85, 88-90, 93-94, 103, 107-108, 111-13, 115, 117, 120-25, 128-29, 133-34, 136, 138-39, 142-44, 146, 151-52, 156, 158-64, 169, 173-77, 181, 185-86, 188, 191-93, 197, 200-201, 203-207, 214, 219, 238, 240, 244, 247
Sydney and East Bay project 69, 107
Sydney and Glace Bay Railway 128
Sydney and Louisburg Railway and Coal Co 41
Sydney and Louisburg Railway Museum 32, 217
Sydney and Louisburg Railway (S&L) 9, 33, 35-37, 41-46, 74, 90-91, 92, 96, 105, 107-108, 111, 113-17, 119-21, 124, 126, 131-35, 137-38, 146-47, 157, 164, 168-70, 172, 174-75, 177-79, 183-84, 186-90, 192-95, 200-201, 208-13, 215-18, 226, 237, 239, 245-47
Sydney Coal Railway (SCR) 208
Sydney Mines 10, 16-30, 46, 85, 87-89, 94, 108, 120, 126, 128, 131, 133, 135, 152, 159, 162, 164, 171, 194, 215, 223-26
Sydney Mines Heritage Society 215
Sydney Mines steel plant 131, 133, 210
Sydney Steel Corp (Sysco) 145-46, 199, 206, 242
Sydney steel plant 37, 46, 71, 90, 113, 142, 144-46, 151, 164, 191, 199, 208, 213, 241

Telford, Thomas 20
The Gull 245
Trenton 116, 133, 135, 146-47, 242, 247
troop trains 159-61
Tupper, Charles Hibbert 62
Tupper, Charles 31, 33, 51, 93-94, 231, 243

Underwood, Jay 167-68, 230-32, 239, 242, 245

Van Horne, W. C. 42, 131, 240
VIA Rail 122, 201-205, 214, 246
Victoria Junction 115, 193, 208, 211
Victoria Mines 30, 46

Webb, Seward 71-72, 74-77, 86, 102, 234-35
Whitney, H. M. 30, 33-34, 41-44, 47, 70-71, 81, 88, 112, 127-28, 130-31, 229, 234, 239, 240
Whitney Pier 113, 115, 134, 147, 187, 191
Wolvin, Roy 132, 133